The Keowee Courier
1849-1851; 1857-1861
and
1865-1868

Edited By:
Colleen M. Elliot

Book Publishers

Southern Historical Press, Inc.
Greenville, South Carolina

Please direct all correspondence and orders to:

www.southernhistoricalpress.com
or
SOUTHERN HISTORICAL PRESS, Inc.
PO BOX 1267
375 West Broad Street
Greenville, SC   29601
southernhistoricalpress@gmail.com

ISBN #0-89308-152-3

Printed in the United States of America

"KEOWEE COURIER"

Edited and Indexed by

Colleen Morse Elliott

Abstracted and contributed by a lover of
genealogy who wishes to remain anonymous.

Abstracted from the available newspapers,
first published at Pickens Court House,
beginning with the issues of May 1849 to
May 1851; April 1857 to July 1861; September 1865 to August 1868. Due to the
division of Pickens District, South Carolina into the present day counties of
Pickens and Oconee, the KEOWEE COURIER
moved its office from Pickens C. H. to
the present town of Walhalla, the county
seat of Oconee county. The first issue
from Walhalla was on Friday, February 28,
1868.

Issue of: Friday May 18, 1849:

Tribute of Respect - HENRY MOREHEAD, student, ...deceased.

Fatal Accident - Two men in this District, says the last "Edgefield Advertiser", by the names of WEBB and ATTAWAY, while turkey hunting a few days since, before the break of day, without each other's knowledge, happened to take their stand in the same wood. Mistaking each other's yelp for the yelping of a turkey. Attaway quietly and on all fours advanced towards Webb, who, being unable in the early twilight of the morning to distinguish him, discharged his gun which emptied its contents into the face and breast of Attaway...causing almost instant death.

Married - On the 26th ult. by Rev. J. L. KENNEDY, Dr. J. W. EARLE to Miss ELIZA ANN, eldest daughter of Maj. W. L. KEITH, all of this Village.

Married - On the 7th instant by A. ALEXANDER, Esq., Mr. G. W. A. SMITH to Miss MARTHA JANE, daughter of JOHN G. MAULDIN, all of this District.

Married - Also on the 15th instant by Rev. J. B. HILLHOUSE, Mr. HENRY R. HUGHES to Miss ELIZABETH F. DENDY, daughter of JAMES H. DENDY, dec'd,all of this District.

Obituary - Died at his residence in the upper part of this District yesterday morning, Mr. ELISHA LEE, aged about 83 years.

Issue of Friday May 25, 1849:

Married - On the 15th inst. by W. S. GRISHAM, Esq., ANDREW J. DORSEY to Miss NANCY ISABELLA COLHOUN, all of this District.

Married - On the 17th inst., by the Rev. JOHN OWEN, Mr. WM. W. GASSAWAY to Miss JANE MC WHORTER, all of this District.

Issue of Saturday June 2, 1849:

Death of Major Gen'l W. J. WORTH on the 8th inst. at San Antonio, Texas.

Married - On the 24th ult., by the Rev. JOHN OWEN, Mr. THOMAS NIX to Miss ELIZABETH, daughter of Mr. W. W. GASAWAY, all of this District.

State of South Carolina, Pickens District - HANNAH CLAYTON, Applicant vs. CHARLES ALLEN and wife, SARAH A. ALLEN, JAMES YOUNG and wife, MARY ELIZABETH YOUNG, JOHN THOS. CLAYTON, ROBERT C. CLAYTON, STEPHEN G. CLAYTON, MARGARET CLAYTON, JESSE M. CLAYTON, Defendants. For the sale of the Real Estate of JOHN CLAYTON, deceased, not disposed of by Will. And it appearing that JOHN THOMAS CLAYTON resides without the limits of this State.

The "Richmond Enquirer" records the death of JOHN M. BOTTS.

Issue of Saturday June 9, 1849:

Married - On the 31st ult., by W. C. LEE, Mr. WILLIAM BOLLES to Miss ELIZABETH, daughter of ANDREW GORDEN, all of this District.

Married - At Earle's Furnace, Cass county, Georgia, on the 10th ult., by Rev. JOHN W. LEWIS, Col. E. M. FIELDS, of Canton, to Miss CORNELIA M. HARRISON, formerly of Greenville, S. C.

In Equity - JANE BARTON and P. ALEXANDER, Adm'x. and Admr. vs. JOHN LADD and WILEY REAVES and Heirs at Law of B. BARTON, dec'd. It appearing to my satisfaction that BENJ. F. BARTON and JOAB LEWIS and Wife, PHALBY, Defendants to this Bill of Complaint, reside from and without the limits of this State.

1

Issue of Saturday June 23, 1849:

Death of JAMES K. POLK, ex-President of the United States on the 15th in-stant, at Nashville.

Death of Miss MARIA EDGEWORTH, 83, popular novelist, on May 21, at Edge-worthtown, in the County of Longford, Ireland.

Death of Major General EDMUND PENDLETON GAINES. (Long sketch)

Issue of Saturday June 30, 1849:

Death of AMORY SIBLEY - We learn from the "Hamburg Republican", that Am-ory Sibley, of Augusta, Georgia, died at his residence in that city, on the 22nd inst., after a short illness, aged 58 years. As a merchant and a man of integrity his loss will be regretted by an extended circle of friends.

(Note: In this issue there was a notice stating the death of Col. JACK HAYS in San Antonio,Texas , but in the following issue of July 14th, the paper printed a retraction.)

Issue of Saturday July 7, 1849:

Married - Near Oconee Station, on Thursday evening 28th ult., by L. N. ROBINS, Esq., Mr. JOHN H. REID to Miss SUSAN MORGAN, all of this District.

Obituary - JAMES AMBLER, SR., citizen of Pickens District, departed this life 26th June, 1849, being over ninety years of age. He was a Virginian by birth, and a graduate of William & Mary's College, Va. Having a lib-eral education, he came to Edgefield District, S. C. and engaged his ser-vices as a teacher in private families for some years, he then turned his attention to farming, in which his industrious habits and his fine judge-ment ensured success. He spent the last 26 years of his life in Pickens District. He retained his consciousness to the hour of dissolution, and had the consolation of seeing all his children around his dying bedside. As a neighbor, friend, father and husband he was kind, social, and affec-tionate; and leaves a wide circle of friends, relatives, and acquain-tances to mourn his loss.

Obituary - Died on Tuesday 3rd inst., at his residence near Pickensville, after an illness of 4 or 5 days, Mr. JOHN P. ARCHER, aged about 43 years.

Obituary - Died in Pickens District, June 30th, after an illness of sev-eral months, Mrs. REBECCA VERNER, aged 75. The subject of this notice was born in Pennsylvania, and after residing a few years in Iredell, N.C. removed to this State in 1792. She was married to JOHN VERNER, Esq., the next year, having been his consort 56 years. Her chief characteristic was conscientiousness. The first question with her was not, what will others think of this conduct? but will my conscience approve. Having lived the life of a consistent christian, at its close she witnessed a good confession. A week before her death the words, "Come ye blessed of my Father inherit the kingdom prepared for you", she said, ran through her mind all day. A day or two after, when suffering much, she said,"It is a hard thing to die, but death has no terrors to me; Jesus can make a dying bed feel soft as downy pillows are". She is added to that cloud of witnesses, which, in every age, have borne their testimony to truth and piety. That evidence which the Saviour often gives, that He is about to receive the dying sufferer into mansions of eternal rest, was satis-factory in this case. Heaven often, ..."Owns her friends
                    On this side death, and points them out to men;
                    A lecture silent but of sovereign pow'r;
                    To vice confusion, and to virtue peace." J. B. H.

Issue of Saturday July 14, 1849:

Married - On 11th inst. by W. S. GRISHAM, Esq., Mr. SAM"L Y. MC WHORTER to Miss RACHEL W. RUSK, youngest sister of the Hon. THOMAS J. RUSK, of Texas, both of this District.

Issue of Saturday July 21, 1849:

Obituary - Departed this life on the 13th inst., at his residence in this
District, Mr. THOMAS HESTER. He has left a family and a large circle of
friends and relatives to mourn his early death.

Died - Mrs. ARMINDA COPELAND, consort of LEMUEL J. COPELAND, on the 1st
inst., at his resident in this place. Mrs. Copeland was born in Pendleton (now Pickens) District, S. C., 20th of March, 1822. In 1840, with
her parents, ALBERT and SUSANNAH ROBINS, emigrated to this county. She
professed religion in the fall of 1843, and attached herself to the Cum-
berland Presbyterian Church. She was married to Mr. Copeland March the
16th, 1847. During a long and painful illness the deceased manifested
great fortitude. And when fully sensible of her approaching dissolution,
none who saw her will ever forget the almost superhuman serenity of her
countenance; her confidence in the goodness of God, and particularly
the melody of her voice, as she spoke of her blessed Saviour, into whose
presence she was impatient to fly, and when the dark moment of her death
arrived, Jesus with smiling face breathed immortality into her departing.
She fell asleep..."As fades a summer cloud away.../As sinks the gale
when storms are o'er/As gently shuts the eye of day,/ As dies a wave a-
long the shore."...She has left to mourn her loss, a large circle of devoted friends...two affectionate brothers, an aged mother, a small son,
and a husband in the bloom of life, who feels in the bitterness of his
soul: .."Like one who treads alone/ Some vacant hall deserted;/ Whose
lights are fled, whose inmates dead,/ and all but him departed."...The
deceased was a consistent christian, a firm friend, devoted wife and affectionate mother. Farewell! Soft be thy pillow and thy slumbers, till
"God bid thee arise to hail him in triumph Descending the skies!"
                                              "Fulton (Miss.) Monitor"

Issue of Saturday July 28, 1849:

Married - On Thursday evening, 19th inst., by Rev. A. W. MC GUFFIN, Mr.
GRAFTON ADAIR to Miss ELIZA, eldest daughter of Mr. JAMES FERGUSON, all
of this District.

Married - On the 22nd inst., by WM. C. LEE, Esq., Mr. JOHN DAVIDSON, of
Anderson District, to Miss PERMELIA GOODEN, of this District.

Issue of Saturday August 4, 1849:

Death by Drowning - We are credibly informed that Mr. JAMES ROWLAND, a-
bout 40 years of age, put an end to his existence, last week, by drowning himself, in Seneca River, a short distance above Cherry's Bridge, in
this district. Mr. R. was laboring under mania portu, and made his escape from the custody of his friends on Sunday 22nd July; diligent search
was immediately made for him, without effect, until several days afterwards, his shoes and pantaloons were discovered on the bank of the river.
After a laborious search in the water, his body was recovered on Wednesday last, where it is supposed to have lain about eleven days. As we
have not been favored with the report of the Jury of inquest, we forebear further remarks.

Obituary - Departed this life, on Monday evening 16th July, at his Fathers residence in Anderson District, Major JOHN JAMES NORRIS, aged 25
years, 6 months, 27 days, of typhus fever. (Long eulogy)

Issue of Saturday August 18, 1849:

Married - On the 12th inst., by JOHN ADAIR, Esq., Mr. WM. B. COMPTON, to
Miss MARY BREWER, all of this District.

Issue of Saturday August 25, 1849:

Married - On Thursday last, by Rev. J. B. HILLHOUSE, Mr. RUSSEL DEAN to
Miss MARY MELINDA, daughter of Mr. ARTHUR CRAIG, all of this District.

Issue of Saturday September 1, 1849: (see next page)

3

Married - On the 26th inst. by JOHN KNOX, Esq., Mr. WILLIAM BARNES, to
Miss MARY CURTIS, both of Macon County, North Carolina.

Issue of Saturday September 8, 1849:

Murder - Mr. JESSE WEATHERFORD, who lived in this Village, was shot on
Monday night last by a negro man named Joe, belonging to Mrs. R. BLALOCK,
at her plantation about 3 miles from this place. The negro borrowed the
gun and amunition from a neighbor in the name of his young master. But
his real object, as afterwards discovered, was to kill another negro.
Weatherford and two others went with the view of arresting him and taking the gun from him. The party being detached to await the approach of
the negro, Weatherford encountered him single handed, which resulted in
his death ... the whole load of the gun entering his arm and breast near
his heart. Mr. Weatherford was a quiet, peaceable man, and went in search of the negro at the request of the negro's owner. The negro made his
escape and is still at large. "Edgefield Advertiser"

Sudden Death - We are informed that WILSON WALLACE dropped dead in the
streets of Anderson on last Monday. He had been afflicted for years with
asthma, which caused his death.

Married - On the 29th August, by Rev. W. W. REID, Mr. JOHN DODGEN to Miss
MARY CROW, both of Macon county, N. C.

Married - On the 6th inst., by Rev. GIDEON ELLIS, Mr. HAMILTON BURDINE,
of Mississippi, to Miss LOUISA HUGHES, of Pickens District.

Issue of Saturday September 15, 1849:

Tribute of Respect to THOMAS M. SLOAN, deceased.

Married - On 12th inst., by Rev. A. W. MC GUFFIN, Mr. HENRY SMITH, of
Spartanburg District, to Miss ARMINDA, eldest daughter of DANIEL BROOM,
of this District.

Issue of Saturday September 22, 1849:

Married - On the 12th ult., by W. D. STEELE, Esq., Mr. G. W. DODD to Miss
A. M. HUNNICUTT, all of Pickens District.

Obituary - Died on the 9th inst., in this District, Lt. Col. F. M. REID.
On the 10th ult., at his residence in this District, Mr. CHARLES WILLIAM-
SON. He was a Revolutionary Soldier, and has left but few of his compa-
triots behind him.

Another Murder - Our District seems to be getting back to the days of
Weems, and the events of the last four months cry aloud for reform. It
was only in our last number we were called upon to record the death of
a citizen at the hands of a negro man. Now we are called upon to record
another most diabolical murder. It appears that Mr. JOSHUA HAMMOND and
three ruffians by the name of GREEN, were engaged playing cards, when a
dispute arose which led to blows and resulted in the death of Hammond,
the other three having beat him to death with clubs. The murderers are
all in Jail, and we trust that justice will be meeted out to them that
their fiend like conduct merits.
....Rep. Hamburg, S. C. Sept. 12

Melancholy Suicide - Mr. WILLIAM S. RUSSELL, a respectable mechanic of
Grainiteville, put an end to his existence on Wednesday last by cutting
his throat with a razor.

Issue of Saturday September 29, 1849:

Distressing Accident - A most painful occurrence took place on Tuesday
last in Brick Range, by which a life was lost. A little girl, a daughter
of Mrs. A. TARRAR, about three years of age, playing on the back steps
of the second story, fell and received so severe an injury that she expired from the effects of it early Wednesday (yesterday) morning.*

(Note: *The previous story was dated Sept. 20..Col. Telegraph.)

Death of T. J. WRIGHT, Esq. - The "Camden Journal" of Wednesday last says
..."It is with deep regret we record the death of Maj. THOMAS J. WRIGHT,
one of the leading members of the Bar of Lancaster, and a prominent member of the Legislature from that district. He died on Thursday morning,
13th inst., at 4 o'clock, after a very short illness. He was known as a
good lawyer, in the enjoyment of a large practice, and the confidence of
an extended circle of friends; a writer, a sound Democrat, and a sterling Carolinian, as unostentatious in his manners as he was kind hearted
and devoted in his attachments. He had been a member of the Legislature
for about three years; and his liberal views, sound judgment, and close
attention to his duties induced his friends to believe that a wide field
of future usefullness was opening before him. He had secured the confidence of his District, and there are but few in it whose death would
have proved a severer loss.

Married - On Thursday evening last, by Rev. WM. M. MORTON, Mr. PHILEMON
ANSEL CRANE to Miss GEORGIANA AMANDA MELVINA, daughter of JOHN KNOX, Esq.
all of this District.

Issue of Saturday October 20, 1849:

Shocking Event - JOHN A. COLELOUGH killed by RICHARD MARSHALL.
                              "Summerville Banner" Oct. 3
Obituary - "Man that is born of a woman, is of few days and full of
trouble. He cometh forth like a flower, and is cut down; he fleeth also
as a shadow, and continueth not."....Departed this life on Tuesday evening the 16th inst. at his residence on Keowee River, in Pickens District,
Major ANSALEM ALEXANDER. He died of fever and languished on the bed of
affliction near five weeks. Major Alexander was a native of Pickens District, where he lived, not far from the place of his birth, until his
death; a wide circle of relations and friends grieve because he is num-
bered with the dead; and a widowed wife with three small children, in
the bitterness of her unutterable woe, realises her loss, as irreparable.
It was impossible in a short obituary notice, to do full justice to our
departed friend; let it suffice that in all the relations of life Major
Alexander manifested the most umcomprising integrity of chaacter; as a
citizen he was ever prompt, patriotic and conscientious in the discharge
of all his duties...as a neighbor, he was benevolent, social and charitable...as a friend, he was faithful and true...and as a husband and
father he was deeply and intensely affectionate. An omniscient God has
cut him down in the meridian of his manhood, and his sorrow stricken
friends have carried away his mortal body and consigned it to the cold,
remorseless ground. It is a religious duty to bow in solemn, reverential
acquiesence to this afflicting dispensation of Providence, and a mournful privilage to remember his many virtues, and to sorrow most of all because we shall see his face no more. In contemplating this bereavement,
the reflection is peculiarly consolatory, that throughout his entire life
Major Alexander's morality was pure and stainless, and that he exhibited
during his last illness, indubitable evidences of that change of heart
and faith in the Gospel of our Lord Jesus Christ, which divests death of
its sting and the grave of its victory.

Died- of Typhoid Fever in this District on the 8th inst., Mr. ELISHA
PHILLIPS, in the 33rd year of his age. The deceased possessed a vigorous
constitution and stalwart frame, that promised long life and sound
health, and his exit from earth in the meridian of his days, is another
solemn memento of the uncertainty of life. The subject of this brief
notice was strikingly distinguished for his mild and pacific mould of
character and the complaceney of his character, by which he secured the
friendship and esteem of all who knew him; and his loss will be sorely
felt in the circle in which he moved. He had not entered the connubial
state more than nine months before his death, and has left a widowed
wife to grieve over her early bereavement.

Issue of Saturday October 27, 1849:

Married - On the 23rd inst., by Rev. W. G. MULLENIX, Mr. JOHN M. LAURENCE

(October 27 cont'd:)

to Miss ELIZABETH L. CLAYTON.

Married - On the 24th inst., by Rev. J. S. MURRAY, Mr. WM. E. WEBB of Anderson District to Miss ESTHER C. LAURENCE, of this District.

Issue of Saturday December 1, 1849:

Married - On the 21st October by Rev. J. R. HUNNICUTT, Mr. JAMES HAYS of Pickens District to Miss MELISSA MARSHALL of Anderson District.

Married - On the 30th October by Rev. J. R. HUNNICUTT, Mr. LEVI BREWER to Miss NYMAY MOORE, all of this District.

Married - On the 15th November by Rev. J. L. KENNEDY, Mr. W. A. TEMPLE-TON of Pickens District to Miss M. A. M., youngest daughter of Dr. W. K. HAMILTON, of Cobb County, Georgia.

Issue of Saturday December 8, 1849:

Married - On Thursday the 29th ult. by O. E. BARTON, Esq., Mr. ALFRED MC CRARY of North Carolina to Miss REBECCA REAVES of this District.

Issue of Saturday December 15, 1849:

Married - On Thursday evening last, by W. D. STEELE, Esq., Mr. BASIL S. PORTER of Lumpkin county, Georgia, to Miss SARAH I. O'BRIANT, of this District.

Issue of Saturday December 22, 1849:

Married - On Thursday evening last by W. D. STEELE, Esq., Mr. HENRY HES-TER to Miss MELISSA CLAYTON, all of this District.

Married - On the 20th inst., W. S. GRISHAM, Esq., Mr. J. BAYLIS MOSS to Miss SARAH CAROLINE, oldest daughter of JOS. FINLEY, all of this District.

Married - On the 4th inst., by Rev. NIMROD SULLIVAN, Mr. JOHN BREWER to Miss SARAH COMPTON.

Married - On Tuesday evening last, by the Rev. J. L. KENNEDY, Rev. JOS-EPH B. HILLHOUSE to Miss ESTHER L., eldest daughter of Mr. JAMES STEELE, all of Anderson District.

Issue of Saturday January 19, 1850:

Obituary - Died at Pickensville, S. C. on the 29th December, Mrs. DORCAS BARTON, in the 88th year of her age. The deceased was a native of Virginia, but removed to this State with her husband, Mr. BENJAMIN BARTON, about the year 1780. Her husband did good service for his country in its struggle for Independence ... he took a part in the affair at Cowpens, where the British were so signally defeated. Mrs. Barton was remarkable for the affability of her manners and the strength of her understanding. Her last illness was of several months duration and of a very painful character. In death she was peaceful, calm and resigned. For althou' she had never united herself to any branch of the church, yet the christian's hope soothed and sustained her in passing through the valley and shadow of death. K.

South Carolina, Pickens District - HARRIET VANZANT, Applicant, vs. AMAN-DA JANE VANZANT, JEPTHA VANZANT, ROBERT WILLIAM VANZANT, LAVINA ELIZA-BETH VANZANT, GEO. THOMAS VANZANT, Defendants. It appearing to my satisfaction that the Defendants all reside without this State, it is therefore ordered that they do appear to the division or sale of the Real Estate if WILLIAM VANZANT, deceased, on or before the Eighth day of April next, or their consent to the same will entered of record.

W. D. STEELE, O. P. D.

Issue of Saturday January 26, 1850:

Married - On Tuesday 15th inst., by Rev. D. HUMPHREYS, Mr. T. G. TRIMMIER
to Miss MARY L., daughter of Dr. M. THOMSON, all of Anderson District.

Issue of Saturday February 2, 1850:

Murder - Mr. G. FOWLER, was murdered in Raleigh on the 3rd inst., by
CHRISTOPHER SCOTT, who inflicted three mortal wounds on him with a knife.
Scott is in jail, and bail refused him. The deed was committed at the
house of the devil, or ill fame.   "Ashville Messenger"

Issue of Saturday February 9, 1850:

Sad Death of a Child - A Child, aged 9 years, of JACOB HILES, at Lafayette, N. J., got access to a jug of liquor in the house, last week, and
drank so much that he died next day.

South Carolina, Pickens District - TYRE L. ROPER and wife, MELINDA ROPER,
Applicants, vs. WM. EDENS, ALEXANDER EDENS, PASCAL SOUTHERLAND and wife,
ESTHER SOUTHERLAND, JESSE ADAMS and wife, POLLY ADAMS, Defendants, for
the sale of Real Estate of SAMUEL EDENS, dec'd. And it appears that
Jesse Adams and wife, Polly, reside without the limits of this State.

Issue of Saturday February 23, 1850:

Suicide - On the evening of the 19th inst., the body of NATHANIEL RANKIN,
late of Georgia, was found near the dwelling house of Col. JOHN RANKIN,
three miles from this place, with a shot gun by his side, the contents
of which it was very apparent had been discharged through his head car-
rying away and mutilating almost the entire head. Mr. R. was about 60
years of age and subject to occasional fits of insanity. He was living
with his brother, and having had the misfortune many years ago to lose
one of his legs, was unable to participate in the engagements of the farm
and having been left alone at the house for the evening, seized that opportunity of putting an end to his earthly existence. There was evidence
before the jury of Inquest that the gun had been left in the house on the
rack, and not loaded...that there was powder in the house, but neither
shot nor bullets, and there was no perceptible evidence that the gun had
been charged with lead, though a portion of wad consisting of paper and
rags was found near the body. The conclusion is that the deceased loaded the gun himself with powder and wad, run a small limb of a bush thru'
the guard before the trigger, sat down, held the muzzle to his right ear
with the left hand, and with the right drew up the gun with sufficient
force to pull down the hammer, the fatal spark ignited the powder, and a
heavy charge was driven through his head, scattering fragments of the
skull to a distance of 30 yards. 0, it was a shocking scene...a loath-
some and melancholy duty that jury of Inquest had to perform in view of
that horribly mutilated body, the verdict was that the deceased came to
his death by shooting himself.

Issue of Saturday March 2, 1850:

Married - On Thursday the 21st ult. by JNO. KNOX, Esq., Mr. SAMUEL LOV-
INGOOD to Miss MARY LAY, eldest daughter of Mr. JAMES LAY, all of this
District.

Married - On Wednesday evening 20th ult., by J. E. HAGOOD, Not'y. Public,
Mr. CYRUS YOUNG, JR. to Miss LOTTY SUGGS, daughter of Mr. JESSE SUGGS,
all of this District.

Issue of Saturday March 9, 1850:

Married - On Saturday the 23rd Feburay, by the Rev. NIMROD SULLIVAN, Mr.
M. BROOM to Miss EMILY BUTLER, all of this District.

Married - On Thursday evening 28th February, by JOHN ADAIR, Esq., Mr.
WILLIAM BROOM to Miss ELIZABETH BUTLER, all of this District.

7

Issue of Friday March 22, 1850:

Married - On Thursday evening the 7th inst., by the Rev. J. SCOTT MURRAY, H. M. HALL to Miss CAROLINE, daughter of Col. A. RICE, all of Anderson District.

Issue of Friday April 5, 1850:

Death of JOHN C. CALHOUN - Mr. CALHOUN IS NO MORE...he died in Washington the 31st March, at half past 7 o'clock, a. m. As our mail was very late in coming in last evening, we have barely time to make a few extracts on the subject of Mr. Calhoun's death. He failed gradually, and died calmly, composed and free from pain...3 hours before he remarked that he was fast going...he retained the full possession of his faculties almost to the last moment, and when speech failed him, he showed his consciousness by taking each of his friends by the hand for the long last farewell. His face, since death, is perfectly lifelike.

Married - On the 24th March, by JOHN KNOX, Esq., Mr. JAMES E. COWAN, to Miss LUCINDA E. MAULDIN, all of this District.

Married - On the 24th March, by JOHN KNOX, Esq., Mr. DAVID VINCEN to Miss MARGARETT CHASTAIN, all of this District.

Issue of Friday April 12, 1850:

Married - On Thursday 4th inst., by Rev. WM. G. MULLENIX, Mr. BAILY A. BARTON, of Pickens District, to Miss CAROLINA RAREDON, of Greenville District.

Issue of Friday April 26, 1850:

Death of Maj. O'BRIEN - We regret to learn of the death by cholera of this gallant officer, at Indianola, Texas, on the 2d inst. Major, then we believe Lieutenant O'Brien, was the officer who distinguished himself so highly at Buena Vista, in command of the artillery.

Married - On the 23rd inst., by Rev. J. L. KENNEDY, Mr. L. W. ALLEN, of Abbeville, to Miss ELIZABETH, daughter of Maj. W. L. KEITH.

Issue of Friday May 10, 1850:

Married - On the 2d inst., by JOHN SHARP, Esq., Mr. WILLIAM HOLTZCLAW to Miss RANY FRICKS, all of this District.

Issue of Friday May 17, 1850:

Married - On Thursday 7th inst., by Rev. PHILIP CHAMBERS, Mr. CALLOWAY WHISTENANT to Miss KEMLY, daughter of JABEL CARVER, all of this District.

Obituary - Died, on 28th ultimo, near Jacksonville, Florida, whither he had gone with the hope of restoring his health, JAMES HARRISON HOLLAND, of this District. Extracts of a letter written by Dr. HENRY D. HOLLAND, his Physician, to his brother:
"By the request of Mr. PALMER, at whose house your brother, J. H. Holland, was a sojourner, I have to communicate the demise of your brother. He died on Saturday the 28th April at sun down and his remains were accompanied to the cemetery by many friends and mourners for his untimely fate, on Sunday, 5 p. m. In communicating this mournful intelligence I cannot refrain from saying that he had every comfort that man could ask for under the hospitable roof in which fate had placed him,and the respect and love of all who knew him."

Issue of Friday June 7, 1850:

Death of Hon. (U. S. Senator) FRANKLIN H. ELMORE.

Issue of Friday June 14, 1850:
(see next page)

8

(June 14 cont'd:)

Married - On the 9th inst. at the residence of Col. ANDERSON BEEN in this county, by Rev. J. N. CAROTHERS, Mr. W. D. LAWRENCE (of South Carolina) to Miss MARTHA A. BEEN of Chickasaw county, Mississippi.
"Southern Patriot"

Issue of Friday June 21, 1850:

Suicide - ALVIN, or CALVIN SMITH of Greenwood, Anderson District, committed suicide on Friday last by shooting himself.

Issue of Friday June 28, 1850:

South Carolina, Pickens District - Bill for Part., Discov., Act and Relief In Equity - JAMES YOUNG and wife and others vs. WM. G. CARADINE and others...It appearing to my satisfaction that BIRD CARADINE, HIRAM P. CARADINE, THOS. C. CARADINE, ARTHUR BARRET and wife MARY BARRET, FLEMING THOMPSON and wife ELIZABETH THOMPSON, JANE MILLER, JOHN WEBSTER and wife MARGARET WEBSTER, DANIEL HULL and wife CATHERINE HULL, the heirs at law of NANCY REID, dec'd, who intermarried with HUGH REID, heirs at law of ANDREW CARADINE, dec'd. , defendants to this bill, and heirs at law of THOMAS CARADINE, dec'd, reside from and without the limits of this State.

Issue of Friday July 5, 1850:

Married - On 30th ult. by WM. L. KEITH, Esq., Mr. HARVEY HUGHES to Miss ELIZABETH O'NEAL, all of this District.

Issue of Friday July 12, 1850:

Married - On 4th inst., by W. S. GRISHAM, Esq., Mr. D. S. BREWER to Miss SARAH SUSANNAH O'NEAL, all of this District.

Issue of Friday July 26, 1850:

Sudden Death - It is with pain we announce the sudden death of one of our most esteemed citizens...Hon. ALEXANDER M. MC IVER, who died in this place on Wednesday evening. Mr. McIver had been in delicate health for some time but previous to his death, nothing had occurred to particularly excite the fear of his friends. Mr. McIver was a Solicitor for the Eastern Circuit, to which office he was elected for the third term by the last Legislature. We hope to receive, in time for our next paper, a more extended obituary, from a friend well qualified to perform the melancholy duty.   "Cheraw Gazette"

Married - On the 17th inst., in Augusta, Georgia, by the Rev. JEFFERSON PEARCE, Mr. JOSEPH A. GURLEY of Hamburg, S. C. to Miss S. M. WHITE of Augusta, Ga.

Married - On the 23d inst., by the Rev. STEPHEN POWELL, Mr. JEREMIAH PRICE, to Miss MARTHA LEE, all of this District.

Issue of Friday August 16, 1850:

Married - On 15th inst., by W. S. GRISHAM, Esq., Mr. HENRY MYER, of Charleston, S. C. to Miss MARY ANN, daughter of MATTHIAS FRICKS, Esq., of this District.

Issue of Friday August 23, 1850:

Married - On the 15th inst., by JOHN KNOX, Esq., BRIGHT BURREL, of N. C., to NANCY A. BROWN, of Georgia.

Obituary - Died 11th ultimo, Mrs. MARGARET HALLUM, aged 50 years, consort of Mr. THOS. HALLUM, of Pickens District, S. C. While recording this, the exit of this most estimable friend, from this, to the brighter abodes of bliss, mingled emotions of grief and joy arise in our hearts. For an agonized family that feels the irreparable loss of a most kind, tender

9

(Hallum, contd:)

and faithful partner and parent, our sympathy must flow, amid neighbors
and friends within an extended circle, we cannot but lament that such an
one should so soon be removed from our society, in which she moved like
an angel of mercy, with a mind active, vigorous and prompt to plan for
good...with a heart ever ready "to rejoice with them that weep"...with a
hand just as ready to minister to the wants of the needy, and to relieve
the afflicted...and with a tongue that never failed to defend an absent
friend, when need required, and that with a noble discretion. That branch
of the christian church, which was her early choice, feels that a noble
spirit has been transferred "to the abodes of more than mortal freedom".
Her last wish was to unite, once more, in the worship of God on earth...
she said, I have given up the world, and manifested an anxiety only in
the way of conjugal solicitude and maternal tenderness. Let those unite
with her in society, on earth, use all diligence to meet the offended
God, as she did, in Christ; and thus prepare, by union in a common Media-
tor, for an eternal re-union, when "the vital spark of heavenly flame,
to mount and soar to realms of endless day". ..."Thy art gone to the grave,
but we will not deplore thee;/Though sorrows and darkness encompass the
tomb,/The Saviour has passed through its portals before thee,/And the
lamp of his love is thy guide through the gloom./Thy art gone to the
grave, but'twere wrong to deplore thee,/When God was thy ransom, thy
guardian and guide;/He gave thee, and took thee, and soon will restore
thee,/For death has no sting, since the Saviour has died."

Issue of Friday August 30, 1850:

Married - On Thursday, 22nd inst., by W. C. LEE, Esq., Mr. JOSEPH BURNS
to Miss SARAH JEANS, all of this District.

Issue of Friday September 6, 1850:

Married - On Thursday the 29th ult., by Rev. DAVID HUMPHREYS, Mr. JOSEPH
R. SHEALER to Miss REBECCA VERNER, all of this District.

Married - On Sunday evening, 1st inst., by L. N. ROBINS, Esq., Mr. WIL-
LIAM RANKIN to Miss MINERVA, daughter of Mr. GEORGE HEAD, all of this
District.

Married - On the 1st of September by the Rev. J. R. HUNNICUTT, Mr. RANSOM
A. ONEAL to Miss ELIZABETH BREWER, all of Pickens District.

South Carolina, Pickens District - DAVID LESLY and wife, Applicants vs.
WM. MC WHORTER and wife, and others, Defendants. Whereas it appears to
the Ordinary of said District, that MATHEW KYLE, HENRY KYLE and some of
the children of JAS. KYLE, deceased, vs. JAMES KYLE and HUNTER KYLE, the
children of JOHN LAUGHLIN and WM. KYLE, deceased (names not known) and
the heirs of CATHERINE KYLE, widow of ROBERT KYLE, deceased (names not
known) parties, defendants, reside without the limits of this State: It
is therefore Ordered and Decreed that they do appear and object to the
Partition of the Lands described in the Petition in this case.

Issue of Friday September 13, 1850:

Married - On Tuesday evening last by E. ALEXANDER, Esq., Mr. WILLIAM MC-
ALLISTER to Miss ARMINDA WILSON, all of this District.

Married - On 3rd inst., by JOHN ADAIR, Esq., Mr. JOHN HULL to Miss CARO-
LINA MC GUFFIN, all of this District.

Issue of Friday September 20, 1850:

Married - On the 15th inst., by Rev. _____, Mr. WM. WHITE, of N. C., to
Miss SARAH ANN, daughter of SAMUEL BUSLARK, of this District.

Married - On Thursday the 12th, by W. C. LEE, Mr. SQUIRE SANDERS to Miss
ELIZABETH SMITH, all of this District.

Issue of Friday September 27, 1850: (next page)

(Sept. 27 cont'd:)

Married - On the 24th inst., by the Rev. T. B. MAULDIN, Mr. D. von EITZEN to Miss MARGARET, daughter of MARTIN MOSS, all of this District.

Issue of Friday October 4, 1850:

Married - On the 22nd of September by the Rev. J. R. HUNNICUTT, Mr. WILLIAM WHITEFIELD to Mrs. SILLAR BRADAY, all of Anderson District.

Married - On the 22nd of September by the Rev. DRURY KNOX, Mr. JAMES WALL of Rayburn county, Georgia, to Miss MARTHA MOSELY of this District.

Issue of Saturday October 19, 1850:

Married - On Thursday evening last, by W. D. STEELE, Esq., Mr. NATHAN NEWTON to Miss JERUSHA A. MC CAY, all of this District.

Issue of October 26, 1850:

Death of Judge RICHARD GANTT, 87, at his residence in Greenville District. He was a native of Maryland but at an early age moved to Augusta, Ga., when after a short time he again removed and settled in the practice of law at Cambridge, in this State.

Issue of Saturday November 2, 1850:

Death of JESSE E. DOW - Jesse E. Dow, poet and politician, died suddenly at Washington on the night of the 23d inst.   "Carolinian"

Issue of Saturday November 9, 1850:

South Carolina, Pickens District. Bill for Partition. In Equity - BENJAMIN F. KILPATRICK and wife and others vs. THOM. H. JONES and wife and others. It appearing to my satisfaction that THOMAS H. JONES, DAVID JONES SUSAN C. JONES, LUCINDA J. JONES, REBECCA C. JONES, NANCY JONES, MARTHA M. JONES and MATILDA C. JONES: defendants to this Bill, children of HARTWELL JONES and MARY his deceased wife, formerly MARY STRIBLING, and heirs at law of JESSE STRIBLING, dec'd, late of this District, reside from and without the limits of this State.

Issue of Saturday November 16, 1850:

Married - On 3d inst., by Rev. DRURY KNOX, Mr. J. CLARK TERRELL to Miss MELISSA BROWN, all of this District.

Married - On the 14th inst., by W. L. KEITH, Esq., Mr. JOHN GRIFFIN to Miss ALETHEA ANN KIRKSEY, eldest daughter of Mr. C. KIRKSEY, all of this District.

Issue of Saturday November 23, 1850:

Homicide - It is our duty (says the "Edgefield Advertiser") to record another act of violence in this District. Mr. BRITTON MC CLENDALL was stabbed to death, at his residence, on Monday afternoon last by his stepson, PHILIP HUBBURT. Is it not time for the good men among us to do something to put a stop, if possible, to these shocking occurrences in our District?

Issue of Saturday November 30, 1850:

Death of Y. J. HARRINGTON - We learn from the "Newberry Sentinel" that Y. J. Harrington, of that District, died suddenly on the night of the 11th inst., of pulmonary apoplexy, in the 68th year of his age. He had held the office of Clerk of the Court of Common Pleas of that District about 43 years and was a man of great moral worth.

Married - On 21st inst., by Rev. WM. CARLISLE, Mr. S. H. LANGSTON to Miss LUCY J., eldest daughter of A. O. NORRIS, Esq., all of Anderson District.

(November 30 cont'd:)

Married - At 'Walhalla', on 24th inst., by W. S. GRISHAM, Esq., Mr. HEN-
NING SIEBERN of Charleston to Miss FRANCES FRICKS of this District.

Married - On 21st inst., by Rev. J. R. HUNNICUTT, Mr. WM. MC DUNNIE to
Miss RACHEL SANDERS, all of this District.

Married - In Wilmington, N. C., on the 18th inst., by Rev. Dr. DRANE, Gen.
WADDY THOMPSON, of S. C., to Miss CORNELIA, eldest daughter of Col. JOHN
D. JONES.

We regret to notice, by a Mobile paper, that the lady of Hon. SETH BARTON
died with cholera a few days since in New Orleans.

Issue of Saturday December 7, 1850:

Obituary - Died, on 28th November, 1850, JOSEPH HENRY, youngest son of
Rev. T. B. and ELIZABETH MAULDIN, aged 11 months and 6 days.

Died, suddenly, on the 13th Nov., Mrs. ESTHER STEELE, who was many years
an inhabitant of this town. Mrs. Steele was born June 14, 1770, in Augusta county, Virginia, baptized in the Tinkling Spring Church in that
county and removed with her parents to Carolina after the Revolution.
She has been a consistent member of the Presbyterian church for nearly a
half century and has well sustained the character and profession she assumed. She died at the advanced age of 80 years, as she had lived, full
of faith and good works, and calmly awaiting the coming of her Lord.
                                                    "Pendleton Messenger"
Pickens District, In Equity - Bill for Partition and Sale, etc.- WILLIAM
HUNT and MASON BURDINE, Adm'r. and others vs. JAMES W. HUNT. For sale of
two tracts of land on Dodd's Creek, waters of Saluda River, belonging to
HENSON HUNT, dec'd.

Notice - My wife MATILDA MYERS having left my bed and board without any
just cause or provocation, I hereby forewarn all persons whomsoever from
harboring her, or trading and trafficking with her in any way whatever,
as I shall not be accountable for any debts contracted by her nor for any
property trade by her. HENRY MYERS

Issue of Saturday December 21, 1850:

Married - On the 12th inst., in Greenville, by Rev. T. S. ARTHUR, Miss
CAROLINE MATILDA LEWIS and WM. H. CAMPBELL, Esq.

Married - On the 18th inst., by W. D. STEELE, Esq., Mr. JAMES C. O'BRIANT
to Miss HANNAH A., daughter of DANIEL M. ALEXANDER, all of this District.

Married - On 12th inst., by Rev. EDMUND ANDERSON, Maj. A. C. PICKENS, of
Pickens District, to Miss MARY J. BOONE, of Anderson District.

Issue of Saturday December 28, 1850:

Married - On the 19th inst., by Rev. D. H. KENNEMUIR, Mr. SAMUEL STEVENS
to Miss JOANNA SMITH, all of this District.

Married - On the 22nd inst., by Rev. J. R. HUNNICUTT, Mr. ALFRED HEMBREE
to Miss LUCY J. MURRY, all of Pickens District.

Married - At Whetstone on 20th inst. by SAM'L MOSELEY, Esq., Mr. JOHN
SMITH of Chauga, to Miss REBECCA SHED, daughter of JOEL SHED of Bone Camp
and all of this District.

Married - On the 24th inst., by Rev. E. COLLINS, Mr. HENRY D. WILLBANKS,
of Georgia, to Miss LEVINA BEARDEN, of Pickens District.

Issue of Saturday January 4, 1851:

Married - On Sunday evening 29th ult., by O. E. BARTON, Esq., Mr. WM. H.

(January 4 cont'd:)

ANDERSON to Mrs. NANCY R. ANDERSON, all of this District.

Issue of Saturday January 18, 1851:

Married - On Thursday evening last, at the house of Mr. JAMES SMITH, by
MILES M. NORTON, Esq., Mr. WILLIAM ROSS O'NEALL and MARY ANN, daughter
of Rev. LEWIS FINDLEY, all of this District.

Married - On Thursday evening last by W. D. STEELE, Esq., Mr. WM. B. MC-
CAY to Miss R. CATHARINE BELL, all of this District.

Married - On Thursday 9th inst., by W. C. LEE, Esq., Mr. ALEXANDER GRAHAM
to Miss TEMPERANCE ABBOTT, all of this District.

Married - On Thursday 9th inst., by Rev. ANDREW MC GUFFIN, Mr. DANIEL
BROWN to Miss MARTHA KANNADY, all of this District.

Issue of Saturday January 25, 1851:

Married - On the 12th inst., by JOHN KNOX, Esq., Mr. MARION J. BECK to
Miss CAROLINE RIDER, all of Pickens District.

Issue of Saturday February 8, 1851:

Obituary - Died, in Anderson village on the 7th of January ult., ELIZA
FOSTER, eldest daughter of the Hon. JAMES L. and MARY J. ORR, aged six
years, two months and fourteen days. A lovely flower faded before its
bloom was unfolded. The doom of early death was pronounced upon her and
her sun went down whilst it was yet day. We may well exclaim in the
touching language of Moore....(Poetry).

Married - Near the Oconee Station, on '30th ult., by L. N. ROBINS, Esq.,
Mr. JEPTHA HEAD to Miss SARAH, eldest daughter of EDWARD RANKIN.

Married - On 22nd January, by Rev. J. R. HUNNICUTT, Mr. ELIJAH HEMBREE
to Miss MARY BALLDON, all of Pickens District.

Married - On 30th ult., by Rev. J. R. HUNNICUTT, Mr. J. MOOR to Miss N.
K. LUMPKIN.

Issue of Saturday February 22, 1851:

Married - On the 14th inst., by Rev. JOHN SMITH, Miss VALENTINA SMITH to
Mr. JOHN SMITH, all of this District. If this does not locate John Smith
at last, we humbly desire to know what will.....Ed.

Obituary - Died, at their father's residence in the neighborhood of Bachelor's Retreat, THOMAS B. HUGHES, in the 22nd year of his age; and GEORGE
B. HUGHES, in the 19th year of his age. Thomas died on the 30th Jan. and
George on Thursday following. I assure, Mr. Editor, that I scarcely know
what to say on the contemplation of an event so strikingly awful. A few
hours before they were called on to change worlds, the bounding blood of
youth coursed its way through their veins, with a glee of life which is
always expressive of good health, to them the land scape of the future
was as richly ominous of long life, and many earthly blessings, as they
probably thought of, or wished for. But Thomas and George are gone. No
more shall we sit together around our firesides and talk of things common. Those brother-like and friendly voices, that used to make delightful a parent's home; are now hushed forever. We stood by them...bade
them farewell and saw them die. O, what a farewell was that. Earth's
brightest hopes are blighted...the two young men are dead! The only relief the living now have is to walk beside their tombs...breathe a sigh
...shed a tear and think of that same mournful word...Farewell! Oh,that
the spirit of absent would whisper to the hearts of their associates,
never to scoff at Religion; tell them too, that religion will not harness
a chariot of an earthly conquest, nor spread the canopy of an earthly em-
pire; but more than all and better than all, it lives at the sick man's

13

Feb. 22 cont'd:

bed...kneels down by the side of the tomb...and points the dying pilgrim
to this endless rest.   S.

Issue of Saturday March 1, 1851:

Obituary - Departed this life, on 12th ult. at 4 o'clock a.m., at the
residence of her mother in Pickens District, Miss MARY P. GAINES. With
christian patience she bore a most painful illness of four weeks; she
leaves an aged mother and many relations to lament her early death. The
subject of this notice was an ornament in the church of which she was,
for many years, an attentive member, and during her illness gave many evidences of a strong faith in the christian religion. When much cufeebled
she would often say: "I have enjoyed the spring of life, endured the
toils of summer, culled the fruits of autumn, am now passing through the
dreary winter, and am not forsaken of my God. I see the dawn of a new
day...the first of a spring that shall be eternal, it advances to me, I
hasten to embrace it. Welcome, welcome eternal spring! halleljah!

South Carolina, Pickens District   - JNO. MYERS and HENRY MYERS and others,
Applicants, Against the heirs of ROBERT HONNEA. It appearing to my satisfaction that part of the heirs of Robert Honnea reside without the limits of this State, it is therefore ordered that they do appear and object
to the division or sale of the real estate of HENRY MYERS.

Issue of Saturday March 8, 1851:

From Texas - The following extract is from a letter received by a gentleman in this neighborhood, from his son in Texas. The young man alluded
to was, we believe, the son of Col. BENJAMIN BARTON, formerly of Pickens
district, who moved to Texas several years ago. He was the descendant
of a gallant race, and died without dishonoring it. (Messenger)
Laredo, Texas   Jan. 29, 1851
    "We are again troubled with our friends, the Indians. They commenced
about two days since by killing three of our citizens within six miles
of town, and drove off a large amount of stock. Lieut. WALKER, of Fords
Rangers, overtook, killed three and retook 70 odd mules...he had one man
wounded. Two days after a party of the same company, under Lieut. E.
BURLESON, encountered fifteen, and with eight men gave them battle...
a desperate encounter ensued in which one American was killed and six
wounded, (Burleson was shot in the head). But two of the Indians escaped
unhurt, although but two were left dead on the ground. The wounded here
and will do well. The poor fellow killed was WM. B. BARTON, a native of
Pendleton, S. C. He was one of my old soldiers and a noble fellow. From
the battle of Monteray, where he was badly wounded, to the present time,
he has been in active service on this frontier, and died fighting gal-
lantly. He is related to all the Pendleton Bartons, and I believe has
left a wife. Let a notice be written and published in the Pendleton paper. A part of his family reside in eastern Texas. "The fight was on
this (western) side of the Nueces river."

Dastardly Murder - On Friday last a woman by the name WALL, residing in
St. Lukes Parish, Beaufort District, South Carolina, was shot dead in
her own house by some cowardly assassin, who made his escape without having been discovered. We hope the murderer will yet meet retributive justice.

Married - on Thursday evening the 20th ult., by the Rev. T. M. WILKES,
the Rev. L. R. L. JENNINGS, of Pendleton, S. C., to Miss SALLIE E. STOW,
of Eatonton, Ga.

Married - On the 6th inst., by Rev. W. MC WHORTER, Mr. JOSEPH M. DEVENEAU
to Miss CAROLINE M. HOWARD.

Issue of Saturday March 15, 1851:

An Aged Couple - Mrs. NANCY GORDON died at Rockaway, N. J., on the 16th
inst., aged near 90. Had she lived till March 14, she would have seen

14

(March 15 cont'd;)

the seventy first anniversary of her marriage. During the whole time she
and her husband, who still survives her at the age of 92, have lived within sight of Rockaway Church. This aged pair have had nine children, of
whom five survive; forty nine grandchildren, of whom thirty three survive;
one hundred and three great grandchildren, of whom seventy four survive,
and two great great grandchildren, both still living, making in number
their descendants, living and dead, one hundred and sixty three of whom
one hundred and fourteen still survive.

Issue of Saturday March 22, 1851:

South Carolina, Pickens District. In Equity - Bill for Partition and
Sale of Real Estate. ISAAC HOLDEN and wife JANE vs. JANE NICHOLSON, widow, EVAN NICHOLSON, et al. The Complainants having filed their Bill in
my Office, and it appearing to my satisfaction that EVAN NICHOLSON, JAMES
LOVELESS and wife SARAH, WILLIAM HOLDEN and wife MARTHA, WILLIAM NICHOL-
SON, MORDECAI COX and wife MALINDA, parties Defendants to the said Bill
of Complaint.

South Carolina, Pickens District. In Equity - Bill for Partition of
Real Estate. JAS. MULLIKEN and wife MALINDA vs. MARTHA NORTON, ROBERT
WILSON and wife SARAH, et al. The complainants having filed their Bill
in my office and it appearing in my satisfaction that the heirs of ZIP-
PORAH FORBES, deceased, viz. ELMINA, ADOLPHUS, NELSON FORBES and others,
and the heirs at law of MARTHA FORBES, deceased, viz: JEPTHA, ELIZA,
GOERGE FORBES and others, reside from and without the limits of this
State.

Issue of March 29, 1851:

Married - On Thursday evening, 27th inst., by Rev. WM. MC WHORTER, Col.
E. R. DOYLE to Miss SUSAN DENDY, all of this District.

Issue of Saturday April 12, 1851:

Greenville Court - On Wednesday, ENOCH MASSEY passed through the most
terrible ordeal to which frail humanity can be subjected, he being in-
dicted and found guilty of murder. On Thursday...the father and two
brothers of Enoch Massey were to be arraigned as particeps criminis.
Enoch Massey was sentenced to be hung on the 27th of June next.

Issue of Saturday May 3, 1851:

Obituary - Died, at West Union, on 28th inst. at 3 o'clock A.M., Mrs.
MARTHA JOSEPHINE, wife of Maj. WILLIAM S. GRISHAM, aged twenty-one years,
two months and nine days. Her illness lasted about six weeks, and was
very severe. She has left a husband, many relatives, and numerous friends
to mourn their loss. Having lived at West Union only a few years she
gained for herself the esteem of all her acquaintances and truly they
who knew her best loved her most. In every relation of life she was am-
able, affectionate and kind; as a christian, she lived, and always recommended the religion she professed and enjoyed, by a pious deportment
and well ordered conversation. As she lived so she died...full of faith,
and in full assurance of a blessed immortality. Her sun sunk not behind
a cloud, but a star in midheaven she seemed, shined away by the brighter
glories of the rising sun. She often spoke during her illness of her
approaching dissolution, with calmness and with confidence that she was
going to a better world, and when the final hour came she met the King
of Terrors with becoming Christian fortitude...breathed her last without a struggle, and fell asleep in Jesus.

Married - On the 30th April, by Rev. DAVID HUMPHREYS, Mr. ISHAM W. TAY-
LOR to Miss NARCISSA C., daughter of Col. JOHN MC FALL, all of Anderson
District.

Issue of Saturday May 10, 1851:

Melancholy Suicide - On the 9th inst., Mrs. MARY GAINES, an aged widow,

15

(May 10 cont'd:)

and for many years a member of the Methodist Church, committed suicide
by hanging herself with a hank of thread to the beam of a loom. Mrs. G.
had been for for sometime partially deranged in mind.

Sad Accident - On Tuesday, the 6th inst., Mr. C. BULWINKLE, of Walhalla,
in this District, together with Mrs. BULWINKLE and child were thrown
from a vehicle in which they were driving by the horse taking fright, and
were so badly injured that Mr. B. and his child died a few hours after
the accident occurred; Mrs. B. though seriously hurt is said to be recovering. Mr. Bulwinkle was an intelligent and enterprising German, one
of the chief of the German settlement, and his loss will be severely felt
and sorely lamented by his countrymen.

Obituary - Died, April 28th, 1851, in Pickens Dist., S. C., Mrs. ISABELLA
REID, relict of JOSEPH REID, deceased. The subject of this notice lived
to the advanced age of 91 years; and although unable to walk for a great
length of time, yet she was resigned to the will of her Maker, in whom
she had a good hope eternal life thro' Christ Jesus, having adorned her
profession, as a member of the Presbyterian Church, for sixty years; tes-
tifying to the grace of God and the suffiencey of Christ's atoning blood
to save the chief of sinners. Like a shock of corn fully ripe, she was
as we trust, gathered to the garner of heaven, "where the wicked cease
from troubling, and where the weary are at rest".

Issue of Saturday April 25, 1857:

Death of Col. JOSEPH GRISHAM - The numerous friends of this gentleman
will be pained to learn that he departed this life on the 9th instant.
The sad event was not unlooked for by his family, and occurred at his
residence near Canton, Ga. His death is supposed to have been caused
from the effects of an injury received, in 1837, by being kicked on the
leg by a horse and from which he never fully recovered. Latterly, his
sufferings were very great, but it will be gratifying to his friends to
know that they were borne with Christian fortitude and resignation. He
died with the heavenly promise bright before him. Col. Grisham was born
in Anderson district, in 1789, but was, for a long number of years, a
useful and prominent citizen of Pickens. His industry and energy, combined with punctuality and stricktly temperate habits, amassed for him
a large property, notwithstanding heavy losses by fire and flood. In
public affairs, he took the same active interest that characterized him
in the management of his private concerns; ample evidence of his success
in which may be seen. in the workings of our district police, at this
time. His integrity was above reproach, and his patriotism undoubted.
He was a friend to the deserving, and his charities, public and private,
accorded harmoniously with his ability to give. It is impossible, in a
passing newspaper article, to do justice to his life and memory; therefore, we leave it for more competent and appropriate hands.

South Carolina, Pickens District. In Equity - Bill for Partition, Account, Relief, &c. AERAHAM DUKE, HARRIET DUKE and RANSOM DUKE vs. JO-
SEPH DOLLESON, MELINDA DOLLESON, BENJAMIN CANNON, WASHINGTON CANNON, CAR-
TER CANNON, JAMES CANNON, MARGARET MARCHBANKS, JUDY or JUDITH KENDRICK,
ELIJAH CANNON. MARTHA BROWN and WILLIAM GILSTRAP. The Complainants having filed their bill of complaint, and it appearing to my satisfaction
that Joseph Dolleson, Melinda Dolleson, Benjamin Cannon, Washington Cannon, Carter Cannon, James Cannon, Margaret Marchbanks, Judy or Judith
Kendrick, Elijah Cannon and Martha Brown, defendants to said bill, reside without the limits of this State.

Issue of Saturday May 2, 1857:

Lynched to Death - BILL JOHNSON, a desperado, was lately lynched by the
citizens of Waco, Texas, and the Coroner's Jury reported that he came
to his death by means of a rope and a gun in the hands of persons unknown.

Dead - Lieut. WM. GARDNER, of the U. S. Navy, died very suddenly in Aug-

(May 2 cont'd:)

usta, Georgia on Wednesday last, of disease of the heart. He was about forty years of age and leaves a large circle of relatives and friends to mourn his loss.

Married - on the 25th inst., by W. S. GRISHAM, Esq., Mr. DANIEL J. KENNEDY to Miss LETTIE ANN GILBERT, all of Tunnel Hill.

Married - On the 26th inst., by W. J. PARSONS, Esq., Mr. JOAB LEWIS, of Texas, to Mrs. VILANTY COBB, of Pickens District.

Married - On the 29th ult. by JOHN KNOX, Esq., Mr. WM. J. CRANE to Miss ELIZABETH MC ALISTER, both of Pickens District.

Obituary - Died, in Texas, on the 24th of March last, of flux, STEPHEN J. CLAYTON, in the 24th year of his age. Death, at all times, is a solemn event, but more especially does it weigh heavily, when the young and promising fall by its insatiate shaft. The subject of this notice was a native of Pickens district, and son of PHILIP CLAYTON, Esq. He was young in years and full of promise; and, but a short time previous to his death had removed to (....torn....) there to begin life with a confident hope of success, in the very spring-time of manhood. But alas! for prospects bright and hopes human. They, with the manly form of our friend, are entombed to the grave...his dust in a strange land, and his soul,we trust, with the God who gave it. His death was sudden, and it fell with heart piercing grief upon his family here, while his numerous relatives and friends mourn their loss; but they mourn not as those without hope. "For the Lord giveth and the Lord taketh away, blessed be the name of the Lord".

Issue of Saturday May 9, 1857:

Murder - We regret to learn that Mr. WARREN REID was killed by a man named TURNER, at ROWLAND's old store, in Greenville district, on Saturday last. A knife was the instrument used, entering the body near the heart, and causing death almost instantly. Turner was arrested immediately, and has been committed to jail. Reid was a native of Pickens, and leaves a wife and four children.

Burned - A little daughter of T. H. DeGRAFFENREID, of Chester, was burned to death by her clothes accidentally taking fire out in the yard at play. She lingered but two or three hours.

Lynched - Two men, named WM. FERGUSON and C. N. JOHNSON, concerned in robbing and murdering Chinese in Butte county, California, were hung by the populace on the night of the 1st ult.

Obituary - Died, at Tunnel Hill, on the 24th ultimo, EDMUND MARTIN, in the 60th year of his age. The deceased was a native of Anderson district but, for many years previous to his death had made Pickens his home. He had been connected with the Baptist church, as a member, for forty years, and died in the full enjoyment of the christian's final hope, and receiving the rewards of the faithful Christ. For several years before he was called hence, he discharged the responsible duties of Magistrate with equal justice to all, and satisfaction to the public generally. He leaves a family and many relatives and friends to mourn his death, but they sorrow not as those without hope.

Issue of Saturday May 16, 1857:

Death of Maj. WHITFIELD - We are pained to learn that Maj. J. T. WHITFIELD died on Tuesday last, at Anderson C. H. The immediate cause of his death has not reached us, but he had lived to a ripe old age. He represented Pendleton district in the Legislature for a number of years, and, at the time of his death, was the oldest lawyer on the Western circuit.

Married - In Yorkville, on Tuesday morning last, by the Rev. W. W. CAROthers, SAMUEL W. MELTON, Esq., (co-editor of the "Yorkville Enquirer")

(May 16. cont'd:)

and Miss MARY H. GOORE, both of Yorkville.

Died - Suddenly, from the effects of poison by eating bee-bread, at his
residence in Wilkinson county, of the 20th ult., JESSE L. RUSTON, leaving a distressed wife and five little children to mourn his loss.

Sad - The name of the fireman killed at the recent railroad collision
near Memphis, was Mr. D. LYNCH. The accident was caused by his brother,
an engineer, who disobeyed orders in running his engine to endeavor to
make a connection at Moscow.

Married - On the 30th ult., by JOHN KNOX, Esq., Mr. JOSEPH WHITE to Miss
FRANCES E. ROGERS, all of Pickens District.

Married - On Sunday evening 10th inst., by L. N. ROBINS, Esq., THOS. W.
FINDLEY to Miss LUCINDA, daughter of WM. WHITMIRE, all of Pickens.

Obituary - Departed this life, on Saturday, the 2d inst., at the residence of her brother, Col. WILLIAM L. CALHOUN, in Abbeville District,
MARTHA CORNELIA CALHOUN, in the 31st year of her age. The deceased was
the youngest daughter of Mrs. FLORIDE CALHOUN and the late JOHN C. CAL-
HOUN. Her death was very sudden and unexpected to her friends; but she
met her fate with that calm and resigned spirit which characterizes the
death of the true christian. She was a communicant of the Episcopal
Church, and we cannot doubt is now realizing the reward of a well spent
life. The deceased was a lady of marked intelligence, and was strongly
characterized by amiability and mildness of disposition. She died, we
think, without an enemy. We would not add a fulsome eulogy on the character of the deceased, as this would be unnecessary to those who knew
her, and would but disparage her true worth with those who did not know
her.

State of South Carolina, Pickens District. In Equity - Bill of Partition.
MARY ANN COUCH vs. ROBERT COUCH and others. It appearing to my satisfaction that the heirs at law of ELLENDER BAKER, to wit: JOHN BAKER, the
heirs at law of MARY ANN WILLIAMS,   FORRESTER and wife ELIZABETH,
WILLIAM BAKER, LUCINDA BAKER, ROBERT BAKER, RICHARD BAKER, CRAWFORD BAK-
ER and LEWELLEN BAKER, defendants to this bill of complaint, reside
without the limits of this State.

Issue of Saturday May 23, 1857:

Dead - THOS. G. KEY, Esq., a practicing lawyer at Edgefield C. H., died
there last week. He was for several years, editor of the "Hamburg Journal".

Death of JAS. BOATWRIGHT - This venerable citizen of Columbia, aged more
than four score years, is dead. He was an estimable citizen in all the
relations of life.

Man Shot in Georgia - JOHN EDWARDS, a citizen of Talbot county, was shot
at Talbotton on the 2nd inst., by one WM. GIDDINGS. Mr. Edwards lingered until Monday the 4th, when he died.

Obituary - Died, at his residence in Pickens district, on the 17th inst.,
after a lingering illness, A. P. WRITE, in the 47th year of his age. The
deceased was an honest, upright and honorable man ..kind and affectionate to his family, and a good neighbor. He leaves a large family and
many relatives to mourn his loss.

Married - At Tunnel Hill, on the 19th instant, by A. B. BOWDEN, Esq., Mr.
JULIUS HOFFMAN to Miss TALITHA STILWELL, all of Pickens.

Issue of Saturday May 30, 1857:

Death of Dr. D. T. HOLLAND - We are pained to learn the death of Dr. DAVID
T. HOLLAND, which occurred in Florida, on the 11th inst., where he had
gone for the restoration of his health. His disease was consumption.

Married - On the 24th inst., by Rev. W. G. MULLENIX (Mullinnix), Mr. MAR-
CUS M. ARNOLD to Miss LOUISA M. MADDEN, all of Pickens District.

Issue of Saturday June 6, 1857:

Death of Senator BUTLER - The Hon. A. P. BUTLER, Senator in Congress from
this State, died at his home in Edgefield district, on the 25th ult., of
dropsy of the chest. His illness was of several weeks duration, and was
borne with fortitude and resignation. Judge Butler has, during his official career, filled various offices of high trust and public importance.
He was born in 1798, graduated in the South Carolina College in 1817, and
was admitted to the bar in 1818. He was elected a Law Judge in 1833, and
in his administration of the law and justice, none were more highly esteemed and respected. In 1846, he was elected to the U. S. Senate, and
at once took a high position. At the time of his death he was Chairman
of the Committee on the Judiciary, and his reports were almost always
concurred in. The deep feeling and gloom which pervaded the public mind
on this sad announcement attest the hold he had upon the esteem and affections of the people. Socially, he was inferior to no man, and his
eminent ability had made a reputation for him co-extensive with the country, of which any man might be proud. South Carolina had not laid aside
the mantle of mourning for her BROOKS, ere she wraps herself in it again
and bewails the demise of the much loved, pure-minded and distinguished
Butler.

Homicide - JOHN W. GREGORY was killed on Tuesday last, in Lancaster District, by JONATHAN B. DOUGLAS. WILLIS T. GREGORY, the son of the murdered man, offers a reward of two hundred dollars for the apprehension
of Douglas.

Death of a Preacher - Rev. C. F. R. SHEHANE, well known in the South as
a champion of the Universalist denomination of Christians, died at his
residence, near Notasluga, Ala., on the 17th ult.

Issue of Saturday June 13, 1857:

Married - On the 3d inst., by Rev. W. G. MULLINNIX, Mr. F. H. THURBER,
to Miss MATILDA A. GASAWAY, all of Pickens.

Married - On the 4th inst., by Rev. J. SCOTT MURRAY, Mr. T. J. WEBB to
Miss E. F. WILLIAMSON, of Anderson.

Married - On the 7th inst., by W. S. GRISHAM, Esq., Mr. J. A. SHIELDS to
Miss WADE, all of Pickens.

Obituary - Died, on the 26th ult., in Pickens district, Mrs. EMILY SLOAN,
consort of A. J. SLOAN, aged 34 years and 19 days. She was received into the communion of the Presbyterian church, at Bethel, in 1841. For
over sixteen years she followed her Ssviour through evil as well as good
report. She died in the triumphant hope of a blessed immortality. She
patiently bore her sickness, being confined to her bed for three weeks,
showing to all who saw her that she had been changed, and that her hope
was in God. As her life was consistent, her death was peaceful, passing
away without a groan or struggle. Her bereaved husband, with two little
children, mother and a large circle of relatives and friends, are con-
soled in our irreparable loss, in the hope that our loss is her eternal
gain. Will the Lord lead us so to live that our last end my be peace.
"Blessed are the dead who die in the Lord".   A Friend

Issue of Saturday June 20, 1857:

Death of a Veteran - SETH INGRAM died at Matagorda, on the 12th ult.,
aged sixty-seven. His life, like those of most old Texans, was full of
vicissitudes. He was a volunteer in the last war between England and
the United States, and severely wounded in the battle of Lundy's Lane.

Married - On the 3d inst., at Orange Springs, Florida, by the Rev. J. M.
QUARTERMAN, D. B. BOYD, Esq. of S. C., to Miss MARY P., daughter of ROB-
ERT ANDERSON, esq., formerly of Greenwood, S. C.

Death of LANGDON CHEVES - This truly great man died in Columbia on the
26th ult., in the eighty-first year of his age. He was a native of Abbeville, and entered public life when young. As a lawyer, he took high
position; then he was sent to Congress, where, during the war of 1812,
he distinguished himself in debate, advocating the cause of his country
against our natural enemy. He was afterwards elected Speaker of the
House. On returning home, he was elected Judge. And afterwards appointed President of the United States Bank. The Carolinian says his frame
was Herculean, and his intellect massive and powerful, and he bore within himself Roman sternness and Roman greatness. He was one of the noblest sons of South Carolina. She has in the last fifteen years lost a
HAYNE, a LEGARE, a MC DUFFIE, a CALHOUN, a BUTLER...all great men in the
enlarged sense of the term...and now again she is called on to mourn for
Langdon Cheves, one of the purest and most glorious of her sons. Peace
to his ashes ... the Goddess of Fame leans on his tomb.

His Birth Place - the Hon. A. B. MOORE, of Marion, Ala., Democratic nom-
inee for the Governorship of that State, is a native of Spartanburg, S.
C., which has still many more of the same sort of sons.

Distressing Casuality - At Danville, Sumter county, Ga. on the 10th inst.
the Ferry House, together with its contents, was consumed by fire, and
Mrs. MC KINLEY and her step daughter burned to death.

"Old Grimes Dead" - Mr. S. D. GRIMES died recently in Georgia, at the
great age of one hundred and ten years. He never was sick.

JOHN LAPOINT, for the murder of ROBERT WHEATON; ISRAEL SHOULTZ for shooting JOHN ISHAM, and JACOB WOESLIN, for killing his wife, were executed
in the jail yard in St. Louis, Saturday, and at Edwardsville, Illinois,
GEO. W. SHARPE and JOHN JOHNSON were hung for the murder of BARTH.

The Largest Man - MILES DARDEN, of Henderson county, Tenn., has just departed this life. He was the largest man in the world. His height was
seven feet six inches; two inches higher than PORTER, the celebrated
Kentucky giant. His weight was a fraction over one thousand pounds!

Married - On the 25th ult. by J. B. SANDERS, Esq., Mr. THOMAS J. GRANT
to Miss ZILPHA JACKSON, all of Pickens District.

Issue of Saturday July 11, 1857:

Executed - JAMES A. PRICE, who murdered Mr. JOSEPH HUGHES,Sen., in Union
District, four years ago, was executed on the 26th ult., near Unionville,
in presence of an immense concourse.

Death of Hon. W. L. MARCY - Death loves a shining mark! A telegraphic
dispatch to the Columbia papers advise of the death of Hon. W. L. Marcy,
Secretary of State under President PIERCE. He died at Ballston, N. Y.,
suddenly on the 4th of July. He was found in his room, having died a-
lone...perhaps of apoplexy.

Issue of Saturday July 18, 1857:

Drowned - We regret to learn that Mr. WILSON MC KINNEY, of this District,
was drowned in Keowee river, near his residence, on the 12th inst. It
appears that he entered the stream for a specific purpose, and, although
being an expert swimmer, he was unable to save himself. A lad was standing by at the time, but he was too small to do more than give the alarm.

Shooting Affair - We learn from the "Mountain (Ga.) Signal" of the 11th
inst., that an affray took place in Union county on the 4th between J. K.
WOODY and WM. DOCERY. Woody, who was armed with a rifle, shot his antag-
onist thro' the breast, and his life is despaired of. The affray grew
out of a law suit.

A Ripe Old Age - Mrs. SARAH LANCASTER, a lady aged one hundred and one

(Mrs. Lancaster cont'd:)

years five months and seven days, departed this life, near the village of Spartanburg on the 7th instant. Mrs. Lancaster came to Spartanburg before the Revolution, and has been there ever since.

Death of Gen. HERNANDEZ - The Jacksonville News announces the death of Gen. JOSEPH M. HERNANDEZ, of Florida, who was the first delegate to Congress while in the territorial condition, a leading member of the terr. Legislature, and on the breaking out of Indian hostilities, was made a Brigadier General in the United States service.

Tribute of Respect - To. W. T. MC JUNKIN, deceased, by Pendleton Lodge, A.F.M.

Issue of Saturday July 25, 1857:

Killed - Mr. B. S. MIDYETT, of Hyde Co., N. C., was killed by lightning on the 29th ult., while returning from his daily occupation to his family. Mr. Midyett was a mechanical engineer, and at the time of his death had charge of Mr. ROSS's steam-mills.

Married - On the 12th inst., by WM. S. WOOLBRIGHT, Esq., Mr. PRIESTLY ABLES, of Pickens, to Miss MARY KING, of Anderson.

Obituary - Departed this life, on the 22nd inst. of chronic affection(?) after an illness of six weeks, Mrs. DILLEY CHAPMAN, in the 47th year of her age. The subject of this notice had been, for many years, an exemplary member of the Methodist Church, and died in the fullest confidence of reaping the reward of her labors in her Master's service, and finding a home in Heaven. Some years since, Mrs. Chapman had the misfortune to lose her husband by death. Left with four small children dependent upon her exertions, she has struggled on till death has severed the connection. Before her spirit passed away, she committed them to the protecting care of the "Father of the fatherless", and may He guide and protect them.

Issue of Saturday August 1, 1857:

Married - On the 21st ultimo, by W. S. WOOLBRIGHT, Esq., Mr. THOMAS E. CLARK to Miss ELIZABETH GRANT, all of Pickens.

Issue of Saturday August 8, 1857:

Married - On the 23rd ult., by Rev. J. R. HUNNICUTT, Mr. WM. RAY, to Miss ANN DEALE, all of Georgia.

Married - On the 26th ult., by the Rev. Hunnicutt, Mr. WM. HOLLBROOK to Miss CAROLINE HOLMES, all of Pickens.

State of South Carolina, Pickens. Summons in Partition - E. and E. M. FIELD vs. J. D. FIELD and others. It appearing to my satisfaction that JOHN D. FIELD, B. W. FIELD, JOSEPH DONALDSON and wife, JAMES M. FIELD and AMOS L. SOUTHERLAND and wife, reside without the limits of this State. (Sale of Real Estate of JEREMIAH FIELD(S), deceased.)

Issue of Saturday August 15, 1857:

Death of Hon. THOS. J. RUSK - The recent intelligence from Texas is truly astounding as well as melancholy. On the 29th ult., THOMAS J. RUSK, United States Senator, committed suicide by shooting himself through the head with a rifle. Senator Rusk was a native of this district. He emigrated to Georgia when quite young, and removed to Texas during her struggle for independence, and took an active part in the trying scenes of that period. Gen. Rusk was a man of ability, and greatly beloved by the people of Texas. His popularity South was also great, and his name had been connected with the Presidency by men of position and influence. His death, under any circumstances is to be lamented, but more especially in the manner in which he deprived himself of life. The following is the

(Rusk cont'd:)

only particulars we have seen: "No special case was assigned for the
deed, but it is supposed that the mind of Senator Rusk has been much dis-
turbed lately in consequence of some alleged connection of his brother-
in-law with forgeries on the Land Department. The matter, it is surmised,
prayed upon him to such an extent as to induce this terrible result."

Dead - Hon. JOHN RIVERS, a distinguished and aged citizen of Charleston
district, died on the 3d inst., in the 73d year of his age.

Dead - Hon. J. C. DOBBIN, a member of President PIERCE's cabinet, died
in North Carolina last week.

Killed by Lightning - JOHN TRAPP, a young man residing near Milledgeville,
Ga., was instantly killed by lightning last Friday week.

Married - On Sunday morning the 9th inst., by Rev. M. CHASTAIN, Mr. T. M.
ALEXANDER to Miss ANGALINA BARTON, all of Pickens.

Issue of Saturday August 22, 1857:

Inquest - On the 16th inst., an inquest was held over the dead body of
ADALINE GREY, in this District. The jury was empanneled by J. G. C.
KRUSE, Esq., in the absence of the Coroner. The verdict of the jury
was, that she came to her death from want of medical attention and proper nursing.

Issue of Saturday August 29, 1857:

Accidental Death - We regret to learn that Mr. JOHN ERSKINE, a respected
citizen of this District, says the Gazette and Advocate of the 26th, died
on Wednesday last, from an accidental injury received on the side of the
head. He was cutting down a tree at the time, which, in the act of falling broke off a limb which struck him upon the head, producing a con-
cussion of the brain. The injury was a severe one, and he survived it
only a week.

Married - On the 13th inst., by E. HUGHES, Esq., Mr. FRANCIS DUVAL to
Miss N. T. DAVIS, all of Pickens.

Married - On the 27th inst., by Rev. W. G. MULLINNIX, Mr. H. W. M. BOGGS
to Miss MARY C. KNOX, all of Pickens.

Issue of Saturday September 5, 1857:

Mrs. DANIEL - The last "Anderson Gazette" announces the death of Mrs.
MARY E. DANIEL, a most successful teacher in the Johnson Female University at that place.

Caged - IVY FORTNER, who killed FOUNTAIN SNOW in Lumpkin county, Ga.,
some time ago, has been arrested and lodged in jail.

Death of Col. BRANNON - Col. JAMES BRANNON, formerly of Spartanburg district, died at Marietta, Ga., on the 20th ult. Col. B. commanded a company in the war of 1812, and was a member of the Legislature from Spartanburg. For the last few years he had resided in Georgia.

Dead - Hon, JOHN LONG died in Randolph county, N. C., on Tuesday, of last
week, from a fall while climbing a fence. He was formerly a member of
Congress from North Carolina and had, until lately, been a prominent politician in that State.

Obituary - Died, in Tallapoosa county, Ala., on the 8th day of May last,
Mrs. SARAH THOMPSON, in the 70th year of her age. The subject of this
notice was a native of Spartanburg district. In company with her family,
she removed to Pendleton district, and in 1825 to Gwinnet county, Ga.
Afterwards she removed with her youngest son to Alabama, where she
breathed her last peacefully and happily. In early life, she connected

(Thompson cont'd:)

herself with the Methodist church, and continued to the end an upright
and consistent member. She was a loving wife, an indulgent mother, and
kind neighbor. She leaves many relatives and friends to mourn her decease, but they mourn not as those without hope. "Blessed are the dead
who die in the Lord".

Issue of Saturday September 12, 1857:

Hanged - CHESLY BOATWRIGHT was hanged at Camden on the 4th instant, for
murder. He warned the crowd in attendance against bad company and drinking to excess.

Obituary - Died, in Cheohee, on the 30th ult., of flux, JOHN KNOX, after
painful illness of a few days. Mr. Knox had passed the meridian of life,
but was still hale and hearty when attacked with the violent disease that
proved fatal. In all the relations of life...as son, Magistrate, husband, father and neighbor...he was exemplary. He leaves a family, and
many relatives and friends to mourn their loss. But we trust their loss
his eternal gain. Peace to his memory.

Died, at the residence of his grand-father, in Cheohee, on the 9th of
August last, of flux, JNO. WINFIELD, son of SAMUEL LOVINGOOD, Esq., aged
three years, four months, and eleven days. "Suffer little children to
come to me, and forbid them not, for such is the kingdom of heaven."

Issue of Saturday September 26, 1857:

Killed - A man by the name of GRAVES was knocked down with a brick bat
on the 2d instant, at Aberdeen, Miss., by a young man named MOORE, and
died of the wound.

Married - On the 17th inst., by W. S. WOOLBRIGHT, Esq., Mr. GEORGE L.
KING to Miss HELENA PALMER, all of Anderson.

Married - On the 13th inst., by Rev. JESSE DEAN, Mr. WILSON HIGGINS of
Greenville, and Miss MARGARET WILLIAMS, of Pickens district.

Married - On the 31st ult., by the Rev. ROBT. KING, Mr. Z. MINTON to Miss
MALICA HASE, both of Pickens.

Married - On Thursday evening, 10th inst., in Abbeville district, by Rev.
J. SCOTT MURRAY, Mr. THOMAS S. CRAYTON, of Anderson, and Miss HATTIE N.
WHITLOCK, of Madison C. H., Florida.

Obituary - Departed this life on the 1st inst., at the residence of his
father, in Pickens district, BAYLIS JAMES MAXWELL, son of JOHN and ELIZ-
ABETH MAXWELL, aged 27 years. The deceased was a young man of worth and
promise, tenderly beloved by his relatives, and most highly esteemed by
numerous friends and acquaintances. As a son, he was affectionate and
dutiful, devoted to the interests of his father...as a brother, kind and
obliging...as a friend, ardent and constant. Those who were favored with
his confidence and regard could best appreciate his noble, manly traits,
and they most deeply feel his loss. In the midst of youthful vigor and
brightening prospects of usefulness...when his presence seemed most to
be needed at home, and fond parents more trustingly leaned upon him,
death marked him as his victim, and with one fell stroke severed the
cords which affection had twined around him and laid him prostrate in
the dust. (Poetry)

Obituary - It becomes our painful duty, among many others, to announce
the death of Misses AMANDA and MARTHA, daughters of BENNET MOODY, living in Pickens district, South Carolina. The former 19, the latter 17,
years old. The former, after 18 days of intense suffering, which she
bore without a murmur, but with Christian religion and submission, gave
full evidence of her acceptance with God and died in the arms of her
Saviour. A few minutes before her death, she said the Master calls and
I am ready and willing to go; she then bade her parents, brothers, sis-

(Moody cont'd:)

ters, cousins and friends all an affectionate farewell, and exhorted
them to meet her in Heaven. She said she saw Gabriel's Gate open to her.
Though having ever been an affectionate and obedient child she asked her
parents to forgive her for anything she might have done or said wrong to
them. She then closed her own eyes and mouth, crossed her hands on her
bosom, and fell asleep in Jesus. (1 verse poetry)
Martha's sufferings, for days, were equally as intense as Amanda's, and
for two days before her death she was out of her mind. They were cut
down in the vigor and beauty of youth: yes, they shall no more visit our
Sabbath School, of which they were punctual and beloved members; no more
shall they be with and cheer the hearts of their bereaved parents, whose
loss is irreparable, but we hope this loss is their daughter's eternal
gain. But be this as it may, God's will is accomplished and let us say
"thy will and not ours be done". When we walk into our gardens we like
to pluck the lovliest rose, and shall not God do the same in his garden?
We deeply sympathize with the parents and all to whom the deceased were
dear, and may we all meet in Heaven where parting shall be no more. "Be
ye also ready, for in such an hour as ye think not the Son of Man cometh". B. W. M.

Died on the 14th inst., IRA ONSLOW, youngest son of LUKE J. and NANCY
ARIAIL, aged two years, nine months and one day.

Committed Suicide - We regret to hear that the youngest daughter of PET-
ER KING, of this District, hung herself with a hank of yarn, on Tuesday
of last week. For a week previous the family noticed that her mind was
affected, but apprehended no danger. On Tuesday morning she attended to
her duties as usual...brought water for her mother, and her father proceeded to the fodder field, expecting that she would come to his assistance as usual. Her not doing so, drew him to the house to ascertain
the reason of her delay; not finding her there, the family became alarm-
ed and made a search when they found her suspended to a bush dead.
                                                    "Anderson Gazette"

Issue of Saturday October 3, 1857:

Death of a Revolutionary Soldier - The "Sumter Watchman", records the
death of WILLIAM VAUGHN, the last in that District of the Revolutionary
soldiers. He died on last Monday, at the residence of his daughter, Mrs.
DARGAN, four miles from Sumterville. The "Watchman" says that Mr. Vaughn
was born in May, 1764, and had, therefore, reached his ninety-fourth year.
He joined the army when in his 16th or 17th year, and was with MARION
and SUMPTER in several of their most severe engagements. He was married
to the wife who survives him on the 10th of February 1790. They had
lived together as husband and wife for near sixty-eight years. Few more
generous and brave men than William Vaughn have ever lived. Although
infirm, and tottering under the weight of his many years, a bare allusion
to the stirring scenes of the past, would cause his dim eye to flast with
almost unnatural brightness, while the sound of fife and drum seemd to
inspire within the bosom all the fire's of Patriotism that burned so
brilliantly there during the days of his youth. It was said that his
hatred for the Tories was proverbial, and that the mention of them in
his presence, even during the last years of his life, would also draw
from him some expression of his feeling toward them.

Accident - Mr. JOHN GASTON, of Abbeville district, met his death on the
19th ult., by being crushed by a tree which he was felling.

Murder - DAVID GUNN, of Columbus, Ga., was murdered on Friday last about
a mile from that city. Five or six stabs and cuts were on his body, and
the carotid artery of the neck was severed. A man by the name of DOZIER
is supposed to be the murderer, and strychnine whiskey and the "green-
eyed monster" the exciting causes. Dozier is in jail.

Married - On the S. C. bank of Cattooga, on Thursday evening 17th ult.,
by L. N. ROBINS, Esq., Mr. B. F. HOLDEN to Miss JEMIMA, daughter of EVAN
NICHOLSON, of Rabun county, Ga.

Married - On the 27th ult., by Rev. WM. MC WHORTER, Mr. MASON DUNCAN to Miss NANCY ANN, daughter of Capt. DANIEL RILEY, all of Pickens.

Married - On the 15th ult., by Rev. A. W. CUMMINGS, D. D., at the residence of the bride's father, Col. JOHN L. LONAS to Miss MARIA L., daughter of JOHN B. LOVE, Esq., of Jackson county, N. C.

Obituary - Died, on the 27th ult., after suffering a few days, WILLIAM DE WITT, youngest son of FRANCIS F. and MATILDA C. SHARP, aged two years and twenty three days. Sweet babe, rest in the arms of Jesus. (Poetry)

Died - on the evening of the 14th Sept., at half past three o'clock, of dysentery, JNO. THOMAS, infant son of JOSEPH T. and JULIA A. LATNER of Habersham County, Ga., aged 1 year, 2 months and 4 days. (Poetry)

Issue of Saturday October 17, 1857:

Married - On Monday evening, the 12th inst., on the road to Texas, by THOS. H. BOGGS, Esq., Mr. JAMES T. KELLEY to Miss ANN MURPHEE, all of Pickens.

Married - On the 8th inst., by the Rev. J. H. ZIMMERMAN, Mr. M. B. DENDY to Miss M. L. PENNY, all of Pickens district.

Married - On the 8th inst., by Rev. J. R. HUNNICUTT, Mr. W. R. DAVIS to Miss ELIZABETH CLEAVELAND, all of Pickens.

Obituary - Died, at Anderson C. H., the first day of October, in the 32nd year of her age and after a protracted illness, Mrs. ANNA E. HARRISON, wife of FRANCIS HARRISON, and daughter of Rev. A. W. ROSS. Possessing all those qualities of the mind and heart which both enoble and adorn the character, she was at once an affectionate daughter, devoted wife, kind and gentle mother, and constant friend. But loved as she was, by all her associates, and esteemed by all who knew her, she has been cut down in the pride and vigor of womanhood; yet receiving in exchange for this early separation from her friends on earth, a christian's reward above.

Issue of Saturday October 24, 1857:

Accidental Death - We regret to learn that Mr. ROB'T. STEWART, JR. of this District, met his death by accident or mischance on Sunday morning last. He was found near Ball mountain, with his rifle lying across his neck. Upon examination by a Coroner's jury, it was ascertained that his neck was broken...whether by the fall or the weight of the rifle is not known. He leaves a wife and several small children.

Death of IBZAN J. RICE - Recent intelligence from Kansas brings us the melancholy tidings of the death of IBZAN J. RICE, Esq., formerly of Anderson district. His death was caused by a fall, he surviving the accident about two hours. Mr. Rice was editor of the "Southern Rights Advocate" for several years, and more recently of the "Leavensworth Journal", in Kansas. He was a young man of more than ordinary talent, devoted in his friendship, with flattering prospects before him.

Married - On Thursday evening the 15th instant, by Rev. J. L. KENNEDY, Mr. ROBERT E. BOWEN, of Pickens, to Miss M. A. A. OLIVER, of Anderson.

Married - At Walnut Ridge, on the 15th inst., by W. S. GRISHAM, Esq., Mr. G. W. WOODRUFF, of Spartanburg, to Miss NANCY WADE, of Abbeville.

Issue of Saturday October 31, 1857:

Killed - The Coroner held an inquest over the dead body of WM. FLETCHER on the 28th inst., and from him we gather the following particulars: On the 27th, the deceased and one JAMES S. CHANEY were gambling in the woods near Walhalla, when a difficulty arose between them. Whereupon, Chaney struck Fletcher a blow with his hand that broke his neck. Chaney made his escape, although several persons were present. The finding of the jury was in accordance with these facts.

(Oct. 31 cont'd:)

Obituary - Died, at Walhalla, on the 25th of October, JOHN MC DOWELL, infant son of J. WESLEY and CARRIE E. TERRY, aged eleven weeks and twelve hours.

Departed this life, on the 14th inst., Mrs. MARY DICKSON, relict of WM. DICKSON, in her 76th year. The deceased was a consistent member of the Presbyterian church over 30 years. She was afflicted with paralysis for several years, suffered greatly; but, by the grace of God, was enabled to bear it with christian patience and resignation. Thus exemplifying the power of the gospel to support the soul in the deepest distress, and in the prospect of death, the last enemy to be conquered.

Issue of Saturday November 7, 1857:

Article on death of SAMUEL W. LEWIS, at Pendleton, S. C.

Another Hero Gone - JAMES HEAD, a soldier of the Revolution, died in Scott county, Virginia, on the 4th inst., at the advanced age of 90 years.

Married - On the 22nd ult., by Rev. FLETCHER SMITH, Mrs. AMANDA J. MARTIN, daughter of Mr. S. and Mrs. E. MC CULLEY, of Anderson, and Mr. L. W. ALLEN, of Pickens.

Married - On the 25th ult., by Rev. J. R. HUNNICUTT, Mr. E. T. BROWN to Miss MARTHA E. COBB, all of Pickens.

Married - On Sunday, the 25th ult., by the Rev. R. P. FRANKS, Capt. JOHN E. HOKE to Mrs. MARTHA E. CLAMPET, all of Anderson district.

Married - On the morning of the 27th ult., by Rev. B. JOHNSTON, Mr. SAMUEL H. OWENS to Miss JANE ROBINSON, both of Anderson village.

Married - On the 29th ult., by W. J. PARSONS, Esq., Mr. ADAM EVATT to Miss ARTEMISSA A. CATER, all of Pickens.

Married - On the 29th ult., by Rev. C. F. BANSEMER, Mr. JOHN H. KLENIBECK to Miss SOPHIA ZELLE, both of Pickens District.

State of South Carolina, Pickens. Summons in Partition - JONAS PHILLIPS, JR. vs. HENRY GASAWAY, et als. It appearing to my satisfaction that JOHN GASAWAY, JAMES GASAWAY, RACHEL GASAWAY, IRA GASAWAY, WILLIAM GASAWAY, JEREMIAH SUTTON and wife SARAH, WESLEY GASAWAY, BRYANT BANDY and wife PHOEBE, NATHAN PHILLIPS and wife MAHALA, EDWARD WILLIAMS and wife MARY, reside beyond the limist of this State. (Division or sale of real estate of HENRY GASAWAY, dec'd)

Issue of Saturday November 14, 1857:

Obituary - Died, at her father's residence, in Pickens district, on the 19th of October, of Flux, Miss MARY MARGARET MC KINNEY, 23 years and 13 days old. Margaret was a young lady of good disposition and beloved much by those who knew her. To know her was to be acquainted with one that was naturally amiable, modest and retiring in all her deportments. She joined the M. E. Church, the 15th of March, 1856, as a seeker of religion but did not obtain the pearl of great price till after she was taken sick. Some 4 or 5 days before her death she obtained peace by Faith through our Lord Jesus Christ. When first taken sick she seemed desirous to get well but after she obtained religion she was more than willing to die. She spent the most of the time in talking to and exhorting her friends to prepare to meet her in Heaven, assuring them that she was prepared for and was going to rest on high. Thus has passed to the rest of God's people one more witness that God can be just and the justified of them that believe in his Son Jesus Christ. "Let me die the death of the righteous, and let my last end be like his." L.S.

Issue of Saturday November 21, 1857:

Inquest - On the 2d inst., an inquest was held over the dead body of

(Nov. 21 cont'd:)

ALMAN POWELL, an aged citizen of the district. E. HUGHES, Esq., acted as Coroner. From the evidence before the inquest, it appears that he retired to his room on the 31st ult. in his usual health, and was found, on the morning of the 1st instant, in his bed a corpse.

Sudden Deaths - We learn that WILLIAM BOWEN, SR., an aged citizen of the district, fell dead at the breakfast table on the morning of the 8th inst Mr. G. W. YOUNG, also of this district, dropped dead in the road on the same day.

Married - On the 15th inst., by E. HUGHES, Esq., Mr. DAVID HANCOCK, to Mrs. ELIZABETH GARRISON, all of Pickens.

Married - On the 15th inst., by Rev. D. HUDSON, Mr. JOHN NICHOLS to Miss CHARITY WILSON, both of Pickens.

Obituary - Died, in Pickens district, on the 2d November, 1857, Mrs. MARTHA MC GUFFIN, wife of Rev. A. W. MC GUFFIN, after an illness of a few days. She leaves a husband and eight children, with many relatives and friends to mourn her loss. The deceased was a pious member of the Baptist church for 20 years or more, and she has now gone to rest to join the saints in glory. She has gone the way of all the earth, and let it be an admonition to those who die in the Lord, for they shall inherit the eternal life. (1 verse poetry)

Died, in Pickens county, Ga., on the 10th of October last, an infant daughter of Capt. JOHN and MARY C. GEURIN, aged ten days.

Issue of Saturday November 28, 1857:

Married - On the 19th inst. by JOHN ADAIR, Esq., Mr. JAMES MC GUFFIN to Miss BURNETTA MASON, all of Pickens.

Obituary - Died, at THOMAS D. MORGAN's in Pickens district, on the 9th of November, 1857, after a long and painful illness, of Paralysis, Mrs.MARY CANNON, wife of the late JAMES CANNON, in the 84th year of her age. The deceased had been a member of the Baptist church for upwards of thirty years, and showed by her walk that she understood the teachings of the Spirit. Her affliction, though of a painful character, was borne with fortitude and resignation becoming the truly pious, and it might be truly said with emphasis that she was a mother in Israel. She leaves many relations and friends to mourn her loss, but believing at the same time that their loss is her eternal gain. In all her relations in life, as wife, mother, mistress, neighbor and friend, she had no superior, and it might be truly said of her that she had not an enemy upon earth, but she is gone to enjoy that rest prepared for the people of God; and let us who survive endeavor to profit by her example and be ever ready to take our departure in peace. D.L.

Departed this life, on the 18th of October, after a severe illness of several weeks, JOHN MC WHORTER, in the 57th year of his age. The subject of this notice has long been a consistent member of the Baptist church, in which he lived an exemplary life, until the day of his death. His hand was ever ready to aid in the cause of Christ, and his house a home for the minister. Thus in his death, the church has lost a devoted member, the country a good citizen, and his family a kind husband and affectionate father. During the last six weeks of his life his sufferings were great; yet, he bore them with christian fortitude and resignation, thus exemplifying the power of the religion of Jesus Christ to support the soul in the deepest distress; and in the prospect of death, the last enemy to be conquered. He would often exclaim in the midst of the most severe suffering: "They will only make my rest the sweeter' one hour in heaven will make up for them all". He often called his family and friends around his bed-side, and exhorted them to live for God, and meet him in heaven. He entreated his weeping children to shed no tears for him, but to rejoice that he would so soon be freed from suffering and care. He would then commit his afflicted companion and affectionate children into

27

the hands of his heavenly father, who has promised to be husband to the
widow, and a father to the fatherless. Thus he passed away, leaving a
devoted family and many relatives and friends to mourn his loss.

Fatal Affair - Maj. THOMAS MULL, several years a member of the Mississippi Legislature, was killed at Memphis, Tenn., on the 9th inst., in an affray with W. R. HUNT, a wealthy gentleman of that place. Six shots were
fired, one piercing Maj. M. through the heart.

Dead - Dr. JOS. A. HUBER died in Washington county, Ala., on the 17th
ult., aged 64 years. He was an assistant surgeon in Napoleon's army and
was with it in the retreat from Moscow. He was a man of fine attain-
ments and much eccentricity.

Issue of Saturday December 5, 1857:

Dead - Col. WM. TONEY died at his residence in Clay county, Miss., on
the 8th ult. in his eighty-second year. He was a native of Virginia and
had resided many years in Greenville, S. C.

Issue of Saturday December 12, 1857:

Matrimonial - We have the pleasure of announcing that Mr. WM. B. CARLISLE
the assistant editor of the "Charleston Courier", was married to Miss
ARABELLA BIRD, on the 3d inst.

Hung - WOODY T. CARTER was hung at Chester C. H. on Friday the 27th ult.,
for the murder of JAMES GIBSON.

Murdered - On Wednesday, the 11th ult., Mr. WM. PIERCE, of Franklin parish, La., was killed by two of his negroes at his plantation in Beauf
Prairie. He attempted to flog them, whereupon they attacked and killed
him.

Dead - "The Spartan" announces the death of SOLOMON ABBOTT, a soldier of
the Revolution, at the advanced age of 100 years.

Married - On the 19th ult., by Rev. W. G. MULLINNIX, Mr. JAMES H. PEGG,
of Anderson, to Mrs. ELIZA BRAZEALE, of Pickens.

Married - On Tuesday evening 24th ult., by Rev. H. M. BARTON, Mr. ROB'T.
A. GILMER, of Pickens to Miss AMANDA F. SWIFT, of Franklin co., Ga.

Married - On the 26th ult., by E. HUGHES, Esq., Mr. W. H. BROWN, of
Floyd county, Ga., to Miss MARY G., daughter of Mr. W. B. DICKSON, of
Pickens.

Married - On Tuesday evening the 1st inst., by Rev. J. R. HUNNICUTT, at
the residence of Capt. J. H. LE ROY, Mr. J. P. WOOLBRIGHT, of Pickens,
to Miss MARGARET E. BROWN, of Rome, Ga.

Married - On the 2d inst., by Rev. M. CHASTAIN, Mr. JOHN T. LEWIS to Miss
ELIZA E., daughter of Mr. JAMES ROBERTSON, all of Pickens.

Married - On Tuesday evening, the 8th inst., by Rev. C. F. BANSEMER, Mr.
MENKE BULLWINKLE to Mrs. C. D. BULLWINKLE, all of Walhalla.

Married - On the 7th inst., by JOHN ADAIR, Esq., Mr. WILLIAM DUNN to Miss
ELIZABETH (blurred) , all of Pickens.

Married - On the 2d inst., by Rev. A. RICE, Mr. THOS. D. BELOTTE to Miss
F. A. MATTISON, all of Anderson.

Obituary - Died, at the residence of her son on the 3d day of December,
1857, Mrs. MARY MC KINNEY, wife of the late JAMES MC KINNEY. Her age is
not exactly known, but supposed to be about 90 years. She joined the M.
E. Church about 20 years before her death. (blurred)

Died - In Jackson county, N. C., Nov. 2d, after an illness of fifty two days, B. P. NORTON, in his 26th year. He leaves a disconsolate widow and one child, besides many relatives and friends to mourn his loss. He was a young man of promise, universally beloved, a kind neighbor and good citizen.

Issue of Saturday December 19, 1857:

Married - On the 10th inst., by JOHN SHARP, Esq., Mr. MICHAEL KENNEDY to Miss MARY M. RANKIN, all of Pickens.

Obituary - Died, in Pendleton village, on the 15th Nov., at the house of his father-in-law, Mr. REUBEN L. TERRY, in the 26th year of his age. Brother Terry was left a poor orphan boy, at a tender age, in Charleston. In 1845, he left the city and came to Pendleton to try and do something for himself. He commenced the Cabinet business with Mr. W. J. KNAUFF, and, after mastering his trade, he married his employer's only daughter, with whose family he continued to live until his death. Brother Terry joined the Methodist Church several years ago, and for the last three years he has been faithful in his attendance at Church. Two weeks previous to his death, I visited him, conversed with him and prayed with him, and left him in a happy state of mind. I visited him the next evening and stayed with him through the night and found him still peaceful, though gradually sinking. Every attention that love and friendship could suggest was paid to him, but all to no avail. His attachment to his wife was as great as I ever witnessed. He requested her not to leave him as long as he lived, and, after he had talked with his friends and exhorted them to meet him in heaven, he took his wife by the hand and placed it upon his breast, shouting and giving glory to God, and in this frame of mind he continued till death had done its work. On the 17th, his Masonic brethren met in their room and marche in procession to the house of the deceased, from thence to the Methodist church, and placed his corpse near the altar. His funeral was preached to a large and respectable congregation, from Phillippians, ch. 1, v. 21st: "For me to live is Christ, but to die is gain." From thence his body was carried to the grave and buried with Masonic honors. Brother Terry has left a wife and two small children, with many friends to mourn their loss, but doubtless their loss is his eternal gain. (Poetry)

Died, in Anderson district, on the 24th Nov., Mr. JOHN S. SWORDS, in the 62nd year of his age. Brother Swords has been a member of the Methodist Episcopal Church, South, some thirty odd years, and has been a very study church going and hard working man all the time. He raised a large and respectable family. It was doubtless his greatest delight to meet his brethren in the house of God and worship with them. We have often heard him relate his experience and tell of the dealings of God with his soul, but his work is done and he is gone to recap his reward. The disease of which he died was of a typhoid nature, and so violent that his reason was dethroned, and as such was not able to give his friends and family his dying prospects; but when we call to mind his manner of life, we doubt not that he triumphed in death. Brother Swords has left a wife and twelve children with many friends to mourn their loss, but their loss is his eternal gain. W.G.M. (1 verse poetry)

Issue of Saturday December 26, 1857:

Accident at Tunnel Hill - The second fatal accident occurred at Tunnel Hill on the 17th inst. At Shaft No. 2, HENRY KELLY, a bankman, fell from the top of the shaft, and, in his descent, (the bucket ascending at the same time with JAMES COLLINS) he knocked him out, and both were precipitated to the bottom. Collins was instantly killed, and Kelly breathed but a few minutes after being removed. Kelly fell a distance of about one hundred and seventy-five feet!

Married - In Glenville, Ala., at the residence of Mrs. MARY R. RICHARDSON, on Thursday evening, 3d inst., by Rev. Mr. DOUGLASS, Mr. SAMUEL E. MAYS, of Pendleton, and Miss KATE E. MOSELY, of Glenville.

Married - On Tuesday evening, the 22d inst., at Oconee Station, by Rev. WM. MC WHORTER, Mr. J. FREEMAN AULD, of Ga., to Miss RACHEL, daughter of Capt. S. R. MC FALL, of Pickens.

29

Married - On the 22d instant, by Rev. W. G. MULLINIX, Mr. ELIJAH OWENS, of Anderson, to Miss LUCINDA CRENSHAW, of Pickens.

Obituary - Departed this life, near Clarkesville, Ga., on Friday the 18th instant, Mrs. BELLE VANDIVER, after a short illness.

Died, at his residence, in Anderson district, on the 1st Nov. last, Mr. JAMES JOHNSON, in the 37th year of his age. Brother Johnson, in 1849, joined the Methodist Episcopal Church, South, and from that time till the day of his death he was regarded as a consistent member of the same... faithful in his attendance and liberal in support of the gospel. Brother Johnson was taken sick soon after his return from the Pickensville camp meeting, and, although he had the attention of one of the most experienced physicians in the district, and his wife, as an angel of mercy, attended at his bed side by day and by night. His neighbors, too, showed their strong attachment which they bore to himself and family by their devoted attention to him. Yet it was evident that he was constantly sinking. When I first visited him, he was in a happy frame of mind. He requested me to have prayer, and, when we commenced singing the praise of God, his countenance showed that his soul was happy. I visited him the next day and found him still calm and peaceful. After this, late one night he expressed a desire to see the minister who received him into the church.On the minister's arrival, he appeared much gratified. Although enfeebled by sickness, he conversed with the minister, in a low voice, giving his hopes and prospects. While thus engaged his soul was happy...he tried to shout, but his voice and strength failed. He then pressed the minister to his form, and reluctantly released him. He then affectionately embraced his wife, consoling himself with the belief that if he could not remain with her and their children, they at least could come to him. It was observed that if, in his restless moments, those around him would sing, he appeared to forget his misery, and commune more deeply with his God; and in this frame of mind he continued till speech failed him. He continued to give signs of his faith in God to the last. Brother Johnson has left a wife and two children, with relatives and friends, to mourn their loss, but their loss is his eternal gain. A Friend (1 verse poetry)

Died, in Cherokee county, Ga., on the 5th inst., WILLIAM COBB, in the 74th year of his age. He had formerly resided, for many years, in Pickens district, and, having lived a pious life, he died in the full hope of a better world.

Issue of Saturday January 12, 1858:

Found Dead - JOHN SOSEBEE, says the "Spartanburg Express", was found dead in that district a few days ago. A Coroner's jury agreed that whiskey was the cause.

Death of Mr. BAKER - Rev. DANIEL BAKER, President of Austin College, Texas, died recently in his sixtieth year. He was a great revivalist.

Dead - Gov. H. G. RUNNELS, of Texas, died on the 17th ult. He was a native of Mississippi, and had been Governor of that State.

Died of Yellow Fever - THOS. HUFF, of Lumpkin county, Ga., aged 15 years, was one of five passengers by the Star of the West , who died on the passage from New Orleans, of yellow fever contracted during the stay at Havana.

Homicide - We learn that IRA HAMMOND killed EDWIN HOLLIS, in this district, on Thursday 24th ult. Hammond is in jail. As the matter will be investigated. we forebear going into further particulars.

Homicide - On last Wednesday afternoon, a man by the name of CROLY was killed by a person named PELTIER. A piece of shingle was the weapon used. Coroner CHAPMAN empanneled a jury, which rendered the following verdict: " That JOHN CROLY came to his death, from a blow inflicted by WILLIAM PELTIER." As the case will undergo a judicial investigation, we forebear further remarks.   "Pee Dee Herald"

30

Married - At Tamossee on Sunday evening, 20th ult., by L. N. ROBINS, Esq.,
Mr. J. M. WHITMIRE to Miss LEATHA F., daughter of MARTIN MAHATHEY, all of
Pickens.

Married - On the evening of the 24th Dec., by A. B. BOWDEN, Esq., Mr.THOS.
GERARD to Miss MARY BEARD, all of Tunnel Hill.

Married - On the 27th ult., at Dr. A. J. ANDERSON's by Rev. THOMAS LOOPER,
Mr. H. D. HUNT of Pickens to Miss E. A. MC CARROLL of Greenville.

Married - On Tuesday the 29th ult., by E. H. COX, Esq., Mr. THOS. M. FRED-
ERICK to Miss SARAH ANN CASEY, all of Pickens.

Obituary - Died, of Typhoid Pneumonia, on the 14th of November last, in
Hart county, Ga., near Hartwell, at the residence of Mr. JAMES MASSEY,
HENRY HOWARD, aged 70 years and some months. The subject of this humble
tribute was born in Union District, S. C., where he resided until he was
thirty-five (35) years old, he then migrated to Pendleton District with
his family where he settled and lived until the division of the district
which took place in 1829. Being by trade, a Carpenter and being much beloved as a man and mechanic, he was selected as the one most capable, by
the contractors of the public buildings at Pickens C. H. to commence
building up a village in the mountain forest. As soon as the contractors
made him acquainted of their selection he removed from Pendleton and settled about one mile from the site of the contemplated village in Pickens
district. And soon the hills and valleys around, were made musical with
his cheerful songs, the sound of his mighty axe and the felling of the
proud pines, and scampering of the wild deer running away from sounds so
unusual to his untaught ears. The sound of his axe and hammer ceased not
until the Court House and Jail were completed with several other buildings; he then bade farewell his fellow mechanics, put away his tools and
turned his attention to farming for several years, not forgetting at the
same time to send his children to school, and to train them up in the
paths of virtue and honesty. A few years ago the plow and hoe were laid
aside, and the deceased again took up the tools of his early life and
when death came for him, he was busily engaged in rearing up improvements
in the vicinity of Hartwell. As soon as he was taken ill he wrote to his
children who now reside in Cass County, Ga., apprising them of his indis-
position, and his desire to go home and see them all once more. Two of
his sons went after him; but alas, when they arrived he was gone! Oh, yes,
forever gone; gone to God...he was dead and buried. And the disconsolate
sons could only repair to his grave, and shed their mingled tears over
the fresh clods that enwrapped his cold remains. Oh, it was truly a heart
melting scene to see those brothers...strangers, as they were, in a
strange land, weeping over the dust of a departed parent. The deceased
had many friends, and although he died among strangers, he lacked not for
attention; every thing that man could do was done for him, but nothing
could stay the hand of death. A few days before he expired, he was asked
by his pious friends if he felt willing to die. He replied "yes", "I
know that I am going to die, and my way before me is as clear and bright
as noonday. I am going to a world of happiness". His sons not being willing to leave him so far away from them, dug him up and took him home with
them, and intered him near them in the Kingston Grave Yard, where the wife
and children can repair at will, and think of him who has gone before
them, as they drop and humble tear over the grave of the father and husband. (1 verse poetry) Kingston, Ga. Dec. 1857 C.

Issue of Saturday January 16, 1858:

Inquest - Mr. Coroner GANTT held an inquest over the dead body of ANSEL
GODFREY, on the 10th inst., From the evidence adduced on the inquisition
it appears that the deceased came to his death by a fall, which dislocated the neck. He was supposed to be intoxicated, from the articles found
on the body, at the time of his death. The supposition is that the death
occurred some two weeks before the body was found. A dreadful death from
too common cause.

Dead - The "Edgefield Advertiser" announces the death of Mr. J. ELDRED
SIMKINS at Silverton, on the 17th ult. He distinguished himself in the
Mexican War, having been one of the few, in the forlorn hope, at the

storming of Chepultepec.

Suicide - The "Spartanburg Express" says that Mrs. CLARY, wife of LEWIS CLARY, living near Limestone Springs, in that District, hung herself on the 30th of December last. She had shown symptoms of insanity for some days previous.

Married - On the 31st ult., by Rev. J. M. RUNION, Dr. F. A. MILES, of Greenville, and Miss ELIZA, daughter of Col. BENJAMIN HAGOOD, of Pickens.

Married - On the 5th inst., by Rev. T. L. MC BRYDE, D. D., Rev. D. CHAL-MERS BOGGS, of Pickens, and Miss HENRIETTA R., daughter of Rev. J. L. KEN-NEDY of Anderson.

Obituary - Departed this life on the 31st of December, 1857, JOSEPHINE E. infant daughter of HANCKE and LUCY AMELIA GISSEL, of Walhalla, aged three months and 27 days. (Poetry)

Issue of Saturday January 23, 1858:

Fatal Accident - We regret to learn that another fatal accident occurred at Tunnel Hill, on Thursday morning last, at 2 o'clock a.m. An Irishman, named JOHN MC GRAW, a bank man, fell from the top of Shaft No. 4, a distance of about 185 feet, and was instantly killed. We understand the body was horribly mangled.

Hung - We learn from the "Georgian" that JOHN BLACK was hung at Clarkesville, Ga., on the 8th inst., for the crime of murder. Some three or four thousand persons witnessed the execution.

Married - On the 18th Sept. last, by E. P. VERNER, Esq., Mr. A. S. COLE, to Miss ESTHER ADDIS, all of Pickens.

Married - On the 12th Oct. by the same, Mr. WM. PERKINS to Miss AMERICA KNOX, all of Pickens.

Married - On the 15th inst., by the same, Mr. W. K. TANNERY to Miss ME-LISSA LAND, all of Pickens.

Married - On the 24th Dec. by Rev. J. F. PETERSON, Mr. DAVID U. SLOAN to Miss JULIA JENNINGS, of Edgefield.

Married - On the 12th inst., by Rev. W. G. MULLINNIX, Mr. ROB'T. M. HUT-CHINS to Miss SARAH A. MC WHORTER, all of Pickens.

Married - On the 10th inst., by Rev. H. T. ARNOLD, Mr. B. F. ROBERTSON to Miss D. J. BOWEN, all of Pickens.

Issue of Saturday January 30, 1858:

Married - On the 22d Dec. 1857 by the Rev. Mr. STILLAMN, Hon. J. A. ORR, of Houston, Miss., to Miss CORNELIA, daughter of the late Hon. W. J. VAN de GRAEFF of Gainesville, Alabama.

Married - At Tunnel Hill, on the 7th inst., by A. B. BOWDEN, Esq., Mr. JAMES H. WHITING, of Habersham County, Ga., to Miss NANCY E. FOWLER, of Pickens.

Married - On the 21st inst., by Rev. WM. MC WHORTER, Mr. DANIEL S. HULL to Miss CAROLINE JENKINS, all of Pickens.

Married - On the 26th inst., by Rev. W. G. MULLINNIX, Mr. JOHN W. BURDINE to Miss LUCINDA MC WHORTER, all of Pickens.

State of South Carolina. In Ordinary, Pickens. Summons in Partition. ROB'T. POWELL and wife vs. J. M. BLACK el als. It appearing to my satisfaction that J. M. BLACK and Z. JOHNS and wife NICEY, parties in this suit reside without the limits of this State. It is ordered therefore that they do appear and object to the division or sale of the Real Estate if ALLEN BLACK, Dec'd.

Death of a Revolutionary Soldier - The "Anderson Gazette" announces the death of Mr. WM. HUBBARD of that district, age 97 years. He was an old revolutionary soldier, distinguished for the active part taken in the "times that tried men's souls".

Dead - RICHARD SONDLEY, Esq., an estimable gentleman, aged 58 years, died suddenly in Columbia, of disease of the heart, on the 27th ult.

Dead - Mr. WM. TAYLOR SMITH, late foreman of the Carolinian Job Office, died in Columbia, on Sunday night last, after a long illness.

Married - Col. WADE HAMPTON, JR. of Columbia, has married Miss MARY S., daughter of the late Hon. GEORGE MC DUFFIE.

Married - On the 7th ult., by Rev. H. M. BARTON, Mr. LEWIS B. GAINES, of Madison county, to Miss D. O. GRUBBS, of Hart co., Ga.

Married - On the 14th, by the same, Mr. WM. H. WHITWORTH, of Franklin co., to Miss NANCY E. GRUBBS, of Hart co., Ga.

Married - On the 19th ult. by Rev. J. R. HUNNICUTT, Mr. MARSHFIELD HOLMES to Miss M. ELIZABETH CAPE, all of Pickens.

Old - The oldest man in the State, (so the "Courant" says) died at his residence on Bull Swamp, Orangeburg district, last week. His name was JAMES KNIGHT, and his age was one hundred and one.

Issue of Saturday February 13, 1858:

Dead - The "Anderson Carolinian" announces the death of KENON BRAZEALE, of that district, age 106 years.

Married - On the 26th ult. by Rev. E. T. BUIST, D. D., Mr. JAMES D. SMITH of Pendleton to Miss MARY E. BATES, of Greenville.

Married - On the 2d inst. by Rev. W. G. MULLINNIX, Mr. ROBERT E. MAW to Miss MALINDA B. FREEMAN, all of Pickens.

Married - On the 4th inst. by E. HUGHES, Esq., Mr. JOBERRY HUNNICUTT to Miss MARY PULLEN, all of Pickens District.

Issue of Saturday February 20, 1858:

Death by Strangulation - Mr. HENRY COATS died suddenly in Griffin, Ga. on the 29th ult. in a very remarkable manner. He had gone into a small grocery store and while engaged in eating, undertook to swallow a piece of beef, too large for the capacity of his throat, and was choked to death before medical assistance could be rendered.

Married - On the 16th inst., by W. S. GRISHAM, Esq., Mr. JAMES R. MILLER to Miss ELIZABETH ANN EATON, all of this district.

Homicide - On Thursday evening last a Coroner's inquest was held over the body of SOPHIA PHILLIPS, of this place, who was found dead in bed. The verdict of the jury was, that deceased came to her death from a blow on the head with a piece of iron, inflicted by her husband, GEORGE PHILLIPS. Phillips is now confined in jail to await his trial. Both drunk.
"Dahlonega Signal" 13th inst.

Issue of Saturday February 27, 1858:

Married - On the 16th inst. by Rev. NIMROD SULLIVAN, Mr. JOSEPH PELFREE to Miss MARTHA A. WATKINS, all of Pickens.

Married - On the 18th inst. by Rev. WM. MC WHORTER, Mr. ROB'T. STEELE,JR. of Anderson, to Miss ELIZA J. MC ELROY of Pickens.

Married - On the 21st inst., by Rev. J. R. HUNNICUTT, Mr. T. BROWN to

Miss DEBORAH LILES, all of Pickens.

Married - On the same evening, by the same, Mr. JOHN ELBERSON to Miss D. NORRIS, all of Pickens.

Married - On the 28th ult. by Rev. A. H. CORNISH, Capt. J. B. E. SLOAN to Miss MOLLIE SEABORN, all of Pendleton.

Married - On the 25th inst., by JAMES E. HAGOOD, Esq., Mr. JASPER CRANE to Miss KEZIAH GIBSON, all of Pickens.

Inquest - The Coroner held an inquest on Sunday last, over the remains of a man identified to be those of HENRY CARVER. From the evidence, it appears that his death occurred a few days before Christmas, and was caused probably by the recurrence of an asthmatic affection to which he was subjected. There was no evidence of foul play, or that attempts had been made to conceal the body. The jury returned a verdict that deceased came to his death by means to them unknown.

Death of Col. EASLEY - It is our painful duty to announce the death of Col. JOHN A. EASLEY, JR., of this district. Typhoid fever, with aggravated complications, produced a speedy dissolution. He was confined to his room on the 16th, and breathed his last peacefully on the 22d inst. Col. Easley was a young man of high promise and more than ordinary ability. His friends elected him twice to represent the district in the Legislature. The manner in which he discharged his duty, both as a public and private citizen, is still fresh in the memory of all and requires no commodation at the hands of any one. He was public spirited and useful, and zealously attached to his friends.

Death of a Palmetto - THOS. L. YOUNG, a member of the Palmetto Regiment, died in Winnsboro last week. He entered the army, says the "Herald", at the tender age of sixteen years, and was in the thickest of the fight on every such occasion. Peace to his remains, and all honor to his memory.

Death of Col. THOMSON - "The Spartan" announces the death of Col. H. H. THOMSON of Spartanburg, aged fifty-three years. He was a lawyer of note.

Dead - Col. HUGH ARCHER, formerly of South Carolina, died in Florida on the 23d ult.

Venerable Man Dead - ADOLPHEUS BAKER, a classmate of DANIEL WEBSTER in Dartmouth College, and father of Col. ADOLPHEUS BAKER, of Abbeville District, who is well known for his eloquent appeals in behalf of Kansas, died lately in Columbus, Ga., in his eighty-seventh year.

Issue of Saturday March 6, 1858:

Killed - On Thursday week, Mr. ANDREW HARRISON, of Spartanburg District, was instantly killed by a rafter of a smoke-house, which he was building falling upon him.

Married - On the 27th Oct. last, by WM. S. WOOLBRIGHT, Esq., Mr. JOEL VAUGHN to Miss SARAH A. CLELAND, all of Pickens.

Married - On the 18th ult.,by the same, Mr. GEORGE GRANT, of Pickens, to Miss ELIZABETH SIMMONS, of Anderson.

Married - On the23d ult. by Rev. J. L. KENNEDY, Mr. J. W. CALLAHAN, of Abbeville, to Miss MARTHA HALLUMS, of Pickens.

Obituary - Died, on the 5th February last, Mrs. ARMINDA A. MC ALISTER, wife of DAVID MC ALISTER, and daughter of Mr. GRAFTON and Mrs. REBECCA JENKINS, aged twenty-four years and some months. The deceased was a member in good and regular standing in the Presbyterian church, having lived in the faith of the gospel of peace and salvation, she died with a good hope of enjoying the rest prepared for the people of God beyond the grave.

Issue of Saturday March 13, 1858: (next page)

Frozen to Death - The Wilkes county (Ga.) "Republican" states that WILKES WELBORN of that county, went to Augusta last week to sell his cotton,and was frozen to death on his return. His body was found about 18 miles from his residence.

Married - On the 4th inst., by Rev. W. G. MULLINNIX, Mr. HARRISON DILLARD to Miss MARGARET HAMILTON, all of Pickens.

Married - On the 7th inst., by W. S. GRISHAM, Esq., Mr. ANDERSON DORSEY, formerly of Texas, to Miss ELIZABETH JANE, daughter of Mr. WM. KING, of Pickens.

Obituary - Departed this life on the 17th ult., MARTHA LOUISA, daughter of JOEL and RACHEL MOODY, aged one year and five days. Also on the 22d ult., SARAH HARRIET MOODY, aged three years and three months.

Departed this life on the 9th ult., SARAH A., daughter of LUCY and B. B. MOSELY, aged eleven years, eight months and thirteen days. The amiable qualities of our young friend made her a favorite with all who knew her. She suffered much during her illness, and seemed conscious that death was fast approaching. (Poetry)

Died, at the residence of her parents, (Mr.and Mrs. T. DICKSON) near Pendleton, Mrs. SARAH ANTOINETTE, consort of Mr. THOMAS J. STEELE, on the 5th of January, 1858, in the 22d year of her age. The subject of this notice was justly endeared to a large circle of acquaintances dearly loved by her parents and other kindred. Having a heart susceptible of social soul-endearing friendship, she had a year previous to her death become the partner of a kind and tenderly affectionate husband, was a mother to a sweet and lovely infant. To these and to parents, sisters and brothers, she was linked in all that endearing tenderness of heart, which combined kindred together on earth. Thus we might truly say for her life here was desireable indeed. But the all-wise God whose rights and claims are paramount in his unsearchalbe wisdom, saw it best to take her from this sin blighted world. Her illness was hort, cut off sudden- ly in the spring time of her life, reminding us that "in the midst of life we are in death" and of the uncertainty of all earthly happiness. But we hope she is now chanting the praises of her Redeemer in that "hap- py, happy land", she loved so much to speak of. May He "who tempers the wind to shorn lamb" soothe the bereaved sorrows, and sanctify their af- fliction. "Earth has no sorrows that Heaven cannot heal". "Christ is your richest treasure: He can give Strength to the feeble, joy to the distressed, He saves the lost, He bids the dying live, And guides the weary soul to perfect rest."

Departed this life in Clarkesville, Ga., on the 22d day of February, 1858, Mrs. HESTER ANN PAYNE, daughter of T. J. and LUCINDA HUGHES. She was born on the 17th day of October, 1832, at Anderson Court House, S. C., and was married to JOHN B. PAYNE on the 28th day of July, 1850. The de- ceased had never united herself with any church, but had long since pro- fessed a hope in the christian religion and to know her Maker through faith. And although during her sickness, nature exhibited unmistakeable evidences of the most excruciating suffering, yet she uttered not a sing- le murmur at the fate which she said was fast approaching, and evidently awaited her. Kindred and friends crowded around the death bed of this good woman, and tried to console her with words of hope that she might recover; but being truly convinced, in what she thought, she was taught from above, she continued to exhort them, that her time had come, and that she was going; that her mother, who had died some four years ago, was present, and was calling her home, to live with her in Heaven. And when the moment of her dissolution approached, she expired without a groan or struggle, leaving a husband and three small children to mourn her loss. H. (1 verse poetry)

Issue of Saturday March 20, 1858:

Convicted - We learn that THOS. GOLDEN was tried at the Superior Court of Marion county, Geo., last week, for the murder of NICHOLAS JORDAN some time last winter and was convicted.

Horrible - A little son of Mr. J. B. THOMAS, of Clarkesville, Tenn., fell
into a vessel of boiling soap on Tuesday week, and was so severely burned as to cause his death next day.

Married - On the 7th ult. by Rev. W. B. SINGLETON, Mr. MARSHALL CHILDERS
to Miss JANE SATTERFIELD, all of Pickens.

Married - On the same day, by the same, Mr. JOHN HOLLINGSWORTH to Miss
FRANCES FREEMAN, all of Pickens.

Married - On the same day, by the same, Mr. HENRY HARPER to Miss LUCINDA
HOLLINGSWORTH, all of Pickens.

Married - On the 21st ult., by LEONARD ROGERS, Esq., Mr. JEPTHA REESE to
Miss V. WILSON, all of Pickens.

Married - On the 4th inst., by the same, Mr. JAMES CHASTAIN to Miss ELIZ-
ABETH RIDLEY, all of Pickens.

Married - On the 14th inst., by the same, Mr. T. J. CHASTAIN to Miss HAN-
NAH WEST, all of Pickens.

Issue of Saturday March 27, 1858:

Fatal Accidnet - Mr. JOHN RUDLER, of Augusta, Ga., was killed by a fall
from a buggy on Sunday afternoon last. The horse ran away and threw him
out.

Drowned - JOSEPH A. MC JUNKIN, of Union district, was drowned in Broad
River, last week, while fishing.

Death of a Senator - Hon. R. L. TILLINGHAST, Senator from St. Luke's
Parish, died recently. He was a lawyer, and a man of talent.

Dead - Mr. GALLOWAY MONTEITH, a prominent citizen of Columbia, died in
that city, a few days since in his 53d year.

Horrible Death - Mr. JACOB SMYER, owner of a mill in Floyd county, Ga.,
was caught in his machinery, a few days ago, drawn in between two cog
wheels and crushed to death. He was a worthy citizen.

Married - On the 18th inst., by Rev. W. G. MULLINNIX, Mr. W. B. GAINES,
of Pickens, to Miss LUCY A. M., daughter of Col. H. HAMMOND, of Anderson.

Married - At Mount Zion Church, on the 23d inst., by the same, Mr. A. T.
CLAYTON to Miss T. C. CLAYTON, all of Pickens.

Obituary - Departed this life on the 8th inst., Mrs. ELIZABETH A. MULLI-
NIX, wife of JOHN G. MULLINNIX, in the fortieth year of her age. For
the last six months, it was plain to be seen that she was constantly
sinking, and, although she had been piously brought up, and united with
the Church when young, yet she lived without the comforts of religion
until within two months of her death. When her friends saw that she
could not long stay with them they were concerned about her situation,
and, when they inquired as to her spiritual prospects, she replied that
she was without hope. In order that she might be encouraged to trust in
Christ, we appointed service at her house, and tried to preach on the
office of the spirit, but still there was sadness in her countenance.
We continued, however, to pray with her and for her until her faith began to take hold, and God was pleased to speak peace to her soul. From
then to the time of her death all was well. She entreated her friends
not to do as she had done...not to live without the comforts of religion,
but to seek it in youth. She requested that her body might be buried at
the church where she held her membership; and, a very short time before
she closed her eyes in death, she requested the writer to preach her
funeral, and then asked her mother-in-law to take care of her children.
The last word that she was heard to speak was "glory"...I have no doubt
the last on earth and the first in heaven. The deceased leaves a sor-
rowful husband and five children, with many friends and relatives to

lament their loss. But they sorrow not as those who have no hope. M
(1 verse poetry)

Issue of Saturday April 3, 1858:

Suicide - We learn that on Saturday last, a Mr. JOHN AUTREY, living a-
bout 18 miles from this place, in Greenville District, committed suicide.
The particulars, as we have heard them, are, that in the morning, becoming intoxicated, he attempted to kill himself by placing the muzzle of
his gun to his head and his foot on the trigger; but his wife thwarted
his efforts then, and ran to the neighbors for assistance. She did not
return until the afternoon, when he threatened violence to her unless
she gave him the powder and balls taken from him in the morning. As
soon as he received these, he re-loaded his rifle, and stepping into the
yard, placed himself in the same position as before, and fired, the ball
passing through his forehead. He lived about twenty hours afterwards.
"Anderson Gazette"

Married - On the 17th ult. by Rev. S. SISK, Mr. J. M. MURPHREE to Miss
MARY F. MC KINNEY, (daughter of the late DAVID MC KINNEY of this district) all of Habersham co., Ga.
Married - On the 18th ult. by Rev. C. BANSEMER, Mr. A. BRENNECKE to Miss
___(torn)___ BIEMAN, both of Walhalla.

Married - On the 25th ult. by J. C. WHITEFIELD, Esq., Mr. ABNER HUTCHINS
of Pickens, to Mrs. NANCY JOHNSON, of Anderson.

State of South Carolina, Pickens. Bill of Partition - JAMES ROGERS vs.
EDWARD ROGERS et als. It appearing to the satisfaction of the Commissioner that EDWARD ROGERS, TEMPERANCE MC WHORTER, JOHN MC WHORTER and
wife SARAH, WILSON DRENNAN and wife PRUDENCE, AMES ROBINSON and wife
NELLY, HUGH ROGERS, and the heirs-at-law of JOHN ROGERS, to wit: ___?___
ROGERS, his widow, EMERSON BLACK and wife ELIZABETH, _____ MOORE and
wife SARAH, JAMES ROGERS, ZACHARIAH ROGERS, WILLIAM ROGERS, JOHN ROGERS
and DAVID ROGERS, defendants to complainant's bill of complaint, reside
beyond the limits of this State.

Issue of Saturday April 10, 1858:

Death of Indian Brave - TUCK-A-LIXTAH, or "The man that has many horses",
a brave of the Pawnee tribe of Indians, died on the 20th ult., in Washington, where he was sojourning, with a number of his tribe, on business
with the government.

Obituary - Died, on the 19th February, in the 19th year of his age, WIL-
LIAM T., son of BURRELL and ELEANOR PERRITT. Another immortal spirit
has left its earthly habitation, and has been wafted upon scraphic wings
to the glorious habitation of God and His angels. Our young friend was
dutiful and affectionate, and ever ready to perform his duties to his
parents. He did not belong to any branch of the church, yet when death
came he was ready. What a consolation it was to you, bereaved parents,
when the last spark of life was almost extinct, to hear him shouting,
glory! glory! glory!...a term of praise found in the vocabulary of celestial language, and which is always resounding in the heights of heaven!
On the 28th, the Rev. Mr. WALKER paid a beautiful tribute to the memory
of the deceased, in which his relatives and friends found a panacea for
their wounded hearts, for they believed that while they listened to the
soul-stirring eloquence of the speaker, the departed spirit of a child,
a friend, was joining in the celestial melody of praise to God. J.B.W.
(2 verses poetry)

Married - On the 6th inst. by Rev. WM. MC WHORTER, Mr. J. T. HALL to
Miss MARTHA J. JENKINS, all of Pickens.

Married - On Thursday the 1st int., by Rev. J. R. HUNNICUTT, Mr. R. L.
ADAMS to Miss MARY BROOM, all of Pickens.

Married - On the same day, by the same, Mr. D. A. LILES to Miss JANE
BLACK, all of Pickens.

Suicide - Mr. JAMES DILLARD, a farmer living near Elizabethtown, Kentucky, committed suicide on Monday week. He was an industrious, hard-working man. He silently went up stairs, and his family, on missing him searched and found him lying with his throat cut, a corpse.

Obituary - Departed this life, on the 6th Feb. last, at his reidence in Cherokee county, Ga., after a severe illness of 46 days, of typhoid fever, WILKINSON JAMESON, in the 42nd year of his age. The subject of this notice was born and raised in the eastern part of this district. In the 24th year of his age, (in 1840) he removed to where he resided until his death. In a few years after his last removal, he attached himself to the Baptist church, of which he continued to live a faithful member until his death. On the 3rd day, according to his request, he was buried near his residence with Masonic honors. He bore his afflictions with as much patience as any man could. We mourn not as those who have no hope, for we believe our loss is his eternal gain. His faith was strong, and, through all his afflictions, he was resigned to the will of our Heavenly father. His only desire to live was to raise his children and settle his affairs in this world. Thus he passed away, leaving a devoted wife, and children, and many relatives and friends to mourn his loss. J.J.

Died, at the residence of her father, W. C. LEE, Esq., on the 27th March last, after an illness of thirty hours, Mrs. ELIZABETH J., consort of J. W. F. THOMPSON, of Walhalla. The suddenness of this dispensation of Providence was truly fearful; but, she, who had been a dutiful and affectionate daughter, and a kind and loving wife and mother, was prepared for it. Years before, she had become a member of the Methodist Episcopal Church, and had walked uprightly therein to the day of her death. Unrelenting death is, at all times, claiming its victims, and bows our head in humbleness and makes the heart sick with sorrowing; but, when that victim is youthful, amiable and faultless, in all the relations of life, it is heart rending in the extreme, and drives us to His bounty in this our greatest affliction. But hope, that never failing anchor of the soul, comforts us with its solaces and future promises. A devoted husband and two little children, with many relatives, mourn their loss, but they sorrow not as those without hope. (4 verses poetry)

Issue of Saturday April 24, 1858:

Death of Mr. ARCHER - The numerous friends of Mr. A. H. ARCHER will regret to learn that he expired at his residence, in this district, on Wednesday last. Some ten days before, he had been dangerously injured by being kicked by a vicious mule, and lingered on until relived by death. He leaves a young and interesting family, and many bereaved friends.

Dead - Col. WM. MAYBIN, of Newberry, died of appoplexy, on the 14th inst. He had represented Richland in the Legislature, and filled the office of Mayor of Columbia.

Married - In Pickens co., Ga., on the 1st inst., by J. M. BEDFORD, Esq., Mr. W. J. MURPHY to Miss ELIZABETH JOHNSON, both formerly of Pickens.

Married - On the 6th inst., by Rev. W. G. MULLINNIX, Mr. WM. B. HUTCHINS of Anderson and Miss CONSTANTIA C. ELLIS, of Pickens.

Issue of Saturday May 1, 1858:

Died, at the house of WM. SANDERS, SR., on the 13th ult., ELIZABETH SANDERS, being ninety-one years, nine months and eight days old. She was a consistent member of the Baptist Church, and had lived a christian life for many years. The death of the old is a timely lesson for the young and middle aged.   A Grandson

Departed this life, on the 21st ultimo, at 1 o'clock A.M., Mr. ANDREW H. ARCHER, in the 30th year of his age. On the 13th, he was kicked by a mule just above the ear, which broke his skull. From that time, his mind was much affected, so much so as to be unable to relate the particulars of the accident. The deceased was a man of energy and perseverance, and had, by industry and economy, acquired an education so as to

prepare him for any common business of life. In 1855, he was happily
married to Miss PARMELIA T. BARTON, and had within the last few months,
settled himself as a farmer. Mr. Archer was a man of high sense of hon-
or, pleasant in his manners, peaceable in his neighborhood, kind and com-
panionable as a friend, and devoted as a husband. We had often hoped
that he would connect himself, in good time, with the people of God, but
alas! how suddenly he has been called away, and we can but hope that in
man's extremity is God's opportunity. He leaves a wife and two small
children, with relatives and friends to mourn their loss. But the comfort of the wife was she would meet him in heaven. (1 verse poetry)

Issue of Saturday May 8, 1858:

Murder - SAMUEL LANDRUM, of Benton county, Ala., was murdered on the 8th
inst. near Atlanta by three men names JONES, COBB and CROCKETT. Crockett
was sentenced to be hung on 18th June next.

Dead - Col. WM. R. CANNON died in Columbus, Miss., on the 15th ult. He
had served in the House and Senate of that State. He was a native of
Darlington district.

Married - On the 25th ult., by JOSHUA JAMESON, Esq., Mr. JESSE GARRETT
to Mrs. MARY SHERMAN, both of Anderson.

Married - On the 23rd of April, by A. B. BOWDEN, Esq., Mr. TERRY WHITLEY
to Miss SARAH L. DEAL, all of Tunnel Hill, S. C.

Obituary - Died, at Blue Creek, White co., Ga., on the 24th ult., FRAN-
CIS L., son of Maj. YOUNG and NANCY DAVIS, aged about four years. Frank
was a sprightly intelligent child, much beloved by all who knew him.His
death was caused doubtless by accident, though he survived it three
months. His sufferings are now at an end, however, and his relatives
and friends sorrow not as those without hope, having the assurance of
the word of God that he sleeps in Jesus, with his sainted little sister,
who preceeded him something over a year ago. J.Q (poetry)

Issue of Saturday May 15, 1858:

Dead - W. J. WILSON, a member of the Palmetto Regiment, died in Camden
on the 1st inst.

Married - At the residence of JOHN S. LORTON, Esq. in Pendleton, on the
29th ult., by Rev. A. W. ROSS, Mr. J. W. LIVINGSTON, of Abbeville, to
Miss CLARA KILPATRICK, of the former place.

Married - At the house of the bride's father, on Sunday evening the 2nd
inst., by D. P. ROBINS, Esq., Mr. ANDREW J. CAPPS to Miss NANCY ANN DUN-
CAN, all of Pickens.

Married - On the evening of the 9th inst., at the house of Mr. PAYNE, by
A. B. BOWDEN, Esq., Mr. SQUIRE A. GILBERT to Miss LUCRETIA PAYNE, all of
Pickens District.

Married - On the same day, by the same, Mr. HENRY ROACH to Miss SARAH
PEARCE, all of Pickens.

State of South Carolina, Pickens. Summons in Partition - ISHAM SIMMONS
and wife vs. HENRY TROTTER and others. Henry Trotter resides without
the limits of this State. Division or sale of the real estate of JAMES
GILLILAND, deceased.

Issue of Saturday May 22, 1858:

Sudden Death - We regret to learn that Mr. WILLIAM ABBOTT, an aged citizen of this district, fell from his horse, it is supposed, on the 10th
inst., and expired suddenly. He was traveling the road by himself near
Mr. N. J. F. PERRY's at the time of the occurrence. To his bodily infirmity, we are informed, may be added aleination of his mind.

Suicide - Mr. THOMAS REED, of Estill co., Ky., drowned himself on Tuesday of last week, by attaching a piece of pig iron to his neck and jumping into a creek.

Affairs in Texas - ALEXANDER COCKREL, of Dallas county, Texas, was killed on the 3d ult. in a conflict with a constable. W. E. HARREL, of Washington, was also killed in a fight on the 10th ult.

Obituary - Died, on the 26th April, at his residence in Gilmer* of Congestive chill, Mr. THOS. J. HALLUM, aged 52 years, eight months and 1 day. The deceased was born and raised in Pickens district, whence he emigrated with his family to Texas* in 1852, where he continued to reside until his death. Several years previous to this he attached himself to the Methodist church, and was noted for his quiet unobtrusive method of living. He leaves a large family to mourn his decease, yet it is hoped that their loss will be his eternal gain.

Married - On Tuesday evening, 4th inst., by Rev. RICHARD FURMAN, Mr. THOMAS D. LONG to Miss SUSAN PERRY, both of Greenville.

Married - At the same time (as above), by the same, Mr. J. G. HAWTHORNE of Fairfield, to Miss SUSAN FOSTER, of Greenville.

Married - On Sunday evening the 16th inst., by D. P. ROBINS, Esq., at Long Creek Church, Mr. ROBERT HIX, of Pickens to Miss SARAH SMITH, of Rabun county, Ga.

Issue of Saturday May 29, 1858:

Dead - Gen. PERSIFER F. SMITH, of the U. S. A., died at Leavenworth city on the 16th inst. He had distinguished himself in the Mexican war.

Dead - The Pensacola papers announce the death in that city, on the 29th ult., of ARNOLD GUILLEMARD, Esq., at the age of seventy years. He was an old citizen, having been an officer in the Spanish army before the cession of Florida to the United States.

Dead - "The Edgefield Advertiser" laments the death of H. R. SPANN, Esq., of that district. He was an able lawyer. He died in Texas, whither he had gone on business.

Accidentally Killed - The Hon. S. B. PIERCE, a lawyer, and formerly member of the Legislature, was killed recently, in Perry County, Mississippi by being thrown from his horse, while on a deer hunt, the fall causing his gun to discharge its contents in his person, producing instant death.

Married - On the 20th inst., by Rev. GIDEON ELLIS, Mr. PRIER ALEXANDER, JR. to Miss VICTORIA COTTRELL, all of Pickens.

Married - On the 20th inst., by Rev. W. G. MULLINNIX, JOHN C. WHITFIELD, Esq., to Miss SUSAN FINLEY, both of Anderson village.

Married - On the 20th inst., by Rev. JOHN CORN, Mr. WM. J. NEVILLE, of Clayton, Ga., to Miss SALLIE R., daughter of Maj. JOSIAH CARTER, of Townes county, Ga.

Married - On the 27th inst., by J. E. HAGOOD, Esq., Mr. JOHN HAWKINS to Miss CAROLINE DODD, both of Pickens.

Obituary - Died, in the Lunatic Asylum, at Columbia, on the 1st May, inst., MILTON STUBBLEFIELD, of this District.

State of South Carolina, Pickens. Summons in Partition. JOS. MERCK and wife vs. JOEL CHAPMAN et als. It appearing to me that THOMAS MC KINNEY and wife MARY, JOEL CHAPMAN, O. J. WIGGINTON and wife RUTH and ISRAEL CHAPMAN, defendants in this case, reside without the limits of this State. Division or sale of the real estate of JOSHUA CHAPMAN, deceased.

Issue of Saturday June 5, 1858:

Death of Capt CALHOUN - We are pained to learn that Capt. PATRICK CAL-

HOUN, a gallant officer of the U. S. Army, died at Pendleton on Tuesday last. He had been in the service for a number of years. Consumption, with its lingering fatalness, ended his career, which promised much at man's estate. He was a son of the lamented JOHN C. CALHOUN. The Pendleton Dragoons escorted his remains to the grave.

Death of a Venerable Matron - "The Edgefield Advertiser" announces the death of Mrs. SOPHIA BONHAM, at the residence of her son, the Hon. M. L. BONHAM, on the 18th of May. The "Advertiser" says: "Mrs. Sophia Bonham was born on the 18th of December 1780, in the midst of our Revolutionary War. She was a daughter of JACOB SMITH and SARAH SMITH...the former the brother of SMALLWOOD SMITH, the latter the sister of JAMES BUTLER, who fell at Cloud's Creek in defence of American liberty. Her husband was Capt. JAMES BONHAM. Becoming a widow at the age of thirty-five, she employed the remainder of a long life in the service of her God, and in devotion to the well being of her children and grand-children. In 1831, she attached herself to the Baptist Church, at old Red Bank in this District, of which communion she was a member up to the time of her death. Truly may we say, that a mother has fallen in Israel, and many are the hearts, both here and in distant land, that will receive the intelligence with deep emotion.

Aged - Mrs. GANTT, says the "Due West Telescope", being a worthy member of Little River Baptist Church, in Abbeville district, died, at her residence on Little River, on the 22d ult., at an extreme age, being in her one hundred and third year.

Married - On the 4th of February last, by ALFRED DELANY, Esq., Mr. JOHN T. RAY to Miss F. E. JANES, all of Mississippi.

Married - On the 8th of April, by Rev. M. C. BARNETT, Dr. G. H. KING to Miss E. E. BREWTON, all of Spartanburg.

Married - On the 31st ult. by JOHN SHARP, Esq., Mr. THOMAS BRADLEY to Miss SARAH E. KIMBRELL, all of Pickens district.

Married - On the same day, by the same, Mr. CHAS. MAHEW to Miss MARY A. MORGAN, all of Pickens.

Obituary - Died, on the 11th ult. after a severe illness, Mrs. ELIZABETH CLEVELAND, consort of Mr. JONATHAN R. CLEVELAND of this district, in her 28th year. The deceased was exemplary in all relations of life. She leaves a devoted husband, with five small children, and many relatives and friends to mourn their irreparable loss. But they sorrow not as those without hope.

Issue of Saturday June 12, 1858:

Death of An Aged Citizen - We regret to learn that Mr. SARGENT GRIFFIN, an aged citizen of our district, died at his residence on Monday last, of the prevailing disease...flux. He was a man of noble mien, scrupulously honest, and a good neighbor. He lived through fourscore years, attached to himself many friends, and then sunk peacefully into the grave.

The Outrages in Kansas - The persons killed by the late outrage in Linn county, Kansas, were JOHN F. CAMPBELL, of Pennsylvania; WM. STILLWELL, of Iowa; _____ COLPETZER of Pennsylvania; MICHEL ROBINSON, of Iowa, and PATRICK ROSS. Rev. C. REED, Baptist missionary from Wisconsin, is among the wounded.

Hung - NEWTON S. HAWKINS, convicted of murder at the last Superior Court of Gordon county, Geo., was hung at Calhoun on the 21st inst.

Accident - JAMES MC DEARMAN, says the "Newberry Conservatist", was run over by the train of the Greenville and Columbia Railroad, near Boazman's Turn Out, on the 20th ult., and instantly killed. His own imprudence caused the fatal accident, by lying down across the track.

Married - At Tunnel Hill, on the evening of the 30th, by A. B. BOWDEN, Eq.

Mr. FIELDING PRICE to Miss DELIA ANN GARRISON, all of that place.

Obituary - On the 22nd of April, 1858, at the residence of his mother,
in this district, Mr. ROBERT A. STEELE, after an illness of nearly four
weeks, departed this life, aged about 20 years. He was the only son of
the late WM. D. and Mrs. MARGARET STEELE. Although a boy in years, at
the death of his father, in December 1855, he took upon himself and man-
aged with the skill and prudence of a man, the domestic affairs of the
family. He left a widowed mother and two sisters to mourn his early decease...but thanks be God our Saviour! They mourn not without hope that
their loss is his eternal gain. About ten days before his death, he expressed to the writer the expectation that he should never recover, and
his readiness to meet his God in Judgement. He was the affectionate son,
the loving brother, the steadfast friend, the obliging neighbor, and the
gentlemanly acquaintance; insomuch that none knew but to love, admire
and respect him. From us he has gone never to return. Let us endeavor
to gain that heavenly abode where we may reasonably expect to meet and
enjoy forever the society of our departed friend.

Departed this life, in Ramer, Alabama, Mrs. SUSAN D. MC DANIEL, formerly
of this district, consort of Rev. J. C. MC DANIEL, on the 9th of April,
1858, after a few hours suffering from injuries received by a tornado
blowing down their house. Thus cut off in the prime of life, she leaves
a husband and five small children, an aged mother, brothers, sisters,
and many friends, to mourn her loss. They have every assurance by her
professing religion, when quite young and her daily walk, and her last
words, that our loss is her eternal gain. S.A.C.

Issue of Saturday June 19, 1858:

Obituary - Died, in Williamston, S. C., May 28th, of Typhoid Dysentery,
SAMUEL C. REID, in the sixth year of his age. "It is well with the
child." Also, at the same place and of the same disease, June 3rd, Mr.
GEORGE M. REID, in the twenty-six year of his age. Though Mr. Reid had
lived regardless of the claims of religion, on his death-bed he was, we
trust, brought to repentance and a saving faith in Christ. He was baptised at his request, thus renouncing the world, and taking upon him the
profession of God. He declared his trust in the Lord, and even rejoiced
in the love of God and the hope of Heaven. Thus, after two weeks of
separation, parent and child are, we trust, reunited in the Paradise a-
bove.

Issue of Saturday June 26, 1858:

Death by Drowning - "The Greenville Patriot" states that Mr. R. T. BAIL-
EY, a citizen of Greenville village, was drowned in Reedy River, on last
Sunday. Mr. Bailey has left a widow and several children.

Dead - Judge W. A. HIGGINS, a distinguished member of the Masonic fraternity, and for many years Chief Justice of Washington county, Texas,
died at his residence at Brenham, on the morning of the 20th ult.

Obituary - Died, on the 12th inst., LELAH C., infant daughter of J. E.
and E. HAGOOD, aged eleven months and ten days.

Died, on the 5th June, instant, CAROLINE M. LANDERS, consort of R. P.
LANDERS, in the 28th year of her age. Her health had been feeble for
the last five years. She became a member of the Methodist Church at
Mount Zion, in this district, at the early age of thirteen years. Shortly afterwards she professed religion, and has ever since striven to walk
in His ways, and with apparently complete success. The deceased leaves
a husband and one child, with many relatives and friends, to mourn their
loss. But they sorrow not as those without hope.

Married - On the 2d inst., by Rev. W. E. WALTERS, Mr. JOHN W. ROBINSON,
of Anderson, to Miss REBECCA WATT, of Fairfield district.

Married - On the 10th inst., by Rev. J. H. FIELDS, Mr. JAMES MC NEVILLE,
of Pickens, to Miss MARGARET DILLARD, of Rabun, Ga.

Married - On the 20th inst., at sun-rise, by W. J. PARSONS, Esq., Mr.
JOHN SWINEY, of N. C., to Miss SARAH COLLINS, all of Pickens.

Issue of Saturday July 3, 1858:

Death of Gen. COFFEE - We regret to learn that Gen. EDWARD COFFEE, of
Rabun county, Ga., died on the 30th ultimo, of dropsy in the chest, in
the 65th year of his age. Gen. Coffee was a native of this district. He
removed to Rabun on his arriving at manhood, where he lived an exemplary
and upright life. For many years, he represented Rabun in one or the
other branch of the Legislature. At the time of his death, he was the
Senator from that county.

Married - On the 15th ult., by Rev. J. J. O'CONNELL, Mr. JAMES CONNELL
to Miss ANNIE GUNN, all of this district.

Married - On the 30th ult. by Rev. D. H. KENNEMUR, Mr. WM. B. FANT to
Miss ELIZABETH CHAPMAN, all of Pickens district.

Obituary - Died, in Cherokee county, Ga., on the 17th ult., WILLIAM FORT,
infant son of P. H. and SUSAN M. BREWSTER, aged two months and two days.

Issue of Saturday July 10, 1858:

Married - On the 4th inst. by W. S. GRISHAM, Esq., at the residence of
ALEX. MOOREHEAD, Mr. JOHN CARVER to Miss HANNAH R. HUGHES, all of this
district.

Married - In Pendleton village, on Sunday morning, June 27, by J. E.
BELOTTE, Esq., Mr. JOHN S. PATTERSON and Miss SUSAN CAMANADE.

Obituary - Died, at his residence in Chickasaw county, Mississippi, on
the 18th of June last, Mr. THOMAS B. REID, in the 72nd year of his age.
Mr. Reid was a native of this State, and removed some twenty-three years
ago to the West. He maintained, in all the relations of life, a character unsullied, and was highly respected and esteemed by all who knew
him. In early life, when his country called for soldiers to chastise
the Indians, he entered the service as an officer and discharged his
duty like a soldier and patriot. Conspicuous in the settlement and advancement of the section of country which he last made his home, with
his simplicity of manners and kindness of heart, endeared him to a large
circle of friends. Thus, he died as he had lived...an honest man, and
is mourned by many relatives and friends.

State of South Carolina, Pickens. Summons in Partition. JAMES M. AB-
BOTT vs. NOAH ABBOTT and others. It appearing to me that NOAH ABBOTT
and JNO. DOWIS and wife SARAH, defendants in this case, reside without
the limits of this State. Division or sale of the real estate of WIL-
LIAM ABBOTT, deceased.

State of South Carolina, Pickens. Summons in Partition. J. W. KELLY vs.
JAMES J. KELLY et als. It appearing to me that JAMES J. KELLY resides
without the limits of this State. Division or sale of the real estate
of ANDREW KELLY, deceased.

State of South Carolina, Pickens. To Prove Will in solemn form..W. R.
BOWEN and others vs. JOHN BOWEN, Ex'or., et als. Whereas W. R. BOWEN
and others have applied to me to have a paper purporting to be the last
Will and Testament of WILLIAM BOWEN, deceased. It appearing to my satisfaction that T. H. BOWEN, JOEL WELLBORN and wife MARTHA, THORNTON BEN-
SON and wife ELIZABETH and T. H. BOWEN and wife NANCY, defendants in this
case, reside without the limits of this State.

Issue of Saturday July 17, 1858:

Death of Gen. CLEVELAND - "The North East Georgian" furnishes us with a
fuller history of Gen. BENJ. CLEVELAND, of Habersham, Ga., whose death
we briefly announced last week. He was a native of South Carolina, and
was the descendant of Col. Cleveland, who commanded a division of the
Revolutionary army at the battle of King's Mountain. He was a kind hus-

band and father...a good neighbor, and an upright man. Of the seventy-
six years that he lived, fifty or more were spent in the Baptist church.
In 1814, he organised a company, and fought the Indians at Autassee and
the Callibee swamp. During the campaign he was advanced to the position
of Major. Retiring from the army in 1815, he was elected to the Legislature, either in the capacity of Representative or Senator, oftentimes,
his last service embracing the session of 1853-4. He was buried with
military honors, in the midst of those who respected and esteemed him
while living, and who will cherish his memory after death.

Dead - MATTHEW DICKSON, of Townville, in his 89th year, died on the 28th
ult. He was a native of North Carolina and had been a member of the
Presbyterian Church for about 55 years.

Old and Young - Married, in Gibson county, Tenn., on the 10th ult., Mr.
DENNIS THOMPSON, aged 93, to Miss SARAH F. KOONCE, aged 13 years!

(Note: This next issue of the paper was misfiled in the 1861 group.)

Issue of Saturday July 24, 1858:

Obituary - Died, in Pickens district, on the 8th inst., BRATTON M., son
of W. B. and H. L. DICKSON, aged ten months. Thos lovely rose of ours
that was loaned to us ten short months, and upon which we doted so tenderly, has been taken from our arms by the blessed Jesus, who says: "Suffer little children to come unto me and forbid them not, for of such is
the kingdom of Heaven". J.R.H.

Departed this life on the 16th inst., of flux, ANGUS MARCELLUS, infant
son of J. H. and Z. A. AMBLER, aged eleven months and 16 days.

Issue of July 31, 1858:

A Wife Murdered - On the 11th inst. WESLEY FISHER, residing in Ottawa,
LaSalle county, Ill., shot his wife dead at her mother's house in that
town. He then made an attempt to escape, and jumped into a canal, but
was dragged out and put in jail. Jealously is said to have been the
cause of the murder, and the victim bore the reputation of being "fair
and frail".

Drowned - Mr. JOHN ABBOTT was drowned in Owl creek, Cherokee county, Ga.
on the 5th inst.

Married - On the 15th inst. by the Rev. N. H. PALMER, Mr. THOMAS J.HUGHES
Esq. and Miss LOUISA M. HORSHAW, all of Clarkesville, Ga.

Obituary - Died, on the 25th of June,last, FLORENCE, only child of Dr.
T. S. and H. MILLER, aged eleven months and fifteen days. (Poetry)

Issue of Saturday August 7, 1858:

Dead - The "Yorkville Enquirer" reports the death of Col. I. D. WITHER-
SPOON, of York District. He died at the White Sulphur Springs, Va., on
the 20th ult. He had been a member of the State Senate and House of Representatives for many long years.

Large Reward - WM. TAYLOR, Esq., of Montgomery, Alabama, offers a reward of $10,000 for the apprehension of the murderer of his son, ABNER
C. TAYLOR.

Married - On the 1st inst., by W. J. PARSONS, Esq., Mr. C. C. PORTER to
Miss MALINDA ROBERTSON, all of Pickens.

Married - On the same day, by the same, Mr. F. V. G. PARSONS to Miss
PHOEBE HERD, all of Pickens.

Married - On Sunday morning, the 25th ult., by J. E. BELOTTE, Esq., Mr.
JOHN H. BLEVIN and Mrs. ELIZABETH AMICK, all of this district.

Married - In the village of Pickens, on Thursday norning, 5th instant,by

J. E. HAGOOD, Esq., Mr. JOEL R. B. BUCKESTER to Miss NANCY A. ALBERSON, all of Pickens.

Obituary - Departed this life, on the 22d of July, Mrs. JANE H. KENNEDY, wife of Rev. J. L. KENNEDY, in the 48th year of her age, esteemed and be- loved by all who knew her, and in the full assurance of a blissful im- mortality beyond the grave. She was a native of Spartanburg District, and connected herself in early life with Nazareth Presbyterian church, then under the pastoral charge of the Rev. Michael Dickson, and ever a- dorned her profession by a godly walk and conversation. She was not on- ly a consistent Christian, but zealous in every good work, especially in the cause of Sabbath Schools, whose interests and labors she delighted to promote by every means in her power. To her beloved husband she was a helpmate indeed; encouraging him in his arduous labors as preacher and teacher, and managing their domestic affairs with prudence and industry. "Her children (twelve in number) arise up and call her blessed; her hus- band, also, and he praiseth her." Her last illness was long and painful, yet she bore it with Christian patience and submission. Soon after she was taken sick, she had a presentiment that the messenger of death had come for her, but she had not then to prepare for his coming, for she had on the wedding garment and was ready. When asked how the Saviour ap- peared unto her, she replied: "Altogether lovely, precious indeed, my all and in all"; and in reference to her great sufferings, she said "they were nothing compared with what she deserved, and the greater her suffer- ings the sweeter did rest appear to her". Whilst speaking of leaving her husband and children, she manifested deep emotion, but said, "not my will but thine be done". When she lost the power of speech and was asked "if her way was clear" and if "she enjoyed comfortable assurance of peace with God", to which, with a smile, she nodded assent; and thus she left this world to enter upon that rest which remaineth for the people of God.
A Friend

Died, in this district, on the 24th ult., MATILDA HARRISON, aged about sixty years. She died in peace, with the hope of a blessed immortality.

State of South Carolina, Pickens. Summons in Partition. G. F. COX vs. EDWARD COX et als. It appearing to my satisfaction that JOHN COX, MAR- INDA COX, GABRIEL COX, ROBERT COX, LITTLETON EDGE and wife MINERVA, GEORGE NAVES and wife JANE, GEORGE GLOW and wife RHODA, reside without the limits of this State. Division or sale of the real estate of JOSHUA COX, deceased.

State of South Carolina, Pickens. Summons in Partition. DANIEL ALEXAN- DER vs. JAS. ALEXANDER et als. It appearing to me that JAMES ALEXANDER, WM. DURHAM and wife MELINDA, and SALLY BOATNER, defendants in this case, reside without the limits of this State. Division or sale of the real estate of THOMAS ALEXANDER, deceased.

Issue of Saturday August 14, 1858:

Killed by a Sheep - J W. SHAW, of Winnsboro, S. C., was killed on the 2d inst., by a but(t) on the neck from a sheep.

Dead - The Charleston papers announce the death of A. DELLA TORRE, an old merchant of that city. He was a native of Italy.

Married - On Tuesday evening, 3rd inst., by Rev. ALBERT A. MORSE, at Ri- voli, the residence of Col. JOHN T. SLOAN, in Anderson district, W. H. WHITNER, Esq., to Miss ESSIE M. SLOAN.

Obituary - Died, on the 14th ult., Mrs. MARTHA M. BALLINGER, consort of WM. D. BALLINGER, in the 30th year of her age. Although she had never attached herself to any religious denomination, yet from her exemplary walk through life, patient resignation and christian-like fortitude which she bore in her last illness, left a well-grounded hope with her friends that she has gone to inherit eternal rest. She left a large circle of relatives and friends, who sympathize with her bereaved husband and chil- dren for their irreparable loss. F.

Brutal Murder - GEORGE IVEY, of Columbus, Ga., murdered his wife in a brutal manner on Sunday last. He has escaped.

Married - On the 22nd ult., by THOS. H. BOGGS, Esq., Mr. MARK LIVELY to Miss ELIZA PILGRIM, all of Pickens.

Married - On the 15th inst., by the same, Mr. ANDREW B. DURHAM to Miss MARTHA J. MILWEE, all of Pickens.

Death of a Veteran - Col. HENRY KING, a native of North Carolina, who fought as a private at New Orleans, and was on the electoral ticket of Alabama in Gen. JACKSON's first presidential campaign, died on the 13th ult. in Marengo county, Ala. He was for many years a member of the Alabama Legislature.

An article on the murder of a JOHN SMITH, late of Georgia, by one or more Irishmen at Tunnel Hill on Sunday last. They were drinking and a difficulty arose between Smith and the Irishmen.

Obituary - Died, in Rabun county, Ga., on the 21st of July, AUGUSTUS NAPOLEON, son of H. A. H. and CATHERINE GIBSON, aged one year, eight mon's and fifteen days. His little body "sleeps that sleep which knows no waking" until the last trump of God shall sound. His pure spirit has winged its flight to that "house not made with hands, eternal in the Heavens",...it has gone to Him who said, "Suffer little children to come unto me, for of such is the kingdom of heaven". That darling flower that we loved so well has faded on earth, to bloom in the celestial garden of Paradise...no more on earth will his little bright eyes meet our gaze.
(Poetry)

Departed this life, on the 13th of August, 1858, after eight days suffering of rheumatic inflamation, SARAH A. HUGHES, daughter of EDWARD and ASERETT HUGHES. She was a true member of the Baptist church, professing religion and a strong faith in her Saviour, while very young. She was a kind and obedient daughter...an affectionate sister...one who was ever ready to soothe the pains of the sick and afflicted. None knew Sarah but to love her. A short time before her death, she kindly admonished her brothers to forsake the world and look to Jesus Christ for their salvation, and to pray for themselves and for her, and to meet her in heaven. She tenderly implored her mother and sisters not to weep for her; the best of friends must part...and then she closed her eyes and fell asleep, and without a struggle her immortal spirit was wafted to its eternal abode. E.F.H. (Poetry)

Issue of August 28, 1858:

Shocking Murder - "The Chattanooga Advertiser" of the 10th inst., says: On Saturday evening last, a man by the name of HAMMOND, was inhumanly beaten to death, in the upper part of this city. When found, he was just able to tell that his brother-in-law, JOSHUA NORMAN, was his murderer.

Weldon, N. C., Aug. 18 - EDWARD YARBOROUGH, son of Col. Yarborough, the well known hotel proprietor at Raleigh, committed suicide last night, by cutting his throat. He was a Lieutenant in the late Mexican war, and leaves a wife and three children.

State of South Carolina, Pickens. Bill for Partition &c. AVARILLA GRIFFIN vs. THOS. GRIFFIN et als. It appearing to the Court, upon bill filed that J. B. MANSELL and wife VASHTI, BARTON GRIFFIN, BENJAMIN GRIFFIN, SARGENT GRIFFIN, R. H. GRIFFIN, H. A. BILLINGSLY and wife MINERVA; the heir-at-law of BAILEY GRIFFIN, deceased; to wit: AVARILLA GRIFFIN, SARGENT J. GRIFFIN, JOSEPH GRIFFIN; and the heirs-at-law of WILLIAM GRIFFIN, dec'd, namely: AVARAILLA A. GRIFFIN, NANCY V. GRIFFIN, ELIHU H. GRIFFIN, RASANNAH M. GRIFFIN, G. B. GRIFFIN, MARY L. M. GRIFFIN, BAILEY B. GRIFFIN, THOMAS V. GRIFFIN, MARGARET T. GRIFFIN, MARTHA F. D. GRIFFIN, and JANE M. S. GRIFFIN, reside without the limits of this State.

Obituary - Departed this life, on the 15th of August, Mrs. JULIA E. NEV-

VILLE, wife of JOHN C. NEVILLE, and daughter of S. R. and ANNA MC FALL, in the 25th year of her age. The deceased, cut down in the prime of life was dedicated to God by baptism in infancy, trained by pious parents and the subject of many prayers. She was naturally gentle, quiet and lovely in her dispostion and beloved by all who knew her. For some months prevous to her last illness, which was long and painful, she had manifested more than ordinary concern for the salvation for her soul. Soon after she was taken sick, she spent a season of the most intense anxiety and inquiry what she must do to be saved. During this period she was constantly visited and instructed by ministers and pious friends. At length she obtained relief from her distressing fears and expressed a desire to connect herself with the church. Accordingly an examination was entered into, by a minister and ruling elder present, which proved both interesting and satisfactory to all who heard it. These officers, believing her to be a sincere and true christian, and in compliance with her desire and urgent request to be permitted openly to acknowledge Christ, received her as a member of the Presbyterian church. In a short time after these solemn services, which were peculiarly gratifying and consoling to her friends; after most affectionately entreating her husband to give himself to Christ and walk in the path of righteousness and peace; after a tender farewell to her "precious little ones", and directing that they should be trained for the Lord, she bid adieu to her earthly friends and passed, in the triumphs of faith, to the abode of the blessed above. Thus we have left us a bright example of the power of divine grace to sustain and console in the very hour and article in death. She leaves a bereaved husband, fond parents, affectionate brothers and sisters, with many friends and neighbors to mourn her loss. But let all such comfort themselves with the blessed assurance that their loss is her unspeakable and eternal gain.   A Friend

Issue of Saturday September 4, 1858:

Killed - JAMES GREEN killed a man named DANER, of Mobile, at Warrenton Sprongs on the night of the 23d, with a bowie knife, in a rencontre. The same parties were recently arrested in Washing, and prevented from fighting a duel. Both are young men. Green is in custody.

Dead - The Abbeville papers announce the death of THOMAS R. COCHRAN, sheriff of that district. He died of consumption.

Married - On the 24th ult. by L. ROGERS, Esq., Mr. J. M. WILSON to Miss ELIZABETH HUDSON, all of Pickens.

Obituary - Departed this life in Pendleton, July 10th, 1858, JINCY E. CAMPBELL, daughter of Mr. H. E. CAMPBELL, in the 24th year of her age. Her illness was protracted but she bore it with Christian patience and resignation, and gave strong evidence of her preparation through faith in our Lord Jesus Christ to meet the summons to leave the earth. May her family and friends receive her death as a call from God to them to prepare for eternity, and may their end be as hopeful as hers.   A Friend

Died, in Pickens district on the 2d May, 1858, CORNELIA C., daughter of W. and M. E. BURKETT, aged nine months and fifteen days. This lovely rose of ours that was loaned to us for a short period, and upon which we doted so tenderly, has been taken from us by the blessed Jesus, who says his word: "Suffer little children to come unto me, and forbid them not, for such is the kingdom of Heaven". Weep not bereaved parents for little Cornelia C., for while her body has been lowered to the grave, her spirit has found a home in Heaven. "Home sweet home", we all have friends in Heaven.

Issue of Saturday September 11, 1858:

Fatal Accident - THOMAS B. JARRAT, employed in a mercantile house at Murfreesboro, Tenn., was killed by a falling wall last week.

Married - On the 2d inst., by E. ALEXANDER, Esq., Mr. E. B. ALEXANDER to Miss RUTHA ALEXANDER, all of Pickens district.

Issue of Saturday September 18, 1858:

Married - At the residence of J. W. PRATHER, Esq., on Wednesday evening
the 8th inst., by Rev. J. L. KENNEDY, Dr. R. J. GILLILAND, of Pickens,
to Miss J. ANNA TURNBULL, of Habersham co., Ga.

Married - On the 14th inst., by E. H. COX, Esq., Mr. J. R. CLEVELAND to
Miss ELIZABETH LE ROY, all of Pickens.

Issue of Saturday September 25, 1858:

Death of Col. CALHOUN - We are pained to learn that Col. WILLIAM L. CAL-
HOUN, (a son of the lamented JOHN C. CALHOUN) died at his residence in
Abbeville district, last week. His remains were interred at the Stone
Church, in this district, on Thursday last. The memory of one, so well
and favorably known in the walks of private life, requires no tribute
from the pen of the public journalist. Peace to his dust!

Married - At Long Creek Church, on Sunday the 19th inst., by Rev. BURREL
WALL, Mr. JAS. SMITH to Miss ELIZABETH LONG, all of Pickens.

Married - At the same time and place, by the same, Mr. ARTHUR MC CRACKIN
to Miss FRANCES LOWRY, all of Rabun county, Ga.

Issue of Saturday October 2, 1858:

Fatal Affray - The "Enterprise" states that a fatal affray occurred in
Greenville district, between two of her citizens...JOHN FOWLER and FELIX
ROGERS in which Rogers lost his life. Fowler is in jail.

Married - On Thursday the 23d ult. by Rev. J. R. HUNNICUTT, Mr. ROBERT
SPENCER to Miss EMILY DEATON, all of Pickens district.

Obituary - Died, of yellow fever, on the 20th of September, on Mrs. JOHN
L. NORTH's farm, near Pendleton village, Mrs. EDWARD N. THURSTON, of
Charleston. Her bereaved family have the sympathy of this community.

Died, June 22d, of cholera infantum, MARY ESTELLE, infant of Col. P. H.
and Mrs. J. Y. PRATHER, aged 10 months. The family of her grandparents
in Abbeville were anticipating a visit from her parents, and the joy of
seeing and caressing little Mary was not the least in the pleasure of
reunion, but her little coffin was all we were permitted mournfully to
meet. Yet when we made room for her among the flowers and thought of her
as a seraph in the spirit land, we little knew that she had only gone
before, and in a few short weeks would welcome to her glorious home, one
who loved his little neice on earth, and is still more nearly allied to
her in heaven. (Poetry)

Died, in Pine Bluff, Arkansas, July 22d, of passive congestion of the
bowels, after an illness of five days, R. HENRY DRENNAN, Esq., son of
Capt. WM. L. and Mrs. M. D. DRENNAN, aged 22 years, three months and
five days. In writing a memorial of one so much beloved, we do not feel
that we are intruding private griefs upon an unsympathizing public. For
though so young, he had won for himself the respect and admiration of a
large circle of friends and acquaintances, and the tribute of many a sigh
has been wafted to the far west, where he nobly fell in the discharge of
duty, and where his body lowly lies, awaiting a removal to his native
land. Endowed with superior abilities which had been highly cultivated
...with noble principles which had been preserved pure and intact...with
a high sense of honor, which was cherished bright and unstained...with
a heart so filled with generous impulses that envy, malice and guile had
no dominion there. Henry, our precious boy, was an example of all that
is noble, true and of good report. A selfish act, an unkind word, or
an expression of detraction was never heard from him...so truly was he
noble, so nobly was he true to his God, himself, and his neighbour. His
most intimate associates, his nearest and dearest relations, even in the
most secluded hours of social intercourse, never heard him utter a peev-
ish or passionate word, and if the faults and shortcomings of others
were never made a subject of conversation in his presence, it seemed to

give him pain. Thus, we can look back upon his life as a pure and sparkling stream, making sweet music as it flowed along, undimmed by a single shadow, unstained by passion or vice; reflecting the beautiful, the
glorious, and good, until it met and mingled with the pearly river, which
"makes glad the city of our God". A graduate of Erskins College at the
early age of nineteen, Mr. Drennan commenced the study of law, and amidst the circle of "loved ones at home", amidst its music, its flowers,and
its fireside enjoyments, "Blackstone" was read, and many a pleasant jest,
encouraging word, and pictured hope brightened its dry pages, making
them more a pleasant employment than a hard study to him. A few months
only, under Gen. MC GOWAN and Maj. PERRIN, at Abbeville C. H., towards
whom for their kindness to him his friends shall ever feel grateful,
completed his course, and in December, 1857, at Columbia, he was licensed to the practice of the law in his native State. But feeling that in
the west a wider field for the employment of his talents was opened to
him, in the following February, he bade adieu to his boyhood's home, and
with the blessings and the prayers of loving hearts attending him, he
sought and obtained a situation in Pine Bluff. There, under the kind advice and encouragement of Gen. JAMES, a distinguished lawyer of the
place, he earnestly pursued his profession, and his assiduity, talents
and general deportment was such that even strangers prophesied for him
a brilliant, as well as useful career. But, alas! these prospects were
only allowed to bud, betokening the beauty and fragrance of the plant
from which they sprung, when Death, with relentless hand, crushed them
all; and the skill of physicians, the prayers of weeping strangers who
had learned to call him friend, nor the agony in store for hearts en-
twined around him, could save him from the Destroyer. In answer to the
inquiries of friends, we would say that from letters received from Rev.
J. I. BOOZER and others, of Pine Bluff, we learn that his sickness was
thought to be superinduced from taking a bath after tea, and eating hear-
tily of peaches. That he suffered very little comparatively...that he
met the communication of his extreme illness with characteristic patience
and fortitude. He gave his keys and papers to the keeping of Mr. Boozer, designated the spot in which he preferred burial, repeated two verses of a favorite hymn, "On Jordan's stormy banks I stand", and asked
the remainder to be read...sent a farewell to his friends at home, and
spent his dying breath in prayer. From an obituary written by some kind
stranger in an Arkansas paper, we extract a few paragraphs. "If good
conduct, generous demeaner, and a wiilingness to perform good deeds promise long life, Mr. Drennan possessed them all. He was somewhat reser-
ved among strangers, but his good and amiable deportment impressed all
who came within the circle of his acquaintance. His attachments of
friendship were strong, devoted and faithful. His tongue was never employed in evil speaking towards any one, and in this he was worthy of
the highest imitation. Although he had not time to establish a reputation in his difficult profession, yet he displayed some of the surest
elements of success; close application, strict attention to business,
perfect sobriety and high integrity. If close attention to his sickness
can afford any consolation to his bereaved parents, relatives and friends
they may know he had it from the hands of the purest and most anxious
friends". And now from crushed and bleeding hearts a prayer arises that
the best of all blessings may descend upon each one who thus ministered
to our beloved, our precious boy. L. (5 verses poetry)

Issue of Saturday October 9, 1858:

Accident - A fatal accident occurred at Tunnel Hill, on the 29th ult. At
shaft No. 4, as Mr. JOHN COIL was ascending from his work, he fell from
the bucket, a distance of about one hundred feet, breaking his head. He
survived only a few hours. The facts are in accordance with the finding
of the jury of inquest.

Married - On the 5th inst., by Rev. J. L. KENNEDY, Mr. ALEX. SHELOR, of
Pickens, to Miss SUE SCOTT, of Habersham Co., Ga.

Issue of Saturday October 16, 1858:

Melancholy Death - A gentleman by the name of J. L. BROOKS, died at the
residence of a friend in Rankin county, Mississippi, a few days ago, under very painful circumstances. He went from Mobile to be married, but

was seized with the yellow fever, and instead of reaching the Hymeneal alter, found an untimely grave.

Dead - Col. S. A. WALES, at one time a resident of Habersham Co., Ga., died in Columbus recently, aged about sixty years.

Man Murdered - Mr. THOMAS BAGBY, JR., was fatally stabbed at a camp ground near Macon, Ga., on Sunday, the 26th of September.

Issue of Saturday October 23, 1858:

Married - On the 14th inst., by WM. J. PARSONS, Esq., Mr. SAM'L. A. A. PARSONS to Miss AZINA M. GARVIN, all of Pickens.

Obituary - Departed, this life on the 14th inst., WM. FRANKLIN, son of RANSOM and ELIZABETH O'NEAL, aged 2 years 4 months and 15 days. This tender tie was soon severed, and alas! how painful; but we yield..."suffer the little children to come unto me and forbid them not", was the language of him, who knows best when to take them. M.A. O'N. (5 verses poetry)

Sudden Death - The force of the oft repeated quotation ..."In the midst of life we are in death"...was never more fully realized than on Tuesday morning last. Early in the morning, Mr. ALFRED HESTER, who was in attendance as an officer on the grand jury, fell suddenly to the earth and expired in a few minutes. An affection of some one of the vital organs, probably the heart, was the cause of his death. The Coroner, with a jury empanelled, held an inquest over the body of the deceased.

Fatal Affray at Edgefield Court House - An affray occurred at Edgefield Court House, on Wednesday night last, in which a young man named MAT. JONES, a son of LOUIS JONES formerly Sheriff of Edgefield district, was fatally stabbed, by THOS. MARKEY, formerly of this city. We did not learn the cause of the quarrel or the cincumstances of the affray but it seems to be the general impression that Markey was, at the time, acting on the defensive. He was arrested and committed to jail to await an examination. "Augusta Chronicle"

Suicide - Mr. W. J. LENOX, of Natchez, committed suicide on the 1st inst. He was afflicted with a cancer; his physicians had given him up, and in despair he put an end to his life.

Sad - ELIZABETH FITZGERALD, aged 3 years, daughter of WM. G. and M. C. SOMERVILE, of Culpepper county, Va., died on the 10th inst. This makes the sixth child recently taken from this afflicted family...all died of scarlet fever.

A Tribute to a Woman - "The Troy (Ala.) Bulletin" notices the death of Mrs. ANN LOVE, land-lady of a hotel in that place. So much had she endeared herself to the citizens, that every store was closed at her burial.

Issue of Saturday October 30, 1858:

Suicide - A young lady named ANNA HOLT committed suicide at Wilmington, Del., on Monday, by taking strychnine.

Obituary - Died, of scarlet fever in this place on the 23d inst., after an illness of five days, ELLA JANE, youngest child of W. E. and E. C. HOLCOMBE, aged two years and one month. The subject of this notice had just reached that period of her age at which children are most interesting, not only to their Parents and immediate family but to their relations and friends generally. Little Janie, (as she was called) was an extraordinary child, I knew her well, she filled a large space in the family circle. Her death has created a vacuum, which will be long and deeply felt. She was the idol of a doting mother, a devoted father, a loving sister and affectionate brothers. But little Janie is no more! Her little form has been laid in the cold, cold Grave, and her spirit has gone to that God who gave it. Those bright and sparkling eyes, which so often sent a thrill of joy to a mothers heart are now dimmed and

50

closed in death. That sweet peculiar voice which fell in such delightful accents on a fathers ears, has been silenced on earth, and so attuned as to accord with the harps of Angels in Heaven. I know it was hard to give her up...that the Messenger of death was an unwelcome guest, but remember the grave cannot keep her. While you, her father and mother, sister and brothers are sheding bitter tears, over her departure, she is singing praises to the Lamb that was slain, and hath redeemed her to God by his blood. Think of her then not as a prisoner of the Tomb, but as a redeemed saint in Glory, such a though will afford joy and not grief, and will enable you to say the Lord giveth and the Lord hath taken away, blessed be the name of the Lord.

Issue of Saturday November 6, 1858:

Died of Injuries - WM. HOUNSCHILD, the German who was so badly injured by the explosion of powder on the Railroad, died on the 24th ult. He was buried by the Walhalla Riflemen, of which corps he was a member.

Murder - "The Grayson (Va.) Patriot" states that DANIEL DAVIS, who was tried in that county for murder of SPENCER ISOM and acquitted, started with his wife after the trial, for Jonesville, North Carolina, and both were murdered on the road. He was married but a few days ago.

Homicide - The "Pee Dee Herald" of the 26th ult. states, that JOSHUA ALFORD was shot and instantly killed, in Marlborough district, by ZION ODOM last week. Odom has been arrested.

Married - On Wednesday morning the 27th ult., by Rev. R. C. KETCHUM, ROBERT A. THOMPSON, Editor of the "Keowee Courier", to Miss V. ROSE STARRITT of Clarkesville, Ga.

Married - On the 28th ult., by E. ALEXANDER, Esq., Mr. THOS. J. ELLENBURG to Miss SUSAN MURPHREE, all of this District.

Issue of Saturday November 13, 1858:

Fatal Kick - The "Yorkville Enquirer" says that Mr. I. N. SADLER was kicked by a horse on the 3d inst., and died from its effects on the succeeding Sunday.

Killed - THOMAS SCILEY fell from the new bridge, which is being erected over the Savannah river at Hamburg, and was drowned, on the 30th ult.

Married - On Thursday the 4th inst., at Whetstone, by D. P. ROBINS, Esq. Mr. WM. J. HAMBY of Rabun Co., Ga. to Miss MARY COMPTON, of Pickens.

Married - On the 4th inst., by L. ROGERS, Esq., Mr. N. B. LUSK to Miss R. E. CORBIN, all of Pickens.

Married - On the 24th ult., at the residence of Col. J. L. BOYD, by Rev. E. COLLINS, Mr. JOHN BEARDIN to Miss MATILDA SMALL, all of Pickens.

State of South Carolina, Pickens. In Equity - Bill for Relief, Discovery, Account, &c. EPHRAIM PERRY vs. JAMES ROBINSON, Adm'r., JOHN MC KINNEY, Adm'r., et als. The complainant having this day filed his bill in the above stated case, and inasmuch as the following defendants reside without and beyond the limits of this State; to wit: JAMES MC KINNEY, SARAH MC KINNEY and her husband JAMES MC KINNEY, PRESTON MC KINNEY, GEORGE W. MC KINNEY, NANCY MC KINNEY, JAMES D. MC KINNEY, MARY MURPHY and her husband _____ MURPHY, FRANCIS MC KINNEY, PRESTON MC KINNEY, JR., NANCY MC KINNEY, JR., MARY ERNEST and WILLIAM MC KINNEY.

Issue of Saturday November 20, 1858:

Married - On the 14th inst., by Rev. A. MC GUFFIN, Mr. CHARLIE B. JEANS to Miss ELIZA A. BARTON, all of Pickens.

Married - on the 24th ult., by T. H. BOGGS, Esq., Mr. SAMUEL PERRY to Miss MARTHA FERGUSON, all of Pickens.

Married - On the 28th ult. by the same, Mr. JOHN T. HINTON to Miss N. E. FENNEL, all of Pickens.

Married - On the 4th inst., by the same, Mr. JOSEPH MOORE to Miss REBECCA J. HAMILTON, all of Pickens.

Obituary - Departed this life, on the 22nd day of September last, at the residence of her son, A. B. SARGENT, Mrs. SARAH SARGENT, aged about 90 years. Mrs. Sargent was born in Virginia, and in early life passed through the trying scenes of the revolution, often taking shelter in the woods with her mother and young brothers and sisters, from the unnatural enemies of the county, (the tories) while her father and elder brother were in the army, faithfully combatting for the rights of their country. She joined the M. E. Church in 1808, of which she continued a member until 1848, when she joined the Baptist church at Pleasant Hill, in whose fellowship she continued until her death. She was a dutiful wife, a kind mother and an exemplary christian. She was blind for nearly three years before her death, yet she bore her affliction with that fortitude and composure, which none but the christian know. Thus she has passed away from earth, to that upper and better world, "where the wicked cease from troubling, and the weary are at rest". K.

Drowned - THOMAS BALTRELL, son of Judge Baltrell, of Tallahassee, Fla., was drowned at Apalachicola, on the 30th ult., by leaping from a steamer to rescue a drowning child. The child was saved but the young man lost his life.

Issue of Saturday November 27, 1858:

Deceased - Maj. J. H. WRIGHT, a native of Virginia, and who was wounded at the battle of New Orleans, died at Greensburg, La., on the 9th inst., of yellow fever.

Sudden Death - The "Mobile Register" announces the sudden death of JOHN B. TRINCHARD, commercial editor of that paper.

Married - On the 12th inst. by E. ALEXANDER, Esq., Mr. E. J. NIX to Miss HARRIET FORRESTER, all of Pickens.

Issue of Saturday December 4, 1858:

Married - On Sunday evening the 14th ult., by Rev. BURRELL WALL, Mr. ALEXANDER ORR to Miss SOPHRONIA COX, all of Pickens.

Married - On Thursday the 18th ult. by the Rev. J. H. ZIMMERMAN, the Rev. J. H. GLEASON, of the South Carolina Conference, to Miss OPHELIA L. MC MASTERS, of Anderson district, S. C.

Married - On Friday night, the 12th ult. at THOMAS ERWINS, by D. P. ROBINS, Esq., Mr. DECATUR POWELL to Miss MARTHA E. LANGSTON, all of Georgia.

Married - On the 18th ult. by W. S. WOOLBRIGHT, Esq., Mr. JORDAN SIMMONS, of Anderson to Miss MARTHA GRANT, of Pickens.

Issue of Saturday December 11, 1858:

Horrible Death - JOHN G. WALSINGHAM was found dead on Saturday morning, says the "Barnwell Sentinel". We learn that he had been intoxicated the night previous, lay down by the fire and was burnt nearly up. This happened at the house of one JOHN LAMBERT, near the village.

Deplorable - The "Edgefield Advertiser" says that Miss SARAH TOWLER committed suicide in that District on the 16th ult., by hanging herself. No cause is assigned for this terrible act.

Married - On the 18th ult. by E. ALEXANDER, Esq., Mr. HENRY GROGAN to Miss SARAH SMITH, all of Pickens.

Married - At the residence of D. E. SMITHSON, on the 2d inst., by L. H. VERNER, Esq., Mr. JOHN M. BOWMAN to Mrs. ELIZABETH TELFORD.

Obituary - Departed this life, on the 29th November last, in the fifty-
fifth year of his age, WILLIAM ROBINSON, of dyspepsy and dropsy of the
chest. The subject of this notice has been a member and deacon of the
Baptist Church for many years, and died in full faith of meeting his Saviour in peace. He remarked, on his dying bed, that he was only waiting
his Maker's will to go. "Blessed are the dead who die in the Lord, for
they shall see God". He was a kind husband and affectionate father, and
leaves a large family and many friends to mourn their loss. A few days
before his death, he called for his little children, and told them to be
good and obey their mother; then extended his hand to his wife, and called on the Lord to bless and take care of her in this world, and enable
her to meet him in Heaven. E.E.R.

Issue of Saturday December 18, 1858:

Married a Fortune - Mr. CHARLES P. TALIAFERRO and Miss CAROLINE FORTUNE,
of Brownsville, Tenn., were united in marriage on the 24th of November.

Death of an Aged Man - Mr. REUBIN GRAY, aged 97 years, died at Brooks-
ville, Maine, last Tuesday. He was the first male white child born on
the Peninsular of Castine. He voted for Gen. WASHINGTON and for every
Democratic candidate for President up to the present day.

Bloody Work - The "Darlington Flag" says that WM. RHODES killed SIMON
KELLY, in that district, on Tuesday last. WM. WALTERS also mortally
wounded WM. BEASLEY a few days before.

Married - On the 13th inst., at the residence of REUBEN GAINES, by E. G.
MULLINNIX, Mr. E. CLARK, of Anderson, to Miss G. A. GAINES, of Pickens.

Married - In this village, on the 16th inst., by J. E. HAGOOD, Esq., Mr.
THOMAS DODD, JR., to Miss LIZZIE COX, all of Pickens.

Married - At the residence of H. HUGHES, on the same evening by the same,
Mr. WILLIAM HUNNICUTT, of Clayton, Ga., to Miss AGNES O'NEAL, of Pickens.

Issue of Saturday December 25, 1858:

Obituary - We regret to notice the announcement of the death of Col. AL-
BERT PIKE of Arkansas. He was a distinguished lawyer, poet and scholar.
He commanded "C" company of the Arkansas Cavalry in Mexico, and was a
brave and determined soldier. It will be remembered that he succeeded
the lamented Gen. QUITMAN in the exalted masonic office.

Married - On the 12th inst. by Rev. W. MULLINNIX, Mr. JOHN HENDRICKS to
Mrs. CYNTHIA COUCH, all of Pickens.

Married - On the 14th inst., by Rev. T. L. MC BRYDE, D. D., Dr. JOHN HOL-
LAND, of Abbeville, to Miss MARTHA, daughter of J. P. HARRIS, Esq., of
Anderson.

Murder - A brutal murder was committed upon ROB'T. MORRISON, in Chester
District, on the 9th inst., by WM. HODGES and JOSEPH HOWERTON, who have
fled the country. One hundred dollars reward is offered for their apprehension.

Issue of Saturday January 8, 1859:

Married - On the 21st Oct. last, by Rev. D. H. KENNEMUR, Mr. JAMES A. DAR-
NOLD to Miss L. J. KILBURN, all of Pickens.

Married - On the 23d ult., by the same, Mr. E. M. MADDEN to Miss OPHELIA
A. ARNOLD, all of Pickens.

Married - On the 30th ult. by J. E. HAGOOD, Esq., Mr. WARREN R. CANNON
to Miss HARRIET POWER, all of Pickens.

Married - On the 23d ult. by Rev. A. W. MC GUFFIN, Mr. W. W. POLLARD, of
Spartanburg, to Miss T. P. BALLINGER, of Pickens.

Married - On the 23d ult. by Rev. J. R. HUNNICUTT, Mr. WM. WILSON to Miss ELIZABETH MASTERS, all of Pickens.

Married - At Long Creek Church, on the 19th ult., by Rev. BURREL WALL, Mr. ELI MOORE, JR. to Miss EMILY SHED, all of Pickens.

Married - On the 23d ult., by D. P. ROBINS, Esq., Mr. ROBERT BLACKWELL to Miss RHODA ANN ROTHELL, all of Pickens.

Married - On the 23d ult. by J. M. QUILLIAN, Esq., Mr. W. J. SUTTLES to Miss MATTIE A., daughter of THOMAS KELLEY, Esq., all of Clayton, Ga.

Obituary - C. ADDIS, daughter of SAMUEL and EUINICE ADDIS, departed this life the 9th day of December, 1858, aged 20 years, 6 months and 14 days. She was a member of the Baptist Church, at Westminster. She gave satis-factory evidence that she departed in peace, and in hope of eternal life. "Blessed are the dead which die in the Lord; yea, from henceforth saith the spirit they rest from their labors and their works they do follow them".

Departed this life on the 12th Dec., 1858 after a few days suffering of scarlet fever, SUSAN REESE, aged two years and six months, infant daugh-ter of M. S. DOYLE, consort of ELI R. DOYLE, deceased. This little one who was so much loved by her fond mother, two little sisters and many relatives, has passed away, but while this lovely little flower faded on earth, it was transplanted in Heaven to bloom eternally, and when her bright eyes were closed in the tranquil slumber of death, we could only say, "O! death where is thy sting; O! grave where is thy victory'. Al-though it seems hard to see death throw its cold and icy mantle around these tender ties and sever them from the kind embrace of their Parents, yet, we must yield to the mysterious ways of a kind Providence and say all is well. For while we mourn her loss on earth her pure spirit has ascended on high to a land of pure delight to unite with the celestial choir in singing the praises of the redeemed forever. (2 verses Poetry)

Issue of Saturday January 15, 1859:

Sudden Death - GEORGE M. NEWTON, of Augusta, Ga., among the most distin-quished anatomists of the Union, died on the 6th inst., of lockjaw.

Issue of Saturday January 22, 1859:

Married - In Chester, at the residence of Rev. L. C. HINTON, C. S. BRICE, Esq., editor of the "Standard", to Miss FANNIE HINTON. "Chester Standard"

Married - On the 16th inst., by E. ALEXANDER, Esq., Mr. JEFFERSON ALEX-ANDER to Miss MALINDA REEVES, all of Pickens.

Married - On the 4th inst., by Rev. A. RICE, ISAAC WICKLIFFE, Esq., of Pickens, to Miss CELESTINA WAKEFIELD, of Anderson.

Married - On the 11th inst., by Rev. W. G. MULLINNIX, Mr. JOHN P. TRAY-NUM to Miss MARTHA A. SMITH, all of Anderson.

Married - On the 23rd ult. by A. B. BOWDEN, Esq., Mr. D. D. RICHEY to Miss EMALINE DARBY, all of Pickens.

Married - On the 18th inst., by the same, Mr. JAMES NETTING to Miss CATH-ERINE KING, of Forsyth county, Ga.

Married - On the 6th inst., by Rev. A. W. MC GUFFIN, Mr. JAMES MILLER to Miss DELILAH C. DUNLAP, all of Pickens.

Obituary - Departed this life, on the 2d January, inst., Mrs. FRANCES GAINES, consort of Rev. ROBERT GAINES, in the 78th year of her age. The deceased was a native of Virginia, was raised in North Carolina, but spent the most of her days in this State. Having been afflicted in body for many years, she was, a few days before her death, attacked by a stubborn cold, which proved fatal. Mrs. Gaines had been a member of the

Methodist church for 62 years, and has left behind her a large family
connection and many friends, bereaved and sorely afflicted. "Blessed are
the dead who died in the Lord".

Died - On the 1st inst., of Pneumonia, after an illness of thirteen days,
LIZZIE JANE, daughter of JAMES A. and MARTHA DOYLE, aged two years, eleven months and twenty-seven days.

Issue of Saturday January 29, 1859:

Death - Hon. JAMES E. BELSER, a native of this State, but for many years
a resident of Alabama, died there on the 6th. He was in his 53rd year.

Married - On the 2d inst., by Rev. WM. MC WHORTER, Mr. E. C. LUSK to Miss
E. S. ALEXANDER, all of Pickens.

Married - On the 2d ultimo, in Sarepta, Calhoun co., Miss., by Rev. J. M.
BARTON, Dr. JOHN M. LYLES, of Sarepta (formerly of Newberry district, S.
C.) to Miss MARY E. REID, of Pickens.

Obituary - Departed this life, Dec. 22d, 1858, Mr. JOS. BREWER, in the
43rd year of his age. The deceased attached himself to the Methodist
Episcopal church, sometime in the year 1840, and soon after became the
subject of the converting grace of God. His life was ever such, as to
correspond with the sanctity of the Christian religion, discharging
faithfully the duties of a member of the Church of Christ. For several
years of his christian life, he served the church in the capacity of
circuit steward; the duties of which his health forbade active life. He
was the victim of severe and protracted affliction for several months
previous to his death. He bore his affliction with much patience, being
resigned to the will of his Heavenly Father. The writer of this sketch
visited him frequently during his sickness, and conversed with him freely on the subject of death; he expressed himself ready for the solemn
event...only manifesting concern for his family, which seems to be the
only existing tie to earth. He died in peace, and no doubt has realized
the saving efficacy of redeeming grace beyond the grave. He leaves a
wife, four small children, aged parents, to whom he was an obedient and
affectionate son, brothers and sisters, with many friends and relatives
to mourn their loss, but their loss is his eternal gain. P.

Issue of Saturday February 5, 1859:

Melancholy Death - The "Greenville Patriot" announces the melancholy
death of young, beautiful and interesting daughter of the Hon. B. F. PER-
RY, who died in the 17th year of her age, lamented and beloved by all.
Her disease was Consumption. Two columns of that journal manifest the interest and sympathy felt in the community in the deceased .

Married - On the 5th ult, in Brussels, Miss STROTHER, of the United
States, was united in marriage to Baron PHILLIPS FAHNENBERG de BURGHEIM,
of Germany.

Married - On the 16th ult. by H. J. ANTHONY, Esq., Mr. WYATT HUDSON to
Miss MARGARET M. BLACK, all of Pickens.

Married - On the 30th ult. by E. ALEXANDER, Esq., Mr. WILLIAM MURPHY to
Miss SARAH E. ALEXANDER, all of Pickens.

Issue of Saturday February 12, 1859:

Shocking Patricide - WM. MOODY, an old citizen of Oxford, Ky., was killed on the night of the 24th ult., by a blow from a club in the hands of
his son, JOSEPH MOODY. The murderer, who was crazy from liquor at the
time, was arrested.

Died - The Charleston papers announce the death of Mr. JAMES CHAPMAN,
formerly a most successful merchant of that city.

Suicide - Mrs. JANE SOSEBEE, of Spartanburg District, S. C., an unfortunate lunatic, committed suicide on the 10th of Jan., by hanging herself.

Married - On the 13th Jan. last, by WM. HUNT, Esq., Mr. WM. D. ROCHESTER to Miss CORNELIA FREDERICKS, all of Pickens.

Married - By the same on the 3d Feb., Mr. MALACHIA WHITTEN to Miss MARY J. BURKET, all of Pickens.

Married - On the 1st inst., by Rev. M. CHASTAIN, Mr. R. C. CLAYTON to Miss M. ELIZABETH KIRKSEY, all of Pickens district.

Married - On Tuesday, the 27th ult., by the Rev. A. B. MC GILVARY, Mr. JAMES M. SPENCER, to Miss AMANDA, daughter of Mr. JOHN BROWN, all of Pickens.

Obituary - It is with feelings of deep grief, we announce through your columns the death of our esteemed friend, WILLIAM SOUTHERLAND. He depar- ted this life on the 22nd ult., supposed cause of death was cold and palsy. The deceased was born on Dan river, in Rockingham County, N. C. where his father lived till he was twelve years old, from thence he with his father removed to within the neighborhood of Table Rock, where he re- sided respected and esteemed by his neighbors till his death. He was warm in friendship, social in his intercourse with his fellow citizens, a kind and an affectionate husband, a doting parent and a lenient and kind mas- ter. He possessed all the principles which constitute in a high degree the philanthropist. When the poor have been in a state of sufferance, no one administered more liberally to alleviate their wants. The above, al- though not a member of any church professed previous to his death full faith and a firm reliance in our Lord and Saviour Jesus Christ, and de- clared his willingness to join with the departed spirits who have gone to that world from whose bourne no traveller returns. The deceased has left his aged widow and her family to mourn his loss. But we trust that their loss may be his eternal gain and that they may all meet in heaven where parting and grief shall be no more.

Died, at the residence of Col. W. S. GRISHAM on the 1st inst., JOHN OVER- TON WATSON, in the 24th year of his age. John suffered for 15 days beyond description. His disease was Typhoid Pneumonia, baffling the skill of the best medical aid, and the attention of his solicitous friends; but all could not stay the hand of the "insatiate monster"; the fiat had gone forth, and nothing short of grasping him in his icy arms, and placing him in a lonely church-yard home would appease. To give even a synopsis of the many noble and manly traits that actuated this excellant young man would lengthen this beyond the limits of an ordinary obituary notice. Suffice it, then, that we say, that in his manners he was unassuming, po- lite and courteous; in his dealings punctual and honest; in his attach- ments warm, kind, faithful and confiding. In his death, his widowed moth- er has been bereft of a dutiful son, his brothers and sisters of an af- fectionate brother, and the district has lost a promising young man. S.

Issue of Saturday February 19, 1859:

The Altar and the Grave - Gen. THOS. FLOURNOY, who had been married about 72 hours, died on the 31st ult., at Eufaula, Alabama.

A Palmetto Gone - A communication in the Abbeville papers state that Mr. RICHARD WATSON, one of the bravest members of the Palmetto regiment, died in that district recently.

Death of Dr. TOGNO - The "Abbeville Press" announces the death of Dr. JOSEPH TOGNO. He died suddenly of apoplexy on the 5th inst., aged about 70 years.

The Lost - Dr. THOMAS CURTIS, of Limestone Springs, was lost in the burn- ing of the steamer North Carolina. He was an English by birth, and the principal of the school at that place.

Married - On the 17th January last, at the residence of E. S. CAPPOCK,Esq. in Newberry village, JAMES H. JOHNSON, Esq., of Ocala, Florida, to Mrs. R. N. SCHUMPERT, of the former place.

Obituary - Died, on the 1st inst., Mr. SAMUEL MC WHORTER, in the 84th

year of his age. He was a native of North Carolina, but early in life
was brought to Abbeville district, and there educated. Thence he moved
to Pickens district, in which he resided till his death. He has left many
kindred and friends to whom he was endeared, by an amiable disposition,
ardent affection, upright deportment; and, above all, by devotion to a
sovereign saviour God. United in spirit to the Presbyterian Church, he
embraced her systems of doctrines as apostolic, and departed as a good
old soldier of the Cross of Christ, having that peace, "which passeth
all understanding" through the atonement. Though this record, which is
sanctioned by the custom of ages, is soon to pass away as all earthly
records must, yet we cherish the pleasing hope that he hath a record on
high, lasting as eternity...bright and fair in the Book of Life, amid
those of patriarchs, prophets, apostles and martyrs, yea, of all the redeemed who have gone to the abodes of the blessed...the mansions of rest
prepared by an ascending Lord and Redeemer.

Died, in Franklin county, Ga., on the 1st of January, Mrs. MARTHA EDDINS,
aged 84 years and 26 days. Mrs. Eddins was born, raised and married to
Mr. WILLIAM EDDINS, in Abbeville District, S. C., and soon after came
to Georgia, where he died about 25 years before her. She raised nine
children, but only seven of them survived her. Her person was remarkable
for corpulence, and on this account she was deprived of many pleasures,
not being able to go out of doors for several years before her death.She
has been a consistent member of the Baptist Church for over fifty years;
and although unable to attend public worship during the last years of
her life, yet her piety did not abate, for she still rejoiced at the
prosperity of the Church, and the conquests of the Redeemer's Kingdom.
During her numerous afflictions, she was not heard to murmur at her sad
lot, but was always cheerful and resigned. She was charitable to the
poor, in supplying their wants; and among her numerous relations and acquaintances, she was highly esteemed and respected. To know, was to love
her. She sent words of comfort to her afflicted and dying friends, saying "She also looked forward for years with tranquility, to the hour of
her exit, when she would be wafted by angels to that great and blessed
beyond. But at length after an illness of sometime, the solemn crisis
came. When the cold and icy hand of death layed hold of her mortal frame,
and as her earthly twilight darkened, the sweet aurora of Heaven burst
forth as she fell asleep in Jesus. How rich the consolation that she has
gone to that bright abode where, "The stars are but the shining dust."

Issue of Saturday February 26, 1859:

Sad Occurrence - We are grieved to learn that an interesting little
child, aged about eighteen months, of Mr. THOS. J. SLOAN, who resides
near Fair Play, in this district, was drowned on Saturday last. The particulars, as we learn them are, that the child, becoming seperated from
its nurse, wandered to a stream near-by, was precipitated by accident or
itself into the water, and drowned before it was discovered.

Death of an Old Soldier - The "Lancaster Ledger" states that Mr. ALEXAN-
DER MONTGOMERY, of that district, died on the 13th inst., aged one hundred and five years! He is the last survivor of the revolutionary fathers in that district. It is made to appear that he was with Sumter in
his marches, and participated heroically in the battles of Fishing Creek,
Blackstocks and Eutaw Springs. This indeed is a career of usefulness and
glory, of which but few, very few men now living can boast. And we drop
a tear to his memory.

Homicide - On Sunday evening last, says the "Montgomery (Ala.) Mail", we
learn that Mr. J. S. GRAVES was killed at Dublin, in this county, by a
man by the name of DOUGLAS, who is now in jail in this city.

Married - On the 18th ult., by Rev. D. H. KENNEMUR, Mr. ANDREW C. SIMS
to Miss ELIZABETH S. SMITH, both of Pickens.

Obituary - Died, in Franklin co., Ga., JAMES BUCHANAN, son of GEORGE and
AMANDA TODD. Howconsoling are the words of the Prophet to the bereaves..
thus saith the Lord: "Refrain thy voice from weeping and thy eyes from
tears, for they shall come again from the hand of the enemy"...which is
death.

Issue of Saturday March 5, 1859:

Married - On Wednesday evening, February 23d, by the Rev. JAMES M. CHILES, Mr. GEORGE E. ROBINSON, of Pendleton, to Miss SALLIE R. CHILD, of Abbeville district.

Married - On the 10th ult. by A. B. BOWDEN, Esq., Mr. ELIAS BOTTOMS to Miss POWELL, all of Pickens.

Married - On the 27th ult. by the same, at Tunnel Hill, Mr. THOS. SMITH to Miss MARY D. SMITH, all of Tunnel Hill.

Married - On the 21st ult. by Rev. WM. MC WHORTER, Mr. JAMES A. MC KEE to Miss EMILY E. PERRY, all of Pickens.

Married - On the 10th ult., by the Rev. WM. T. GREADY, Mr. T. J. HUGHS to Miss ELIZABETH J. HALL, all of Pickens.

Issue of Saturday March 12, 1859:

Married - On the 3d inst., by Rev. WM. MC WHORTER, Mr. JOHN HARRIS to Miss CHARLOTTE JEANS, all of Pickens.

Married - On the 8th inst., by Rev. C. F. BANSEMER, Mr. WM. HENRY PIEPER to Miss JOHANNES AHRENS, all of Walhalla.

Married - On the 9th inst., by Rev. J. R. HUNNICUTT, Mr. JAMES E. COMPTON, of Greenville, to Miss REBECCA BREWER, of Pickens.

Parricide - STEPHEN P. BRADHAM, of Onslow county, N. C., killed his father DANIEL BRADHAM, on Thursday last, by striking him over the head with a fence rail. The murderer made his escape.

Horrible Death - A white woman named MARY MC EACHERN, fell into the fire at Wilmington, N. C., on Tuesday, while under the influence of liquor, and was burned to death.

Issue of Saturday March 19, 1859:

Accident - We regret to learn that an Irish operative, named JAMES BURNS, was killed at Tunnel Hill on the 9th instant. He was ascending from the bottom of Shaft No. 3, when he came in contact with the descending bucket, which knocked him back, and so severely wounded him that he died in a few hours. We learn that he failed to give the proper ascending signal and paid thus dearly for his omission.

Suicide - The "Edgefield Advertiser" states that SOLOMON ELENBERG, of Edgefield District, hung himself with a rope attached to the limb of a tree, some ten days since. The unfortunate creature was some 70 years old, and not sound in mind.

Sad Accident - A little child of Mr. WM. HORTON, says the "Yorkville Enquirer", was so severely scalded recently that it died soon afterwards.

Killed Himself - We regret to learn that the death of Mr. W. M. BELSER, a member of the State Legislature from Williamsburg Dist. Death was caused by an overdose of an anodyne.

Murder at Little Rock - On the 10th ult., a young man named LESTER, from Georgia, was murdered at Little Rock for his money, something less than $1,000, by an Irishman named CHAS. COSGROVE; the latter was arrested, and came near being lynched.

Murdered - A Correspondent of the "Ashville News" that B. S. MATTOCK, of Macon, Co., N. C., was murdered on the 24th ult. by an unknown person.

Death of Capt. McWILLIAMS - The Charleston papers announce the death of Capt. ARCHIBALD MC WILLIAMS, of that city. He was born in Ayreshire, Scotland, in 1778, and in 1795 came to this country, which has since then been his home.

Homicide - The "Marion Star" says that on the 26th ult., in a fracas between G. FORD and R. ROGERS, the latter was stabbed in the neck and died
in a few minutes. Ford is at large.

Homicide in Edgefield - A correspondent of the "Augusta Dispatch", writing from Edgefield, on the 10th instant, relates the following: "A most
lamentable affair came off near the Red Oak Grove Church, in this district, yesterday morning at 8 o'clock A.M. LEVI H. MC DANIEL was killed
by three balls fired by JOHN H. JONES (a well digger) from a revolver.
The whole neighborhood has since been the scene of intense excitement.
The evidence in substance, was, that there having been an old feud between them for several months, and having met in the road, the deceased
said he could whip Jones, and got off his horse and pulled off his coat,
and made at Jones, whereupon Jones fired three times. The deceased walked about thirty yards, fell and expired in a few minutes. The verdict
of the coroner's inquest is, that Levi H. McDaniel came to his death from
the effects of pistol balls fired by the hand of John H. Jones. Jones is
not arrested up to this time."

Obituary - Miss FRANCIS WELBORN departed this life on the 8th of February,
1859, at the residence of her father, near Glassy Mountain, Pickens District, S. C. Francis was the daughter of Col. W. E. and H. WELBORN,aged
sixteen years, five months and thirteen days. She was an affectionate
and an obedient child, amiable in her deportment, possessed of a meek
and quiet spirit; delighted in obedience to her parents; beloved by all
who knew her; but, better than all, she had obeyed the Heavenly injunc-
tion..."Remember thy Creator in the days of thy youth",&c. She made a
profession of her faith in Christ Jesus in September, 1855, and was Baptised into the fellowship of the Baptist Church of Christ at Big Creek,
Anderson District, S. C., by the writer of this notice. She died in full
communion with the Church where ever she was known. She has left a bereaved father and mother, brothers and sisters, and many relatives to
mourn their loss in her death, but they mourn not as those who have no
hope, but rejoice, believing that "their loss is her eternal gain"; and
when Christ, who is her life, shall appear, then shall she also appear
with him in Glory. Brother and sister, your much loved daughter is gone
from the evils to come and rest in hope of a better resurrection, for
those who sleep in Jesus will God bring with him. Blessed are the dead
that die in the Lord.   W. P. MARTIN

Died, at his father's residence, in Cherokee county, Ga., on the 24th instant, of inflammation of the brain, ALEXANDER H. MOSS, in the seventeen-
th year of his age. The deceased was very promising young man, of high
moral worth, a dutiful son, and an affectionate brother. He was confiding in his attachments, obliging in his manners, and highly esteemed by
those who knew him. He leaves many relatives and friends to mourn his
loss. S.

Died, on the 12th of February, in Elbert co., Ga., BEVERLY ALLEN HENRY,
JR., eldest son of Dr. B. A. and Mrs. MARY A. HENRY, aged five years,six
months and five days. This brief tribute is recorded for the immediate
consolation of parents overwhelmed and crushed by the sudden loss of
their first-born...none can appreciate the magnitude of their loss, and
the bitterness of their grief, but those who have experienced the same
calamity. A bright, intelligent, affectionate boy gave promise of a hop-
ful future, and enshrined himself within the inner sanctuary of the parent's hearts...when, lo! a blight fell on that boy and he withered...dis-
appointment and darkness settled on that household...and grief, deep and
poignant, ravaged the hearts of parents. The doings of Providence are
well nigh always inexplicable, and therefore should never be judged by
reason or sense. Revelation, which alone contains the mind of God, as-
sures us that God is the disposer...from him cometh only good and perfect gifts. Providence, then, are the dealings of God, as graciously benevolent as they are wonderous wise. How important then to be enabled
to say, "The Lord gave, and the Lord hath taken away", for then only can
we exclaim, "Blessed be the name of the Lord".   A Friend   (1 verse of
poetry)

<u>Issue of Saturday March 26, 1859</u>:(next page)

(Mar. 26 cont'd:)

Hung - The "Columbia Carolinian" states that JAMES GOINGS was hung in
that city on the 13th inst., He had been convicted of murder.

Fatal Affray - The "Colleton Sun" relates a difficulty between JAMES
STRICKLAND, and his nephew, ABRAHAM STRICKLAND, which occurred last week.
It resulted in the death of James Strickland, by being stabbed six or
seven times with a knife. The survivor was lodged in jail.

Terrible Leap - While Rev. THOMAS P. CALHOUN, Presbyterian minister, and
his wife, were crossing a bridge at St. Cloud, Minnesota, in a sleigh, on
the 20th ult., the horse became unmanageable, and jumped from the bridge
to the hard frozen bottom below, a distance of thirty feet, killing Mr.
Calhoun and severely injuring his wife.

Fatal Duel - At New Orleans, on the 12th inst., EMILE HIREAT, a reporter
of the Delta, killed C. LOQUET, a French cotton broker, in a duel.

Suicide - The "Fairfield Register" states that JOHN MC GRADY, of that district, committed suicide on the 13th inst., by drinking laudanum, after a
few days of drunkenness.

Married - On the 6th inst., by J. JAMESON, Esq., Mr. J. B. STEPHENS to
Miss SARAH MC COY, both of Pickens.

Married - On the 13th inst., by the same, Mr. A. F. SHEARMAN, recently
of New York, to Miss MARY E. LIDDELL, of Anderson District.

State of South Carolina, Pickens. In Equity - Bill for Partition. J. M.
BLACK et al vs. ISAAC RICE, et al. The Complainants having filed their
bill in this case, and, it appearing therefrom that JAMES J. BLACK; MAR-
GARET CRANE, HARPER CRANE, DAVIS CRANE, A. P. CRANE, and L. ORR CRANE,
representatives of ELIZABETH CRANE, formerly ELIZABETH BLACK, defendants
in this case, reside from and without the limits of this State.

Issue of Saturday April 2, 1859:

Obituary - Died, on the 23d inst., at his residence in Pickens District,
S. C., near Glassy Mountain, Mr. JAMES FERGUSON, SR., aged 54 years and
6 months. He expired in the immediate neighborhood of his birth, and in
which he spent his whole life, and was well known to be one of the kind-
est and most provident of husbands, a tender, loving father, an indulgent master, a generous neighbor, and one of the most useful citizens in
bearing the public burthens, and by his example of unceasing, honest industry and economy. In addition to a liberal share of literature, he also taught his children by his own acts...honesty, sobriety, industry, e-
conomy, charity and to attend places of public worship. His name was not
registered in any church book kept by man, but I feel justified by the
word of Christ, in saying that his name was and is known by God as a
child of his; for our Lord says that, he who is not against us is for us,
and we need only to take a glance at Secona Church, in which his coffin
set containing his lifeless body, while his funeral was preached, and
ask ourselves, whose liberality contributed largely to its erection, for
a proof that he was not against believers in Christ Jesus. His many generous contributions to the support of the Gospel, and for all religious
purposes, testify to the same. And not only cups of cold water, but man-
y cups of coffee and every necessary food have been bestowed on the ministers of the Gospel and believers in Christ by him, and entitle him to
a believer's reward. A weeping widow and children, sons-in-law, a brother, sisters-in-law, many relatives and acquaintances composed the assembly who bedewed the place with their tears, around the grave in which
his body was consigned; and tears were caused more freely to flow by the
surviving companion bowing to kiss his lifeless cheek, and exclaiming,
in a tone of grief, "James, I hope to meet you in Heaven". A little daughter also sprang forward to the open coffin and imprinted her last kiss
on the forehead of him who had so oft kissed her own. To the bereft family in whose ranks the dread appointment, that man must died has been so
recently demonstrated. The writer would say that he is glad to know that
he has a heart which feels to weep and mourn with you. But our mourning

is not without hope, for, notwithstanding, that after death is the judgment. A God, who has manifested his love for us by dying in our stead, and in thousands of other modes, is to be the judge; this gives high and consoling hope. That we must follow the deceased companion, father and friend, if we are prepared, is also a consoling thought. K. (3 verses of poetry)

Died, on the 20th ultimo, of croup, WILLIAM J., son of W. J. PARSONS,Esq, aged about four years. "Suffer little children to come unto me, and forbid them not, for such is the Kingdom of Heaven".

Issue of Saturday April 9, 1859:

Married - On the 20th March, by the Rev. GIDEON ELLIS, Mr. BERRY FORRESTER to Miss LETITIA L. NIXON, both of Pickensville.

Married - By the same, on the 24th March, Mr. CHARLES ROPER to Miss LUCINDA WATSON, both of Pickens.

Married - On the 3d ult., by Rev. B. F. MAULDEN, Maj. R. H. GRIFFIN, of Pickens, to Miss LUCY J., daughter of Mr. GRIFFIN BRAZEALE.

State of South Carolina, Pickens. In Equity - Bill for Discovery, Ac't, &c. JOHN H. TROWELL and wife et al vs. ELIZABETH B. KEITH, Ex'trix. et al. It appearing to the Commissioner that B. F. HOLLAND and wife PENELOPE, ELLIOTT M. KEITH, CHRISTOPHER KIRKSEY, DAVID GARVIN and wife NANCY; the heirs at law of JARED KIRKSEY, deceased, to wit: ISAIAH M. KIRKSEY, JARED E. F. KIRKSEY, MARY L. M. P. KIRKSEY, the minor heirs of THOMAS J. HALLUM, namely: THOMAS J. HALLUM, WILLIAM HALLUM, FAIR K. HALLUM, CELESTIA B. HALLUM, CATHERINE HALLUM, _____ HALLUM, defendants in this case, reside from and without the limits of this State.

Issue of Saturday April 16, 1859:

Fatal Accident - We have been informed, at rather a late day, of a fatal accident at Tunnel Hill. On the 24th ult., two men, JOHN HUGHES, a citizen of the district, and HUGH RANEY, an Irishman, were instantly killed. It appears that portions of the fixture and earth at the top of Shaft No. 3 gave way, falling on these persons, with the above unfortunate result.

Death of W. D. ROBINSON - It is with extreme sadness, says the "Laurensville Herald", that we announce the death of Mr. WARREN D. ROBINSON,while prosecuting the duties of his profession as a lawyer, near Montgomery, Ala. He was in our midst last year, as a law student, and endeared himself to all who knew him, by the delicacy of his feelings, his modest demeanor and high-toned principles of right and honor. Blessed with the gift of rare and bright talents, his friends predicted for him, in due time, a high place among the gifted and honored of our land. This our hope has been crushed; but it should bring consolation to the bereaved parents to know that "their boy" won golden opinions for himself wherever known.

Inquest - ABEL ROBINS, Esq., acting as Coroner, held an inquest over the dead body of Mrs. ELIZABETH SMITH, on the 9th inst. She was found dead in her bed. The verdict of the jury was, that the deceased came to her death by means to them unknown.

Death of a Naval Officer - A letter from Hong Kong, dated January 29th, states that Lieutenant CHARLES W. PLACE, of the U.S. ship Germantown, died at Manilla on the 9th of that month. He had got his leg mashed while trying to secure the guns in a gale of wind, and the limb was afterwards amputated. He survived the operation only a few days.

Fatal Affair - Mr. JAMES A. FOLKES, a respectable citizen of Vicksburg, Miss., was killed a few days ago by the accidental discharge of a gun in the hands of his nephew.

Death of HOPKINS (TAGALO) HOLSEY - This gentleman, for several years a representative in Congress, and afterwards editor of the "Athens Banner", died in Taylor Co., Ga., the 31st ult.

Dead - A. LANDRUM, Esq., well known throughout the South, as the publisher of a weekly journal in Columbia, during the days of Nullification, died on Sunday last, aged about 70 years.

Burned to Death - Mrs. POTTER, two sons and a grand child, were burned to death at Bangor, Me., on the 6th instant. It is supposed that they suffocated, as the house was burned with them.

Homicide - A homicide took place in Cobb county, Ga., on Saturday night. A man named FINNEY killed another named YEARWOOD, while the latter was taking improper liberties with the wife of the former. The head of Yearwood was severed from his body with an axe by Finney. This is acting with the right kind of spirit.

Married - On the 19th February last, by WM. HUNT, Esq., Mr. C. W. MILLER to Miss SARAH GRISHOP, all of Pickens.

Issue of Saturday April 23, 1859:

Dead - BILLY BOWLEGS, the celebrated Indian chief, is dead.

To be Hung - A. J. LINGO, has been convicted at Marietta, Ga., of the killing of ROBERT DUNCAN, and sentenced to be hung on the 27th of May.

Sudden Death - The "Darlington Flag" says that Mr. EDWARD WOODWARD fell dead in the streets of Marion village on a few days since.

Dead - A dispatch from Milwaukie, dated 12th inst., announces the death of Hon. E. V. WHITTEN, Chief Justice of the Supreme Court of Wisconsin, who died at his residence in Janesville on the afternoon of that day.

Married - On the 10th inst., by Rev. A. W. MC GUFFIN, Mr. WM. DICKSON to Miss LOUISA P. FULLERTON, all of Pickens.

Married - On the 14th by the same, Mr. CORNELIUS PALMER to Miss RHODA SANDFORD, all of Pickens.

Married - On the 17th inst. by D. P. ROBINS, Esq., Mr. JACOB HYDE to Miss ARMINDA LOWERY, all of Pickens.

Married - On the 12th inst., by E. G. MULLINNIX,Esq., Mr. F. M. LANGSTON to Miss D. A. Hopkins, both of Pickens.

Obituary - Died, on 10th inst., at the residence of her husband, near Bachelor's Retreat, in Pickens district, S. C., Mrs. SUSAN AMANDA DAVIS, wife of JAMES G. DAVIS, in the nineteenth year of her age. The deceased was a daughter of RANSOM and NANCY A. KELLY. She was born in Anderson district, but her parents removed to Pickens district some years ago,and she married at an early age, but was soon to bid adieu to this world and all that was dear to one yet in the bloom of life. Hersufferings though great, during her illness of some weeks, were borne with a meek and christian-like spirit, and as long as she had strength she often praised her Maker and sung different hymns of praise, among them which were the following lines: "Farewell, farewell to all below,/My Saviour calls and I must go". She never connected herself with any church but accorded with the Baptist faith in her belief, and died not without a well grounded hope of that peaceful rest in Heaven, which she so calmly contemplated in her last moments. She leaves an affectionate husband, a little infant, and many friends and relatives to mourn so untimely a loss.
                                                                    A Friend

Issue of Saturday April 30, 1859:

Murder at New Orleans - A peaceable old German named MICHAEL DEDINGER was brutally murdered at New Orleans on Friday last, by a ruffian named EUGENE ADAMS, who stabbed him a number of times with a bowie knife in the presence of his family.

Fatal Accident - The "Barnwell Sentinel" states that WM. A. COX, a highly esteemed citizen of that District, residing in the neighborhood of

Bamberg, was almost instantly killed a few days ago, by the falling of a
tree.

Dead - Hon. TILGHMAN TUCKER, ex-Governor of Mississippi, died at the residence of his father in Marion county, Alabama, on the 3d instant, aged
about 60 years. He was elected to the State Senate in 1838, and was e-
lected Governor of the State in 1841, and a member of Congress in 1843.

Married - On the 27th ult. by Rev. W. G. MULLINNIX, Mr. JAMES D. GASSA-
WAY to Mrs. MARIA GAINES, all of Pickens.

Married - On Thursday evening 21st inst., by LEVI N. ROBINS, Esq., Mr.
BAYLIS NICHOLSON to Miss ELIZABETH, daughter of Mr. DANIEL WHITMIRE,all
of Pickens.

Married - At the house of the bride's father, on Sunday evening the 24th
inst., by D. P. ROBINS, Esq., Mr. DAVID QUARLES to Miss MARGARET RICHEY,
all of Pickens.

Obituary - Died, on the 25th January, 1859, of liver disease, Mr. JOSEPH
DURHAM, in the 52nd year of his age. Mr. Durham was an affectionate husband and father, and has left a large family and wife to mourn their loss,
but their loss is his gain. He lived a worthy member of the M. E. Church
for over 35 years. He told the writer a few days before his death that he
had always tried to live as he wished to die, and said that he had a
bright prospect of heaven as soon as he was done with this world. E.G.

Notice - Mr wife, MALINDA CARVER, having left my bed and board, I shall
not be held responsible for any debts she may contract in my name.
                                                      MARTIN STADTLER

Issue of Saturday May 7, 1859:

Information Wanted - The heirs of JAMES CLARK, deceased, who removed
from Virginia in 1820-'25, and whose mother's maiden name was MITCHELL,
will hear of something to their advantage by applying at this office by
letter or otherwise.

Death of the Kentucky Giant - JAMES PORTER, the celebrated Kentucky giant
was found dead in his bed at Shipping port, Ky., on Monday morning last.
He was about 49 years of age and 7 feet and 9 inches high. His coffin
was the largest ever made in Kentucky, being over nine feet in length,
and two feet across the breast.

Married - On the 3d ult., by A. HUNTER, Esq., Mr. JOHN H. BLACKSTONE to
Miss ELIZABETH M. BRAZEALE, all of Pickens.

Married - On the 1st inst., by the same, Mr. WM. J. YOUNG to Miss ELIZA-
BETH J. BLACKSTON, all of Pickens.

Obituary - Died, at my residence, near Pickensville, on the 16th ult.,
Mrs. ELLEN BRADLEY, wife of JOEL BRADLEY, in the 55th year of her age.
Her illness was long and painful, yet she bore it with that unmurmuring
patience that well characterizes the devoted Christian. She leaves behind her an aged mother, her husband and ten children besides numerous
relatives, neighbors and friends to mourn her loss, but the loss of an
affectionate daughter, of a loving companion, of a kind, tender and affectionate mother, is her eternal gain. The deceased has for many years
been inpossession of that religion that is pure and undefiled and fadeth
not away. Altho' she made no public profession of religion until last
summer when she attached herself to the Baptist Church at Enon where she
lived a consistent member until her death; after she could no longer attend to going to church, she requested that brother ARIAIL should come
and preach at her house, which he kindly attended to after the congregation dispersed. I asked her how she felt; she replied in words like
these' "O, it is so good to hear about Jesus". Some few days after I
visited her again, she took me by the hand and told me she must die. I
said to her Mrs. Bradley I hope you are not afraid to die, "O, no said
she, I am only waiting my Saviours time". I then repeated those beautiful lines of the Poet to her. "Jesus can make a dying bed feel soft as

downy pillows are". Ah, yes and he will soften mine said she. Some days
after this I visited her again and stayed all night, in the morning which
was Monday before her departure, when I was ready to start home she expressed a desire to go home with me, I was very fearful that it would in-
jure her, but she insisted and I made the best preparation I could to
render her comfortable and started the trip, it did not seem to fatigue
her any at all, but on the contrary she seemed to mend all the week and
on Saturday morning just before she died she ate more than usual and was
quite lively not more than one or two minutes before she died. Thus did
our beloved mother and sister in Christ fall asleep in the arms of Jesus
without a struggle or a groan and her immortal spirit took its flight to
the spirit world where the wicked cease from troubling and the weary are
at rest. "Blessed are the dead which die in the Lord yea saith the spirit
for they rest from their labours and their works do follow them. During
her illness she begged her aged mother and weeping children not to grieve
after her, "for", said she, "while you are weeping and grieving after me
I shall be up yonder at rest with my loving Jesus." She told her sons to
be obedient and kind to their father, who is not on the decline of life,
and exhorted them to choose the good part that Mary chose, and be prepared to meet her in heaven where parting will be no more. She requested
to be buried at Enon, by the side of little SALLIE and little EMMA, her
two little grand daughters, the latter infant daughter of A. J. BRADLEY,
of North Carolina. But ah, says the reader, whose little Sallie? that
sweet little prattling babe was mine. Father or mother, have you lost
your babe? If you have, listen what the Saviour says: "Suffer little
children to come unto me, and forbid them not, for of such is the Kingdom of Heaven." The Lord gave and the Lord taketh away, and blessed be
the name of the Lord."   T.R.G.   (1 verse poetry)

Issue of Saturday May 14, 1859:

An Inquest - A jury of inquest was held over the dead body of THOMAS
MONTGOMERY an aged and respectable citizen of this district, residing
near Pickensville. His death is ascribed to the effects of intemperance.
The verdict of the jury of inquest was, that he came to his death by the
visitation of God.

Poisoned - Miss ELIZABETH BROWN, residing in the upper part of Laurens
district, says the "Enterprise", committed suicide recently by taking
strychnine.

Burned to Death - A little son of Capt. JAMES A. RIDGEWAY, of Talbott
county, Md., was burned to death last week, by his clothes taking fire.

Homicide - A fatal affray occurred at Columbus, Miss., last Saturday,be-
tween COLUMBUS LANCASTER and P. H. DELANY. Lancaster was instantly killed by a pistol shot through the body. Both residents of Columbus, and
journeymen tinners.

Married - On the evening of the 5th inst., by S. H. JOHNS, Esq., Mr.HEN-
RY BURDIT to Miss DELILAH PRICE, all of Pickens.

Married - On the 3d ult., by WM. HUNT, Esq., Mr. JERRY SMITH to Miss
CELIA JANES, all of Pickens.

Married - On the 10th ult., by the same, Mr. JAMES MOORE to Miss MARY
HARDEN, all of Pickens.

Married - On the 5th inst., by E. P. VERNER, Esq., Mr. WM. MARTIN to
Miss SARAH ANN FRANCES, daughter of MARY HONEA, of Pickens.

Obituary - Died, at his residence, near Bachelor's Retreat, after a few
days illness, Mr. JOHN M. BOWMAN, in the 81st year of his age. He was an
upright, honest man, a true friend and a worthy and respectable citizen.
The community has lost a useful man. He left a widow and a large circle
of friends to mourn his loss. F.

Issue of Saturday May 21, 1859:

To be Hung - SAMUEL SIMMONS, convicted of the murder of NATHAN SIMMONS, a relative, has been sentenced to be hung on the 27th of May, at Wilmington, N. C.

Dead - Dr. TOMLINSON FORT of Milledgeville, Ga., is dead. He was formerly a member of Congress, and a distinguished medical practitioner, widely known and universally esteemed.

Issue of Saturday May 28, 1859:

Death of Gen. WALLACE - We are pained to learn that Gen. DANIEL WALLACE, of Union, died on the 16th instant. Previously his health had been bad, and, on the morning of the 16th, while walking the floor, he suddenly fell dead. Gen. Wallace was a self-made man, and rose to high position. He was a native of Laurens district. He held the office of Commissioner in Equity, and represented his district in the Legislature and Congress. Other positions, civil and military, he filled most acceptably. Gen. W. was possessed of a gallant and chivalrous spirit, generous to his opponents, and true to his principles. Ability of no ordinary character, was long since conceded to him, which, with other sterling qualities of the head and heart, endeared him in a high degree to his friends and fellow-citizens. Peace to his memory!

Hymeneal - Hon. L. M. KEITT led Miss SUE SPARKS, of this State, to the hymeneal altar recently. They proceeded to Europe immediately, where, we trust, the "honey-moon" will shine with undimmed lustre o'er their happiness.

Lamented Death - We learn from the "Pendleton Messenger" the death of Mrs. ESSIE M., consort of W. H. WHITNER, Esq., at the residence of her father, Hon. J. T. SLOAN, on Tuesday evening the 17th instant, in the 22d year of her age, after a painful illness of six weeks.

Terrible Storm at Gainesville, Ala. - A letter from Gainesville, Ala., dated the 10th instant, reports a dreadful storm in that vicinity, causing the death of Mr. J. W. M. BERRIEN, a brother of the deceased U. S. Senator, and agent for the house of SACKETT, BELCHER & Co., of N. Y.

Dead - Judge F. H. CONE died at his residence in Greensboro, Ga., on the 18th inst. He was an eminent lawyer and widely known.

Dreadful Homicide - STEPHEN PETTY killed his mother-in-law, Mrs. MARY AIKENS, a defenceless old lady aged some eighty years, in the eastern part of Cherokee county, Ala., last Sunday week. He stabbed her with a pocket knife in some five or six places, killing her almost instantly. No cause is assigned for the diabolical deed. Petty has been a preacher, and heretofore regarded as a peaceable and orderly man.

Married - On the 22d inst., by D. P. ROBINS, Esq., Mr. JACKSON QUARLES to Miss SARAH ANN DUNN, all of Pickens.

Married - On Thursday morning the 26th inst., by Rev. D. C. BOGGS, Dr. O. M. DOYLE to Miss MARY RAMSEY, all of Pickens.

Issue of Saturday June 4, 1859:

Dead - JESSE HAYNES, a pauper Lunatic from this district, died in the Asylum, at Columbia, recently.

Body Found - The body of DAVID DUNBAR, of Memphis, Tenn., was recently found packed in a barrel, which was floating in the Mississippi river. He was murdered, it is said, by a man named MOORE.

Killed - The "Marion Star" says that TRISTAME COTTINGHAM shot and killed himself accidentally, in that district, on the 19th inst. A pistol was the weapon so carelessly handled.

Married - On the 22d ult. by E. P. VERNER, Esq., Mr. WM. D. BALLINGER to Miss SARAH ANN HOLLY, all of Pickens.

Married - On the 26th ult., by Rev. W. G. MULLINNIX, Mr. WM. M. FENNELL to Miss MARY A. E. CHAPMAN, all of Pickens.

Married - By J. E. BELOTTE, Esq., at his residence on the evening of the 24th inst., Mr. JOHN L. BROWN, of Andersonville, and Miss NANCY G. CAMP-BELL, of Pendleton.

Obituary - Died, in Texas, on the 16th of April last, of Hemorage of the Lungs, ABBY GUERIN, formerly of Pickens District.

Issue of Saturday June 11, 1859:

Died - Mrs. WILKES, one of the parties poisoned in Newberry, died recent-ly from effects of the poison so administered.

Married - On the 26th ult. at Feasterville, by JACOB FEASTER, Esq., Mr. WM. S. WILLIAMS, of Pickens, to Miss. S. C. FEASTER, of Fairfield.

Married - On the 23d ult. by E. HUGHES, Esq., Mr. CHESLEY A. TISHER to Miss LETTYANN DAVIS, all of Pickens.

Married - On Sunday 26th May, by Rev. Mr. CONNER, Mr. MONROE MULLIGAN to Miss MARY C LAYTON, all of Pickens.

Obituary - Departed this life, at Pendleton, on the 30th ult., in the blessed hope of a glorious immortality, Mrs. ANN E. SHANKLIN, wife of J. V. SHANKLIN, Esq., and mother of the late Rev. J. A. SHANKLIN, in the sixtieth year of her age.

Obituary - Died, on the 6th inst., in Cheohee, JOHN LAY, aged forty-one years. The deceased was one of the noblest works of God...an honest man.

Horrible - A brutal affair took place in the upper portion of this dis-trict, near Thomas'Cross Roads, on the 14th of May ultimo, between THOMAS and WILLIAM OWENS, brothers, the latter at the time being very drunk, which resulted in the death of WILLIAM on the 24th, from the wounds re-ceived. From some cause or other, THOMAS OWENS struck his brother twice with a large stick, cutting severe gashes about the neck and head, and fracturing the skull obliquely across the union of the parictal and oc-cipeted bones. The verdict of the jury of inquest on the dead body, was that, "the deceased come to his death by blows inflicted upon his face, neck and head, with a large stick in the hands of Thomas Ownes, on the evening of the 14th day of May, 1859." We understand that Thomas Owens, the perpetrator of this unnatural deed, has fled to parts unknown.
                                        "Laurensville Herald" 2d inst.

Issue of Saturday June 18, 1859:

Married - On the 5th inst, by J. B. SANDERS, Esq., at Five Chesnuts, Mr. BARTLEY HARVEY to Miss MARY MEREDITH, all of Pickens.

Married - On Wednesday morning the 15th inst., by Rev. J. L. KENNEDY, Mr. H. S. VANDIVIER, of Clarkesville, Ga., to Miss M. ROSE LAWRENCE, of Pickens, S. C.

Married - On the 12th inst., by the Rev. P. MOORE, Mr. W. M. ROACH to Miss CATHARINE HOBBS, all of Pickens.

Married - On the 12th inst, by the Rev. C. F. BANSEMER, Mr. WARREN COBB to Miss LOUISA MULLER, all of Pickens.

Issue of Saturday June 25, 1859:

Obituary - Died, on the 24th of April last, GEORGE W., infant son of Mr. G. W. and MARY C. VANZANT, aged about three years.

Died, on the 7th inst., of dysentery, WILLIE THOMPSON, infant son of T. F. and MARY DAVIS, aged eleven months and twenty one days. "Suffer lit-tle children to come unto me, and forbid them not, for of such is the kingdom of Heaven."

Issue of Saturday July 2, 1859:

Executed - The "Colleton Sun" says that ABRAHAM STRICKLAND, who was convicted at the April session of the Walterboro' Court, for the murder of
his uncle, suffered the extreme penalty of the law on the 17th ult.

Suicide - J. R. MIMMIS, bookkeeper for CRESAP and MC MILLAN, committed
suicide in a house of ill fame, at Columbus, Geo., on Friday. Cause unknown.

Drowning - The "Due West Telescope" reports that CARO, aged six years,
daughter of Prof. YOUNG, of Erskine College, at Due West, Abbeville District, was drowned on the 14th inst., in an artificial pool in her father's garden.

Murder and Suicide - A man named JAS. ASLEY killed J. N. CARMACK, near
Belton, Texas, on the 23d of last month. He shot him down like a dog;
was pursued by an armed mob; when in his desperation, he poisoned himself.

Killed by a Rattlesnake - Mr. N. R. RUSHING was bitten by a rattlesnake,
at his place, near Gillisonville, S. C., and died in eight hours from
the effects of the wound.

Obituary - We know not when we have been called upon to discharge a more
painful task than to write "GEORGE MILLER is dead". He died at the residence of Dr. J. M. CROSS, in Wheeling, Holmes county, Miss., on the 11th
of June, 1859, of typhoid fever; he was born and raised in Pickens district, and removed to Mississippi in the fall of 1858. He was a useful
and highly esteemed mason, a just and upright man, a true and faithful
friend; and his memory will always be cherished by the order of which he
was a member, and by the society of which he was one of its most shining
ornaments. Singularly modest in his deportment, of gentle manners and
warm attachments...brave, generous and forgiving...he is gone, and the
memory of his virtues are the onlu solace left them who loved him while
living and mourn him dead. For the family who have been thus smitten,
when they least expected a blow, we have no words to express our sympathy. We feel assured that the death of no man in this whole community
could be more worthy of a heart-felt sorrow than was George Miller. Every attention and kindness was shown him, that friendship could suggest
or his wants demand.   C.

Died, in White county, Ga., on the 13th ult., Mrs. N. M., wife of E. A.
ALEXANDER, formerly of this district.

Died, at the residence of its parents in Cherokee county, Ga., on the
19th June 1859, PAUL, infant of Rev. P. H. and SUSAN M. BREWSTER, aged
4 days.

Died, at Pickens C. H., on the 14th ult., JAS. PRESTON, infant son of
Mr. and Mrs. G. W. KING, aged 18 months.

Issue of Saturday July 9, 1859:

Suicide - JOHN HOGAN, an Irishman, committed suicide at Walterboro, in
this State, last week. He was laboring under excitement produced by an
undue use of intoxicating liquors.

Killed by Lightning - The "Columbia Carolinian" learns that on Saturday
last, Mrs. LEONORA JOHNSON, wife of the overseer of Maj. STARKE, was
struck by lightning and killed instantly. She was standing alongside of
the dairy.

Married - On the 30th June last, by Rev. W. G. MULLINNIX, Mr. DANIEL MA-
GILL, of Anderson, to Miss MARY C. CAMPBELL, of Pendleton.

Issue of Saturday July 30, 1859:

Suicide - JOHN MARTIN, a citizen of this district, committed suicide on
the 23rd inst., by hanging himself. No cause is known or excuse given

for the commission of the act. The verdict of the Coroner's inquest was in accordance with these facts. The deceased leaves a young family, in an almost destitute condition.

Sun Stroke - JOHN FISHER, aged about 32 years, died in Charleston, on the 19th inst. of sun stroke. He was a sailor, and a Scotchman by birth.

Married - On the 14th ult., at Woodlands, near Pendleton, by the Rev. J. MAXWELL PRINGLE, Mr. A. C. CAMPBELL to Miss LIZZIE P., daughter of the late Rev. JASPER ADAMS, D. D., all of the above place.

Married - On the evening of the 13th inst., at Walhalla, by JNO. ADAIR, Esq., JAMES HULL to Mrs. SARAH SATTERFIELD, all of Pickens.

Married - At Walhall, by Rev. J. R. HUNNICUTT, on the 21st, WM. REID to SARAH E. HULL, both of Pickens.

Married - By D. P. ROBINS, Esq., on the 24th inst., Mr. WM. BOYD LONG to Miss JEMIMA SMITH, all of Pickens.

Obituary - Died, at his residence, in Pickens District, near Pickens-ville, on the 10th inst., of Billious Typhoid fever, Mr. ELIAS MULLIN-NIX, in the 54th year of his age. His illness was very painful and pro-tracted, being five weeks and some days confined to his bed. The de-ceased leaves a large circle of relations and friends to mourn his loss. He was a man of high moral worth, of industrious habits and very econo-mizing, by which means he accumulated much of this world's goods. Though close in his dealings, he was strictly honest, charitable and obliging to those by whom he was surrounded. He made no profession of Religion, yet we mourn not for him as though we had no hope; for while he retained his proper mind during his illness, he appeared to be much concerned a-bout the salvation of his soul, and was often _____ hath said in his word, "Let the wicked forsake his way, and the unrighteous man his thoughts, and let him return unto the Lord, and he will have mercy upon him; and to our God for he will abundantly pardon". Yes, he pardoned the thief upon the cross, and we hope that he heard and answered the prayers of our deceased friend, and pardon all his sins, and that while worms are preying upon his lifeless body, his immortal spirit is with the Angelic Choir praising the Lord for redeeming grace and dying love in the Paradise of God. A Friend

Issue of Saturday August 6, 1859:

Fatal Mistake - JOHN CHARLES, from South Carolina, died suddenly in Mont-gomery, Ala., on Tuesday, from taking by mistake, a dose of morphine for quinine.

Dead - Ex-Gov. JOHN GAYLE, of Ala. (a native of this State) died on the 21st inst., near Mobile.

Drowned - JAMES H. CHAMBERS, of Charleston, a young man of promising and generous traits of character, was drowned on Friday last while on a plea-sure excursion in the Bay.

Married - On the 30th of June last, by Rev. JNO. COFFEE, Mr. WM. H. LAND, of Pickens, to Miss MARTHA L. WALL, of Rabun, Ga.

Married - On the 31st ult. by W. J. PARSONS, Esq., Mr. WM. BYRON to Miss SARAH RIGDON, of Pickens.

Married - On the 31st ult. by the same, Mr. JNO. WALKER to Miss GANTT, daughter of MARTIN GANTT, all of Pickens District.

Married - On the 2d instant, by Rev. WM. MC WHORTER, Rev. J. L. KENNEDY, of Anderson, to Mrs. ELIZABETH SIMPSON, of Laurens.

Issue of Saturday August 13, 1859:

Distressing Accident - WM. L. FAIRCHILD, of Hinds co., Miss., was return-ing from the house of a neighbor, on the 17th ult., with his wife and

child in a buggy, when a tree fell on them, causing instant death to the
three persons.

Married - On July 31st, by the Rev. GIDEON ELLIS, JAMES D. BEACHAM, M.D.,
to Miss EUGENIE A. DOUTHIT, all of Pickens.

Married - On the 24th of July, by the Rev. J. R. HUNNICUTT, Capt. D. B.
SULLIVAN to Miss ELIZABETH JOHNSON, all of Pickens.

Sudden Death - An old citizen of this District, Mr. NEHEMIAH FRANKS, who
lived a few miles above this place, died very suddenly on the 27th ultimo. He was a hale old man, and had laid down in the afternoon to sleep,
with no one but a little negro attending him, as the family was attending church, when unusual symptoms of pain and disease being exhibited,
the nearest neighbour was sent for. Before the arrival of any white person, however, he, with a few short struggles and moans as of intense
pain, had died. It is supposed he had disease of the heart. Truly, in
the midst of life we are in death. "Laurensville Herald"

Issue of Saturday August 27, 1859:

Dead - DAVID NUCKOLLS, of Tuskegee, Ala., died from the effects of a pistol shot received while arguing politics. The affair created intense excitement, involving bitter party feelings.

Married - On the 14th instant, by WM. S. WOOLBRIGHT, Esq., Mr. JAMES A.
MOORE to Miss SARAH J. GIBSON, all of Pickens.

Issue of Saturday September 3, 1859:

Dead - CORNELIUS DONHOE, originally from Laurens District, of this State,
but for sixty years a resident of Georgia, died on the 15th instant, in
Cobb county, at the very advanced age of 102 years.

COBB-WEBB - Last week, JOHN COBB married Miss KATE WEBB. A prospecting
editor says their house will, without doubt, be full of cob-webs!

Death of Col. BROCKMAN - Col. THOMAS P. BROCKMAN, of Greenville, died
last week of Paralysis. The Greenville papers, making the announcement,
state that he was elected to both State conventions held in the State in
'32 and '52...served in the State Senate four years, and in other prominent positions in that district.

Killed - J. TIEL was killed in Campbell co., Ga., last Monday, by JOHN
and THOMAS YANCEY. Tiel was the only sober man in the affray, which
caused his death.

Dead - JOHN BLAKE WHITE, Esq., an old citizen of Charleston, died Wednesday.

Married - At Itonia, on the 30th ult., by Rev. D. C. BOGGS, Mr. I. J.
LONG, of Danville, Ky., to Miss CALLIE P., second daughter of Rev. J. L.
KENNEDY, of Anderson.

Issue of Saturday September 10, 1859:

Suicide - Mrs. BIRD FITZPATRICK committed suicide at Union Springs, Alabama, on the 20th ult., by hanging herself. She rose before daylight
from the side of her husband, and going into the yard in her night dress,
hung herself to the limb of a tree. She was dead when discovered.

An old Saw not Sharp - "A rolling stone gathers no moss." A very doubt-
ful adage. We have just seen, in a country paper, the marriage of PEL-
EG ROWLINSTONE to Miss OPHELIA MORSE.

Married - On the 25th inst., by the Rev. A. H. CORNISH, at the residence
of her mother, Mrs. SOPHIA WARLEY, near Pendleton, S. C., Mrs. E. G.
SCHLUZ to Mr. C. J. BOURN, of Bristol, England.

At the residence of the bride's father in Pendleton, on Thursday the 1st

September, by the Rev. J. SCOTT MURRAY, Dr. T. J. PICKENS to Miss SUSAN J., only daughter of Mr. and Mrs. S. E. MAXWELL.

Married - On the 11th ult., by the Rev. JOHN GOLDEN, GEORGE G. ELROD, of Habersham county, Ga., to ELEANOR C. HARRIS, of Anderson.

Married - By the same, on the 30th ult., THOMAS C. MARTIN to MARTHA OWEN, all of Anderson.

Married - By the same, at the residence of A. P. WATSON, MC DUFFIE HAM-ILTON, of this District, to Miss AMANDA CAROLINE COUCH, second daughter of Mrs. SARAH A. COUCH, of Anderson.

Married - At the same time and place, by the same, JNO. Q. A. COUCH to Miss MARY JANE ELLISON, eldest daughter of WILLIAM ELLISON, all of this district.

Married - On the 1st instant, by Rev. W. G. MULLINNIX, Mr. JAMES A. GAINES, of Pickens, to Miss MARY A. PEGG, of Anderson.

Issue of Saturday September 17, 1859:

Married - On the 1st instant, by Rev. D. H. KENNEMUR, Mr. THOS. E. MAD-DEN, to Miss NANCY A. ALEXANDER, all of Pickens.

Issue of Saturday September 24, 1859:

Obituary - Died, on the 6th of August last, at his residence in Pickens District, SIDNEY MC DOW, aged forty years. The deceased had noble traits of character...he was honest, a good neighbor, an affectionate father and a dutiful husband. If errors he had (and who is without them?) let the mantle of charity cover them in the silence of the grave. He leaves a sorrowing family, and a large circle of friends to mourn his early de-mise.

Issue of Saturday October 1, 1859:

Killed by a Broomstick - The broomstick in the hands of an enraged wife, is a standing jest, but there are exceptions. On the 11th inst., JAMES SHAW, a resident of Vicksburg, Mississippi, was struck by his wife with a broomstick, and, staggering into the yard, fell dead. The murderess was arrested.

Dead - J. M. SMITH, a member of the Palmetto Regiment, died in the Asy-lum, at Columbia, on the 23rd ult.

Homicide - The "Laurensville Herald" of the 23d ult., says that an af-fray occurred near Cross Hill, in that district, between WM. FULLER and JAMES BENJAMIN, in which the latter lost his life. Fuller has been ad-mitted to bail.

Drowned - Col. R. W. FOSTER drowned himself on the 18th ult., as we learn from the "Spartanburg Spartan". The cause is not given.

Married - On the 22nd ult., by the Rev. J. H. ZIMMERMAN, Mr. JOHN W. F. THOMPSON, of Walhalla, to Miss ALICE A. BRUCE, of Anderson.

Married - By the Rev. J. R. HUNNICUTT, on the 22nd ult., Mr. W. D. BLACK to Miss NATHANY RIDER, both of Pickens.

Married - At the same time, by the same, Mr. NATHANIEL RIDER to Miss H. ARENAY STANDRIDGE, all of Pickens.

Married - On the 18th ult., by Rev. W. B. SINGLETON, Mr. W. G. BLASSIN-GAME to Miss MARGARET ANTHONY, all of Pickens.

Married - By the same on the 20th ult., Mr. ABNER HOWARD to Miss NANCY NORMAN, all of Pickens.

Married - On the 21st ult., by Rev. W. G. MULLINNIX, Mr. GEORGE L. CHAP-

MAN to Miss MATILDA N. MC WHORTER, all of Pickens.

Married - On the 4th ult., by Rev. THOMAS LOOPER, Mr. JAMES B. HESTER to
Miss LUCETTIE MAULDIN, all of Pickens.

Issue of Saturday October 8, 1859:

Accident - A lamentable accident occurred in Franklin county, Ga., on the
30th ult. Two persons...JAMES MABERRY and W. MABERRY, his uncle...were
out turkey hunting, when the latter shot the former by accident, suppos-
ing him in the thickett to be a turkey. The wound was so serious that
Jas. Maberry is supposed to be dead.

Death of a Venerable Lady - We pen with sincere regret the death of Mrs.
CATHERINE CRAIG, relict of the late JOHN CRAIG, which occurred near this
place, on the 29th ult. Mrs. Craig was, in some respects, a remarkable
woman. Her great age, (she being about ninety-two at the time of her
death) invested her presence with cherished memories, linking the past
with the present. Her recollection of Revolutionary history and incidents made her an object of great interest, whilst her sterling qualities
and womanly virtues commanded the respect, and won the esteem of those
who were best acquainted with her. But it was as the wife, mother and
christian that she exhibited those incomparable traits of character most
prized by the virtuous and good. Her life, long and chequered, witnessed her country's deliverance from tyranny and misrule, and an entrance
upon the pleasures of peace and the enjoyment of liberty and the protec-
tion of the citizen. Her example may well be treasured, as a bright and
shining light, to guide the footsteps of the daughters of the present day,
and of their sex from them descending. The family have our sympathies in
their great bereavement.

Death of a Veteran Soldier - Colonel JOHN DUVAL, who had represented
Scott county, Ky., for many years, in the Legislature of that State, died
there on the 7th inst. He was a captain in the war of 1812, and served
a campaign under Gen. HARRISON.

Suicide - Maj. CHAPMAN, U.S.A., committed suicide by cutting his throat,
at Fortress Monroe, Baltimore.

Homicide - The "Haynesville, Ala., Chronicle" says that a difficulty occurred near Helicon, Lowndes county, on the night of the 17th inst., between JOHN MITCHELL and JOHN A. PETRIE, at the house of the latter, which
resulted in the death of Mitchell.

Sad Honeymoon - W. W. WESTON, who was killed recently at Hopkinsville,Ky.,
in an affray growing out of politics, was a native of Memphis, Tenn., and
had been married only two months, to a daughter of the Hon. J. W. UNDER-
WOOD, of Kentucky.

Dead - Dr. J. P. BARRETT, a worthy and respected citizen of Abbeville,
died recently in that district.

Dead - Gen. E. B. WHEELER, aged sixty years, and Ordinary and Clerk of
the Court of Marion district for thirty-three years, died suddenly on the
24th ult.

Suicide - Gen. CRUTCHFIELD, in prison in Greene county, Ga., for the murder of his wife, committed suicide on the 20th ult., by cutting his
throat.

Obituary - Departed this life on the 23d ult., in Pickens District, HAN-
NAH ELIZABETH, eldest daughter of W. M. and T. C. ALLEN, aged seven years.
Although little Hannah will be greatly missed by all who knew her, we
hope that her parents will be comforted by the words of our Saviour,
"Suffer little children to come unto me, and forbid them not". P.
(1 verse poetry)

Issue of Saturday October 15, 1859:

Dead - Col. HUGH MILLER, one of the gallant band of the Palmetto Regiment, died recently at Winnsboro, in this State.

Homicide - The "Darlington Flag" states that D. LADSON STUCKEY was killed by HENRY D. HEARON his brother in-law. The particulars are not giv-
en.

Sudden Death - We learn from the Abbeville papers that Mr. EDMUND COBB,
a hotel keeper in that place, committed suicide by taking laudanum last
week. No reasonable account is given for the commission of the act.

Longevity - Mr. PATRICK RIORDAN was born in Kilmare, Ireland, in 1756.
Twenty years ago he emigrated to New Orleans, where he has since resided.
He died on the 20th ult., aged 103 years; a most remarkable age to ar-
rive at in that climate.

Suicide - MARIA VAN RENSALAER, committed suicide at Charleston, on the
1st instant, by taking poison. She was a native of Albany, N. Y.

Dead - JAMES W. A. HENDERSON, a practical printer, and one of the veter-
ans of the Palmetto Regiment, died in Charleston on the 21st ult.

Awful Tragedy - The "Georgia Citizen" of the 31st, has the following: A
horrible occurrence took place, yesterday, in Jones county, a few miles
above Macon, which resulted in the death of two brothers, of the name of
JACK and GUS ROBERTS, each by the hand of the other! Between these two
brothers a feud had, for some time previous, existed, about a piece of
land, and when they met yesterday, for the purpose, with others, of working on the public road, an altercation arose and one of them drew a pistol and shot the other, when the latter, in the act of falling dead,
fired at the former and shot him in the breast, killing him instantly.

Married - On the 4th inst., by Rev. JOHN CORN, Mr. JOSEPH G. NEVILLE, of
Clayton, Ga., to Miss NANNIE L. CARTER, daughter of Major JOSIAH CARTER,
of Thomas county, Ga.

Married - On the 6th inst., by Rev. D. H. KENNEMUR, Mr. ELIAS F. ALEXAN-
DER, of Pickens, to Miss MARY GREEN, of Jackson county, N. C.

Take Warning - I hereby forewarn all persons from harboring or trading
with my wife, NANCY CHAPMAN, as she has left my house without just cause
or provocation, and I will not pay any debts of her contracting from and
after this date.   ENOCH CHAPMAN

Issue of Saturday October 22, 1859:

Death of Mr. JONES - We are pained to announce the death of Mr. JABEZ
JONES, an aged and highly esteemed citizen of this district. He died on
the 15th instant, aged about ninety years.

Married - On 13th inst., by Rev. J. L. KENNEDY, P. D. CURETON, M. D., of
Greenville, to Miss JANE C., eldest daughter of Mr. LEMUEL HAMILTON, of
Pickens.

Married - On the 5th inst., by Rev. W. B, SINGLETON, Dr. WILLIAM T. FIELD
of Pickens to Miss E. JENNIE BLASSINGAME, of Anderson.

Married - On the 5th inst., by Rev. J. L. GIRADEAU, Mr. J. J. LEWIS, of
Pendleton, to Miss CAROLINE C., daughter of the late JEREMIAH DICKINSON.

Obituary - Died, in Cherokee county, Ga., on the 26th Aug. 1859, FRANCES
CAROLINE, daughter of NATHAN W. and MARTHA A. ELLIOTT, aged three years,
eight months, and twenty-one days.

Died, in Cherokee co., Ga. on the 10th inst., GEORGE WASHINGTON, son of
JOHN and ANGELINA GARRETT, aged one year, six months and twenty-three
days. G.W.H. (2 verses poetry)

Notice - All persons are hereby forewarned not to trade with or trust my
wife LUCINDA HARPER, and her child, SARAH J., on my account, as I will
not be responsible for their debts. My wife left my bed and board with-

72

out just cause or provocation. Persons harboring these parties will be dealt with as the law directs. HENRY T. HARPER

Issue of Saturday October 29, 1859:

Death of Mr. GARVIN - Death is busy with our old citizens. It is our melancholy duty to announce this week the death of Mr. THOMAS GARVIN. He died on the 11th, of dropsy in the chest, aged eight-five years. He was Commissioner of Locations, for this district, for many years. Well known and highly respected whilst living, his departure, even at a ripe old age, is mourned by many relatives and friends.

Tribute of Respect to JAMES I. HOLLINGSWORTH, deceased.

Fatal Duel - We learn by a dispatch to the "Mobile-Tribune", that a fatal duel was fought in the vicinity of Columbus, Miss., on the evening of the 8th inst. The parties were Mr. MOORE, a merchant of Greensborough, Ala., and a Dr. WILEY. The latter was shot through the head.

Married - On the 17th inst., by J. B. SAUNDERS, Esq., Mr. JOHN TEAGUE to Miss TEMPERANCE POOL, all of Pickens.

Married - On the 22d inst., by Rev. T. B. MAULDEN, Mr. WILSON MOSS to Miss JENNIE CALDWELL, all of Pickens.

Issue of Saturday November 5, 1859:

The Accidnet at Tunnel Hill - The accident at the Tunnel, referred to last week, was of a more serious nature than we were at that time apprized of. There was, however, no explosion. On the night of the 26th ult. at shaft No. 4, the stop cock of the engine flew out, emitting the steam which scalded six men badly. Since, WM. HUMPHREYS and FRANCIS MC KIEMAN two of the men, have died.

Sudden Death - Mr. H. E. CAMPBELL, of Pendleton, favorably known as a kind and accommodating host, died suddenly on the morning of the 28th ult. An affection of the heart is supposed to have caused his death, which was so sudden that no relief could be extended. Kind, hospitable and obliging, he will be long remembered by a large circle of friends. His family has our sympathy in their great bereavement.

Homicide - The "Cheraw Gazette" says that TOM CRAWFORD shot and killed DANIEL MELTON, at his own house, last week. Crawford has been arrested.

Killed - An affray occurred at Doctor Town, in Wayne county, Ga., on Wednesday last, between two men named PATRICK FISHER and BARTLEY O'DONNELL, in which the latter stabbed the former, killing him instantly.

Murder - DAVIDSON VICK deliberately shot JOHN T. FORD, in Haywood county, N. C., on the 20th ult. Vick has escaped. A reward is offered for him.

Issue of Saturday November 12, 1859:

Killed - It gives us pain to record another fatal accident. On the 3rd inst., at Dr. COAT's Saw-mille, just in the edge of Anderson District, a worthy man, by the name of ALLEN BAILEY, was killed. It appears that in adjusting a piece of lumber near the Saw, (which was running) it was struck by the saw, hurling it with great force against deceased's temple, dashing out his brains, and causing almost instant death.

Married in Russia - JOHN E. BACON, Esq., of Edgefield, Secretary of the United States Legation at St. Petersburg, was married recently to Miss REBECCA PICKENS, daughter of our Minister to Russia, Hon. F. W. PICKENS. The bride and bridegroom are gone to Italy.

Dead - Hon. JAMES C. JONES, formerly Governor of Tennessee, died in Memphis, on the 30th ult.

Dead - Hon. E. BROWNLEE, State Senator from St. Georges Parish, died on the 30th ult., of typhoid fever.

Obituary - Departed this life at my residence, in Cherokee county, Ga., on the 20th of October, of Billious Pneumonia, Mrs. MARY C. GEURIN, in the 26th year of her age. She was seized very ill and painful for eleven days. The deceased leaves a large circle of relatives and friends, and a little infant boy, one year old, and a bereaved husband to mourn her sacred loss. She was very industrious, and economizing, and an obedient child to her parents, and a charitable neighbor, and beloved by all who knew her. She was an affectionate wife, and a loving mother. She was not a member of any Christian church, though she took the Bible for her guide, and tried to live in accordance with it. For the last several years past her prayers were often to God, who hath said in His words, "Let the wicked forsake his and the unrighteous man his thoughts, and let him return unto the Lord, and He will have mercy upon him; and to our God, for he will abundantly pardon". Yes, he pardoned the thief, upon the Cross, and we hope he heard and answered her prayers, though I mourn not her as those who have no hope in the future. I often talked with her about her interest in His mercy, and when she was first taken ill I asked her how she felt, and her prospect of rest in the future, and she told me she believed she would go to rest. I asked her several times during her painful illness, and she manifested the same. She remained in her proper mind until her death. She bore her sufferings with great patience. She requested to be buried at Schedcom Camp-ground, by the side of her little babe, who was buried just two years ago. "The Lord gave and the Lord taketh away, and blessed be the name of the Lord".
A Husband (6 verses poetry)

Married - On the 27th ult., by Rev. JOHN ARIAIL, Mr. ELISHA A. FERGUSON to Miss MARY RICHARDSON, all of Pickens.

Married - On the 1st inst., by the same, Mr. WM. J. HUNNICUTT to Miss ELMINA PERRY, all of Pickens.

Married - On the 3d inst., by WM. S. GRISHAM, Esq., Mr. WM. HENRY BUTLER to Miss SARAH JANE, only daughter of WM. H. WHITE, Esq., of Coneross.

Married - On Tuesday evening, the 18th of October, ult., at the residence of the bride's mother, in Pendleton, by Rev. A. W. ROSS, Mr. G. W. SYMMES to Miss MELLIE POE.

State of South Carolina, Pickens. In Ordinary - Petition for settlement and Decree. D. K. HAMILTON, JOHN WALKER, Adm'rs. vs. JAS. WALKER and others. It appearing to my satisfaction that JAMES WALKER, ALLEN FULLER, and wife ELIZA, and PATSY ALEXANDER, defendants in this case, reside without the limits of this State. Settlement of the estate of JANE WALKER, deceased.

Issue of Saturday November 19, 1859:

Horrible Death - A young lady named BRINKLEY, 18 years of age, was on Tuesday night caught in a sugar mill and crushed to death, about five miles from LaGrange, Missouri.

Issue of Saturday November 26, 1859:

A Duel - A duel was fought in Alabama a short time since by H. C. CHILDERS and C. RANDOLPH, both of Greensboro. Cause, personal insult...... weapons, pistols...damage, Childers wounded fatally. This progresses civilization.

Murder - Madame UEDARD, a fortune teller, was found in New Orleans, on the morning of the 7th inst., lying dead in her chamber, with her throat cut from ear to ear. Her watch and money were missing. She was about 63 years old and a native of Ohio.

Married - In Pendleton on the 19th inst., by J. E. BELOTTE, Esq., Mr. C. A. SWORDS to Miss AMELIA SMITH.

Married - At Tunnel Hill, on the 29th inst., by W. PITCHFORD, Esq., Mr. JAMES WARD to Miss AMANDA CRANE, all of Pickens.

Married - On the 29th inst, in the evening, by W. PITCHFORD, Esq., Mr. JOHN FORSTER to Mrs. V. A. RIPLEY, all of Pickens.

Tribute of Respect to S. J. CHAMBLIN, deceased, by Pendleton Lodge No.34. A.F.M.

Issue of Saturday December 3,11859:

Inquest - THOS. H. BOGGS, Esq., acting as Coroner, held an inquest over the dead body of PETER SHARPE, of this district, who died suddenly on the 26th ult. The verdict of the jury was that the deceased came to his death by the "conjestion of some vital organ, caused by intemperance".

Death of a Hero - Dr. JAS. F. LEE, of Elizabeth City, N. C., died on the 10th inst. Mr. Lee was engaged in some of the late Indian struggles,and served his country faithfully and honorably in the late Mexican War, having borne a gallant part in crowning the American arms with the brilliant victory achieved at Buena Vista.

Convict Killed - The "Wetumpka (Ala) Spectator" says a convict named WM. GRIFFITH was shot while in a state of rebellion, by Dr. BURROWS, one of the lessees of the State prison, on Thursday, killing him instantly.

Married - On the 27th ult., by Rev. D. H. Kennemur, Mr. JAMES BAKER to Miss SARAH ANN WEST, all of Pickens.

Married - On the 27th ult., by Rev. B. WALL, Mr. WM. COX to Miss LIZZIE PHILLIPS, all of Pickens.

Married - On the 5th inst., in Greenville, S. C., by the Rev. F. A.MOOD, Mr. T. O. (or Q.) DONALDSON, Esq., of the "Patriot and Mountaineer", to Miss SUE HOKE.

Issue of Saturday December 10, 1859:

Sudden Death - The certainty of death and the uncertainty of life is forcibly brought home to us in the death of Rev. GIDEON ELLIS, which occurred on the 30th ult. Whilst sitting in his chair before the fire, he was seized with an affection or palpitation of the heart, causing his death almost instantly. He was near his three score and ten years, and had led a most pious and exemplary life. Peace to his manes.(?)

Dead - B. H. OVERBY, a prominent citizen of Georgia and a native of Anderson district, died at Williamston recently.

Married - On Wednesday morning 30th of Nov. by Rev. E. E. PRESSLY, Mr. MILFORD BURRIS, of Anderson, to Mrs. VASHTI GAINES, of Abbeville.

Married - On the 8th December, by THOMAS J. KEITH, Esq., Mr. GEO. W. CHASTAIN to Miss SARAH MORGAN, all of Pickens.

Issue of Saturday December 17, 1859:

Another Sudden Death - Mrs. MARTHA, wife of Mr. PRIER ALEXANDER, Sr., died suddenly on Tuesday night last. She had retired to bed in her usual health, and was seized suddenly with asthma or affection of the heart which terminated in death in a few minutes. A Coroner's inquest, held over the body, elicited nothing else.

Melancholy Death - The "Greenville Patriot" announces the death of Rev. J. W. COOK, formerly a lawyer, but who had gone to Greenville for the purpose of joining the South Carolina Conference.

Married - On the 20th of October last, by THOS. H. BOGGS, Esq., Mr. JACOB SHRUM, of Miss., to Miss ELVIRA G., daughter of JEREMIAH WILLIAMS, dec'd., of Pickens district.

Married - On the 13th ult., by the same, Mr. JAMES A. HAMILTON, of Ga., to Miss MALINDA A. MOORE, of this District.

Married - On the 4th inst., by the same, Mr. JOAB MAULDIN to Miss DEBO-
RAH R., daughter of the late I. J. HOLLINGSWORTH, of Pickens.

Married - On the 11th inst., by JOHN SHARP, Esq., Mr. JOHN M. RANKIN to
Miss EDDIE MOSS, of Pickens.

Married - On the 20th ult., by W. S. WOOLBRIGHT, Esq., Mr. ANDERSON B.
HAYS to Miss ELIZABETH ANN ELLIOTT, all of Pickens District.

Married - On the _____, by Rev. DRURY KNOX, Mr. BENSON HONEA to Miss VI-
NEY E. VINSON.

Married - On the 11th inst., by Rev. J. R. HUNNICUTT, Mr. P. V. WILSON
to Miss ELIZABETH HODGINGS, all of Pickens.

Married - On the 8th inst., by Rev. A. W. MC GUFFIN, Mr. DANIEL A. WARD
to Miss MARTHA S. HOLLEY.

Issue of Saturday January 7, 1860:

Burnt to Death - Mrs. FRED ENGEL was burnt to death at Memphis last week
by her clothes accidentally taking fire.

Married - On the 14th ult., in Cassville, Ga., by the Rev. HENRY BROWN,
Col. J. J. SHARP to Miss M. E. MOSS, all of Cherokee county.

Married - On the 20th ult. at the house of E. L. KEITH, by J. B. SUTHER-
LAND, Esq., Capt. V. B. WILLIAMS to Miss SARAH HARRIS, all of Pickens.

Married - On the 24th ult., by THOS. H. BOGGS, Esq., Mr. ANDREW HAYNES
to Miss JUDITH GILSTRAP.

Married - On the 25th ult., by the same, Mr. WM. H. NIXON, to Mrs. ELIZ-
ABETH BARNETT, all of Pickens.

Married - On the 22d ult., by Rev. WM. M. MORTON, Mr. JAMES MOODY to
Miss RHODA SHED, all of Pickens.

Married - On the 20th December, by H. J. ANTHONY, Esq., Mr. RICHARD HAR-
RIS to Miss NANCY SINGLETON, all of Pickens.

Obituary - Died, on the 17th November, 1859, of Phthissis, Mrs. MARY
DAVIS, wife of T. F. DAVIS, aged twenty-four years. The subject of this
notice had for several years been a professor of religion, and her patience and fortitude during a long and severe illness proved that she
had Divine aid to bear her up in the trying hour of disolution. O.

Issue of Saturday January 14, 1860:

Married - On the 20th Nov., 1859, by Rev. A. P. SULLIVAN, Col. WILLIAM
KNOX of Hart county, Ga., to Miss FRANCES J., eldest daughter of the
late Hon. MATHEW KNOX, of Greene county, Alabama.

Married - On the 25th ult., by Rev. J. R. HUNNICUTT, Mr. WM. S. MC GUFFIN
to Miss L. J. HULL, all of Pickens.

Married - On the 28th ult. by the same, Mr. JOHN H. MC GUFFIN to Miss S.
E. JENKINS, all of Pickens.

Married - On Thursday evening, the 5th inst., by J. E. HAGOOD, Esq.,Mr.
W. F. DODD to Miss SARAH I. SMITH, all of Pickens.

Married - On the same evening, by the same, Mr. DRURY FREEMAN to Miss
NANCY E. BURGESS, all of Pickens.

Married - On the 3d inst., by Rev. D. C. BOGGS, Mr. CARLILE TODD to Miss
JANE DUNCAN, all of Pickens.

Married - On the 27th ult., by Rev. ALBERT A. MORSE, Colonel THOMAS J.
GLOVER, of Orangeburg, to Miss E. TOCCOA WHITNER, of Anderson C. H.

Obituary - Died, at her residence, near Pendleton, S. C., on the morning
of the 30th of December, 1859, in the 77th year of her age, Mrs. ELIZA
PICKENS, relict of EZEKIEL PICKENS...eldest son of Gen. ANDREW PICKENS..
and daughter of GEORGE and MARY BARKSDALE, of Christ Church Parish, S.C.
The deceased in the varied relations of her life beautifully illustrated
all those virtues which dignify and adorn the character of the Christian
matron. She was the devoted and confiding wife, the anxious and affectionate mother, the attached relative and friend, and the kind and con-
siderate mistress. She was for many years a consistent member of the
Presbyterian Church, and liberally supported all the ordinances and in-
stitutions. For more than two years she was a great sufferer from a fall
which she received in her own house, and consequently confined to her
room during the greater part of that time. She bore her sufferings with
great patience and submission to the Divine will,"and lived in constant
expectation of the messenger to call her home, after longing to depart
and be with Christ." By a Providential dispensation all her children
and most of her grandchildren were with her during her last. moments to
smooth her dying pillow; and by them and by a large circle of relations
and friends she will be held in everlasting rememberance. Thus has one
of the last links that binds the present generations of old Pendleton
"to the past, and the bereaved family" to their illustrious ancestor...
one of the patriots and heroes of the Revolution, been broken. May the
mantle of the fathers and mothers fall upon their sons and daughters,and
may the altars enacted by them in these Wescern wilds to the honor and
praise of God's grace, not cease to burn when those who enacted them
have passed away. A Friend

Drowned - Mr. MOSES ROSS, of Masontown, Va., up the Monogahela, was
drowned lately, while attempting to cross the river on the ice, which
broke soon after he left shore, letting him through into deep water.

Accident - Mr. M. C. PENDLETON a sober and industrious young man, of Darlington, shot himself in the abdomen with a pistol, which he was handling
on the 23d ult., and died in 30 minutes after.

Sad - The "Laurensville Herald" states that a Mr. BUTLER, in breaking the
ice around the water wheel of a mill in that district, fell from the top
of it, and died from the effects thereof almost immediately.

Death from Wrestling - ALECK LYTLE, while wrestling with one NATHAN
SMITH, near Glasgow, Ky., was thrown, and endeavoring to turn his antag-
onist, suddenly gasped and died.

State of South Carolina, Pickens. In Ordinary - Petition for final settlement & decree. JEREMIAH CLEVELAND, Adm'r. vs. THOS. CLEVELAND and
others. It appearing to my satisfaction that THOMAS CLEVELAND, GIBSON
HIX and wife NANCY and MARTIN L. LOONEY and wife MIRIAM, defendants in
the above stated case, reside without the limits of this State. Settlement of the estate of BENJAMIN CLEVELAND, deceased.

State of South Carolina, Pickens. In Ordinary - Petition for Partition.
JAMES JENKINS vs. THOS. JENKINS & others. It appearing to my satisfaction that THOMAS JENKINS, the heirs at law of ABNER JENKINS, deceased,
names and numbers unknown. JOHN JENKINS, WILLIAMSON JENKINS, one of the
heirs of ANDERSON JENKINS, deceased, to wit: THOMAS JENKINS, _____
STEWART and wife ELIZA STEWART, reside without the limits of this State.
Division or sale of the real estate of FRANCIS JENKINS, deceased.

Issue of Saturday January 21, 1860:

At Hymen's Altar - Elsewhere we barely noted the fact that Maj. S. D.
GOODLETT had retired from the editorial chair of the "Patriot and Mountaineer". We regret his loss to the fraternity, but welcome him most
cordially in his new character. A brief sentence announces his alliance
with Miss MARY LYLES, of Fairfield. Lucky, my friend, to be relieved of
the editorial harness to enter upon the felicities of the honeymoon.Long
may it continue.

Married - On the 12th inst., by E. P. VERNER, Esq., Mr. JAMES M. HARRI-
SON, of Franklin co., Ga. to Miss NANCY E., daughter of JESSE JENKINS,

(Harrison-Jenkins cont'd): of Pickens.

Married - On the 13th December, 1859, by E. ALEXANDER, Esq., Mr. JOHN MURPHREE to Miss ELIZABETH OWENS, all of Pickens.

Married - On the 4th inst., by Rev. A. W. ROSS, at the residence of the bride's father, near Pendleton, Mr. WILLIAM Y. MILLER, of Abbeville, to Miss SALLIE C. ROSS.

Married - On Tuesday evening, 10th inst., at the residence of the bride's father, by Rev. J. SCOTT MURRAY, Mr. JOHN PETER BROWN to Miss JULIA S., second daughter of Col. J. P. REED, both of Anderson Court House.

Issue of Saturday January 28, 1860:

Married - On the 12th inst., by WM. HUNT, Esq., Mr. F. A. COX to Miss MARY E. BROOKS, all of Pickens.

Married - In La Porte, Oct. 6th, by Rev. G. A. PIERCE, Mr. W. B. STANLEY to Miss JENNIE ROACH, both of Pine Grove, California.

Married - On the 19th inst., by Rev. J. H. BOROUGHS, Mr. JOHN T. JAMES to Miss JANE E. GARVIN, all of Pickens.

Married - By Rev. D. C. BOGGS, Mr. B. N. J. DUNCAN to Miss MARGARET RILEY, of this District.

Obituary - Died, in Texas, on the 17th December 1859, HUGH OSCAR, son of ELISHA and SUSANNA GAINES, aged three years and twenty days.

Died, on the 28th October, 1859, of Cramp Colic, Mrs. NANCY MC ADAMS, wife of JAMES MC ADAMS, in the 37th year of her age. The subject of this notice was for more than twenty years an acceptable member of the Methodist E. Church, and in all the concerns of life she adorned her profession...letting her light shine, so that others might see her good works, and glorify our Father in Heaven. She was at all times willing to do, or suffer the will of God; knowing that if she acknowledged Him in all her "ways", that He would direct her "paths". Her last illness was short and severe; but while disease preyed upon her system, she was not deprived of the presence of that God whom she served continually. She rejoiced in God her Saviour to the last. An affectionate husband and five children, with a large circle of friends mourn her loss, while she "rests where the wicked cease from troubling". V.A.S.

Horrible Murder - SANFORD EVANS, a young man, was murdered some eight or ten miles south of Greenville, Tenn., on Saturday night last by HYRAM COGBURN. The murderer has given himself up.

Issue of Saturday February 4, 1860:

Married - On Thursday evening, 26th inst., at the residence of the bride's father, by L. N. ROBINS, Esq., Mr. T. D. ENTRIKEN, formerly of Laurens, to Miss LUCRETIA PRICE, all of Pickens.

Married - On Sunday evening, 29th inst., at the residence of the bride's mother, by Rev. B. F. MAULDIN, Mr. S. NEWTON WILLIAMS, of Anderson, to Miss M. ANN ARCHER, of Pickens.

Married - On the 29th inst. by J. N. ARNOLD, Esq., Mr. WM. T. GARVIN to Miss MARTHA M. JAMES, all of Pickens.

Married - On Thursday, January 19th, at "The Oaks", Pendleton, by Rev. A. H. CORNISH, Col. THEODORE DEHON WAGNER, of Charleston, to Miss SARAH ELLA, daughter of the late JACOB WARLEY.

Murder of an Editor in Vicksburg, Miss. - W. D. RAY, editor of the Vicksburg "Southern Sun", was murdered Tuesday by SHIPPARD, his defaulting clerk. He was shot through the heart.

Issue of Saturday February 18, 1860: (next page)

Married - On Thursday the 9th inst., at the residence of ROBERT ISBELL, by Rev. S. ISBELL, Mr. WM. G. MARETT to Miss JULIA ISBELL, all of Pickens.

Married - On the 8th inst, by THOS. H. BOGGS, Esq., Mr. B. F. BOGGS to Miss ROSALIE H. WILLARD, all of Pickens.

Married - On the 12th inst., by the same, at Sharon Church, Mr. SHELBY BATES, of Pickens, to Miss TABITHA CRENSHAW, of Anderson.

Married - On the 14th inst. by the same, Mr. JOB F. SMITH to Miss M. ADA-LINE, daughter of the late JOHN FERGUSON, all of Pickens.

Killed - ROBERT AIKEN YOUNG, formerly of Columbia, was killed recently by falling from a trestle on the Northeastern Railroad. His brother was killed a few months since in attempting to get upon a train of which he was a conductor.

Fatal Mistake - The "Abbeville Banner" says that friends of J. L. GRIFFIN will regret to hear of his death. He leaves a wife and two children, with a large circle of friends and relations to mourn his loss. His untimely death is said to have been caused by unintentionally taking too much Laudanum.

Sad Affliction - The Rev. Dr. ROBERTS, Professor in Union Academy, Clifton, Tennessee, has lost four children from sonsumption, in the short' period of twenty months ... three sons and a daughter. Their ages ranged from 13 to 24 years.

Suicide - Mr. J. FOXWORTH, of Marion District, South Carolina, committed suicide on Sunday last. Cause assigned by the "Star"...probable delirium tremens from intoxication.

State of South Carolina, Pickens. In Ordinary - Petition for Partition. JACOB LEWIS vs. CHARLES WOOD, et als. It appearing to my satisfaction that WILLIAM MORGAN and wife SARAH, ALEX. WOOD, JOHN WOOD, ROB'T. WOOD, TILMAN HOWARD and wife ANN, defendants in this case, reside without the limits of this State. Division or sale of the real estate of JOSEPH WOOD, deceased.

Issue of Saturday February 25, 1860:

Married - On the 16th inst., by Rev. T. L. MC BRYDE, Mr. J. THOMAS STEELE to Miss LAURA A. ALEXANDER, both of Pickens.

Issue of Saturday March 3, 1860:

Married - On the 26th inst., by J. N. ARNOLD, Esq., Mr. J. J. BURTON to Miss C. A. MAULDIN, all of Pickens.

Married - On the 12th inst., by E. P. VERNER, Esq., Mr. JAMES CARROLL to Miss SUSAN MASON, all of Pickens.

Obituary - Died, in Pickens District, on the 26th ult., CHARLES HUNT, aged 86 years, 8 months and thirteen days. The deceased had been a member of the Baptist church for the last thirty years, and lived a most upright and honorable life. Age, everable always, is lovely when supported by a consistent christian experience. He leaves many relatives and friends to mourn their loss.

Issue of Saturday March 10, 1860:

Death of Mr. BENSON - The painful duty devolves on us this week of announcing the death of Mr. E. B. BENSON, of Pendleton. He breathed his last on Sunday morning, the 4th instant, of pneumonia, after an illness of several days. Mr. Benson was in his 72nd year, during much of which time he merchandised at Pendleton. He represented Pendleton district acceptably in the Legislature, and was also Sheriff of that district for one term. With pleasing address and kindness of heart, he drew around him many friends. Long service in the church prepared him fitly for the final struggle. He was the respected head of a numerous family, with whom and his widely extended connexion, we, in common with the community at large, mourn the sad event.

Dead - JOHN G. BOWMAN, of Columbia, formerly connected with the press of this State, died on the 5th instant.

Married - On the 1st. inst., by Rev. V. A. SHARPE, Mr. A. MONROE CARPEN-TER, of Lincoln, N. C., to Miss ELIZABETH J., eldest daughter of A. C. and LUCINDA HUGHES, of Pickens.

Married - On the 4th inst., by H. J. ANTHONY, Esq., Mr. HARRISON J. GIV-INS to Miss AVARILLA, daughter of DANIEL HURT, all of Pickens.

Obituary - Died, on the 2d inst., of Catarrhal Fever, EDWARD, son of J. B. and C. J. SITTON, of Pendleton, aged nine months. C. (1 verse poetry)

Issue of Saturday March 17, 1860:

Married - On the 11th inst., by H. J. ANTHONY, Esq., Mr. T. W. HILL to Miss D. A., daughter of DANIEL HURT, all of Pickens.

Married - On the 15th December, 1859, by A. D. B. ALLISON, Esq., Mr. JAMES M. THURSTON to Miss MARIA C. DAVIS, all of Henderson county, N.C.

Issue of Saturday March 24, 1860:

Obituary - Died, in the city of Augusta, Ga., on the 12th inst., MINNIE FLORENCE, daughter of J. A. and S. M. GURLEY, aged 2 years and 8 months. (poetry)

Issue of Saturday April 7, 1860:

Married - On the 8th inst., by WM. STODDARD, Esq., Mr. HAYNES ABERCROM-BIE, of Pickens District, to Miss CLARINDA BABB, of Laurens.

Issue of Saturday April 14, 1860:

Obituary - Departed this life, in the 68th year of his age, WM. H.WHITE, a worthy citizen of the District, at his home on Coneross, on the 27th March, 1860. The deceased was well known in the District, as a School Teacher, and is remembered no doubt, by many, for his lessons in letters and morals. He was a consistent member of the M. E. Church for thirty-nine years, his home being a home for the Minister of the Gospel. It was his delight to be at Church in connection with his brethren, and but few enjoyed themselves better than he in the house of God. When addres-sed, in his last hours, in regard to his peace of mind, being unable to speak, the tears traced each other down his cheeks, and he raised his hand, with a smile on his face, in token of victory. His friends mourn because of his departure, but not without hope. "Blessed are the dead who die in the Lord". A Friend

Departed this life March 13th, 1860, in Tishemingo county, Mississippi, MAVEANN C. MULLINNIX, second daughter of J. H. and RACHAEL MULLINNIX, in the fifth year of her age, after a short illness of what the Doctor cal-led Raseoler, and worms combined. She was a child of the most pleasant manners and extra smartness, and just before she breathed her last, when her doting father was standing over her and trying to help her, she spoke out and said, "You wont let me go", and then in a few moments she said, "I want to go", several times, and soon she fell asleep in Jesus. She was laid in the grave at Lebanon church, in Tippah county, on the 14th, in the midst of a large and weeping crowd. W.G.M. (2 verses of poetry)

Dead - The "Winnsboro Register" announces the death of JOHN OWENS, a gallant member of the distinguished Palmetto Regiment, on the 4th inst.

Issue of Saturday April 27, 1860:

Murder - The body of a man named WALTER WORLEY was found in the public road near Marion C.H., on the 12th inst., brutally murdered. No particulars of the horrible affair is given.

Death of a Veteran - JOHN LUDWIG SNYDER died in Clearfield county, Pennsylvania, last week, at the age of one hundred and thirteen years. He
was a native of Michaelstadt, Germany, and came to the United States in
1758. A paper noticing the event says: He was with Washington when he
crossed the Delaware, on Christmas night, 1776, and was in the battle of
Trenton, the 26th of December. The light of day was just breaking when
the Americans drove in the outposts of the Hessians through a thick
snow-storm. Snyder was in the battle of Brandywine, September 11, 1777,
under LAFAYETTE. He was transferred to the command of Gen. WAYNE, and
was in his defeat near Paoli, September 20, 1777. He was encamped with
WASHINGTON at Valley Forge, December 11, 1777. He has said the winter
of that year was the coldest he ever experienced. Our troops, he told
us, shot squirrels and drew their skins over their feet for shoes. He
was in the battle on Monmouth, June 28, 1774, under Wayne and was with
Wayne at the taking of Stony Point, where the watch-word was, "Remember
Paoli, brave boys". He was with Lafayette at the surrender of CORNWAL-
LIS at Yorktown, on the 19th of October, 1781, and in his own words,
"in many more scrimmages that he could not remember the particulars of".
This warrior left descendants to the fourth generation, and to the num-
of nearly three hundred. He was a gunsmith by trade, and made a perfect
gun when he was 107 years of age. During the last summer, he could read
without spectacles. When he was 90, he walked to Clearfield and back,
a distance of nearly 30 miles...and then back again, a distance in all
of 60 miles, before dark, on one and the same day. He never missed a
Presidential or Gubernatorial election since the very first.

Married - On Thursday evening, the 19th inst., by L. N. ROBINS, Esq.,Mr.
ISAAC STEWART to Miss FANNIE PRICE, both of Pickens.

Obituary - Died, near Dacusville, in Pickens District, S. C., April 1st,
1860, MARY LOOPER, wife of JEREMIAH LOOPER, Sr., in her seventy-eighth
year. Her disease was heart dropsy, of which she lingered about six
weeks, after which time it pleased an All-wise God to remove her from a
large circle of friends and relatives. The subject of this notice joined the Baptist church at Cross Roads in 1836, of which she has been a
member of good standing to the day of her death. Her counsels of religion to her children and friends we hope will not be forgotten in many
days to come. It pleased God to strengthen her path at the approach of
death. She called her husband and children to her bedside and bade them
all farewell and besought them to meet her in heaven, and praised God by
singing the sweet lines, "Religion makes me happy/ And then I want to
go,/ To leave this world of sorrow,/ And trials here below."   T.L.

Departed this life on the 9th inst., CARLOS THADDEUS, infant son of Z.A.
and J. H. AMBLER.

Issue of Saturday April 28, 1860:

Obituary - Departed this life in the 58th year of his age, SAMUEL ADDIS,
a worthy citizen of this district, on the 29th February, 1860. The deceased was well known as an industrious farmer, a good neighbor, kind
husband and an affectionate father. He was for about 25 years a member
of the Baptist church. The writer visited him often, and conversed freely with him about his future prospect. He was resigned to the will of
God, and suffered it in meekness. When addressed, in his last hours, in
regard to his peace of mind, he gave satisfactory evidence that he was
ready for his departure. A short time before he breathed his last, when
asked if there was anything that he wanted, his reply was: "No, I feel
very good, I feel now that I am on my way to Heaven". He has left a
large circle of friends and relations to mourn their loss, yet they rejoice in the thought that their loss is his eternal gain. H. (2 verses
poetry)

Mrs. HARRIET BAKER died at her residence in Pickens District the 28th of
February 1860, in the 56th year of her age. The deceased was for many
years a widow, and notwithstanding the difficulties, and disadvantages
with which she had to contend, she maintained her family in credit,and
at the time of her death had accumulated considerable property. Long ago

she attached herself to the M. E. Church, of which she remained a faithful and consistent member to the day of her death. She loved God's house
and when able to attend the writer never recollects seeing her seat vacant. In God's people she delighted...her house was a home for the preacher. She was a kind and affectionate mother, an obliging neighbor;and
I may say with truth, she was loved and esteemed by all who knew her.
She was much afflicted for near a year previous to her death, in all of
which she manifested a Christian spirit; contented that God's will might
be done. She was anxious to live for her family, and yet willing to die,
if it was the will of her Master. In all her affliction she felt that
God was with her, and to the last her trust was in him. She is gone from
the troubles of this life to the saints everlasting rest in heaven, for
the promise is, "Be thou faithful unto death and I will give thee a crown
of life". Let her children and friends strive to meet her in heaven.
                                                                V.A.S.

J. C. TERREL Executed - In accordance with the sentence of the Court,
JOHN C. TERRELL, who had been convicted of causing the death of his
grand-father, ANANIAS GRAHAM, by poison, was hung at Bennettsville on
Friday last.

Another Palmetto Gone - The "Winnsboro Register" records the death of
another of the survivors of the Palmetto Regiment, Mr. MADISON STUBER.
He was a volunteer in the Fairfield Company and had resided in that District for some years.

Sudden Death - We learn that on the 26th ult., Capt. JOHN BREWER, a citizen of this district, died suddenly. He had been out hunting oxen or
cattle, when, on returning he complained that his head hurt him, and fell
dead!

Issue of Saturday May 12, 1860:

Married - On the 19th ult., by Rev. T. L. MC BRYDE, Dr. J. H. MAXWELL to
Miss MARY ALEXANDER, of Pendleton.

Married - On the 1st inst., at the residence of the bride's father, by
the Rev. W. A. MC SWAIN, Rev. J. H. ZIMMERMAN to Miss MARY E., daughter
of Col. H. and Mrs. E. HAMMOND, of the town of Anderson.

Obituary - Died, at Campobella, near Pendleton village, on the morning
of the 18th ult., COLLIN, eldest son of ARCHIBALD C. CAMPBELL, aged twenty years, nine months, and eighteen days. Mysterious, past finding out
are the ways and works of Almighty Providence. The seemingly premature
departure of this young man has filled many hearts with sorrow. Endowed
with many amiable and excellent qualities of mind and heart, a dutiful
son, an affectionate brother and friend, he was naturally the object of
many fond hopes and expectations. But the spring bud had scarcely unfolded its leaves, and began to exhibit its promised excellance, when it
was plucked and taken away...only, we trust, to bloom more beautifully
in a better clime.

Death of an Estimable Lady - We are pained to learn that Mrs. L. M. GRIS-
HAM, consort of the late Colonel JOSEPH GRISHAM, died, at her residence
near Canton, Ga., on the 26th ult. She was in her 71st year, and, but a
short time before, had the promise of many more useful days. Alas! how
uncertain is human life. Her numerous relatives and friends have our
heartfelt sympathies in their sad bereavement. An appropriate obituary
will be prepared for our columns.

Funeral Service - Rev. J. R. HUNNICUTT will preach the funeral of Mrs.
MARY RUSK at Bethel Church, on the 4th Sabbath in May, instant.

An Old Postmaster - Mr. SAMUEL MELTON died recently at Yorkville, S.C.,
in the seventy-second year of his age. He had served as Postmaster for
thirty-eight years, under the administration of Presidents Adams, Jackson, Van Buren, Harrison, Tyler, Polk, Taylor, Fillmore, Pierce and Buchanan.

Sudden Death - WM. S. DANIEL, Esq., of Savannah, Ga., was attacked while at breakfast Wednesday morning with asthma, it is supposed, as he was subject to it, and expired in about ten minutes. He was a gentleman of affable manners and many fine traits of characrer, which created him many warm friends.

Issue of Saturday May 19, 1860:

Obituary - Died, at her residence in Anderson District, on the evening of the 13th of April 1860, Mrs. JANE WATKINS, relict of JOSEPH WATKINS, and daughter of WILLIAM and DINAH PASSMORE, in the 70th year of her age. The subject of this notice has been quite an orderly and consistent member of the Baptist Church for many years. Few we might say have ever been more humble, meek and devout, in the discharge of christian duties and requirements in all their bearings and relations. Her whole life has been one renowned for the manifestation of much courteousness, benevolence and purity. As a neighbor, she was universally beloved by all her acquaintances...as a mother, she was unwavering in affection and duties...as a mistress, kind and indulgent. She had been for some time apparently conscious of approaching dissolution, and in view of it manifested great anxiety in the welfare of others, having a word of advice and warning to each member of the family. She has left several children and a large circle of friends and acquaintances to mourn her departure. But there is comfort in the hearts of those who mourn. (Poetry)

Married - On the 10th inst., by Rev. WM. MC WHORTER, at Greenway, Mr.W. H. DENDY to Miss S. JENNIE STEELE, both of Pickens.

Married - On the 10th inst. by the Rev. EDWARD F. THWING, Mr. HENRY BIEMANN to Miss CATHERINE HAUSKAMP, both of Walhalla.

Dead - JOHN TILLMAN, who was shot in Edgefield District some two weeks since by GEO. W. MAYS, as we noticed at the time, died on Sunday of his wound.

Dead - The "Anderson Gazette" announces the death of ANDREW N. MC FALL, Esq., an estimable citizen of that district.

A Man of Eighty Commits Suicide - The "Lewisburg Messenger" states that JAMES CLARK, an old and highly respectable citizen of Marshall county, Tennessee, committed suicide on the 25th ult. He was nearly eighty years old and suffered from palsy so much that it was almost impossible for him to put his hands together.

Issue of Sautrday May 26, 1860:

Dead - JEFFERSON CHOICE, Esq., an influential and highly esteemed citizen of Spartanburg, died suddenly in that place last week, of apoplexy.

Obituary - Departed this life, at his residence in Pickens District,ROBERT ANDERSON LATHEM, aged 39 years, 8 months and 10 days. Mr. Lathem departed this world leaving a wife and two children. He was a kind husband, a doting parent, and a good citizen. Having attached himself to no branch of the christian church, yet his short stay on this earth was marked with true piety. Having suffered for four long weeks the most excruciating pain, he was never heard to mourn, but all the time seemed willing to do the will of the Lord. And when it did please the Almighty God to send His messenger Death, and require of our friend that soul that he had given him, he quietly and submissively closed his eyes in death, gave up the ghost and died. Blessed are those who serve the Lord.
J.

Issue of Saturday June 9, 1860:

Obituary - Mrs. MALINDA DURHAM, wife of J. C. DURHAM, of this district, died May the 25th, 1860, aged _____ years, 9 months and 2 days. She was not called to suffer long, though it was very severe; it was borne, however with christian patience and resignation. The deceased connected herself with the Methodist E. Church, at a protracted meeting held ___ September at Bethleham Church, and shortly after found Christ, to the joy and comfort of her heart. Always after her conversion, she seemed "strong in the faith", and in speaking of death, of which she seemed to have a previous presentement previous to her affliction, she expressed her readiness to go at God's command. It was the writer's privilege to see her but a short time before her death, and when the subject of religion was mentioned her countenance lighted up, and in substance said,"I am ready", "I only suffer in the flesh". As I looked upon that face so full of trust in God and so confident of a blessed immortality beyond the grave, I could but exclaim, "Let me died a death of the righteous, and let my last end be like his". She soon passed away in a more gentle clime. On the 25th, her funeral was preached to a large and deeply affected congregation; and there her mortal remains were deposited near the church of which she was a faithful member, to the time when the dead in Christ shall be raised incoruptible. To her bereaved husband, with her kindred and friends, we say: "Follow her as she followed Christ".

Died - On the 17th May, 1860, of Entesitis, SALLIE, daughter of J. M.and MARTHA ALEXANDER, aged one year, eleven months and thirteen days.

Issue of Saturday June 16, 1860:

Obituary - Died, at her residence near Salubrity, on the 1st ult., Mrs. JANE HAMILTON, in the 51st year of her age. Her illness was very painful, though short, being confined only about eighteen hours. The subject of this notice has been for many years a consistent member of the M.E. Church, and died in the full triumph of the faith once delivered unto the Saints; and whilst she is gone home to her Heavenly Father's house to enjoy that rest that remaineth for the people of God, she leaves behind her, to sorrow and mourn, an affectionate son and daughter, besides a large circle of relatives, neighbors and christian friends. But while we mourn our loss in the Church of Christ, and in the family circle, we rejoice that our loss is her eternal gain. Precious in the sight of the Lord is the death of his saints. Yea, Blessed are the dead which die in the Lord from henceforth. Yea, saith the Spirit, that they may rest from their labors, and their works do follow them. And whilst our loved sister died exultingly in the love of Christ, with glory in her soul and Heaven in her view, she exhorted her friends, and especially her only son, to choose the good track that many choose, and be prepared when the Angel of Death should call for them, to meet her in the glory land where the wicked cease from troubling, and the weary are at rest. T.R.G (1 v.p)

Departed this life August 9th, 1859, ELIZA A., youngest daughter of W.W. and E. A. LATHEM. On May 18, 1860, JOHN C., infant son of W. W. and E.A. LATHEM.   E.A.P.L. (3 verses poetry)

Fatal Accident - The eastern bound train on the East Tennessee and Virginia Railroad, ran off the tract Sunday night when seven miles east of Knoxville killing the Engineer, DONALD GRANT, formerly of Lynchburg, and Fireman MOOD.

Issue of Saturday August 11, 1860:

Married - On the 6th May last, by LEONARD ROGERS, Esq., Mr. JAMES WOOD to Miss MARTHA HEAD, all of Pickens.

Married - On the 19th July, ult., by the same, Mr. WM. H. WHITMIRE to Miss SARAH, daughter of Mr. BENNETT MOODY, all of Pickens.

Married - On the 2d inst., by Rev. T. B. MAULDIN, Mr. W. T. JANES, of Pickens, to Miss D. S. RUST, of Franklin county, Ga.

Obituary - Died, at his residence in Pickens District, on the 2d August, inst., AARON TERRELL, in the 72d year of his age. The deceased was a native of the district, and one of its most respectable citizens. Mr. Terrell had a high appreciation of all those qualities constituting a gentleman. He was strictly honest, and punctual in all his engagements. Liberal by nature, his circumstances enabled him to minister to the wants of the poor; many of whom will sincerely mourn his decease. He was kind and indulgent to his family, and loved by them in return. He was an exemplary neighbor. He was inflexible in his devotion to his friends and

his country, and never allowed an honorable opportunity to pass without
durthering the interests of the one, or advocating the cause of the other.
Thus has passed away one ripe in years and good works; mourned deboted-
ly by his family, his relatives and a wide circle of friends.

Suicide - THOS. MONROE CORY, a prominent merchant of New Orleans, lately
committed suicide by hanging himself. Cause...financial embarrassments.

Issue of Saturday August 18, 1860:

Obituary - Died, on the 4th of July, MARY JOANNAH, only daughter of JOHN
W. and S. A. SINGLETON, aged one year, seven months and twenty days.

Departed this life, near Walhalla, S. C., Friday August 10th, 1860, Miss
AVERILLIA ABBETT, in the 52nd year of her age. Miss Abbett left a lonely mother, five brothers, and five sisters, together with a large train
of relatives and friends to mourn their irreparable loss. She was an
affectonate daughter, a kind sister and connected herself with such christian properity in all the relations of life as to gain the esteem and
good will of all that knew her. As she approached the hour of death,the
grace of God was sufficient to enable her to bear her affliction as a
faithful Christian, with the hope of a future world of endless happiness.
To the last hour she seemed to be aware of her departure; when interrogated by her friends concerning her soul, she would reply that there was
nothing on earth to make her wish to remain. She is gone, her afflictions have ended, and her soul is wafted beyond the shores of sorrow and
pain, by the angelic choirs with whom she will be enabled to sing praises
to Him who triumphed over death. J.M.C.H. (2 verses poetry)

Tribute of Respect to Major MILTON MAULDIN, deceased, by Pendleton Lodge
No. 34, A.F.M.

Death of Mr. CLAYTON - We are pained to announce the death of Mr. JOEL
H. CLAYTON, a native of this district, which sad event occurred at Henderson, N. C., a few days ago. Mr. Clayton had been connected with the
press for a number of years, and at the time of his death, was the Editor of the Presage, published at Hendersonville. As there is a bright
side to the picture of life, so there are shadows reflected on the re-
verse. The decease had some qualities of the head and heart that we admired; but he had his failings, and where is the human nature that has
not? Nevertheless, let the grave, as it should, bury those frailities,
and let us only remember those redeeming traits of character which survive and alone shine above the tomb. We sincerely sympathise with his
relatives and friends in their sad bereavement.

Notice - I hereby forwarn all persons from trading with my wife CATHERINE
NALLY, who has left my bed and board without cause or provocation, And I
hereby extend notice to all persons that I will not be responsible for
her contracts. L. F. NALLY

Issue of Saturday August 25, 1860:

Married - On the 16th inst., by Rev. THOMAS LOOPER, Mr. A. B. SATTERFIELD
to Miss ANNA ROPER, all of Pickens.

Married - On the 19th, by the same, Mr. ELIJAH ROPER to Miss ARMINDA SAT-
terfield, all of the same place.

Married - On the 12th inst., by Rev. WM. W. REID, Rev. CHAS. ROPER to
Miss MARGARET L. STEWART, all of Pickens.

Married - Also, at the same time and place, by the same, Mr. ANDREW R.
RIGGINS to Miss GIZZEAL STEWART, all of Pickens.

Obituary - Died, on the 15th ult., CHARLES ANDERSON, son of ANDERSON and
ARZELA IVESTER, aged 8 months and 25 days. (1 verse poetry)

Dead - Rev. G. W. HUCKABEE, a worthy minister of the Methodist church,
died at his residence in Abbeville District, on the 30th July. He was
attacked while preaching on Sabbath, with Paralysis, and died next day.

He was 59 years old, and was regarded as a consistent and faithful christian minister.

Murder - Mr. W. C. HALTREE, living a few miles below the city of Natchez, was shot a few night since, while sitting on his gallery with his family and instantly killed. The assassin was seen running away after the commission of the deed. The identity of the villain, it is believed, will be established.

Issue of Saturday September 1, 1860:

Married - On the 22d inst., by J. N. ARNOLD, Esq., Mr. JOHN MARTIN, of Ireland, to Miss FRANCIS MC ALISTER, of Pickens.

Issue of Saturday September 8, 1860:

Married - On 1st August, by J. JAMESON, Esq., Mr. JOHN R. SMITH to Miss SUSAN BLAKELY, all of Pickens.

Married - On the 8th August, by the same, Mr. WM. CHAPMAN, of Pickens, to Miss NANCY BLOODWORTH, of Franklin county, Ga.

Married - On the 26th of August, by the same, Mr. H. E. ELLISON, of Anderson, to Miss LUCRETIA YOUNG, of Pickens.

Married - The same evening, by the same, Mr. BAILUS SCLETON to Miss SARAH SMITH, all of Pickens.

Married - On the 2d inst., by Rev. WM. W. REID, Mr. ANDREW GRAY, of Cherokee county, Ga., to Miss SUSANNAH ELLINBURGH, of Pickens.

Issue of Saturday September 15, 1860:

Married - On the 13th August last, by H. J. ANTHONY, Esq., Mr. ANDERSON ROPER to Miss SARAH WATSON, all of Pickens.

Married - On the evening of the 2d inst., by J. E. HAGOOD, Esq., Mr. E. G. STANSELL, JR., to Miss ELMINA BANKS, all of Pickens.

Issue of Saturday September 22, 1860:

Married - On Sunday the 9th inst., by J. B. SANDERS, Esq., Mr. WILLIAM NORRIS to Mrs. MARY HALL, all of Pickens.

Obituary - Died, in Pickens District, on the 10th September, MARY JOSEPHINE, eldest daughter of Mr. A. P. and Mrs. CAROLINE COX, aged 16 months.

Departed this life on Friday the 21st of August last, STEPHEN CLAYTON, infant son of Capt. ROBERT F. and MALISSA MORGAN, aged 10 months and 24 days. The subject of this memoir was one of an interesting pair of twins who strikingly resembled each other, which circumstances rendered its loss the more painful to his bereaved parents. But God in his wisdom has taken him ere he had known the sorrows of this world, and transplanted him in the regions of eternal bliss. Farewell, dear child, you can never again return to us, but we have the blessed assurance that we can go to him. "Suffer little children to come unto me and forbid them not, for such is the kingdom of Heaven". (3 verses poetry)

Dead - CHARLES WILLIAMS, Esq., of Laurens District, once a member of the Legislature, died on the 6th inst.

Issue of Saturday September 29, 1860:

Married - On the 20th inst., by Rev. H. M. BARTON, Mr. R. Y. H. LOWERY to Miss MATTIE C. PHILLIPS, all of Pickens.

Hung - ROBERT TUCKER, a notorious horse-thief was hung at Poluxy Springs, Texas, the other day. He made a confession, implicating many citizens of fair reputation.

Death of a Charleston Merchant - The Charleston papers announce the death
of Mr. WILLIAM CALDER, in that city, on Saturday last, in the sixtieth
year of his age.

Issue of Saturday October 6, 1860:

Obituary - Died, near Fair Play, in Pickens district, on the 29th Sept.
1860, Mr. BENJAMIN MEGEE, in the 90th year of his age. The deceased was
a native of North Carolina, but had been a resident of this district for
the last sixty-six years. He was an honest upright man, and had been a
consistent member of the Baptist church for near sixty years. Mr. Megee
was the first corpse that had ever been in his house. He leaves a disconsolate widow and children, and many friends to mourn his loss.

Departed this life on the morning of the 3rd inst., Mrs. MARTHA JANE KEL-
LEY, wife of CHARLES W. KELLEY, and daughter of JOHN and REBECCA ADAIR,
of this district; aged 19 years, 11 months and 15 days. She bore her affliction with christian fortitude. Well might it be said, "The ways of
the Lord are mysterious in taking His children from their troubles to a
perfect home in Heaven". The life of the deceased was a life of true
piety, and was much beloved by all who knew her. She has gone, no doubt,
to rest; for she said she was prepared to die. She is not here...she
is gone: Christ called for Martha. Husband and connection, He will call
for you. Try to meet Martha in Heaven, where you will meet to part no
more. (1 verse poetry)

Issue of Saturday October 13, 1860:

Married - On Tuesday evening, 2d Oct., 1860, by L. N. ROBINS, Esq., Mr.
ISAAC STONE to Miss ELIZABETH DAWSON, all of Pickens.

Married - On the 16th Sept. Ult., by Rev. A. CHASTAIN, Mr. C. C. ADAMS
to Miss C. D. BARTON, all of Gordon co., Ga.

Obituary - Departed this life September 20th, 1860, in Gordon county,
Ga., ANDERSON BARTON, infant son of JOHN C. and JUSTINA A. COOK, aged
eighteen days.

Terrible Tragedy - Mr. STOVALL, a respectable citizen of Fosterville,
Rutherford County, Tennessee, while laboring under insanity, the result
of financial embarrassments, murdered his wife and four children, on
Saturday night last, by cutting their throats, and, after cutting his
own throat, leaped into a deep spring, where his body was found.

Issue of Saturday October 20, 1860:

Married - On Tuesday evening the 2nd inst., by Rev. A. F. MC GILVRY, at
the house of the Bride's Father, ALLEN MC DAVID, Rev. VAN BUREN A. SHARP,
of the S. C. Conference, to Miss ANNIE MC DAVID, of Greenville District.

Dead - Mr. JOHN E. MURPHY, Inspector of Naval Stores, died in Charleston
on Sunday evening.

Issue of Saturday October 27, 1860:

Married - On the 23d inst., by Rev. V. A. SHARP, Mr. JOEL T. O'NEALL to
Miss MARY A. MC WHORTER, all of this district.

Obituary - Died, at the residence of his father in Lauderdale County,
Miss., on the 1st inst., SAMUEL RIED, infant and only son of JAMES T.and
CAROLINE D. RIED, of diptheria, aged 17 months and twenty five days.

Issue of Saturday November 1860:

Married - On Sunday morning the 15th inst., by J. B. SANDERS, Esq., Mr.
JOHN M. SMITH, of Spartanburg, to Miss ARTEMISSA DODSON, of Pickens.

Married - On the 25th ult., by Rev. JOHN S. PRESSLY, Capt. ABEL ROBINS,
of Pickens, to Mrs. ELIZA FELTON, of Anderson.

Obituary - Died, in Calhoun county, Alabama, on the 29th of September, 1860, of fever, JOHN BLACKBURN, aged about forty-seven years. The deceased was a native of Pickens district, and emigrated to the west in early life. He was an honest man, respected by his neighbors, and loved by his family and friends. He had been a member of the Presbyterian church for seventeen years and much of that time ruled as elder of the church; and gave ample evidence in his dying hours that he had lived a christian, proving his faith by his works. His loss to his bereaved family is great, but they mourn not as those without comfort...knowing,full well, that their loss is his eternal gain. May his soul rest in peace.

Drowned - JESSE WATKINS and JOHN WATKINS, his nephew, were drowned near Salisbury, N. C., on the 8th inst., while attempting to cross a ferry while drunk. The body of John, when recovered, bore a bottle of whiskey in one of his pockets.

Lumpkin, Ga., October 26- Dr. J. S. PORTER was shot and killed, by Mr. J. M. CAIN, in Lumpkin, Ga., on last Tuesday, in a personal rencounter.

Execution of Criminals in Texas - Two young men, late of Ft. Smith, Arkansas, FRANK RIVERS and BOB MONTGOMERY, were hung near San Antonio, Texas, on the 30th ult., for horse stealing.

Issue of Saturday November 10, 1860:

Married - On Sunday evening, November 4th, 1860, by L. N. ROBINS, Esq., Mr. T. P. GARRET to Miss ELIZABETH STUART, all of Pickens.

Married - On Sunday evening, 1st of April last, by E. H. COX, Esq., Mr. JAMES A. HEMBREE to Miss C. A. COX, all of Pickens.

Married - On Sunday evening, 15th of April last, by the same, Mr. E. H. BURKET to Miss RACHEL MOORE, all of Pickens.

Married - On Sunday evening, July 29th, by the same, Mr. WILLIAM M. ADDIS to Miss MARY N. E. DAY, all of Pickens.

Married - On Sunday evening, 21st October, by the same, Mr. BRAXTON R. JOHNSON, of Pickens, to Miss MELVIRA J., youngest daughter of ROBERT W. and LOUISA KING, of Anderson.

Issue of Saturday November 17, 1860:

Inquest - Mr. Coroner GANTT held an inquest, on Sabbath, over the dead body of a young man, ARCHELAUS HAMMETT, who fell dead suddenly early that morning. The jury returned a verdict, that the deceased came to his death by the visitation of God. The deceased had been subject to fits of a serious nature.

Issue of Saturday November 24, 1860:

Married - On the 11th inst., by Rev. FLETCHER SMITH, Mr. JOS. W. HOLLEMAN and Miss EMMA E. WHITE, only daughter of J. B. WHITE, Esq., all of Pickens.

Obituary - RICHARD BURDINE was born August 6th, 1773 in North Carolina, and died at his residence in this District, September 18th, 1860. The deceased was well known to many of the citizens of his own, as well as in adjoining Districts; and what is much better, he was known as a faithful and consistent christian. In early life he engaged in the service of his Heavenly Master, having joined the Methodist E. Church at the age of six years, from which time to the day of his death he was known as the self-denying and humble follower of the meek and lowly Jesus. For many years he was a faithful and efficient class-leader in the church of his choice, and his labors in this direction only ceased when his strength was insufficient to the task. His work was not confined to any particular neighborhood, but he "went about doing good". Perhaps no man has a greater impression upon the mind of those with whom he had to do. He, was I believe, universally respected as one in whom there was "no guile". To him the life of a christian was no small thing; consequently, he lived a life of consistencey, so that every one with whom he came in contact "took knowledge of him that he had been with Jesus". No one after having spent a days' time with him would have been surprised to hear that he professed the christian religion. While he was able his seat scarcely ever vacant at church...a place which was dear to him to the very last...one of his complaints in his weakness being that he could not go to church. For the last few months, however, he was able to get to church several times. In July he was permitted to attend a revival meeting for almost every day in the week, at which meeting he seemed to catch new life; and several times he exhorted believers to be steadfast, mourners to look to Christ, and sinners to flee the wrath to come. His presence and labors at that meeting will never be forgotten by those in attendance. It was at this meeting, he said, that he was almost gone, and that he had as well fall there as anywhere else. He was liberal... always ready to respond to the calls of the church and poor. As a husband, he was kind and affectionate; as a father, indulgent, yet firm in his purpose; as a neighbor and friend he was unsurpassed. Thus lived this man of God for 81 years...an exemplary member of the church. When will our District be visited with his equal? To an aged widow, to children and grand children, we say, live as he lived, and bye and bye you will meet to part no more. V.A.S.

Died, on the 5th day of June, 1860, of inflammation of the lungs, ROSANNA ABI, eldest child and only daughter of ANDREW J. and LUCINDA M. C. PENDLEY, of Pickens District, aged 3 years, 2 months and 12 days. E.H. (1 verse poetry)

Issue of Saturday December 1, 1860:

Married - On Sunday evening the 4th ult., by Rev. M. CHASTAIN, Mr. MATTHEW GILLESPIE, of N. C. to Miss RACHAEL HENDRIX, of Pickens.

Married - On the 8th ult., by Rev. SUMPTER DANIEL, Mr. J. C. C. FEATHERSTON of Anderson, to Miss E. A. SULLIVAN, of Laurens.

Married - On the 20th ult., by Rev. J. B. HILLHOUSE, Col. D. C. TEMPLETON to Miss ADDIE DAY, all of Laurens.

Obituary - Died, of Flux, in Bellview, Rusk county, Texas, October 26th, 1860, MARGARET E. H., daughter of NATHANIEL and MARGARET GEURIN, aged six months and four days. J.A. (1 verse poetry)

Issue of Saturday December 8, 1860:

Married - On the 6th of November, last, by H. J. ANTHONY, Esq., Mr. ANDERSON ROPER to Miss SARAH WATSON, all of Pickens.

Married - On the 2d inst., by Rev. W. B. SINGLETON, Mr. R. A. COOPER to Miss Licena Childers, all of Pickens.

Issue of Saturday December 15, 1860:

Married - On 2d inst, by T. H. Boggs, Esq., Mr. WM. H. PILGRIM to Miss AMANDA E. MC KINNEY, of Anderson.

Married - On Thursday evening the 6th of December, inst., by Rev. D. C. BOGGS, Mr. WM. A. BARRON to Miss MARY ELIZA, second daughter of Mr. WM. H. STRIBLING, all of Pickens.

Married - On the 9th inst., by J. N. ARNOLD, Esq., Mr. JAMES W. POWER to Miss MARTHA B. FANT, all of Pickens.

Issue of Saturday December 22, 1860:

Married - On the 4th inst., by Rev. JOHN ARIAIL, Mr. LEANDER JONES to Miss LOUISA JAMESON, all of Pickens.

Married - On the 13th inst., by the same, Capt. JOHN H. BOWEN to Miss MARY E., eldest daughter of R. E. and ELIZA HOLCOMBE, all of Pickens.

Married - On the 20th ult., by E. H. COX, Esq., Mr. ELIHU F. MILLER to Miss BELINDA F. HAL_, all of Pickens.

Married - On Sunday evening the 23rd ult. by J. E. HAGOOD,Esq.,Mr. ELIAS HINKLE to Miss ALSEY A., daughter of Mr. JAMES LEWIS, all of Pickens.

Issue of Saturday January 12, 1861:

Married - On the 18th of December last, at the residence of S. W. AGNEW, Esq., by Rev. J. C. WILLIAMS, Mr. ALONZO M. FOLGER, of this District, to Miss M. ELIZA AGNEW, of Abbeville District.

Married - On the 3d inst., by A. C. HUGHES, Esq., Mr. ABRAHAM GILSTRAP to Miss LOUISA CRANE, all of Pickens.

Issue of Saturday January 19, 1861:

Married - On the 10th inst., by R. A. GILMER, Esq., Mr. JEFFERSON DAVIS to Miss SAFONSBA NIMMONS, all of Pickens.

Married - On the 20th ult., by the Rev. C. H. SPEARS, Mr. A. GIBSON to Miss MARGARET CAPEHART, all of Pickens.

Issue of Saturday January 26, 1861:

Married - On the 23d December last, by Rev. B. WALL, Mr. WILLIAM LYLES to Miss MATILDA BROWN, all of Pickens.

Married - On Thursday evening 10th inst., by J. E. HAGOOD, Esq., Mr.JOHN C. KNOX to Miss ELIZABETH, daughter of Mr. ELISHA ALEXANDER, all of Pickens.

Married - On the 17th inst., by Rev T. B. MAULDIN, Mr. JOHN KEATON to Miss JANE SANDERS, all of Pickens.

Issue of Saturday February 2, 1861:

Married - On the 20th December last, by Rev. W. B. SINGLETON, Mr. JAMES A. GRIFFIN to Miss ZILPHA ALLGOOD, all of Pickens.

Married - On the 24th inst., by Rev. V. A. SHARP, Mr. J. D. MASTERS to Miss SARAH MARGARET, eldest daughter of Mr. WM. A. LESLEY, all of Pickens.

Issue of Saturday February 9, 1861:

Death from Vaccination - We regret to learn that Mr. SAMUEL LOOPER, a worthy citizen of this district, died last week from the effects of vaccination. He had exposed himself more than was prudent, which is probably the cause of his death. Mortification took place on his arm.

Married - On 16th December last, by L. ROGERS, Esq., Mr. W. R. D. CALHOUN to Miss SARAH C. ROGERS, all of Pickens.

Married - On the 3d December last, by the same, Mr. J. W. CANNON to Miss SARAH BRYCE, all of Pickens.

Married - On the 24th January last, by the same, Mr. JAS. ROCHESTER to Miss ARMINDA PEARSON, all of Pickens.

Married - On the 31st January last, by Rev. BENJ. HOLDER, Mr. JESSE M. CLAYTON to Miss MARTHA A. BOWEN, all of Pickens.

Married - On the 21st ult., by Rev. J. E. DU BOSE, Mr. ELIAS E. WHITNER, of Anderson, S. C., to Miss EMMA A. WILLIAMS, of Bell Air, Fla.

Obituary - Departed this life, at her husband's residence, in Pickens

District, S. C., on the 23d January, 1861, Mrs. EMILY M. DAVIS, wife of
THOMAS R. DAVIS, aged 41 years, one month and 23 days. The deceased
leaves a kind and affectionate and now sad and heart broken husband, two
children...one boy and one girl...an aged father and mother, numerous relations and many devoted friends to mourn their loss; but we trust and
believe, her eternal gain. The deceased had many prominent traits of
character; she was industrious, economizing, truthful and scrupulously
honest; an affectionate and devoted wife; a loving and indulgent mother,
and a true and sincere friend. The large weeping crowd that attended
her burial, was unmistakable evidence of how her neighbors and friends
respected her. A Friend (1 verse poetry)

Issue of Saturday February 23, 1861:

Suicide - We regret to learn that Mr. JONATHAN S. HOLCOMBE committed
suicide at Pickensville, on the 14th inst., by cutting his throat with
a razor, in a fit of Mania a potu. The deceased was kind-hearted, genial by nature, and warm in his friendships.

A Melancholy Occurrence - Our heart is pained by the intelligence of the
death of another one of our noble volunteers. JAMES C. ALLEN, of Abbeville District, a member of the company from that section, received an
injury on Tuesday afternoon, which was followed by almost instant death.
The company, of which this gentleman was a member, is quartered at the
Moultrie House, on Sullivan's Island. He and some of his comrades were
engaged in harmless diversion during an interval of leisure. They were
chasing each other from room to room, and while running with all speed
along the long corridor of that building, Mr. Allen came in contact with
a bayonet on a gun in the hand of one of his companions. The weapon entered the right eye and penetrated the brain. The unfortunate young man
survived only a few moments. Mr. Allen was but nineteen years of age.
His character was without a spot, and he was greatly beloved by his brother soldiers. His remains will be conveyed to Abbeville this morning.
This melancholy accident has cast a gloom over the cheerful hearts that
were prepared to lose their friends in noble warfare, but were not ready
to see one so promising and so blessed with virtues thus rudely and suddenly smitten with the hand of the destroyer.   "Charleston Courier"

Obituary - Died, near Pendleton, S. C., on the 5th inst., Mrs. MARGARET
FITZGERALD, wife of ELI FITZGERALD, deceased, after a severe illness of
several weeks duration.

Married - On the 14th inst., by Rev. WM. MC WHORTER, Mr. R. R. STRIBLING
of Franklin county, Ga., to Miss LOU W. DENDY, of Pickens.

Issue of Saturday March 2, 1861:

Killed - We learn that ANSEL CRANE was killed in Jackson county, N. C.,
on the 20th ultimo, by JOHN CALHOUN, JR. The act, we are informed, was
done in self-defense. Calhoun surrendered himself to the Sheriff of the
county, and afterwards obtained bail.

Frightful Tragedy - On the evening of the 25th, near Memphis, Scotland
county, Mo., THOMAS H. RIDGLEY killed his wife and two small daughters
with a knife and axe, knocked down a son 18 years of age with a billet
of wood, wounded a smaller son with a knife, and completed the shocking
tragedy by cutting his own throat from ear to ear with a razor. No
cause is assigned for the act except a supposed fit of insanity.

Obituary - Died, on the 20th February last, after a lingering illness of
chronic affection of the bowels, NATHANIEL LYNCH, SR., in the 71st year
of his age. The deceased was a native of Pickens, and was distinguished
for his high moral and religious character. He had been a consistent
member of the Baptist Church for twenty-five years, and felt the consolations of religion in his expiring hours. In the character of citizen,
neighbor, husband and father his life was exemplary; and, whilst we deplore the loss of one so honest and upright, we are nevertheless cheered
by the belief that our loss is his eternal gain. * March 1, 1861

Issue of Saturday March 16, 1861: (next page)

(March 16 cont'd:)
Married - On the 26th ult. by Rev. V. A. SHARP, Mr. WM. A. WHITE, JR.,to
Miss E. A., eldest daughter of Mr. JAMES M. MC WHORTER, of Pickens.

Married - On the 7th inst., by J. N. ARNOLD, Esq., Mr. JAMES F. C. PRINCE
to Miss MARTHA F. A. GARVIN, of Pickens.

Obituary - Another of the meek of the earth has departed and gone from
time. The Rev. W. G. MULLINIX, formerly of Pickens District, departed
this life in Tippah, Mississippi, on the 11th of November, 1860, after a
painful and severe attack of winter Fever. He was a minister of the Methodist E. Church South, and was beloved and caressed by all orthodox
christians, not so much from the greatness of his preaching as from goodness of the man, though he was truly, in one sense, a great good preacher,
for he combined good sense with a most catholic and christian spirit.
Preaching in all the churches in this (Anderson) and Pickens District...
where he was raised, for he had only lived in Tippah, at the time of his
death, about one year...he married more people, baptised more and funer-
alized more, for the last few years of his sojourn, than any other minister in the two Districts. See what he says in a small account which
he gives of him-self but a short time before he died, under date of June
13, 1860: "I am now in my 55th year, and my days are almost at an end.
I was born in Spartanburg, July 2, 1805, came to Pendleton District in
1809, and when the District was divided, I was cut off in the Pickens
division. Most of my education obtained at Sabbath school, and in the
care of the Presbyterian church at old Pendleton, where my brother and
myself walked six miles to attend every Sabbath. I joined the Methodist
Church in my 16th year, married in 1824, and in a short time was appointed a class-leader. In 1829 I was licensed to exhort, and in September
of the same year, at Sandy Spring, I was licensed to preach. In 1835 I
was ordained Deacon, and in 1842, Elder. I was employed in the year 1835
to ride the Pendleton circuit, in connection with BARTLETT THOMASON. A-
gain, in 1857, I travelled in connection with R. P. FRANKS. I took the
number of people in Pickens District, by State appointment, three years
...'39,'49 and '59. I have spent much of my strength in the church. I
have preached 2,500 times, baptised 500 persons, and married 200. I cannot undertake to give a correct account of the number of funerals I have
attended, but a great many, nor do I know how many I have taken into the
Church, but a great many." Thus you see, my friends, the labors of Brother Mullinix has been great. He was a good man, and much more than a
newspaper sketch could be said in his favor, but let me close this by
saying "Blessed are the dead who died in the Lord, for they do rest from
their labors and their works do follow them". C.L.G.

Issue of Saturday March 23, 1861:

Married - On the 10th February last, by L. ROGERS, Esq., Mr. T. J. SLOAN
to Miss ELIZA MOSS, all of Pickens.

Married - By the same, on the 11th March, Mr. ASHLEY POWELL to Miss C.
SHED, all of Pickens.

Married - By the same, on the 17th inst., Mr. W. W. CRUMPTON to Miss N.
A. ROGERS, all of Pickens.

Married - On the 26th February last, by Rev. B. WALL, Mr. W. T. FINLEY,
of Pickens, to Miss MARY M. HOLDEN, of Rabun, Ga.

State of South Carolina, Pickens. In Equity - Bill for Partition, &c.
JOHN BURDINE vs. PATSY BURDINE et als. It appearing to my satisfaction
that the heirs of POLLY LATHEM, to wit: GEO. LATHEM. T. H. SOUTHWICK
and wife PATSY, J. W. LATHEM, RICHARD M. LATHEM, ANDREW P. LATHEM, ANTHO-
NY G. LATHEM, SAM W. LATHEM, JAS. E. PETIT and wifeJANE E., JACOB ERNEST
and wife BETSY, JOS. BURDINE, SAM'L. BURDINE, ELIJAH ROBINSON and wife
HENRIETTA, defendants in this case, reside without the limits of this
State.

Issue of Saturday March 30, 1861:

Death of a Citizen - We regret to learn from the "Blue Ridge Herald", that ALFRED M. CARPENTER, Esq., a worthy citizen of this district, departed this life at his residence, on Friday, the 22d inst. Mr. C. spent the greater part of his life in the service of God. He was for many years a Class leader in the Methodist Church, in which relation he was untiring in his efforts to do good.

Inquest - A Coroner's inquest was held on Saturday afternoon, says the "Columbia Guardian" of the 25th inst., on the body of JAMES SENN, who, in examining his fish trap in the Congaree river, was drowned. The verdict of the jury was death by accidental drowning.

Obituary - Died, near Pickensville, on the 3d December last, SAMUEL MAULDIN, in the 14th year of his age. He leaves a kind mother, and brothers and sisters to mourn his loss. He was a kind and affectionate brother, a tender and loving son. He was confined to his room about four weeks, and though his sufferings were great, he was continually talking about dying. During his sickness it seemed to be on his mind very much that he was going to die, and felt like he was going to a better world than this. He expressed a willingness to die, but regretted leaving his mother and brothers and sisters behind. (5 verses poetry)

State of South Carolina, Pickens. In Equity - Bill for Partition, &c. TILMAN C. MAGEE vs. MARET MAGEE, et als. It appearing to the Commissioner that MARET MAGEE, N. A. MAGEE, NANCY HUNT; heirs-at-law of FANNY MASON, deceased, to wit: BENJAMIN MASON, ELIAS MASON, EZEKIEL MASON, BENJAMIN BROWN, H. M. SALMON and husband WARD, defendants in this case, reside without the limits of this State.

State of South Carolina, Pickens. In Equity - Bill for Partition, &c.

G. M. LYNCH, et als vs. C. F. LYNCH, et als. It appearing to the Commissioner that WILLIAM J. LYNCH, C. F. LYNCH, CALVIN LYNCH, JASON GILLESPIE and wife ELIZABETH, JOHN LEWIS and wife MARY, WILLIAM BAKER and wife SARAH, RICHARD ROBINSON and wife NANCY, JOHN ROBINSON and wife ELIZA, defendants in this case, reside without the limits of this State.

State of South Carolina, Pickens. In Ordinary - Petition for Settlement. WM. HUNTER, Adm'r. vs. J. M. OWENS and others. It appearing to my satisfaction that J. M. OWENS and wife PERMELIA A., OLIATTA ARCHER and EUGENIA ARCHER, defendants in this case, reside without the limits of this State. Settlement of the estate of ANDREW H. ARCHER, deceased.

Issue of Saturday April 6, 1861:

Married - On Thursday evening, the 28th ult., by J. E. HAGOOD, Esq., at the residence of the bride's father, Mr. GEORGE W. STEWART to Miss ADALINE BAKER, all of Pickens.

State of South Carolina, Pickens. In Ordinary - Petition for Settlement. J. E. HAGOOD, Adm'r. vs. JEREMIAH WHITMIRE and wife ANNA, et als. It appearing to my satisfaction that JAMES ROBINSON, GEORGE ROBINSON, JR., JOSEPH ROBINSON, RANDALL ROBINSON, LYDIA HAGOOD, THOMAS HITT and wife MARTHA, the heirs-at-law of WILLIAM ROBINSON, deceased, (names and number unknown) and the heirs of ELIZABETH REESE, deceased, (names and number unknown), defendants in this case, reside without the limits of this State. Settlement of the estate of HARDY ROBINSON, deceased.

Issue of Saturday April 20, 1861:

Married - On the 9th inst., by H. J. ANTHONY, Esq., Mr. D. M. H. MASSEY, of Anderson, to Miss LUCINDA, daughter of Mr. J. J. HUNT, of Pickens.

Married - On the 14th inst., by A. HUNTER, Esq., at the residence of Mr. JEREMIAH LOOPER, Mr. A. J. DURHAM, to Miss MARY J. TURNER, all of Pickens.

Obituary - Died, at the residence of Mr. JOHN A. ROBINSON, in Pickens District, on the 25th of March last, JEREMIAH LOOPER, SR., in the 85th year of his age. The deceased was a native of the District, and commended himself to his friends, and neighbors, throughout his long career, by the most exemplary conduct . He had been a member of the Baptist Church for about thirty-five years, and was sustained in his last illness by the consolations of the religion of his blest Saviour. The deceased leaves a large circle of kindred and devoted friends, who mourn their loss as his eternal gain.

Issue of Saturday May 4, 1861:

Death of An Aged Citizen - We regret to have to record the death of one of the oldest citizens of the District, Mr. LEONARD CAPEHART, who departed this life on Tuesday, the 23rd ult., being near one hundred years old. The deceased was a native of Virginia. He leaves a large family and numberous friends to weep over his departure.

Dead - Mr. JOHN CALVIN MC DANIEL, who, it will be recollected was severely wounded at the Regimental Muster last summer, by the accidental discharge of the cannon, breathed his last on Saturday, the 27th ult. He suffered much and long, but bore it with the courage and patriotism that becomes a soldier. He leaves many relations and friends to mourn his loss.

Issue of Saturday May 11, 1861:

Married - At Walhalla, on the 26th ultimo, by Rev. FLETCHER SMITH, Mr. A. FISCHESSER to Miss MENA GOTZ.

Issue of Saturday May 18, 1861:

Married - At Atlanta, Ga., on the 2d inst., by Rev. J. P. Payne, Mr.ELIAS HOLCOMBE, formerly of this District, to Miss FANNIE E., only daughter of S. CLEVELAND, Esq., of New Orleans.

Issue of Saturday May 25, 1861:

Married - On Thursday evening, the 16th May, inst., by Rev. C. MC KENDREE SMITH, Mr. WILLIAM STEGALL to Mrs. MARY ANN MONTGOMERY, all of Pickens.

Obituary - Departed this life, on the 3d inst., JOSEPH, son of SAMUEL and G. A. YOUNGBLOOD. The strong tie of affection has been suddenly and unexpectedly snapped. It is oftentimes cut loose by the cold hand of death. How precious and how dear to us are our lovely, innocent little ones. Sweet be their rest until the resurreciton morn, when they will be awakened in immortal youth to greet their kindred and all the sanctified in glory. G.

Tribute of Respect to G. N. FORTUNE, deceased, by members of the Piercetown Guards, 4th Regiment, S.C.V.

Issue of Saturday June 1, 1861:

Married - On the 28th April, by Rev. WM. REID, Mr. CALVIN H. STANCIL, to Miss NANCY ANN CHAPMAN, all of Pickens.

Married - On the 10th inst., at the residence of the bride's father, by Rev. D. MC NEIL TURNER, Mr. F. E. HARRISON, of Anderson, to Miss MARY PERRIN, of Abbeville.

Issue of Saturday June 8, 1861:

Fatal Shooting - In a difficulty at the Depot at Columbia, Tenn., a few days ago, W. C. REYNOLDS shot and killed his brother-in-law, WM. PORTER, and also killed, by accidental shot, Mr. BURGESS, a volunteer from Giles county. In the course of the unfortunate recontre Mr. Reynolds was wounded by a pistol shot in the shoulder, and severely beaten on the head with a stick. Reynolds has been arrested and will be brought to trial.

Married - On the 22d. ult., by L. N. ROBINS, Esq., Mr. W. O. DURHAM to Miss ARTAMISSA JAMES, all of Pickens.

Married - on the 2d June, by the same, Mr. JOHN STEWART to Miss SUSAN

STONE, all of Pickens.

Obituary - Departed this life on the 23rd ult., Mrs. SUSAN NICHOLSON, wife of EVAN J. NICHOLSON, aged 46 years. Mrs. Nicholson leaves a husband and five children, and a large circle of relatives and friends to mourn their irreparable loss; and in her death Mr. Nicholson loses a kind wife, her children an affectionate mother, and the settlement a pious neighbor, and a good example for the rising generation. H.B.

Issue of Saturday June 15, 1861:

Murder - We learn from the "Summerville (Ala.) Democrat" that JAMES EVANS was killed in Morgan county, Ala., on the 20th inst., with a fire-arm. "Circumstances pointed to L. D. EVANS as the man who did the killing."

Dreadful Accident - We learn from the "Pensacola Observer", of the 2d inst., that SAMUEL PETER MC KINLAY, a lad about fourteen years of age, was killed in that town by the accidental discharge of a gun in the hands of a soldier.

Married - On Thursday the 5th inst., by JOHN R. GOSSETT, Esq., Mr. JOHN S. THACKSTON, of Greenville, to Miss MARY, daughter of TILMAN and SARAH C. MILLER, of Pickens.

Married - On Sabbath morning, the 2d inst., by Rev. T. B. MAULDIN, Mr. W. M. V. A. TABOR, of Franklin county, Ga., to Miss NARCISSA P., daughter of EDMUND HERNDON, Esq., of Pickens.

Issue of Saturday June 22, 1861:

Married - On the 16th inst., by L. ROGERS, Esq., Mr. JOHN L. LITTLETON to Miss ELIZABETH H. MOODY, all of Pickens.

Married - On the 13th inst., by L. THOMAS, Esq., Mr. THOMAS DAVIS to Miss MARTHA, daughter of Mr. JOHN HUDSON, all of Pickens.

Issue of Saturday June 29, 1861:

Obituary - Died, at his residence in Pickens District, on the morning of the 13th inst., Mr. G. W. LIDDELL, in the 74th year of his age.

Issue of Saturday July 6, 1861:

Found Dead - MICHAEL FITZPATRICK, of this District, was found dead in his house on Sabbath last. An inquest was held over the body, A. ROBINS, Esq. acting as Magistrate. The verdict of the jury was, in substance, that deceased came to his death by the visitation of God. Fitzpatrick was an Irishman, had been a workman on the Blue Ridge Railroad, and has neither family or kindred in this section.

Married - By Rev. THOMAS LOOPER, on the 4th June last, Mr. DAVID FREEMAN to Mrs. ELVIRA FENDLY, all of Pickens.

Married - On the 26th June last by Rev. V. A. SHARP, Mr. D. A. DAVIS, of North Carolina, to Miss MARY MC CAY, of Pendleton.

Issue of Saturday July 13, 1861:

Homicide - We learn that on the 6th inst., at a place called FARR's Still House, in the lower part of this District, a rencounter occurred between GEORGE TRANUM and EDWARD NORRIS, in which Norris was stabbed and killed by Tranum. An inquest was held over the body of Norris by Magistrate JOHN R. GOSSETT, acting Coroner, the verdict of the jury being in accordance with the above statement. Tranum has been lodged in jail to await a judicial hearing of his case.

Obituary - Died, at his late residence, Kingston, Georgia, June 1st, 1861, Mr. LEONARD TOWERS, aged 59 years. The deceased lived long in this District, and was extensively known, and his many friends will receive the tidings of his death with much regret, and with sorrow for the loss of

his now desolate widow. But it will be a consolation to them to know
that he died not as one without hope, and that his death, though one of
sorrow to those whom he has left, is only a translation to him from a
world of sin and suffering to one of holiness and happiness. A few years
ago, of his own accord, and without any solicitation of others, he determined to make a public profession of religion, as he had long felt it his
duty to do, and attached himself, as a member, to the Bachelor's Retreat
Presbyterian Church. He did not claim to be without sins...as who can..
but he claimed to be a sinner, changed by the spirit, and relying upon
the grace of Christ, in faith and prayer, for pardon and salvation..In
this faith, during his protracted illness, he constantly expressed his
readiness to die, and his belief that he would be saved. With hope, he
looked forward calmly to his passage through the dark valley of the shadow of death. He was an enterpriseing citizen, an ardent friend, generous in his impulses, ready to help the distressed; and if his warm tem-
perment at any time led him to too hasty action, he was gradually led by
force of his better nature, to rectify his errors, and to make amends
for his faults. May He who has styled himself "the God of the widow",
prove himself such to her, who has been made a widow by this bereavement;
and let all the relatives and acquaintances of the deceased be wisely admonished by his death to be ever making ready for the same great change.
But travellers we are to another and never-ending abode, and as travellers should we conduct ourselves.

Issue of Saturday July 20, 1861:

Fatal Accident - We learn from the Greenville papers that, onthe night
of the 10th instant, a young man by the name of HENRY W. FULLENWIDER, of
Shelby, North Carolina, was thrown from his buggy and instantly killed.
He was on a visit to some friends in Greenville, and on the evening a-
bove named, while returning towards town, after having paid a visit, his
horse became frightened, made a sudden jump, and threw him out of his
buggy, causing immediate death.

Obituary - Died, July 4th, 1861, in the forty fifth year of her age, Mrs.
MARTHA DOYLE, wife of JAMES H. DOYLE. She retired to rest at night in
usual health, and before the sun rose again to greet thousands who were
living with the resplendent rays, her spirit had taken its flight to the
regions of immortality. She leaves a husband and ten children to mourn
their irraparable loss; but they should feel that is her eternal gain.
As a kind wife, mother, and mistress, I think she has left few equals...
no superiors. Her husband, who knew her best, loved her most. She has
been an exemplary member of the Presbyterian Church from early youth,
and we feel that we can offer no better tribute of respect to the memory of one possessed of so many amiable qualities, than to strive to im-
itate her many virtues and pious walk through life's perilous journey.
May we strive like her to meet the angel of death without a struggle.
M.S.D.

Tribute of Respect to JAMES W. MARTIN, who died at Leesburg, Va., on the
2d July, by the Piercetown Home Guard.

Issue of Saturday July 27, 1861:

Obituary - Departed this life, on the 3rd of June, 1861, Rev. LEWIS FEND-
LEY, in the 65th year of his age. The deceased left a kind and affectionate wife, a family of dear children and a large circle of friends to
mourn over their loss; but we believe that our loss is his eternal gain
whose life has been a pious and goodly life. He joined the Baptist
Church in early life, and commenced exercising a public gift soon after
he joined the church. He was ordained in or about the year 1840, and
was engaged in the faithful discharge of his calling until the grim monster, death, seized on his frame and laid his body low. E.F. (poetry)

Issue of Saturday September 23, 1865:

Married - At Fair Play, S. C., on the 7th of Sept., 1865, by Rev. H. M.
BARTON, Dr. JOHN N. DOYLE and Miss LOU W. STRIBLING, all of Pickens.

(Note: No issues available between 1861 to 1865...T.C.W.)

Killed - AENEAS HUNTER, a citizen of this District, was killed of Friday
night, the 6th instant. He was shot, we learn, by one or more persons.
Further particulars of this affair are unknown to us.

Married - On Sunday morning, 8th instant, at the house of the bride's
father, by L. N. ROBINS, Esq., Mr. CHARLES DURHAM, of Anderson, to Miss
MARY ANN DURHAM, of Pickens.

Issue of Saturday October 21, 1865:

Married - On the 23d ult., by Rev. FLETCHER SMITH, Mr. A. E. BROWN, of
Anderson, to Miss JULIA M. MILLER, of Pickens.

Married - On the 11th inst., by the same, Mr. SAMUEL MC CALL to Miss M.
E. TEAGUE, of Georgia.

Married - On the 12th inst., by the same, Mr. C. C. PERRY, formerly of
Colleton, to Miss MENA MC CALLIS, of Walhalla.

Married - On the 14th inst., by the same, Mr. HENRY DENNENBERGE to Mrs.
AUGUSTUS FAJEN, both of Walhalla.

Married - On the 6th inst., by the Rev. J. H. SULLIVAN, Mr. G. W. EATON
to Mrs. L. J. MC GUFFIN, both of Pickens.

Issue of Saturday October 28, 1865:

Married - On Sept. 6, 1865, by Rev. J. H. MC KINNEY, Mr. WM. WARREN MOSS
to Miss ARRETHA S. ROBERTSON, both of Pickens.

Married - On Sept. 12, 1865, by the same, Mr. JOHN F. BLASSINGAME, of
Ga., to Miss LENA E. MARET, of South Carolina.

Issue of Saturday November 11, 1865:

Married - On Thursday evening, the 6th Nov., 1865, at the residence of
the bride's father, in Pendleton, Mr. W. PINCKNEY LOWNDES to Miss ANNA,
youngest daughter of Judge FROST, both of Charleston, S. C.

Issue of Saturday November 25, 1865:

Married - On the 16th November, instant, at Bachelor's Retreat, Pickens
District, by Rev. WM. MC WHORTER, Mr. J. W. LESLEY, of Abbeville, to
Miss LOU J., eldest daughter of the officiating Minister.

State of South Carolina, Pickens. In Ordinary - Petition for Partition.
LEVI PHILLIPS and wife vs. JANE WHISENANT, et als. It appearing to my
satisfaction that the heirs-at-law of NICHOLAS WHISENANT, deceased;..
GEORGE WHISENANT: the heirs-at-law of ROBERT WHISENANT, deceased; FLEM-
ING BATES and wife POLLY: _____ DICKEY and wife SARAH: SALINA LILES, JE-
REMIAH JOHNS and wife REBECCA; defendants in this case, reside without
the limits of this State. Division or sale of the real estate of CHRIS-
TOPHER WHISENANT, deceased.

Obituary - Judge A. B. MEEK, of Alabama, a poet, politician, and noted
chess-player, died recently at Columbus, Miss.

Issue of Saturday December 2, 1865:

State of South Carolina, Pickens. In Ordinary - Petition for Partition.
GEORGE I. CHAPMAN vs. W. J. FENNEL & wife, et als. It appearing to my
satisfaction that BENJAMIN P. CHAPMAN and REBECCA SWORDS, defendants in
this case, reside without the limits of this State. Division or sale of
the real estate of SARAH CHAPMAN, deceased.

Issue of Saturday December 16, 1865:

Married - On Sunday evening 10th inst., by Rev. D. D. BYARS, at the residence of Mr. ABNER ODELL, Mr. W. G. FIELD to Miss MARTHA J., daughter of the late JACKSON MULLINNIX, all of Pickens.

Married - On the 10th inst., by Rev. J. H. C. MC KINNEY, Mr. MORGAN H. BRYCE to Miss M. A. MORGAN, all of Pickens.

Married - On the 7th inst., by Rev. HENRY H. PENNY, Mr. STEPHEN P. BARRON to Miss JOSEPHINE L. MC KINNEY, all of Pickens.

Married - On the 3d inst., by Rev. HENRY H. PENNY, Mr. FRANCIS H. CLEVE-LAND to Miss SUSAN F. DAVIS, all of Pickens.

Married - On the 2d ult., by Rev. FLETCHER SMITH, Mr. LOUIS H. BRANDT to Miss MATTIE C. KNEE, both of Walhalla.

Married on the 12th ult., by the same, Mr. J. C. P. J. MILLER to Miss E. C. E. HOLCOMBE, both of Pickens.

Married - On the 23d ult., by the same, Mr. EDWARD F. JOHNSTON to Miss MARY E. JENKINS, all of Pickens.

Married - On the 25th ult., by the same, Capt. J. F. TATHAM, of Macon, N. C., to Miss SALLIE A. FRANCIS, of Pickens.

Married - On the 26th ult., by the same, Mr. W. C. TATHAM, of Valley River, N. C. to Mrs. MARGARET A. BRAZEALE, of Pickens.

Issue of Saturday January 6, 1866:

Married - On the evening of the 14th ult., by Rev. J. R. HAMLIN, Mr. J. W. FENDLEY and Miss CARRIE, youngest daughter of Mr. MARTIN MOSS, all of Pickens District.

Issue of Saturday January 13, 1866:

Married - On the 24th ult. at the residence of Capt. L. ROGERS, by L. N. ROBINS, Esq., Mr. JOHN S. SLOAN and Miss AMANDA SNEAD, all of Pickens.

Issue of Saturday January 20, 1866:

Married - On the 4th inst., by Rev. Mr. GRADAY, Capt. JAMES T. REID and Miss CARRIE, eldest daughter of Mr. WM. H. STRIBLING, of Pickens district.

Issue of Saturday January 27, 1866:

Married - On the evening of the 18th inst., at the residence of the bride's mother, by Rev. J. R. HAMLIN, Mr. SILAS K. CANNON to Miss MARY M., second daughter of Mrs. WILLIAM BROCK, all of Pickens.

State of South Carolina, Pickens. In Ordinary - Petition for Partition. JOHN ROSS vs. JESSE R. ROSS & others. It appearing to my satisfaction that LUNSFORD M. ROSS, one of the defendants in this case, resides without the limits of this State. Division or sale of the real estate of GEORGE F. ROSS, Deceased.

Issue of Saturday February 17, 1866:

Married - On Thursday evening, the 8th inst., by L. N. ROBINS, Esq., Mr. J. C. PARROTT, to Miss LICENA E., eldest daughter of Mr. WATSON STEWART, all of Pickens.

Married - On the evening of the 1st inst., at the residence of the bride's father, by Rev. J. R. HAMLIN, Mr. D. W. CANTRELL, of N. C., to Miss MARY S., daughter of Mr. JAMES PORTER, of Pickens.

Married - By the same, on Sunday the 11th inst., at Antioch Church, Mr. JOSEPH CHAPMAN to Mrs. DARCUS ANN YOUNG, all of Pickens.

Married - On Feb. 1st, 1866, by Rev. N. SULLIVAN, Mr. ROLAND RIDER to Miss SARAH ANN PITTS, all of Pickens.

Married - On the 8th inst., by the Rev. Mr. SPEARS, Mr. W. B. WHITE to Miss SARAH, daughter of HENRY CRENSHAW, all of Pickens.

Notice - My wife, EMILY MOODY, has deserted my bed and board, without cause. This is to give notice to all concerned, that I will not be responsible for any contracts she may hereafter make, and I forwarn all persons not to trust her on my account. W. F. MOODY

Issue of Saturday March 10, 1866:

Married - On the 28th ult., by Rev. W. E. WALTERS, Col. JOSEPH N. BROWN and Miss LIZZIE L., only daughter of THOMAS BRUCE, both of Anderson District.

Issue of Saturday March 17, 1866:

Married - On the 11th inst., by Rev. J. R. HAMLIN, at the residence of the bride's father, Mr. DAVID WINCHESTER to Miss TABITHA ANN, daughter of Mr. WILLIAM CANTRELL, all of Pickens.

Married - On the 18th February by Rev. H. M. BARTON, Rev. JAMES SULLIVAN to Mrs. MARY WOODIN, all of Pickens.

Issue of Saturday March 24, 1866:

Death - We regret to learn that ELIJAH E. ALEXANDER, an esteemed citizen of this place, departed this life on Wednesday morning last. Consumption which has been preying on him for years, was the cause of his death.

Married - On the 18th inst., by Rev. Mr. WHORTER, Mr. C. KEELS MAXWELL to Miss MARY F., only daughter of Mrs. AMANDA SHELDON, all of Pickens.

Married - At the residence of Mr. W. A. CLYDE, March 7, 1866, by Rev.R. N. MAULDEN, Mr. O. CYRUS FOLGER to Miss L. CAMILLA BRAZEALE, both of Pickens.

Issue of Saturday April 7, 1866:

Homicide - We regret to learn that Col. THOS. MILLER, of Henderson county, N. C., was shot in the vicinity of Wolf Creek, in this District, on Monday evening last, as he was on his way to Walhalla. He lingered until Tuesday night, when he died of his wounds. We have not been able to learn the particulars of this unfortunate affair.

Married - On the 1st inst., by J. N. ARNOLD, Esq., Mr. JOHN MC DOW to Miss AMANDA BROCK, all of Pickens.

Issue of Saturday April 28, 1866:

Sentenced - We learn that F. G. STOWERS and JAMES CRAWFORD KEYS, charged with the murder of three Federal soldiers, at Brown's Ferry, were sentenced to be hung, at Castle Pinckney. _____KEYS and ELISHA BYRUM have been sentenced to the penitentiary, at New Hampton, Mass., for life.

Issue of Saturday May 12, 1866:

State of South Carolina, Pickens. In Equity - Bill for Partition, &c. WM. C. KEITH et als vs. MARY R. KEITH and others. It appearing to my satisfaction that BROADWELL W. KEITH, MARY KEITH, DRUCILLA KEITH, SUSANNAH KEITH, and two other minors, whose names are unknown, heirs at law of MARVILLE L. KEITH, deceased, late of the State of Kentucky, defendants in this case, reside without out the limits of this State.

Notice - My wife, JANE COLLINGS, having left my Bed and Board, without provocation, I hereby give notice to all persons not to trade with or trust her on my account, for I do not intend to pay any debts which she may contract. ELIJAH COLLINGS.

Issue of Saturday May 19, 1866: (next page)

State of South Carolina, Pickens. In Equity - Amended Bill for Construction of Will, Discovery, Acc't., Relief, &c.
ELIZABETH HESTER, by her next friend, vs. ELIZ'B'TH HESTER, Ex'trix.,et
als. It appearing to my satisfaction that MALINDA HESTER, STEPHEN C.
HESTER, LAURA A. HESTER and MARY E. HESTER, defendants in this case, reside without the limits of this State.

Issue of Saturday May 26, 1866:

Col. HERBERT HAMMOND, for many years Ordinary of Anderson District, died
on the 19th instant.

Issue of Saturday June 9, 1866:

Married - On the 10th ultimo, by Rev. B. S. GAINES, at the residence of
the bride's mother, Mr. EDWARD HOPKINS to Miss MARY S. MULLINNIX, all of
Pickens.

Married - At the same time and place, by the same, Mr. JOS. J. WERNER to
Miss MARY MC DOW.

Married - On the 25th ult., by Rev. C. H. SPEARS, Mr. JOHN H. MULKEY to
Miss SARAH F. ROCHESTER, all of Pickens.

Died, on Sunday evening the 20th ultimo, Mrs. REBECCA CHAPMAN, in the
eighty-seventh year of her age. The deceased lived to an advanced age.
It was truly affecting to witness the death-bed scene of this aged lady.
She has left the extensive train of connexion to mourn her loss, but they
do not mourn as some without hope. They hope that she has gone to a better world, where she is now chanting songs of praise. Weep not, dear
friends, but prepare to meet your mother in Heaven. J.G.B. (1 verse
poetry)

Issue of Saturday June 16, 1866:

State of South Carolina, Pickens. In Equity - Bill of Reviver for Relief, Partition, &c. ELIZABETH SANDERS vs. B. W. KEITH, et als. The defendants in this case, namely: BROADWELL W. KEITH, MARY KEITH, DRUCILLA
KEITH, SUSANNAH KEITH, and two other minor children, Heirs at law of
MARVILLE L. KEITH, deceased, reside without the limits of this State.

Issue of Saturday June 30, 1866;

Married - On Thursday evening the 21st June, inst., at the residence of
the bride's father, by L. N. ROBINS, Esq., Mr. JAMES B. GRANT to Miss
MARY WHITMIRE, all of Pickens.

Issue of Saturday July 14, 1866:

State of South Carolina, Pickens. In Ordinary - Petition to sell Real
Estate to pay debts. ROB'T. A. THOMPSON, Adm'r. vs. LUCINDA W. MARET,
et als. It appearing to my satisfaction that LUCINDA W. MARET, ELIAS J.
MARET, NANCY E. BRANNON, JAS. W. BRANNON, FREDERICK S. MARET, LUCY E.
BLASSINGAME, JOHN BLASSINGAME, JOHN W. MARET and JOANNA C. MARET, defendants in this case, reside without the limits of this State. (Real estate of BENJAMIN W. MARET, deceased.)

Issue of Saturday July 28, 1866:

Married - On the 27th ult., by JOHN SHARP, Esq., Mr. BEAUFORT R. WHITE
to Miss MARY E. GAILLARD, all of Pickens District.

Married - On the 19th inst., at Bieman's Hotel, by Rev. C. H. SPEARS,Mr.
JOHN H. KIRKOFF to Miss FRANCES LAIDY, all of Pickens.

Issue of Saturday August 4, 1866:

Death of Mr. CAREY - We regret to announce the death of our friend and
neighbor, Mr. JOHN W. L. CAREY. This sad event occurred on Monday morning last, after a protracted illness of great suffering. Disease had been

preying on him for years. Mr. Carey was wellknown to our readers. He had
been Tax Collector for the District for a long term of years, and had
discharged the duties for that office to the satisfaction of the State
and a very large majority of his fellow citizens. As a lesson to the
youth of the country, nothing can be more convincing or interesting than
to state that Mr. Carey rose from obscurity to a position of prime usefulness in the community by his own industry, energy and indefatigable
exertion. He was buried by the Masonic fraternity.

Issue of Saturday August 11, 1866:

The Anderson Prisoners - Some days ago we extracted from the "Charleston
Courier" a statement that the prisioners, Messrs. STOWERS, J. C. and
ROBERT KEYES and BYREM, had been removed from Castle Pinckney, and men-
tioned that we had reason to believe that they were sentenced to be con-
fined in the Dry Tortugas for life. The following official orders con-
firm our statement:
War Department, Adjutant General's Office, Washington City, July 23, 1866
Ordered, that the sentences to be hanged, in the case of FRANCIS GAINES
STOWERS, JAMES C. KEYES, ROBERT KEYES and ELISHA BYREM, citizens of Georgia and South Carolina, be committed for life at the Tortugas.
Maj. Gen. SICKLES, United States Volunteers, commanding the Department
of the Carolinas, will cause the above-named prisoners to be transported
to the Tortugas, and turned over to the commanding officer there, who
will carry this order into effect. By order of the President.
                              (Signed) E. D. TOWNSEND
                                       A. A. General

Married - On Thursday evening, the 2d Aug. inst., by L. N. ROBINS, Esq.,
Mr. WILLIAM BILLINGSLY, of Rabun, Ga., to Miss AMANDA, youngest daughter
of PRIER ALEXANDER, Esq., of Pickens.

Issue of Saturday August 18, 1866:

Married - On the 2d inst., by Rev. WILLIS W. ABBOTT, Mr. WILLIAM ADDIS
to Miss SARAH SANDERS, all of Pickens.

Issue of Saturday September 1, 1866:

Removing to Texas - Among the emigrants from our District, to the West,
we part with our esteemed fellow-citizen, Mr. DAVID S. STRIBLING, of
Fair Play, with sincere regret. He will carry with him, to his new home
in the "far West", the best wishes of his numerous friends in the "old
land", for his future prosperity and happiness.

Explanation - Editor "Keowee Courier" ...Dear Sir: I notice in the last
number of your paper that certain property of T. A. MINTON is advertised
by the Sheriff to be sold at the suit of the undersigned. This is a mistake. I have no claim whatever against Minton. He never owed me a cent
in his life, and probably never will. His property is to be sold at the
suit of his mother-in-law, Mrs. PEGGY BALDWIN, under a decree from the
Court of Equity in her favor, for costs. The only connection I have with
the matter is that I am one of the Lawyers who conducted the suit and obtained the Decree successfully for Mrs. Baldwin. The mistake is a slight
one, in the nature, I presume, of a clerical error, still I think it proper to correct it, and beg that you will publish this with that view.
Respectfully, your ob't. servant. J. M. ADAMS

Issue of Saturday September 8, 1866:

Married - On the 16th August, 1866, by Rev. J. H. C. MC KINNEY, Mr. SAM-
UEL LILES to Miss LOUISA BROWN, both of Pickens.

Issue of Saturday September 15, 1866:

State of South Carolina, Pickens. In Ordinary - Summons in Partition.
MARY J. BLACK, JESSE R. BLACK and NANCY E. BLACK, minors; by their next
friend, JOHN R. BLACK, applicants, vs. WM. MC CRACKIN and SARAH MC CRAC-
KIN, defendants. It appearing to my satisfaction that WILLIAM MC CRACK-
IN and SARAH MC CRACKIN, defendants in this case, reside without the lim-

its of this State. Division or sale of the real estate of WILLIAM G.
BLACK, deceased.

Issue of Saturday September 22, 1866:

Married - On Saturday the 4th ult., at Oakway, by J. B. SANDERS, Esq.,
Mr. JAMES WALDRUPE, of Union District, to Miss MARY CAMPBELL, of Pickens.

State of South Carolina, Pickens. In Ordinary - Petition for final settlement. I. T. BARRON, Adm'r, vs. THOS. BARRON and others. It appearing to my satisfaction that JOHN JONES and wife NANCY, the heirs of HEN-
RY BARRON, deceased, THOMAS BARRON, JOHN BARRON and wife MARY, defendants
in this case, reside without the limits of this State. Final settlement
of the estate of SAMUEL BARRON, deceased.

Issue of September 29, 1866:

Married - On Sunday evening the 23d inst., at Pickens C. H., by J. E. HA-
GOOD, Mr. WM. D. CASSAWAY to Miss ANNA, daughter of Rev. B. S. GAINES, of
Pickens.

Married - at Oakway, on Sunday evening 6th inst., by J. B. SANDERS, Esq.,
Mr. JAMES JOHNSON to Mrs. CAROLINE CHASTAIN, both of Anderson district.

Tribute to a Dead Friend - Miss LORTIE M. CHERRY, the dearest and most
angelic creature, has been removed by the hands of Providence to adorn
the celestial regions above. Her virtues did plead like Angels trumphet
tongued, for all the merits and praises of this world, but she was such
a symbol of innocence and purity that she could no longer claim her
birthright in this transitory career of life. She was the bud of life
that had just blossomed, and was blooming in the hearts and mansion of
her parents...affording the balm of comfort and joy to their old age,and
exhibiting a sweetness and loveliness to all the virtues of love and
pleasure that did surround her golden throne of beauty and happiness,and
shining as one of the brightest ornaments of society from her piety and
moral influence, and commanding the respect and love of all her community. Though nursed in ease and luxury by a kind and doting father, she
always preserved an equanimity of temper and spirit, and lent a grace
and charm to his household. He can now have the sweet recompense in
death of knowing that he was amply compensated, and the great solace that
he has accomplished one of the noblest works of nature, in rearing a
daughter of such truth and simplicity, that she never merited a single
rebuke, or caused him a regret or mortification. May this beautiful and
lovely gem of life, that has left her faith on earth strewn of flowers,
in losing her crown here, have gained one of eternal glory and salvation
in heaven; and may she be wet with the dews of our remembrance each
morning, so that she may be embalmed in the hearts and memory of all her
loving friends. "Friend" (1 verse poetry)

Issue of Saturday October 6, 1866:

Married - At the residence of the bride's father, in this village, on
Thursday evening the 27th ult., by Rev. S. S. GAILLARD, Dr. THOMAS A.
EVINS, of Anderson, to Miss ELIZA E., eldest daughter of W. E. HOLCOMBE,
Esq.

Married - On the 30th ultimo, by Rev. T. B. MAULDIN, Mr. WM. CRENSHAW to
Miss CELIA DUNLAP, all of Pickens.

Married - At the residence of Mr. ABRAHAM TAYLOR, on the 27th ult., by
D. P. ROBINS, Esq., Mr. ANDREW J. M. BILLINGSLY to Miss SUSAN M. TAYLOR,
all of Pickens.

Issue of Saturday October 13, 1866:

We regret to learn that on the night of the 5th inst., Cato, a freedman,
shot and killed JOS. WILLIAMS, of Anderson district. The occurrence
took place, near Salubrity, in this district. The freedman has been arrested, is now in jail, and will, we presume, be tried next week.

Died - MATTHEW SKATES, a Revolutionary soldier aged 108, died near Cowpens battleground, in Spartanburg District, on the 29th August last.

Issue of Saturday October 20, 1866:

Married - On the evening of the 4th inst., at the residence of the brides
father, by Elder J. R. HAMLIN, Mr. J. W. KING to Miss LIZZIE ANN, youngest daughter of JOHN SMITH, Esq., all of Pickens.

Married - On the 14th inst., by Rev. JOHN WEST, Mr. MADISON TAYLOR to
Miss JOSEPHENE FRETWELL, all of Pickens.

Issue of Saturday October 27, 1866:

Another Man Killed - The body of a desperate man, by the name of JOHN HIX,
was found dead in the eastern part of this District, on the 24th inst.
Sometime ago a warrant was issued against Hix for highway robbery. The
Constable, in attempting to arrest him, was fallen upon by Hix, and severely injured. Hix had been dead for some days, and without doubt, met
with a violent death.

Issue of Saturday November 10, 1866:

Married - On the 4th inst., by J. C. C. PARSONS, Esq., Mr. M. T. SMITH
to Miss ELIZA CHAPMAN, all of Pickens.

Tribute of Respect to John M. Moody, deceased, by Keowee Lodge No. 79,
A.F.M.

Issue of Saturday November 17, 1866:

Married - On the 21st ult. by J. N. ARNOLD, Esq., Mr. JAMES P. HOPKINS
to Miss MARTHA REAMS, all of Pickens.

Issue of Saturday November 24, 1866:

Married - At the residence of the bride's mother, on the 11th inst., by
Rev. J. L. KENNEDY, Mr. SAMUEL D. STEWART to Miss E. C. TEMPLETON, all
of Pickens.

Issue of Saturday December 8, 1866:

Obituary - Died, on the 16th of November, 1866, in the 28th year of her
age, Mrs. ELIZA J. STEELE, wife of ROBERT E. STEELE, and daughter of the
late Dr. J. M. MC ELROY. She had been long a child of bodily affliction.
For several years she suffered, and latterly, for nearly two-thirds of
a year, without intermission, she laid upon a bed of languishing and pain,
until her body became too emaciated for life to continue. She was lit-
erally consumed away by a long and slow process of disease. No one could
know her situation but to sorrow with her. But it has never been our
happy lot to witness or to read of a greater triumph of faith over suffering and temptation. We sometimes could not but lose our sorrow for
her bodily sufferings, in our joy for her peace of soul and happiness in
God. She had a clear and joyous view of the way of salvation by Christ
Jesus. She felt assured that she had that good part, which Mary had,and
which could not be taken from her. We saw her often; and never saw her
when, though sighing with pain, she did not express herself as feeling
the comforts of the Saviour's presence. Sometimes her cup of joy was
full to overflowing, and her soul would rise to ecstaries. In her full-
ness,she longed for others to drink of the same cup, exhorting them to
let go the pleasures of the world, to take hold of the pleasures of Christ
assuring them that they cannot enjoy the world and God together, or find
the pleasures of salvation without much faith and prayer. She had evidently learned from her own experience that God takes away the pleasures of
life, that those thus afflicted might by faith and prayer, secure the
heavenly and infinitely superior. Her whole heart was upon heaven. The
future world seemed so glorious to her that she lost the fear of death.
She spake of it, as though she were but going a journey, giving in calmness the minutest details respecting her burial. Dying to her, was, what
it should be to all christians, but going home to her Father's house,

where she would be with Jesus, released from all sin and suffering.
W.F.G. (2 verses poetry)

Departed this life, near Bachelor's Retreat, in this District, on the
10th November last, Miss HARRIET MAHALA WARD, aged 19 years. She was
pious and religious. She joined the Baptist Church at an early age,and
proved to all that religion can adorn the youthful character as well as
the advanced in years; and it will never be known until the day of final
reckoning, how productive of good was her influence over the young with
whom she associated. Lovely in person, unostentatious in manners, and
having those qualities embellished with the beauties of religion, she
endeared herself to all who were favored with much of her company, so
that, after her death, a common expression by her companions, was, "We
loved her so much". But fever had marked her as its victim. She was
confined for four weeks to her room, wasting by degrees, under its bligh-
ting touch. But in all her suffering, she was never heard to murmur or
utter a complaint; the nearer she advanced to the grave the stronger became her faith in the Lord and Saviour, Jesus Christ. Thus passed away
from earth, in early bloom, a beautiful flower...Faith says, to bloom
forever in the happy land. She leaves many friends...for all who knew
her loved her...to mourn her absence. But they know she sleeps in Jesus.
W.G.L. (poetry)

Issue of Saturday December 15, 1866:

Married - On the 6th inst., by Rev. W. P. GREADY, Mr. THOS. H. DENDY to
Miss LUCY A. TERRELL, all of Pickens.

Married - On the 5th inst., by Rev. A. W. MC CUFFIN, Mr. M. ALLEN TERRELL
to Miss S. C. BURNS, all of Pickens.

Married - On the 29th ult., by Rev. FLETCHER SMITH, Mr. EDMUND D. FOSTER
to Miss MARY S. BREWER, all of Pickens.

Married - On the 4th inst., by J. N. ARNOLD, Esq., Capt. F. L. GARVIN of
Co. I, Palmetto Sharpshooters to Miss ETTA, daughter of Mr. AARON BOGGS,
SR., all of Pickens.

State of South Carolina, Pickens. In Ordinary - Petition for Partition.
MATTHEW MANSELL and wife MARY, Applicants vs. SARAH HUGHES and others,
defendants. It appearing to my satisfaction that JAMES MAULDIN, the
heirs-at-law of JOAB MAULDIN, dec'd. (names and number unknown), the
heirs-at-law of ELIZABETH MC CLANAHAN, deceased (names and number unknown), defendants in this case, reside beyond the limits of this State.
Division or sale of the real estate of GODFREY MAULDIN, deceased.

State of South Carolina, Pickens. In Ordinary - Petition for sale of
land for payment of Debts. MALINDA ARCHER, Adm'x. vs. S. N. WILLIAMS and
wife, and others. It appearing to my satisfaction that the heirs-at-law
of VAN ARCHER, deceased (names and number unknown) and the heirs at law
of ANDREW H. ARCHER, deceased (names and number unknown), defendants in
this case, reside without the limits of this State. Division or sale of
the real estate of JOHN E. ARCHER, deceased.

State of South Carolina, Pickens. In Ordinary - Petition for final settlement of the Estate of JOSEPH C. BOGGS, deceased. SAMUEL A. GARY,JAMES
L. BOGGS, Adm'rs. vs. SARAH BOGGS and others. It appearing to my satisfaction that ANDREW BOGGS, Heirs-at-law of NANCY ALEXANDER, dec'd.(names
and number unknown), Heirs-at-law of JOSIAH BOGGS, deceased, (names and
number unknown), defendants in this case, reside without the limits of
this State.

Issue of Saturday December 22, 1866:

Married - On the 13th inst., by Rev. J. R. HAMLIN, Mr. J. B. COLLY to
Miss ELIZABETH SARGENT, all of Pickens.

Terrible Affray - All Parties Killed - A terrible affray occurred on
Tuesday at Sweetwater, Tennessee. Capt. JACKSON, of Marietta, Georgia,
while on business in Sweetwater, was attacked by two men named MC GANGHEY

of Athens, Tennessee, and a third man, name unknown. Pistols were used
by all the men, and Capt. Jackson was mortally wounded. Before falling,
he succeeded in killing one of the McGangheys, and mortally wounding the
other two men. The quarrel grew out of the killing of the father of the
McGanghey's in Athens, Tennessee, in December, 1864, by a raiding party
of bushwhackers, with whom Jackson was supposed to have been connected.

Issue of Saturday January 19, 1867:

State of South Carolina, Pickens. In Ordinary - Petition for sale of
real estate to pay debts. M. F. MITCHELL, Adm'r. vs. JESSE RICKMAN and
wife SARAH, formerly SARAH THRIFT) and others. It appearing to my satisfaction that Jesse Rickman and Sarah, his wife, formerly Sarah Thrift,
defendants in this case, reside without the limits of this State. Sale
of the real estate of J. W. THRIFT, deceased.

Married On Horseback - A Western paper publishes the following marriage
notice: On horse-back, November 18, 1866, by GEO. KINKADE, Mr. WM. BUN-
YARD, late a soldier of Merrill's Horse, and Miss MARTHA E. PRICE, all
of Harrison county, Missouri.

Issue of Saturday January 26, 1867:

Mr. L. A. OSBORNE, a highly respected Christian gentleman, died suddenly
of over exertion and exposure, at the residence of WM. HUNTER, Esq., at
Walhalla, on Saturday night the 10th instant.

Married - At St. Paul's church, Richmond, Va., on the 10th inst., by Rev.
Dr. MINNEGRODE, Mr. AUGUSTUS VAN WYCK, of South Carolina, and Miss LEILA
G., daughter of the late Dr. WM. W. WILKINS, of Virginia.

Married - On the morning of the 13th inst., by Rev. J. R. HAMLIN, at the
residence of the bride's mother, Mr. J. M. WINCHESTER to Miss MARY A.
HOWARD, all of Pickens.

Married - On the evening of the 19th inst., by the same, at the residence
of the bride's father, Mr. ARTHUR R. KNOX to Miss SALLIE L., second daughter of Mr. JOHN WHITMIRE, all of Pickens.

Married - On the 15th inst., by E. P. VERNER, Esq., Mr. J. W. CARTER, of
Chester, to Miss E. E. HAWTHORNE, of Pickens.

Married - On the evening of the 17th inst., at the residence of the
bride's father, by L. N. ROBINS, Esq., Mr. ROBERT STEWART to Miss CANBA,
daughter of Mr. E. M. ALEXANDER, all of Pickens.

Married - On the 9th inst., by Rev. J. H. SULLIVAN, Mr. JAMES HOLLEY to
Miss MARTHA A. BROOKS, all of Pickens.

Married - On the evening of the 10th inst., by the same, Mr. THOS. WILEY
to Miss MOLLIE HOLLEY, all of Pickens.

Married - On the 15th inst., on Cane Creek, by Rev. FLETCHER SMITH, Mr.
SILAS H. BROCK, of Lowndesville, to Miss ELIZA J. JOHNSTON, of Pickens.

Issue of Saturday February 9, 1867:

Married - On the 17th ult., by Rev. B. S. GAINES, at the residence of
the bride's father, Mr. MARCUS SANDERS, of Yorkville, to Miss ARABELLA
C., daughter of THOMAS L. ALLEN, Esq., of Pickens.

Married - On the 24th ult., by Rev. W. B. SINGLETON, at the residence of
Mrs. ANNA HAWTHORNE, Mr. L. R. DURHAM to Miss SALLIE A., eldest daughter
of J. N. HAWTHORNE, deceased.

Issue of Saturday February 16, 1867:

Mr. B. F. SLOAN, SR., a highly respected citizen of Pendleton...died, at
his residence in that place, on the 2d inst., at the advanced age of seventy two years. Mr. Sloan was a public spirited citizen, and, in the

discharge of his duty in the varied walks of life, was actuated by pure motives and a high sense of honor.

Married - On Tuesday evening 5th inst., by Rev. W. E. WALTERS, Mr. WILLIAM N. WHITE, of Pickens District, to Miss BELLE MC CLURE, of Anderson District.

Married - On Thursday 20th September last, by Rev. WILLIS W. ABBOTT, Mr. ELAM HEMBREE to Miss MARTHA J. SANDERS, all of Pickens District.

Married - On Thursday, 2nd November last, by the same at the residence of the bride's mother, Mr. NEWTON MITCHELL, of Abbeville, to Miss MARTHA, daughter of Mrs. HANNAH SANDERS, of Pickens District.

Married - On 5th November last, by the same, at the residence of the bride's mother, Mr. WILLIAM DAVIS to Miss ANNA PATTERSON, all of Pickens District.

Married - On 23rd December last, by the same, at the residence of the bride's father, Mr. J. B. BOYD to Miss LUCY MC DONALD, all of Pickens district.

Married - On 13th January, 1867, by the same, Mr. BALUS FREDERICKS to Miss HARRIET MC KAY.

Issue of Saturday February 23, 1867:

Married - On Thursday the 14th inst., by Rev. FLETCHER SMITH, Mr. WILLIAM A. LOWERY to Miss MARY E. HARBIN, all of Pickens.

State of South Carolina, Pickens. In Ordinary - Petition for Partition. JAMES M. CANNON vs. MARTHA GARRETT and others, JAMES H. REEDER vs. MARTHA GARRETT and others. It appearing to my satisfaction that FRASIER MC CARTY and MILTON GARRETT, defendants in the above case, reside beyond the limits of the State. Division or sale of the real estate of STEPHEN GARRETT, deceased.

Issue of Saturday March 2, 1867:

Married - On Sunday evening, 24th ult., by Rev. FLETCHER SMITH, Mr. JOHN N. GEORGE to Miss SARAH MOODY, all of Pickens.

Married - On Tuesday evening, the 26th ult, by the same, at the residence of the bride's father, Mr. A. R. MARTIN, of Greenville, to Miss SALLIE E. FOSTER, of Pickens.

Married - On the 22d ult., at Cedar Bower, by D. GRICE, N. P., Mr. JAMES WOOD, of Anderson, to Mrs. NANCY MAULDIN, of Pickens.

Mr. ISAAC ANDERSON, an aged and highly respected citizen of Pickens,died at his residence, on Eastatoee, on the 17th ultimo. He was in his 87th year.

Issue of Saturday March 23, 1867:

Married - On the 14th February last, by Rev. C. H. SPEARS, CHARLES D.HILL, Esq., of N. C., to Miss MARY J. CRENSHAW, of Walhalla, S. C.

Married - On the 23rd of February last, by the same, Col. C. P. BRYSON, of Jackson county, N. C., to Mrs. ELVIRA S. JOHNSON, of Pickens.

Obituary - Departed this life, Feb. 13th, 1867, near Pickensville, in this District, ARTA OMEGA ODELL, infant daughter (and only child during nearly 18 years of wedlock) of ABNER and MARY S. ODELL. The subject of this notice was born April 8th, 1866, aged ten months and five days. Her disease was Diptheria; a disease known to be very fatal amongst children. Medical aid was called, but no cure effected. Her disease preyed upon her vitals with such rapidity, that it soon became too intolerable for her infant physical strength and constitution to bear; she becoming exhausted, sank into the paleness and silence of death. Then did she pass through the valley and shadow of death, which dreadful ordeal we have all, ere long, to pass through. That beautiful and lovely form, but a few days previous in health, clothed with beauty, innocence and intelligence ...now lying pale and silent, but not yet cold, in death. That object upon which was centered the future hopes and affections of the doting parents, gone. Now imagine their affliction and their bereavement; how great, how great! I heard them say: Our babe, our only child, is gone, forever gone...nevermore to return. The writer was present during most of her sickness, and can say of a truth, that she was perfectly calm and submissive, and exhibited a degree of knowledge rarely possessed by infants. She was truly a remarkable child for beauty and intellect...was perfectly amiable to all her infant dispositions. Arta is gone beyond the shores of time, and the Pa and Ma are left with tears of grief gushing forth from their eyes; their bosoms almost convulsing with emotion. But, affected and bereaved parents, grieve not, but submit and be thou comforted from the thought of Arta's angelic form being beyond the reach of death, in a state of perfect bliss and happiness; in the immediate presence of her Maker and Redeemer, with all the beauties of Heaven before her eyes, and with the care, attention and company of the Heavenly forever hers. Then, dear parents, be thou comforted from this sublime thought, and from the hope you have of meeting her there. W.G.F. (2 verses poetry)

Issue of Saturday March 30, 1867:

Death of Col. TAYLOR - Col. DAVID S. TAYLOR, an estimable citizen of Pendleton, died suddenly of apoplexy, in that village last week. Col. Taylor, some years since, represented Pendleton District in the Legislature. Both as a citizen and a representative, he obtained the good will of his neighbors and friends through a long period of years. Truly, "in the midst of life we are in death". We drop a tear to his memory.

Obituary - Man is Mortal, and death is the destiny of all that breathe; but when one of more than ordinary character is taken from us, we feel bound to pay more than ordinary respect to their memory. And such was our esteemed citizen and brother, ISAAC ANDERSON, who departed this life on the 17th day of February, 1867, inthe 87th year of his age. The subject of this notice was born in the State of Virginia, in 1780. He moved to this country when quite young. He was one of the first settlers of Big Eastatoe. He settled on this mountain stream over fifty years ago, when it was destitute of roads, mills, schoolhouses or any other improvement whatsoever. He was a pattern of industry. When he settled in this waste, he would work hard all day then build a pine knot fire at night, and grub around it. By his industry and economy he settled the majority of eleven children on the waters of Eastatoe, on good farms.He then was more than ordinary in point of industry. He was a model of true honesty; he lost hundreds of dollars by believing that all men were like him...honest. He was more than ordinary in his kindness to the poor; he made it a point to never turn off the poor empty, especially the widow or orphan. Those who had money might come and buy but it seemed to be more real pleasure to him to accommodate those that had no money. And I would to God that more of our citizens (especially our brethren) had this kind of heart. When upon his death bed, to those of his children that were around him, he said: "Children be good to the poor. I have taught it to you. You know its right; for see, the Lord has always blessed me with plenty." So mote it be. Brother Anderson was not a man of reading; he gave no portion of his mind to politics, or the topics of the day. His motto was: "Plow deep while sluggards sleep". His manner of life was plain and frugal. The visible fruits bespeak piety, but he never made a public profession of religion until September, 1866, when he attached himself to the Baptist Church at Antioch. Then and there he led a procession of thirty-one willing converts into the baptismal fount; and eight of that number his own family, children and grand children. But after speaking of all the good traits of character which were embodied in him whose merits we are rehearsing, now rushes the solomn thought that he is DEAD; and his body lies on the slope of a hill near the old homestead, overlooking the bright waters of Eastatoe, on the banks of which the victim of death spent fifty years of his life. That sleeping body is now waiting the resurrection of the dead, when a re-union will take place; then he will join in aspirations of praise for redeeming

Grace and dying love. And may we all break forth in the language of
Balaam: Let me die the death of the righteous, and let my last end be
like his. J.R.H. (1 verse poetry)

Issue of Saturday April 6, 1867:

Married - On the 31st March last, by W. B. WHITE, Esq., Mr. LEMUEL K.
PITTS to Mrs. NANCY S. BROOM, all of Pickens.

Married - On Sunday, the 4th of November, 1866, at Bethelehem Church, by
Rev. H. N. HAYS, Mr. FRANKLIN DUNCAN to Miss CYNTHIA M. HOOPER, all of
Pickens.

Married - On the 28th November, by the same, at Tunnel Hill, S. C., at
the residence of the bride's father, Mr. WM. T. ROCHESTER to Miss ELIZ-
ABETH VISAGE.

Married - On Sunday, the 17th ult., by the same, at the residence of Mr.
JAMES L. HAYS, Mr. T. DICKENS FRACHEUR to Mrs. LUCINDA WALDEN, all of
Pickens.

Issue of Saturday April 13, 1867:

Married - On the 7th inst., by J. N. ARNOLD, Esq., Mr. JOHN S. HOPKINS
to Miss MARTHA E. DODD, all of Pickens.

Issue of Saturday April 27, 1867:

Death of an Aged Minister - A good man in Israel has fallen! BARNET
SMITH, who, as a minister of the gospel, has labored faithfully for the
church for more than fifty years, has been gathered, ripe as the richest
fruit of autumn, to the arms of his heavenly father. As a citizen, as
a minister, as a friend, he is mourned by the rich, the poor, the high,
the low!

Issue of Saturday May 4, 1867:

Married - At the residence of the bride's father, on Tuesday, April 23d,
1867, by the Rev. A. RICE, Rev. WM. E. WALTERS, Editor of the "South
Carolina Baptist", and Miss ANNA M. MILLFORD, eldest daughter of Dr. W.
J. MILLFORD, both of Anderson District.

Issue of Saturday May 18, 1867:

Dr. M. B. EARLE, eminent as a physician, died at his residence, in the
town of Greenville, on the 3d instant, aged fifty-three years.

State of South Carolina, Pickens. In Equity - Bill for Partition, Relief, &c. EZEKIEL KELLEY et als vs. ELIZA RANKIN, et als. The complainants having filed their bill, in this case, and it appearing to my satisfaction that the heirs at law of SURRY EATON, whose names, numbers and
residence are unknown, WILLIAM CURTIS; heirs at law of NAMAAN CURTIS
whose names and number are unknown; JOSEPH DONALDSON, JOHN DONALDSON;
JERRY YORK and wife PEGGY YORK, _____ LANGSTON and wife BETSEY LANGSTON;
RICHARD TURNER and wife SALLY TURNER; SURRY KELLY and TARLTON KELLY;
SARAH CALHOUN, widow of WARREN; heirs at law of SUSAN BEATTY, names, number and residence unknown; defendants in this case, reside without the
limits of this State.

Issue of Saturday May 25, 1867:

Married - On the 14th inst., at the residence of the bride's father, on
Tugalo, by Rev. J. B. HILLHOUSE, Lieut. WILLIAM STEELE, of Etowa, Ga.,
and Miss N. R. SHELOR, of Pickens.

Death of WM. D. SLOAN - Wm. D. Sloan, Esq., a native of Pickens district,
died, in Pontotoc county, Miss., on the 10th of March, 1867, at the advanced age of sixty years. Mr. Sloan was the first Sheriff of Pickens
district, and emigrated to Mississippi in 1836. He leaves many friends,

with a very large family connexion, to mourn their sad bereavement.

Issue of Saturday June 1, 1867:

Married - On Sunday evening, the 26th ult., by Rev. B. S. GAINES, at the residence of the bride's father, Mr. SAMUEL PROYOR, of North Carolina, to Miss SARAH ANN YOUNGBLOOD, of Pickens.

Death of Col. Elford - We record with sorrow the death of Col. CHARLES J. ELFORD, of Greenville, which sad event occurred at his residence, in that town, on Saturday last. Col. Elford was an eminently useful citizen, in the various walks of life, and his untimely demise will be mourned by many throughout the limits of the State. At some future time we hope to be able to do full justice to his memory.

Issue of Saturday June 8, 1867:

Married - On the evening of the 20th ult., by Rev. FLETCHER SMITH, at the residence of the bride's father, Mr. E. H. CLEVELAND to Miss MILLA M., daughter of RANSOM HUNT, both of Pickens.

State of South Carolina, Pickens. In Equity - Bill for Partition, &c. J. V. JONES vs. J. E. JONES and others. It appearing to my satisfaction that STEPHEN A. JONES, JAMES B. JONES, JOHN C. ELSTON and wife SALINA ELSTON, JOHN N. SLOAN, THEODORE B. SLOAN, WILLIAM D. SLOAN and CLARK D. PERRY, defendants in this case, who reside without the limits of this State.

Issue of Saturday June 15, 1867:

Married - On the 5th inst., by Rev. W. P. GRADY, at the residence of her father, in Pendleton, Miss VIRGINIA E. HUNTER to Mr. J. C. STRIBLING of Pickens district.

Issue of Saturday June 29, 1867:

Poisoned - We regret to learn that a little daughter of Mr. JESSE JENKINS, of this District, caused her own death last week by innocently using strychnine, which had been purchased by the father, and left where it could be had by the child.

Issue of Saturday July 6, 1867:

Married - On the evening of the 25th ult., at the residence of the brides father, in Abbeville District, by the Rev. WM. F. PEARSON, Dr. JAS. M. SLOAN, of this place, to Miss SALLIE J. LYNCH.

Issue of Saturday August 3, 1867:

Married - On Sunday evening, the 28th ult., at the residence of W. H. BURDITT, by J. R. SANDERS, Esq., Mr. WM. G. LEATHERS to Miss SUSAN C. BURDITT, all of Pickens.

Died - On the 23d day of July last, HENRY G., only child of Mrs. _____ and G. Mc.D. THOMPSON, aged fifteen months and twenty five days.

Issue of Saturday October 5, 1867:

Married - On the 1st inst., by Judge WICKLIFFE, Mr. JAMES A. BELL to Miss MATTIE TODD, all of Pickens.

Issue of Saturday October 12, 1867:

Obituary - Died, May 9th, 1867, Mrs. DELILAH FURGUSON, aged sixty one years. The deceased had been an exemplary member of the Baptist Church many years. She was sorely afflicted near three years, during which time she bore her sufferings with christian fortitude, perfectly resigned to the will of Him who doeth all things well. When interrogated a short time previous to her death as to what she wanted, she replied

emphatically: "Nothing but to go home to Jesus"; and calling her family
to her bedside she bade them an affectionate adieu, exhorting them to
meet her in Heaven, and peacefully expired. In compliance with her previous request, her funeral was preached by the Rev. JOHN ARIAIL, on May
the 10th, at Cross Roads Church. Whilst feelings of humanity prompt us
to sympathize deeply with the bereaved family of the deceased, we think
it the duty of all to not indulge immoderate grief o'er the death of one
who has exchanged a world of sorrow for one of ineffable bliss. F.
(3 verses poetry)

Issue of Saturday October 26, 1867:

Married - On Tuesday evening, the 8th inst., by L. N. ROBINS, Esq., Mr.
JOHN DURHAM to Miss JANE COTHRAN, all of Pickens.

Married - On Thursday evening, 17th inst., by the same, Mr. HIRAM ALEX-
ANDER to Miss ELIZABETH CRENSHAW, both of Pickens.

Issue of Saturday November 2, 1867:

Married - On the 30th ultimo, by J. E. HAGOOD, Esq., Mr. WM. E. BOYD to
Miss MARY NEAL, both of Pickens.

Issue of Saturday November 9, 1867:

Married - On the 31st ultimo, by Rev. FLETCHER SMITH, Mr. W. J. HUGHES
to Miss NANCY J. MYERS, both of this District.

Married - On the 3rd inst., by Judge WICKLIFFE, Mr. JESSE MULKEY to Mrs.
MARY PIERCE, all of Pickens.

Issue of Saturday November 16, 1867:

Death of SAMUEL C. REEDER - We are pained to learn that Samuel C. Reeder,
one of our best citizens, died at his residence in this District, on
the 26th ultimo. Unassuming in his manners, he was firm and determined
in adhering to right; and spent much of his time and substance, during
his declining years, in ameliorating the condition of the unfortunate.
Advance in years, he was overwhelmed by the misfortunes of his country,
and the progress of disease.

Issue of Saturday December 7, 1867:

Married - On Thursday evening, 28th ultimo, at the residence of the
bride's mother, by L. N. ROBINS, Esq., Mr. JAMES A. CRENSHAW to Miss
CELIA A. ALEXANDER, both of Pickens.

Issue of December 14, 1867 Saturday:

Married - On the 8th December, instant, by Rev. H. T. ARNOLD, WM. HAMIL-
TON, Esq., aged 72 years, and Mrs. SARAH J. COLLETT, aged 26, all of
Pickens.

Issue of Saturday December 21, 1867:

Obituary - Departed this life on the 9th day of November, 1867, at her
home on Cane Creek, Pickens district, South Carolina, Mrs. MARY D. STRIB-
LING, consort of Mr. THOS. M. STRIBLING, in the fifty-fifth year of her
age. The deceased, after suffering an illness of some four months duration, from dropsy---the latter part of which was painful and severe---
passed quietly from the shores of time to that mysterious bourne from
whence no traveller ever returns. She was a native and resident of this
District. She never made a profession of religion or connected herself
with any branch of the Christian Church,yet, she possessed many enobling
virtues and valuable traits of character. As a neighbor, she was frank
and firm in all her dealings; and as a friend, she was kind, generous,
warm-hearted and true. She has left an affectionate husband, and six
children to mourn their irreparable loss, besides a numerous circle of
relations and friends, who knew her well and loved her. And when the
angel of death unfolds his sable wings in the family circle, and bears

away upon his cold, pulseless bosom, a beloved Mother, we must deeply
sympathise with the bereaved, yet we must always meekly yield to the hand
of a kind and alwise Providence, and say all is well; for, while we
mourn her loss on earth, we hope through the abounding love and tender
compassion of our Saviour, that her spirit, ransomed by the atonement of
his precious blood, has ascended on high to a land of pure delight to
unite with the innumerable host of the angels of God in singing the
praises of the redeemed forever. A Friend

Issue of Saturday January 4, 1868:

Married - On the 31st ultimo, by Judge Wickliffe, at the residence of the
bride's father, Mr. JOHN HOLDEN, of Georgia, to Miss MARY EMMALINE, eldest daughter of Capt. R. F. MORGAN, of Pickens.

Married - on the 25th ult., by J. E. BELLOTTE, Esq., at the residence of
HENRY KEASLER, in the Pendleton Village, Mr. JAS. E. ADDIS, of Pickens,
to Miss M. A. KEASLER.

Married - On the 17th ult., by Rev. W. B. SINGLETON, Mr. W. T. BOWEN to
Miss REBECCA ALLGOOD, both of Pickens.

Married - On the 18th ult., by the same, Mr. W. A. LAY to Miss JANE E.
NIMMONS, both of Pickens.

Married - On the 15th ult., by J. E. HAGOOD, Esq., Mr. W. E. ALEXANDER
to Miss CAROLINE ALEXANDER, all of Pickens.

Married - On the 18th ult., by the same, Mr. JAS. E. H. NIMMONS to Miss
PHALBA LEWIS, both of Pickens.

Married - On the 17th ult., by Rev. M. CHASTAIN, Mr. HENRY LEWIS to Miss
JOSEPHINE STEWARD, all of Pickens.

Issue of Saturday January 18, 1868:

Married - On the 2d day of January, instant, at the residence of the
bride's father, by Elder J. R. HAMLIN, Mr. R. A. STEWART to Miss MOLLIE
E., eldest daughter of Mr. C. C. PARSONS, all of Pickens.

Married - On the evening of the 12th inst., by the same, Mr. M. C. WIN-
CHESTER to Miss NANNIE I., daughter of Mr. ISAAC RICE, all of Pickens.

Notice - MARTHA ELIZABETH JANE NICHOLSON has quit my house, bed and board,
without a cause, and I won't be accountable for any contract she has already made, or for the time to come. J. W. NICHOLSON

Issue of Saturday January 25, 1868:

State of South Carolina, Pickens. In Ordinary - Petition for Partition.
J. B. CARADINE and wife vs. G. W. FREDERICKS and others. It appearing
to my satisfaction that JOS. B. CARADINE and wife SUSAN, defendants in
this case, reside without the limits of this State. Division or sale of
the real estate of GEO. W. FREDERICKS, deceased.

Issue of Saturday February 1, 1868:

Married - On Thursday 2d ult., at the residence of Mrs. MARY A. KING, by
J. B. SANDERS, Esq., Mr. H. A. CHASTAIN to Miss MATILDA PITTS, all of
Pickens.

Married - On Thursday the 23d ult., by Elder J. R. HAMLIN, at the residence of the bride's father, Mr. FRANCIS M. SIMPSON to Miss FRANCES C.
BROOKS, all of Pickens.

Married - On Sunday the 12th ult., by L. N. ROBINS, Esq., Mr. ALFRED MAR-
TIN to Miss N. A. ALEXANDER, all of Pickens.

Married - On Thursday evening, the 16th ult., by the same, Mr. D. M. Mc-
Kinney to Miss REBECCA COTHRAN, all of Pickens.

111

Married - On 25th December last, at Cascade, by Rev. FLETCHER SMITH, Mr.
JAS. B. CARPENTER, of Anderson, to Miss FANNIE E., youngest daughter of
Rev. T. B. MAULDIN, of Pickens.

(Note: Due to the division of Pickens District, S. C., into the present
day counties of Pickens and Oconee, the "Keowee Courier" moved its office from Pickens C. H. to the present day town of Walhalla, county seat
of Oconee county. The first issue from Walhalla was on Friday, February
28, 1868.)

Issue of Friday March 6, 1868:

Suicide - JOHN J. CLAYTON, a prominent merchant of Augusta, committed
suicide Friday evening by shooting himself through the heart. Mental
aberation consequent upon disease super induced the act.

Issue of Friday August 14, 1868:

Sad Accident - Our community was shocked Saturday morning last by the
melancholy intelligence of the death of Mr. ROBERT SEAWRIGHT, about sev-
en miles from this place. It seems he designed going on a drive that
morning, when, in his preparations, his gun was accidentally discharged,
the entire contents entering his leg about the knee joint. The concus-
sion was so great, he survived only a short time.

Melancholy Death - The "Intelligencer" of the 12th inst. records the
suicide of Mr. ROBERT H. HUBBARD, near Greenville C. H., on Friday last.
The circumstances as related are sad indeed. He leaves a large circle
of friends and acquaintances, together with a dependent family to mourn
his death.

Issue of Friday January 8, 1869:

Married - On the evening of the 31st ult., by the Rev. J. L. KENNEDY, at
the residence of the bride's mother, WHITNER SYMMES, Esq., Editor of
"Keowee Courier", to Miss NETTIE, youngest daughter of Mrs. L. ALEXANDER.

Married - On the 30th ult., by Rev. Fletcher Smith, Mr. H. CATER TODD,
of Anderson, to Miss BLANCHE HILLER, of Oconee.

Married - On the 24th ult., by Rev. J. H. SULLIVAN, Mr. JONATHAN R. CLEV-
ELAND to Mrs. SARAH E. MYERS, all of Oconee.

Married - on the 30th ult., by the same, Mr. ROBERT M. CAIN to Miss SAR-
AH L., daughter of J. B. SANDERS, Esq., all of Oconee.

State of South Carolina, Pickens County. In Probate Court. Petition
for sale of Real Estate of WILLIAM BARRETT, deceased. WM. J. KING and
wife MALINDA KING, et als vs. JESSE MC MAHAN and wife CAROLINE MC MAHAN,
et al. It appearing to the satisfaction of this Court that the heirs
at law of BENJAMIN BARRETT, dec'd., to wit: WILLIAM BARRETT, MILTON
BARRETT, BENJAMIN BARRETT and DAVID BARRETT, reside from and without the
limits of this State.

Issue of Friday January 15, 1869:

Married - On Wednesday evening, 6th January, 1869, at Tamossee Valley,
at the residence of the bride's father, by L. N. Robins, Esq., Mr. J.
RILEY GLAZENER, of Transylvania County, N. C. , to Mrs. L. F. WHITMIRE,
of Oconee.

State of South Carolina, Pickens County. In Probate Court. Petition
for sale of Real Estate of WM. HAMILTON, deceased. HARRISON HAMILTON
and WARREN HAMILTON vs. MALINDA HAMILTON, et al. It appearing to my satisfaction that MALINDA HAMILTON, GRIFFIN HAMILTON, the heirs-at-law of
TERRELL HAMILTON, deceased---names and number unknown, reside from and
beyond the limits of this State.

Issue of Friday January 22, 1869: (following page)

(Jan. 22,1869 cont'd)
Married - On the 7th inst., at 10 o'clock, A.M., at the residence of the
bride's father, by the Rev. H. H. PENNY, Mr. T. N. McKINNEY to Miss M.E.
ALEXANDER.

Married - On the same day, at 4 o'clock, P.M., by the same, Mr. T. W.
ALEXANDER to Miss N. C. K. McKINNEY, all of Pickens County.

Married - Gen. ROBERT F. HOKE, of this State, was united in marriage to
Miss LILLIE VAN WYCK, of South Carolina, in New York, on Tuesday of last
week. The ceremony was performed by Rev. Dr. HOUGHTON, in the Church of
the Transfiguration, and the happy bridegroom and bride departed for the
South during the same evening.

Issue of Friday January 29, 1869:

Death of an Old Citizen - We regret to announce the death of Mr. JOHN
CAPEHART, an old and highly respected citizen, which occurred quite suddenly on Saturday morning last, at his residence near this place.

Married - On the 24th of December last, by Elder J. R. HAMLIN, at the
house of Mr. WILLIAM GILSTRAP, Mr. ANTHONY B. LEWIS to Miss EMALISSA AL-
EXANDER.

Married - By the same on the 30th of December, at the residence of the
bride's father, on Six Mile, Mr. JAS. BARRETT to Miss ATHALENDA STONE,
all of Pickens County.

Issue of Friday February 5, 1869:

Married - On the 28th of January 1869, at the residence of the bride's
grandmother, by the Rev. A. H. CORNISH, Mr. J. L. SHANKLIN, to Miss JULIA
F., oldest daughter of the late Col. E. E. DOYLE, all of Oconee.

Issue of Friday February 19, 1869:

Death of Mr. Knee - We are grieved to record the death of this old and
estimable citizen at his residence on the 11th inst., after a protracted
and painful illness. His prominent connection with the founding of Walhalla, his words of kindness and encouragement to the forsaken ones of
the fatherland, in this then wilderness, and his council and wisdom,
which contributed so greatly to its advancement and prosperity, all con-
spire to blend his virtues and sagacity, and draw us nearer to him.
HERMAN HEINRICH KNEE was born in the year 1802, at Bochel, in the Kingdom of Hanover. At the early age of eighteen he emigrated to London,
England where he spent six years of his life. In 1824, he came to Charleston. In 1 54 he removed to Walhalla, then a waste, and uninhabited,
where he remained to the day of his death, filling in the New Settlement
many positions of honor and trust. His adroitness in everything he attended to his readiness to help, wherever there was an opportunity, his
strictly sober habits, his business integrity and his christian and gen-
tlemenly bearing won him the esteem of all, the love of many.

Issue of Friday February 26, 1869:

Sudden Death - Mr. ABIAL FOSTER, an old and respected citizen, died suddenly at his residence at old Pickens C. H., on Monday evening, the 22d
inst. Mr. Foster was a native of the State of Massachusetts and since
his removal to this State has (----blurred--) regard of all who knew him.

Married - On the 17th inst., at the house of Dr. L. B. JOHNSON, in Walhalla, by Rev. WILLIAM MC WHORTER, Mr. JOHN B. PICKETT to Miss MATTIE C.
MC FALL, all of Oconee.

Married - On the 22d inst., at the house of the bride's father, by D. P.
ROBINS, Esq., Mr. ROBERT T. CRAIG to Miss LAURA F. FINCHER, all of Oconee.

Issue of Friday March 5, 1869: (following page)

(Mar. 5, 1869 cont'd):
State of South Carolina, Oconee County. Petition for Partition. PHILO-
MAN CRANE and AMANDA CRANE, Applicants vs. VINEY CRANE and others, Defen-
dants. It appearing to my satisfaction that VINEY CRANE, JOHN CALHOUN
and wife NANCY CALHOUN, LORENZO BARNES and wife MARTHA BARNES, JOHN SAM-
PLES and wife JUDITH SAMPLES, ISAAC CRANE, LEWIS COX and Heirs of GEORGE
BARNES, deceased, defendants in this case, reside beyond the limits of
this State. Division or sale of the real estate of PHILOMAN CRANE,dec'd.

Issue of Friday March 12, 1869:

State of South Carolina, Pickens. In Probate Court. Petition to sell
Lands, pay Debts, for Partition, etc. NANCY ERVIN vs. WILLIAM ERVIN et
al. It appearing to my satisfaction that WILLIAM ERVIN, THOMAS ERVIN
and the Heirs of GEORGE ERVIN, deceased, names and number unknown, the
Heirs of ISAAC ERVIN, six in number, names unknown, reside from and beyond the limits of this State.

Issue of Friday April 2, 1869:

Married - On the 25th inst., at the residence of the bride's father, by
L. N. ROBINS, Esq., Mr. W. A. FENLEY, of Oconee, to Miss LAURA, daughter
of E. M. ALEXANDER, of Pickens.

Issue of Friday April 9, 1869:

Married - On the evening of the 6th inst., at the residence of the brides
mother, by the Rev. W. H. STRATTON, RICHARD LEWIS, Esq., Judge of Probate
of Oconee County, to Miss OLIVIA KATE, eldest daughter of Mrs. L. LAW-
RENCE, all of Walhalla.

State of South Carolina, Oconee County. In Probate. Petition to sell
Lands, pay Debts, for Partition, etc. JOHN WEST, Applicant vs. SUSAN
CATHERINE WEST and others, Def'ts. It appearing to my satisfaction that
SUSAN CATHERINE WEST, JAMES ROGERS WEST, JASPER WEST, MARTIN WEST, STEP-
HEN WEST, MINERVA WEST and CYNTHIA WEST, defendants in this case, reside
beyond the limits of this State. Concerning the sale of the real estate
of ARCHIBALD WEST, deceased.

State of South Carolina, Oconee County. In Probate. Petition to sell
Lands, pay Debts, for Partition, etc. MARY RANKIN, Applicant vs. FRAN-
CIS CAPEHART and others, Defendants. It appearing to my satisfaction
that FRANCIS CAPEHART and MARGARET ELIZA CAPEHART, defendants in this
case, reside beyond the limits of this State. Concerning the sale of the
real estate of EDWARD RANKIN, deceased.

State of South Carolina, Oconee County. Petition for final settlement.
NANCY A. MORGAN, Adm'x. vs. GEO. W. ELLIOTT and MARY E. ELLIOTT, defendants. It appearing to my satisfaction that the heirs at law of JAMES
A. MORGAN, deceased, to wit: GEO. W. ELLIOTT and MARY E. ELLIOTT, reside from and beyond the limits of this State.

Issue of Friday April 16, 1869:

Wanted - Information of the fate or whereabouts of Capt. WM. JOHNSON,
(Blind) who when last heard from, was traveling with a one horse vehicle,
and boy, selling books, maps, etc., thro' Central Tennessee, and Northern
Georgia and Alabama. Any information in regard to him will be thankfully
received; addressed to MARY JOHNSON, care of F. I. DIBBLE & Co., Louis-
ville, Ky. April 5, 1869.

Issue of Friday May 7, 1869:

Married - On Sunday morning, the 25th of April, 1869, at Westminster
Church,.by Elder J. R. HAMLIN, Mr. J. A. NEWELL and Miss SALLIE, daughter
of Rev. ANDREW MC GUFFIN, all of Oconee.

Married - By the same, on the evening of the 27th of April, ult., at the
residence of the bride's father, Capt. R. E, STEELE, of Fort George,

Pickens County, to Miss GEORGIE ANN, eldest daughter of MORRIS MILLER,of Oconee County.

Issue of Friday May 28, 1869:

Married - On the 13th of May 1869, at the residence of the bride's father, by Rev. Mr. SPEARS, Mr. J. F. BURTON, of Georgia, and Miss CECELIA C., daughter of J. W. COBB, Esq., of Oconee.

Issue of Friday June 4, 1869:

Incendiarism and Murder - We regret to learn that, sometime last week a murder was committed in the settlement known as Salubrity, in Pickens County, which exceeds in fiendishness and cowardice anything we ever heard of. We are not prepared to give the particulars, but will state the matter as told to us, which, we doubt not, is correct: The barns and stables of a Mr. WILLARD was discovered to be on fire at a late hour at night, when he and a man by the name of RAMPEY hastened to the scene of conflagration, to arrest, if possible, the devouring flames. On reaching the spot it was found that the fire had made such headway that it could not be stopped, and Willard and Rampey rushed in the stable to rescue the horses and other stock, and while thus engaged were fired upon by unknown persons without. Mr. Willard was struck in the neck by a ball, which resulted in his death in a few minutes. Rampey was struck on the leg, causing a painful wound. We are not informed of any clues as to who the perpetrators were. We hope to give full particulars next week.

In Memory - Of REBECCA HOLLINGSWORTH, who died on the 6th of November last, near Townville, Anderson District, S. C., in the 23rd year of her age. M.T.P. Chicago, Jan. 8, 1869. (5 verses poetry--First line reads: "Oh sister dear! and art thou gone..)

The First Case of Divorce in South Carolina!

The "Greenville Enterprise" says, that three petitions for divorce came up for hearing before Judge ORR on Friday last. Two of the applications were from the wives of wicked husbands, one from the husband against the wife. The first case was from a lady, Mrs. MARY E. CAMERON, residing in Charleston, for a divorce from her husband, ROBERT CAMERON, in Philadelphia, from whom she was by his cruelty compelled to separate several years ago; he having also since the separation unlawfully married another woman in Pennsylvania, with whom he is now living. The unlawful wife on application furnished an affidavit stating that the husband represented himself as a widower; and so she married him in ignorance of the existence of the lawful wife. Judge Orr, after hearing the petition and evidence, readily granted the order of divorce in this case, on motion of PERRY & PERRY, solicitors for the petitioner.
The other parties all reside in this county. The applicants were represented by Messrs. SULLIVAN & STOKES. Judge Orr granted the order of divorce in the case of Mrs. AMANDA C. LENDEMAN from her husband, FRANCIS M. LENDEMAN, who, it was proved, had cruelly treated her and had married and takem up with another woman. In the case of the petition of JOHN W. WALKER for divorce from his wife, MARY J. WALKER, on the allegation of her desertion some six or eight years ago, and her violent temper and abuse which occasioned it, and the hopelessness of a reunion, the Judge was not satisfied that he ought to grant the husband a divorce, but intimated to the counsel that he would further consider the case.
Those are the first cases of divorce that have ever been granted by a law court in this State. To be sure South Carolina was always a barbarous State, and it must doubtless be gratifying to our Down-East friends to witness this giant stride that we have taken in the race of civilazation. It is reconstruction in its most practical sense; that is to say, we are rapidly assimilating ourselves and our laws to Down-Eastern ideas. Who knows but that in a while we may have blue laws, and there is even a possibility that we may in time boast a race of ANNA DICKINSONS. Room for re-constructed South Carolina.

Issue of Friday June 11, 1869:
Married - On the 3d of June, inst., at Mount Ina, at the residence of the

bride's father, by Rev. A. H. CORNISH, Mr. ROBERT YOUNG, of Walhalla, to Miss ANNA W., eldest daughter of Col. H. W. KUHTMANN.

Issue of Friday June 25, 1869:

Married - On the 10th of June, at the house of the bride's father, by the Rev. D. HUMPHREYS, Mr. W. R. SHELOR to Miss R. E., daughter of M. S. STRIBLING, Esq., all of Oconee.

Obituary - Departed this life, on the 31st of May, 1869, at his late residence, on Tugalo River, Oconee County, Mr. ZACHARIAH HALL, SR. His age is not certainly known, but he was, no doubt, an unusually old man, probably passed his four-score. His long life was one of uncommon freedom from sickness and infirmity, but his last year was one of rapid decline, and finally much suffering, which he bore with Christian manliness and fortitude. He is extensively known in his native District, and stood high in the estimation of all his acquaintances, as a man of the strictest integrity, a friendly neighbor, generous to the needy, and hospitable and entertaining to visitors to his home. In his death a good and worthy citizen is lost, as well as a kind and provident father to his children. He did not attach himself to the church until within a few weeks of his death, but we think it was because he feared insincerity. He naturally shrank from anything like pretense. He was long a constant reader of the Bible, often wept over it's pages, and repeatedly declared his reliance upon the Saviour there revealed, who, we trust, has transformed him into the divine image, and taken him into his glorious and blessed presence. W.P.G.

Issue of Friday July 2, 1869:

State of South Carolina, Oconee County, Citation for a Final Settlement and Decree. ALEXANDER ALLGOOD, Ex'or. vs. BANISTER ALLGOOD. It appearing to my satisfaction that BANISTER ALLGOOD, ALVIN ALLGOOD, ELLIS MURPHY and wife JANE, JEREMIAH ELLIS and wife PATSY, FRANCIS HENDERSON, wife of WILLIAM HENDERSON, formerly FRANCIS KENNEMORE, and the heirs of CASANDER MAJOR, deceased, names and number unknown, defendants in this case, reside without the limits of this State. Concerning the final settlement of the estate of BARNETT H. ALLGOOD.

State of South Carolina, Oconee County. In Common Pleas---Equity Side. Bill for Partition of Real Estate. DANIEL S. SMITH, JOHN C. SMITH, et al vs. DANIEL S. HULL, RICHARD CRUMPTON and wife, et al. It appearing to my satisfaction that the defendants, RICHARD CRUMPTON and wife ELIZABETH CRUMPTON, W. J. ROBINSON and wife NANCY ROBINSON, and SARAH DYAR, widow, reside beyond the limits of this State.

Issue of Friday July 23, 1869:

Obituary - On Saturday night, about 12 o'clock, the 12th of June, ult., the messenger of death summoned from our midst Mrs. E. M. DICKSON, the wife of WM. DICKSON, aged 41 years and 3 months. For twenty years she was a member of the Baptist Church, and during her last illness, which lasted about three weeks, she gave much satisfactory evidence of her acceptance with the Saviour of sinners. Fully conscious of her approaching dissolution, she set her house in order. She bore her affliction with christian fortitude and patience---perfectly submissive to the will of her Heavenly Father. While she was willing to go and leave those she loved, she was deeply concerned about their future welfare and happiness. While she was yet rational and possessed the powers of speech, she called her husband and her children to her, one by one, and gave them good and sound advice, exhorting them to make preparation for a better world; said that she was going to leave them, and hoped they would meet her in Heaven, where the wicked cease from troubling and the weary are at rest. She has left a devoted and sorrow-stricken husband, ten children, and a large circle of relatives and friends to mourn their irreparable loss. But we sorrow not as those without hope, for if we believe that Jesus died and rose again, even so them also which sleep in Jesus will God bring with Him. If our loss be her eternal gain, then let us dry up our tears and pray that we too may die the death of the christian. On Monday, the 14th, her remains were carried into West Minister Church, where she held membership, and a funeral sermon was delivered by the writer, from the text: "Therefore be ye also ready".---Mat. 24,44. The discourse was listened to by a large congregation of weeping relatives, friends and neighbors. When the religious services were concluded the corpse was consigned to the grave in the burying-ground near by, there to rest until the last loud trump shall announce that Time shall be no longer. Yes, her remains now sleep in the church-yard at West Minister. May the bereaved husband find strength and comfort in the companionship of Jesus, and may the children remember what a dying mother said, and be gathered as lambs into the fold of the great and good Shepherd, that they may one day rejoin their loved one in the mansions of eternal bliss. J.H.S.

State of South Carolina, Pickens County. In Probate- Petition for Partition.and sale of Real Estate. MACAJAH ALEXANDER vs. DAVID ALEXANDER et al. It appearing to my satisfaction that the heirs-at-law of DAVID ALEXANDER, dec'd, number and names unknown, the heirs of MICAJAH ALEXANDER, JR., 2d, number and names unknown, and three of the heirs of MELVINA ROBERTS, names unknown, defendants in this case, reside beyond the limits of this State.

State of South Carolina, Pickens. In Probate - Petition for Partition and Sale of Real Estate. CLAYTON N. REID vs. ALFRED M. REID, et al. It appearing to my satisfaction that ALFRED M. REID, BARTON GRIFFIN and wife JANE B., OLIVER C. REID and LAWRENCE O. REID, defendants in this case, reside beyond the limits of this State.

State of South Carolina, Pickens County. In Probate - Petition for Partition and Sale of Real Estate of DANIEL LOOPER, deceased. CHARLES HOLCOMBE and wife ARMINDA, Applicants vs. DANIEL LOOPER and others, defendants. It appearing to my satisfaction that JOSEPH LOOPER and wife POLLY, JOHN PRICHET and wife RACHEL, and the heirs-at-law of CAROLINE PHILLIPS, numbers and names unknown, reside beyond the limits of this State.

Issue of Friday August 13, 1869:

State of South Carolina, Pickens County. Petition for Partition and sale of Real Estate. JOHN L. LATHAM vs. JESSE L. DEAN and wife ANNA, et al. It appearing to my satisfaction that Jesse L. Dean and wife Anna, and SARAH LATHAM, defendants in this case, reside beyond the limits of this State.

State of South Carolina, Pickens County. Petition for final settlement and Decree. T. M. ALEXANDER vs. SUSAN ALEXANDER, et al. It appearing to my satisfaction that SUSAN ALEXANDER, CORA TULULA ALEXANDER and M. C. ALEXANDER, defendants in this case, reside beyond the limits of this State. Concerning final settlement of the Estate of FOUNTAIN ALEXANDER, deceased.

State of South Carolina, Pickens County. In Probate Court. MABRY MAULDIN vs. VARDRY MAULDIN, et al. It appearing to my satisfaction that VARDRY MAULDIN, BIRD MARTIN and wife CAROLINE, HARVEY SMITH and wife ADALINE, defendants in this case, reside beyond the limits of this State.

Tribute of Respect to ROBERT STRIBLING, deceased by Fairview Sabbath School. July 25, 1869.

Issue of Friday August 20, 1869:

Married - On Thursday morning, 23rd June, 1869, by L. N. ROBINS, Esq., at the residence of the bride's mother, Mrs.E. B. ALEXANDER, Mr. CHARLEY B. FINLEY, of Oconee, and Mrs. E. KNOX, of Pickens, S. C.

Married - On the 20th of June, 1869, at the residence of the bride's mother, by L. N. ROBINS, Esq., Mr. T. WHITMIRE, of Oconee, to Miss KATE GROGAN, of Pickens.

State of South Carolina, Pickens County. In Probate - Petition for Partition and Sale of Real Estate. SAMUEL CHAPMAN vs. JACOB CHAPMAN, et al. It appearing to my satisfaction that JOEL CHAPMAN, MARY MC KINNEY, the Heirs at law of RUTH WIGINGTON, number and names unknown, and the Heirs at law of ISRAEL CHAPMAN, number and names unknown, defendants in this case, reside beyond the limits of this State.

Issue of Friday September 17, 1869:

Married - On the evening of the 2d inst., by Elder J. R. HAMLIN, at the house of the bride's father, Mr. ANDREW B. WILLIAMS of Pickens County, to Miss SUSAN E., daughter of JOHN WHITMIRE, of Oconee County.

Issue of Friday October 22, 1869:

Married - On the evening of the 22nd ult., at Greenway, the residence of the bride's mother, by Rev. WM. MC WHORTER, Mr. A. H. ELLISON, formerly of Pickens District, to Miss M. AGNES STEELE, of Oconee.

Married - On the 3d inst., by Rev. Mr. DODGE, Mr. HERMANN C. KNICE, of Walhalla, to Miss E. D. MEYER, of Atlanta, Ga.

Married - On Sunday morning, the 10th of October, 1869, by L. N. Robins, Esq., Mr. WM. KELLY, of Anderson, to Miss ARTAMISSA NARCISSA FRANCIS ELIZABETH NANCY JANE DURHAM, of Pickens.

Issue of Friday November 5, 1869:

Married - On the 10th of October, ult., by the Rev. JOHN ARIAIL, Mr. MATTHIAS B. RICHARDSON to Miss MATTI J. YOUNG, all of Pickens County.

State of South Carolina, Oconee County. Petition for Partition. WM. SANDERS, Adm'r. vs. JANE MOORE and others. It appearing to my satisfaction that JANE MOORE, widow and heirs, unknown, MARTHA COX, widow, and heirs, unknown, ELIZABETH SANDERS, widow, and her heirs: MARTHA JANE, FRANCIS C., JOHN W., JOSEPH ORR, MARGARET and JAMES, reside beyond and without the limits of this State. Division or sale of the real estate of WILLIAM SANDERS, deceased.

Issue of Friday November 19, 1869:

Obituary - Collection of thoughts in memory of "sweet little Jimmie", son of JAMES and SALLIE SLOAN, who died at Pendleton of Dysentery, on the 14th of July 1869. It was on the 12th of December, 1868, we received our first born from the Lord, a beauteous boy, not only lovely in the eyes of his parents, but all who saw him were drawn irresistibly by his smiles. His snowy form had expanded into much less symmetry and from the depths of his heavenly blue eyes, beamed a gentle spirit. About his lofty brow law soft golden locks, that formed an image of rare lovliness! Tenderly we cherished him, fondly was he beloved. Brightly we pictured his future, when we should see him walking in the paths of the righteous, luring leis on to God. But a mysterious Providence set a sore trial for our faith. Disease raged in the land, among the victims was this holy child. Oh, how his sufferings smote our hearts, piercing like a sword our very souls. What bitterness there is in recalling those hours of his agonizing pain. Precious lamb! we can ne'er forget when you wildly looked for help and no help could your father give...all had been done which man could do, and in despair he turned away unable to bear the dying gaze that followed him where'er he moved about the room. Clasping those tiny arms about my neck I felt the faint uttering heart heaving its last pulsations. Around that couch were the bowed forms of four beautiful maidens...two that loved him so well...another had been to him a mother in tender care and devoted affection, and one shook in every nerve as she breathed in supplication...asking that when the little spirit fled, bearing their prayers on light wings to lay at Jesus feet, mercy would not be denied. Oh! methinks Jehovah heard and answered those prayers so full of penitence and grief, for one of those girls, the last one of whom I spoke, herself in three short weeks "passed through the Valley and shadow of death", saying to a companion of this self same group, "Oh! sep, I am going..must die...I must go home." And she would

in delirium fancy over and over this death bed scene asking if those
around "did not see little Jimmy, the sweet little baby beside her". I
believe it was even so, and as he had so lately borne to heaven the
prayers of these fair maidens it may be God will send him to bear their
spirits to eternal rest. "Oh, my angel boy...we deplore thee not as
lost, for the bonds that unite us shall exist when the wheel of time
stand still". There was a vacant place in the cherub band and a messenger was sent about midnight for our Darling, bone of our bone, and flesh
of our flesh, we gave him up without a murmur, to him who said: "Suffer
little children to come unto me and forbid them not, for of such is the
Kingdom of Heaven", yet again we hope to hold him to our bosoms, and will
strive to fulfill the promise made in his dying ears, to try to meet him
beyond the vale of tears. Oh! would it not take away the sting of death
and rob the grave of victory, to know that we were going beyond Jordan
and receive in outstretched arms our little babe coming to welcome us to
his blissful home. "A voice seems calling us ever not to forget our
promise...not to forget the form in that little lonely grave...no, my
son not in loneliness and slumbering, for thy fathers heart and mine are
aid with thee in the tomb. (Poetry)

Collection of thoughts in memory of JIMMIE and BELLE, son and daughter
of JAMES and SUSAN CRAWFORD, who died of Dysentery near Pendleton, S.C.
.....The first at 9 o'clock P.M., the 31st of July, the other at 9 o'
clock the following morning, August 1st, 1869. Autumn with its seared
leaves falling and dying around us, vividly recalls those loved ones who
so lately passed away as the grass of the field, and whose glory faded
as the flowers of the morning. None could enter that home from whence
their sunny smiles have fled without realizing and awful calamity had
entered the dwelling...we could not without sympathy from such bereavement, for seldom has an affliction so heartrending betaken a family. That
mother is often missed by the household, and when sought, is found where
she has deposited memorials of her departed. One by one she looks over
the ____   ____ her children and garments they wore, and the gold-
en locks which once adorned the beauteous brows of her dear ones. To
her these are holy moments and communion with those whose voices are no-
where heard and whose seats around the hearth stone are no longer filled
for while affection fondly lingers round memories, thoughts are charmed
away to that bright inheritance they have gone to possess, and Heaven,
becomes more attractive to her since they are there.....................
We will first speak of Belle, the fair creature, round whom so many virtues clung. Just twenty summers had dawned upon her and on the eve of
womanhood, blushing at her own lovliness "none saw her but to admire her,
none knew her to but to love". Beong the idol of her father's heart,
she received the advantages wealth can give, and was cultivated in intellect and polished by society. ....(descriptive passages
of character, etc.) ...Less than a week before her fatal illness, she
was called to the bedside of her nephew, little JIMMIE SLOAN. Fondly
was she attached to this sweet babe.* (*See above notice of "little Jimmie" Sloan) Day and night she wept for him and when she saw he must die
she seemed overcome with the thought, and when life had fled she would
not leave the form, but sat unwatched beside him, till they came to take
him away. She followed on, and when the clods began to fall upon his
breast, she shook in every nerve and was taken from the scene she could
no longer bear. Three days from that time, she too fell a victim to the
same disease, then raging far and wide. Skillful physicians and faithful nurses were in vain to check its ravages.........In another apart-
ment, raging with excruciating pain with the same malady, was her brother JIMMIE, a fragile boy in his tenth year, a dear sweet child....on
account of his natural delicacy and gentle ways. For a week he had been
wild with pain and the physicians and friends ran to and fro to adminis-
ter to one and then the other, , but all proved vain. Early on Saturday
morning, a blood vessel ruptured and every hope fled of our darling Belle.
Soon they told us death, too had seized upon the heart strings of the
frantic child. Language is hushed before this awful scene. Two of one
home lay dying...(poetry)....As night drew on the agony of both increas-
ed..shriek after shriek died away and horror filled every heart, listen-
ing to the delirious child. Then there came an awful calm, and soon it
passed from lip to lip, "Jimmie is dead"......Calm and serene as the
Sabbath morning dawned,,, our beautiful one (Belle) ....died....

Issue of Friday December 3, 1869:

Death of a Brave Woman - Mrs. MILDRED BROWN, for sixty-three years a resident of Howard co., Mo., died at the residence of her husband, ROBERT C.
BROWN, on the 10th inst., after a short illness. She was born January
25, 1796, in Madison county, Ky. When she was scarcely grown, the Indians surrounded Cooper's Fort, (named after her father) in what is now
Howard County, in which were her father, his family and neighbors,
threatening to cut them all off. In this condition MILLY, as she was
called, volunteered to carry the news to Hempstead, a neighboring fort,
which she did successfully, by dashing from Cooper's Fort on a fleet
horse, past a hundred Indians, who sent a hundred rife-balls whizzing
after her. She and her horse escaped unhurt, and the inmates of the
fort were rescued through her courage and daring.

Issue of Friday December 10, 1869:

In telligence has been recieved by State Constable HUBBARD that WILLIAM
K. TOLBERT, accused of the murder of RANDOLPH, was killed last Thursday
night, at a dance in Abbeville County. He was tracked to the home by
constable HOLLINGSHED, with a party of Police, and as soon as they presented themselves , Tolbert commenced firing at Hollingshed, and wounded
him twice, (in the groin and in the thigh) when Hollingshed shot him
through the heart, killing him instantly.. Phoenix.

Issue of Friday December 17, 1869:

In quest- Mr. Coroner HOLLEMAN held an inquest over the body of ROBT. M.
SNIPES, a youth about fourteen years of age, on the 9th inst. Drs. BELL
and JOHNSON were the physicians called in. The verdict of the jury was,
that deceased came to his death by drinking an unreasonable quantity of
liquor.

Issue of Friday December 24, 1869:

Married - On the 5th inst., by Rev. A. B. Stephens, Mr. JNO. B. KING and
Miss LOU M. HAMILTON, eldest daughter of WARREN and CARRIE HAMILTON. All
of Pickens.

Issue of Friday February 18, 1870:

Married - On the 13th of February, 1870, by Rev. JAMES H. SULLIVAN, Mr.
THOS. A. Y. JAMES to Miss M. J. KAY, of Georgia.

State of South Carolina, Pickens County. In Probate Court - Petition
for Partition, Sale, etc. CHARLES DURHAM and wife REBECCA DURHAM vs.
PIERSON MAYFIELD and wife JANE MAYFIELD, et al. It appearing to my satisfaction that PIERSON MAYFIELD and wife JANE MAYFIELD, GEORGE W. MC-
CLANAHAN and B. FRANKLIN MC CLANAHAN, IRA MOREHEAD and wife SUSAN MORE-
HEAD, RICHARD H. TRIPP and wife PIETY TRIPP, defendants in this case,
reside from and beyond the limits of this State.

State of South Carolina, Pickens County. In Probate Court - Petition
for Partition, Sale, Etc. RICHARD REDMAN and wife MELINDA REDMAN vs.
LEWIS REESE, et al. It appearing to my satisfaction that the defendants
in this case, to wit: LEWIS REESE, ROBERT CUNNINGHAM and wife VISA CUN-
NINGHAM, JOHN MINGERS and wife MILLY ANN MINGERS, JOHN TATE and wife
VILENDA SMITH(?), are absent from and beyond the limits of this State.

Issue of Friday April 29, 1870:

Death of an Old Citizen - We are pained to announce the death of Mr.
ELIJAH ALEXANDER, SR., of Pickens County, in the ninety-eighth year of
his age. The deceased, who was one of our oldest and most highly respected citizens, had lived to see his country achieve its independence
and, through the mutations of time, witness its demoralization, degra-
dation and loss of liberty. Mr. Alexander has been for many years a
consistent and useful member of the Baptist Church. He leaves a numerous family connection and many friends to mourn their loss.

Sudden Death - Mr. F. C. BROWN, of this county, died suddenly on Saleday last. He was at Walhalla during the day, returned home, ate his
dinner late, and in the midst of lively conversation, fell from his
chair to the floor and expired immediately. Truly, "in the midst of life
we are in death".

Fatal Accident - We regret to learn that Mr. JOHN SCHUMANN, whilst employed on the steam saw mill of Mr. PARKER, near this place, on the 10th
inst., was caught by the machinery and drawn under the saw, and horribly
lacerated. He lingered a few hours, dying from the effects of the hurt.
The deceased was only nineteen years of age, and could not speak a word
of English. His parents reside near Pomaria, S. C. Light lie the sod
on the grave of the stranger.

Married - On the 5th of May, inst., by Rev. D. McNEILL TURNER, Mr. WM.H.
ANDERSON to Miss CARRIE H., daughter of JAS. M. BEARD, all of West Union.

Issue of Friday May 20, 1870:

Shocking Calamity - One of the most frightful occurrences took place,
near old Pickens, in this County, on the afternoon of the 15th inst.,
which it has been our province to chronicle: Mr. SAMUEL REID, lady and
two grandchildren, started, in a buggy, to this place. One of the little boys, (a son of Col. KEITH) was thrown out and seriously injured.
Mr. Reid and the other grandson, WILLIE REID, were also thrown out and
injured, but not seriously. The injured are doing well.

Married - On the evening of the 12th inst., by Rev. J. L. KENNEDY, at
the residence of the bride's father, at Pickens C. H., Mr. P. McD. ALEX-
ANDER to Miss MARY HAGOOD, eldest daughter of J. E. HAGOOD, Esq.

Issue of Friday May 27, 1870:

Fatal Accident - On the 18th inst., a man named ANDREW BUNCH, of this
county, fell from a house, in town, on which he was engaged as a workman, and killed himself almost instantly.

We learn that EPHRAIM EDINGS, of Franklin County, Ga., on the 21st inst.
whilst under the influence of liquor, fell on his chair, from a standing
posture, and died from the effects of the fall in a short time.

Issue of Friday June 24, 1870:

Married - On the 31st May 1870, at the residence of Capt. F. W. R. NANCE
by the Rev. JOHN M. CARLISLE, Dr. T. A. HUDGENS, of Honea Path, S. C.,
and Miss ELLA GAINES, of Anderson.

Married - At Tip Top, near Pendleton, June 1, 1870, by Rev. J. SCOTT
MURRY, Mr. R. E. SLOAN and Miss S. M. MAXWELL, second daughter of Mrs.
G. L. MAXWELL.

Issue of Friday July 29, 1870:

State of South Carolina, Pickens County. In Probate Court - Petition
for Partition, Sale, Payment of Debts, etc. JOHN L. RACKLEY vs. REDDIN
RACKLEY, et al. It appearing to my satisfaction that the heirs of
WARREN RACKLEY, dec'd, to wit: W. BENSON RACKLEY, MELISSA RACKLEY, R.T.
RICHARDS and wife, ELIZA RICHARDS, reside from and beyond the limits of
this State.

Issue of Friday August 5, 1870:

Obituary - Mrs. M. E. CLEAVELAND, relict of W. T. CLEAVELAND, and daughter of N. J. F. and ELIZABETH PERRY, died at the residence of WM. J. HIX,
24th of June last, in the 27th year of her age. Her health had been declining for nearly one long year. Four months previous to her death she
was confined to the sick room, during which time the best medical atten-

tion was given but all to no purpose..."Death loves a shining mark".She
was early left an orphan, by the death of a kind mother; and having a
mind susceptible of the highest cultivation, the family considered her
a fit subject of moral and literary training, which was well accomplished at quite an early day. After the death of her noble hearted husband, W. T. Cleaveland, graduate of the South Carolina College, she professed religion, and joined the Baptist Church, of which she was an acceptable member at the time of her death. Quiet, amiable and intelligent, she was much loved, and much lamented by her numerous friends and
relatives. She expressed an entire willingness to depart and be with
her Saviour, but for the anxious solicitude felt for the future welfare
of her only child, a sweet little daughter about four years of age.
While dying, her countenance was radiant with the foreshadowings of
Heavenly bliss, and, under the influence of this Heaven born spirit, she
left this world of sorrow to open her eyes amid the glories of Heavens
Eternal Sabbath. (1 verse poetry) C.H.S. Fair Play, S. C.

Issue of Friday August 12, 1870:

Married - August 4th, 1870, in Walhalla, by J. B. SANDERS, Notary Public,
Mr. WM. C. WILLIAMS to Miss MARY ANN HOLDBROOK, all of Oconee.

Issue of Friday August 26, 1870:

Obituary - Died, August 1st, 1870, JOSEPH DOYLE, infant son of J. L. and
JULIA D. SHANKLIN, aged 7 months and 13 days. (1 verse poetry)

Issue of Friday September 9, 1870:

Death of Judge Bleckley - We regret to learn that Judge JAMES BLECKLEY,
of Rabun County, Ga., died at his residence on Monday morning last, in
the sixty eighth year of his age. Judge Bleckley was a highly useful
citizen...honest and devoted to his friends. True in life he has gone
to that "bourne from whence no traveller returns", to realize the great
truth of immortality. Peace to his ashes!

Death of Capt. John Maxwell - We are pained to announce the death of
Capt. JOHN MAXWELL, at his residence, in this County, on the morning of
August 23, 1870, in the seventy-ninth year of his age. He was one of our
oldest citizens. He had been a member of the three constitutional conventions, called for various purposes, in the State, during the last
forty years. He had also been a member of the Legislature; and, in all
these highly responsible positions, discharged his duty to the satisfac
tion of his constituents. Mr. Maxwell was a gentleman of the old
school, connecting the happy past with the overwhelming misfortunes of
the present...honest, ardent, patriotic...idolized by his family, beloved by his friends, and highly respected by his constituents of old
Pendleton District.

Issue of Friday September 23, 1870:

Death of James Lawrence - We announce with regret the death of Mr. JAMES
LAWRENCE, of Pickens County, on the 8th inst., in the eighty first year
of his age. Mr. Lawrence served as a Lieutenant in the war of 1812, and
was subsequently elected a member of the Legislature from Pendleton district. He leaves to mourn his departure, a large family connexion and
many friends.

Obituary - Died, at his residence on Tugaloo River, Oconee County, So.
Ca., on the 25th of August, 1870, of typhoid fever, WARREN R. DAVIS,
youngest son of HARVEY and SALLIE DAVIS, in his 42nd year. ...two weeks
suffering....not a professor of religion, nor a seeker, until a few
days before his death. (Followed by a lengthy eulogy for a paragraph
by "one who was present" and one verse poetry.)

Issue of Friday September 30, 1870:

Married - On Sunday, the 18th of September, by Rev. H. N. HAYES, Mr.DAVID
ELROD, of Oconee County, to Miss LUCINDA MAYS, of Anderson County.

Married - On Sunday, the 15th of September, by Rev. H. N. Hayes, Mr. HEN-
RY DODD to Miss MARGARET NEAL, all of Pickens.

State of South Carolina, Pickens County. In Probate Court - Petition of
Partition, Sale, etc. MARGARET STEELE and JENNIE DENDY, et al vs. JOS-
EPH HARDIN and wife ELIZA HARDIN, HAMPTON WADE, et al. It appearing to
the satisfaction of this Court that BURRELL PACE and wife HANNAH PACE,
HENRY NORMAN and wife HARRIET NORMAN and SAMUEL WADE, reside from and
beyond the limits of this State.

Obituary - Died, at his residence, near Pendleton village, on the morning of August 23d, 1870, Capt. JOHN MAXWELL, in the 79th year of his age,
leaving a devoted wife and children, with numerous other relations, and
an extensive circle of friends, to mourn their loss. He had been declining for several years under a disease of a complicated character,
which baffled the professional skill of his physicians; but being a man
of unusual energy and indomitable perseverance, he kept moving, and re-
sisting the waste of disease as long as he could......he was with Gen.
Jackson in the "Creek War" and also in the war of 1812. In 1861, although seventy years of age, when the late contest commenced at Fort
Sumter, he hastened thither and was present at its surrender. In 1828,
he was elected a member of the State Legislature....held this position
for several successive terms....member of several of the State Conventions, including the Secession Convention of 1860....(followed by a long
eulogy of his character, etc.)

Issue of Friday October 7, 1870:

Married - On Thursday, the 22d of September, 1870, at the residence of
EDMUND HERNDON, (the bride's father), Mr. BENJ. J. JOHNSTON, of Pickens
County, S. C., and Miss L. SUSIE HERNDON, of Oconee County.

Death of an Old Citizen - Another of the old citizens of our County has
passed away. THOMAS DODD, SR., died at his residence near Walhalla on
the 23d ult., at 2 o'clock in the morning, of brain fever, after an illness of two days. The deceased was sicty-three years of age, and respected by all, for his industrious habits and pious walk in life. He had
been a consistent member of the New Hope Baptist Church for many years,
and on the Sunday previous to his death rendered his last earthly service to his Saviour in a happy exhortation to the congregation to his
church.

Issue of Friday October 14, 1870:

Obituary - Died, on the 17th of August, 1870, in Habersham County, Ga.,
SALLIE P. JARRETT, daughter of the late ROBERT and ELIZABETH JARRETT. On
the 2d of the month of her death she completed her 20th year. (Eulogy
follows signed by W. P.G.)

Issue of Friday October 28, 1870:

State of South Carolina, Oconee County. Sale by Probate Court - Peti-
tion for Partition, Account, Relief, etc. DAVID R. ELLIOTT, et al vs.
NANCY ELLIOTT et al. By virtue of an order to me directed, by RICHARD
LEWIS, Esq., Judge of Probate, I will sell to t he highest bidder, at
Walhalla, on Saleday in November next, the Real Estate of ALLEN R. EL-
LIOTT, deceased, on head waters of Beaverdam Creek, containing 100 acres.

Issue of Friday November 4, 1870:

Married - On the 21st of October, 1870, by the Rev. J. A. R. HANKS, Mr.
WM. DICKSON, of Oconee county, S. C., to Miss E. J. FULKS, of Dalton,Ga.

Married - On the 26th utl., by Rev. Fletcher Smith, Mr. WM. D. GOODWIN,
of Greenville, to Miss LIDIE A., second daughter of J. E. HAGOOD, Esq.
of Pickens.

Issue of Friday November 11, 1870:

Married - 6th inst. at the residence of the bride's father, by D. P.

Robins, Esq., Mr. WM. S. FRASIER to Miss SUE E. ROLAND, all of Oconee county.

Issue of Friday November 25, 1870:

Married - In Laurensville, November 23th, by Rev. P. F. KISTLER, THOMAS B. CREWS, of the "Laurensville Herald", to Miss CELIA R. BALLEW, daughter of the late Rev. DAVID L. BALLEW.

Issue of Friday December 16, 1870:

Married - On Sunday, the 8th October, by Rev. H. H. HAYS, Mr. HENRY MC-CLELLAN to Miss MARY ROGERS, all of Oconee county.

Married - On Thursday, 10th November, by the same, Mr. WM. DAVIS to Miss MARANDA JANE ELROD, all of Anderson county.

Married - On Wednesday, 7th December, by the same, Mr. JOSEPH DARBY to Miss SUSAN LEROY, all of Oconee county.

Issue of Friday January 6, 1871:

Married - On the 7th ult., by Rev. WM. MC WHORTER, Mr. D. BUSH, of Banks, to Miss IDA E., daughter of Mr. PATTON JARRETT, of Habersham county, Ga.

Married - On the 15th ult., at the residence of the bride's father, by Rev. A. NORRIS, Mr. E. KEESE and Miss SALLIE J., eldest daughter of Mr. B. F. and Mrs. REBECCA LANDRUM, all of Edgefield.

Issue of Friday January 13, 1871:

Married - On the 22d December, by the Rev. H. N. HAYS, Mr. SCARBER MAUL-DEN to Miss NARCISSA KEASLER, all of Oconee county.

Married - On the 27th December, by the same, Mr. LAWRENCE O. DAVIS and Miss CATHARINE M. GRANT, all of Oconee county.

Married - On the 22nd ult., at Keowee, by FLETCHER SMITH, Mr. A. WILLI-MAN, of Greenville, to Miss HIGHLAND MARY GANTT, of Oconee.

Issue of Friday January 20, 1871:

Obituary - Departed this life, in Walhalla, on the 8th inst., in the 10th year of her age, LILLY, eldest daughter of Mr. and Mrs. A. W. THOMP-SON. Lilly was certainly one of the most intelligent children we have ever known...could converse fluently upon any subject with which she was the least familiar, to the entertainment of older heads....faculty for music was largely developed....illness painful and protracted...long eulogy written by a "Friend".

Issue of Friday February 3, 1871:

Married - On 26th ult., at the residence of the bride's father, by Rev. Fletcher Smith, Mr. F. W. PIEPER, of Charleston, to Miss MAGGIE, only daughter of M. C. WENDELKIN, Esq., of this place.

State of South Carolina, Pickens County. In Probate Court - Petition for Partition, Sale, etc. W. D. EDENS, et al vs. JOHN M. C. EDENS, et al. .....appearing to my satisfaction that JOHN M. C. EDENS, heirs of WIL-LIAM JACKSON EDENS, deceased....number and names unknown..and EVALINE B. GALLAWAY, defendants in this case, reside beyond the limits of this State.

Issue of Friday February 17, 1871:

Married - On Thursday, 12 January 1871, by Rev. H. N. Hays, Mr. WARREN D. MOORE to Miss EVALINE BALDWIN, all of Oconee county.

Married - by the same, on Thursday, 26th January, Mr. WILLIAM CAMPBELL to Miss MARY ANN COX, all of Oconee county.

Married - By the same, on Thursday, 2d February, Mr. WILLIAM PITTS, of
Oconee county, to Miss C. C. PATTERSON, of Anderson county.

Issue of Friday March 3, 1871:

Married - On the 23d of February by the Rev. D. D. BYARS, Mr. JAMES SEA-
BORN to Miss ANNIE MASON, all of Fair Play.

Issue of Friday March 10, 1871:

Fatal Shooting - Near Pickens C. H., on 3d inst., ANDERSON LOOPER and
ZACHARIAH YOUNG fired their pistols simultaneously at each other. The
balls took effect on each near the heart, causing their death instantly.
"Contraband" whiskey is said to be the cause of this unfortunate occur-
ence.

Final Settlement - On Thursday, 16th day of March, 1871, I will apply to
I. H. PHILPOT, Esq., Judge of Probate, at Pickens C. H., for leave to
make a final settlement of the Estate of EUGENIA A. GARY, (formerly E.A.
BRAZEALE) a Minor; and to be discharge therefrom as Guardian. E. H.
GRIFFIN, Guardian.

Issue of Friday March 17, 1871:

Obituary - Died, on the 20th of January 1871, ALEXANDER RAMSEY, Sen.,
...the 30th September last completed his 71st year....born in Old Pendleton, that part now Oconee county, and within the bounds of the Old Stone
Church, where his mortal remains were deposited, among so many of the
hallowed dead, whose memories we love to cherish. Most of his earthly
life was spent in the county of his birth.......member of the Tugalo
Presbyterian Church...left widow and many children...(long eulogy by
W.P.G.)

Issue of Friday March 24, 1871:

Married - On Thursday morning, 16th inst., by Rev. Fletcher Smith, Capt.
M. C. BRAY, formerly of Richmond, Va., to Mrs. E. J. MC GREGOR, of Walhalla.

Issue of Friday March 31, 1871:

Married - On Tuesday evening, March 21st, by Rev. WM. MC WHORTER, Mr.
JOSEPH G. STEELE, of Montana Territory, to Miss S. MATTIE ALEXANDER,
adopted daughter of JAS. A. DOYLE, of Oconee county, S. C.

Off For the West! Our friend, Mr. JOSEPH G. STEELE, of Montana Territory, who has been on a visit to his kindred and friends here, left for
his home in the far West on the 23d inst. A number of the young men of
Pickens and Oconee return with him to better their fortunes in the great
West. But the lines under the "Hymenial" head, best indicate our loss
and the gain of friend Steele. He has taken one of our fairest daughters
to his distant home, to cheer his future and better his bachelor condition. May happiness and prosperity attend them!

Burned to Death - We regret to learn that a little daughter of Mr. WM.
WELSH, of this county, was burned to death last week. The child, as we
understand, was playing in a sedge field, when fire was communicated to
it. The flames spread with such rapidity that the child was unable to
make its escape.

Issue of Friday April, 28, 1871:

State of South Carolina, Pickens County. In Probate Court - Petition for
Partition, etc. JOHN A. CHASTAIN vs. LUCINDA CHASTAIN, NANCY EVALINE
CHASTAIN, et al. ....satisfaction of this court that the heirs of A. M.
CLEVELAND CHASTAIN, dec'd, to wit: NANCY R. L. P. CHASTAIN, and RACHEL
L. CHASTAIN, reside beyond the limits of this State.

State of South Carolina, Oconee County. In Probate Court - Partition
of Real Estate, Account, Etc...PERMELIA G. ROGERS, Plaintiff vs. MARTHA

B. SNEAD, AMANDA C. SLOAN, ARCHIE L. SNEAD, BENJAMIN H. SNEAD, WM. SNEAD and SAMUEL SNEAD, defendants. Concerning the partition of the Real Estate of PHILLIP SNEAD, dec'd.

Issue of Friday May 5, 1871:

Married - On the 1st inst., by Rev. B. HOLDER, Capt. ROBERT GADD, of Charlotte, N. C., to Miss NANCY ANN CARPENTER, of Walhalla.

Issue of Friday May 12, 1871:

Married - On Thursday, 4th May inst., at the residence of the bride's father, by Rev. Fletcher Smith, Mr. B. C. LOWERY to Miss KATE, daughter of Col. M. R. HUNNICUTT, all of Oconee county.

Issue of Friday May 26, 1871:

Married - On the evening of May 10, 1871, by the Rev. A. RICE, at his residence, Mr. JOHN B. PUCKETT, of Oconee county, to Miss MARY F. BROWNE only daughter of J. M. BROWNE, of Anderson county.

Married - In Townville, Saturday, 13th of May, by Rev. H. N. Hays, Mr. W. F. JEANES to Miss MARY S. PALMER, all of Anderson county.

Married - On Sunday, 14th May, by the same, Mr. JAMES BARTON to Miss MARTHA SIMMONS, all of Anderson county.

Death of a Veteran of 1812 - We have received information of the death, on 17th inst., of Captain WILLIAM STEELE, a highly respected citizen of this county........born at old Pendleton Village, his father being one of the first settlers of that place; and at the time of his death, was about eighty years of age. When the war of 1812 broke out, he enlisted in the naval service of the United States and served faithfully through the war. He was a midshipman on the Frigate Constitution, under command of Captain STEWART, when that vessel won...victory over the united forces of the British vessels, "the Cyane and Levant".....1834, he was elected to the Legiislature from Pendleton...at the close of his term, was made tax collector for Pendleton District, in which capacity he served until 1840, when this tax District was divided into two, Anderson and Pickens ...election given to the people. Again elected as Tax Collector of Anderson District.....farmer.....(long eulogy)

Issue of Friday June 2, 1871:

State of South Carolina, County of Oconee. In Probate Court - Petition and Complaint for Relief, etc. WM. MC WHORTER, Adm'r of the Personal estate of MARY MC WHORTER, dec'd. vs. DAVID MC WHORTER, SARAH L. MC-WHORTER, MATILDA MYERS, wife of HENRY MYERS, ANNA BEATY, wife of ROBERT M. BEATY, Distributees of MOSES MC WHORTER, to wit: His widow_____ McWhorter, and daughters, ANNA THOMAS, wife of _____ Thomas, and MARY MC WHORTER, Distributees of JOHN MC WHORTER, dec'd...names and number unknown, and distributees of ISAAC MC WHORTER, dec'd...names and number unknown.

Issue of Friday June 9, 1871:

Death of JOHN BOWEN - We regret to learn that Mr. JOHN BOWEN, a prominent citizen of Pickens county, and formerly tax collector of Pickens District, died on Saturday last, at his residence in that County.

Issue of Friday June 16, 1871:

Obituary - Capt. WILLIAM STEELE departed this life May 17th, 1871; born October 22d, 1796. (see above obituary on Steele)...member of Mt.Zion Church in Anderson District...Elder...1851, removed to Pickens District ....member and ruling elder of Retreat Church...two years since, membership of entire family transferred to Richland Church...Presbyterian... followed by a lengthy eulogy by a "friend".

(Both articles are of some length and almost identical in text...cme)

Issue of Friday June 23, 1871:

Married - On Thursday, 15th inst., by Rev. Fletcher Smith, Col. J. L.
BOYD to Mrs. MARGARET C., daughter of Mr. ROBERT KNOX, all of Oconee.

Issue of Friday June 30, 1871:

Death of ROBERT KIRKSEY- We regret to learn that Mr. Robert Kirksey, of
Pickens county, died on Thursday of last week, aged seventy-one years.

Issue of Friday July 14, 1871:

Obituary - Mr. WILLIAM N. WHITE died of Heart disease, 6th July, at his
own residence, near Walhalla, S. C., aged 34 years. ..native of Oconee
(formerly Pickens) county...reared by pious parents.....youngest son...
(Eulogy written by D. J. McM.)....left wife and two children.

Married - On Tuesday evening, 11th inst., at the residence of the brides
father, by Rev. Fletcher Smith, Mr. WILLIAM H. STROTHER, of Edgefield,
to Miss HASSIE M., daughter of Capt. J. P. MICKLER, of West Union.

(Note: Several years are missing for the "Keowee Courier", unavailable
from either the State Archives or Walhalla office...cme)

Issue of Thursday April 4, 1878:

Killed his Father - On Saturday last, JESSIE MITCHUM and his son, in
company with HENRY W. BLACK, were on their way home from Branchville,
when young Mitchum and Black became involved in a difficulty. The former drew a pistol and attempted to shoot the latter. At this critical
moment, the old gentleman sprang between the two disputants, and while
attempting to arrest the bloody purpose of his son received the ball
from his son's pistol that was intended for Mr. Black, from the effects
of which he died. "Collecton Democrat"

Died - at Seneca City on Wednesday morning, March 27, after a brief illness, Mrs. McCARLEY, the young wife of Mr. T. A. McCARLEY, a merchant of
Seneca. She leaves a young infant about ten days old. Her funeral took
place on Friday amid the tears of relatives and the sympathies of friends.

State of South Carolina, Oconee County. In the Court of Probate. W. F.
CORBIN, as Adm'r and heir-at-law of WM. CORBIN, dec'd., Plaintiff,
against BELONA CORBIN, widow, REBECCA LUSK, EDDY MALINDA FOWLER, MARTHA
JANE MOODY, LEMUEL T. CORBIN, MARY ALICE WILLIAMS, HARRIET GOULDEN,
children; WM. B. F. CORBIN, SARAH JANE CORBIN, FRANCIS MALONE CORBIN and
MARTHA MALINDA WILSON, grandchildren and heirs-at-law of WM. CORBIN,decd.
Defendants-Complaint for Relief, etc.,etc.

Issue of Thursday April 11, 1878:

Townville Locals - Mrs. POLLY LANIER, a respectable widowed lady residing near here, died recently at the ripe age of 84.

Miss WOOD, of Richland County, who shot and killed SAMUEL HENRY, in
November 1877, while assaulting her with criminal intent, was tried in
Columbia last Monday and acquitted.

State of South Carolina, Oconee County. In the Court of Probate. JOHN
N. GRANT, Plaintiff, vs. MALINDA RUSSELL and others, Defendants. - Summons in Partition. To MALINDA RUSSELL, ESTHER HUNNICUTT, heirs-at-law
of PRESSLEY LANIER, dec'd; heirs-at-law of BARTLEY LANIER, dec'd; heirs-
at-law of WILLIAM LANIER, dec'd; heirs-at-law of ALLEN LANIER, dec'd;
NANCY GRANT; heirs-at-law of LEETHE GRANT, dec'd, Defendants. Partition
of the Real Estate of BIRD LANIER, dec'd. (Also BIRD LANIER, Ex'r and
SARAH A. HUTCHINS.)

Married - On Sunday morning, April 14th, by Rev. J. J. NEVILLE, Mr.
ROBERT MATHESON to Miss BETSY GRAHAM, all of Oconee county.

Mr. WARREN LAWRENCE, formerly of this State, and now a resident of Chickasaw county, Mississippi, is on a visit to his old home and relations.

Thursday, April 25, 1878:

Mr. TURNER, living at Burns' Mills, lost a little child on last Friday. It was buried on Saturday in the Baptist Church cemetery at this place.

Thursday May 2, 1878:

W. W. FARROW, a printer from Abbeville, S. C. and at one time the editor and proprietor of the "Banner", of that town, died in Winston, N. C., on Friday of last week, of consumption. He was buried with Masonic honors.

Thursday May 9, 1878:

Oakway Locals - Married, on Sunday morning, 28th day of April last, at the bride's mothers, Mr. DAVID A. STEWART to Miss S. JANE HARGROVES, all of Oconee. J. B. SANDERS officiated.

DANIEL AIKEN, a peaceable, industrious and harmless citizen of Oakway, died recently, after a protracted and serious illness, leaving a wife and many children to mourn their loss. He was buried at New Bethel Church.

Locals - Died, on the 13th April, 1878, at the residence of Mrs. E. E. ROBINSON, Mrs. ELIZABETH GRAY, in the 91st year of her age. She died in full faith of a blessed immortality.

Thursday May 16, 1878:

Locals - Died, on April 13, 1878, Mr. N. H. CARTER, an old citizen of this county, aged 64 years.

ANTHONY MAY was hung at Darlington on the 3d inst. for the murder of ROBERT SUGGS, nearly ten years ago. He was convicted at the last term of the court upon confession made to different persons at different times. The execution was private. Years ago CYRUS COACHMAN was hung for the same murder.

JEFF DAVID, colored, was convicted at the last term of court at Abbeville of the murder of GEORGE and DRUCILLA FRANKLIN, December 20th, 1877. He will be hanged the 17th inst. The evidence against him was all circumstantial.

Thursday June 6, 1878:

Oakway Locals - Rev. J. J. NEVILLE, P.C. of the Walhalla and Seneca City Circuit, preached at Centre Church on Saturday evening last, and on Sunday preached the funeral sermon of Mrs. CHARLOTTE COLE, who died last September.

Thursday June 13, 1878:

Locals- Mrs. SULLIVAN, the wife of Mr. J. F. SULLIVAN, died on Tuesday of last week. She had been sick and bed-ridden for two or three years, and no doubt death was a relief to her. She was buried in the Baptist cemetery at the Baptist Church on last Wednesday.

Thursday June 20, 1878:

Married - On Thursday evening, June 6, 1878, by Reb. B. HOLDER, Mr. ANDREW JONES to Miss FRANCIS CANE, all of Oconee.

Married - Near Richland Church, at the residence of the bride's father, M. S. STRIBLING, June 11, 1878, by Rev. S. L. MORRIS, Mr. T. B. WYLY and Miss ANNA STRIBLING.

Suicide in Edgefield - Mr. WM. E. BRYAN, a young man residing at Edgefield C. H., shot and killed himself with a pistol in his room, in the village, at half-past 10 o'clock A.M., Friday. The ball entered the right temple and passed to and lodged in the left temple. He left letters addressed to his mother, the Edgefield Rifles, Dr. BLAND and others. In one of these letters he assigned pecuniary embarrassment as the cause of his committing the rash act.

We are in receipt of a copy of the "Gazette", daily and weekly, edited and published by D. MC NEIL TURNER, JR., Esq., at Corpus Christi, Texas. "The Gazette" appears to be in a flourishing condition and reflects credit upon Mr. Turner. Mr. Turner was formerly a citizen of Walhalla and is well remembered by many of our citizens.

We regret to announce the death of JONAS PHILLIPS, SR., which sad event occurred at his residence, in this county, on Thursday morning last. Mr. Phillips was, we learn, over ninety years of age and was one of the first settlers above the Indian boundry line. Mr. Phillips had resided where he died for many years, his place being noted as the centre of the section where he lived. Mr. Phillips leaves a large family and many friends to mourn his death.

Thursday June 27, 1878:

Locals - Mr. THOMAS BROOM was kicked severely by a horse on Monday last. He lingered until the next day, when he died from the effects of the hurt. Mr. Broom was over fifty years of age and one of our finest citizens.

We regret to learn of the death of the infant son of Mr. and Mrs. L. B. LEE, aged about twenty months, which occurred at their residence on Keowee River, on the 25th inst., after a short illness.

Thursday July 4, 1878:

Locals - Mr. JOHN SUTTLES, of Walhalla, departed this life this (Wednesday) morning at 3 o'clock. Mr. S. was over seventy years of age.

Mrs. THOMAS CHASTAIN, living in the neighborhood of Richland Church, died on Last Monday and was buried in the Baptist Church yard at Walhalla on Tuesday.

Thursday July 11, 1878:

Locals - Died, in Greenville, Texas, on the 21st June, 1878, MARGARET VINETTA, infant daughter of FRANK P. and GEORGIA A. ALEXANDER, at the age of three months and twenty days.

Col. T. C. WEATHERLY, a well known citizen of Marlboro, and formerly member of the Legislature, died at Glenn Springs.

Thursday July 18, 1878:

We chronicle with regret the death of Mr. JOHN ROSS, one of the esteemed citizens of our county, which occurred on the 12th inst., at his home, near Salem Church. The immediate cause of his death was cancer of the face. Mr. Ross has for thirty years been a resident of Oconee and was over eighty years old at the time of his death.

We regret to announce the death of Dr. T. S. MILLER, which occurred at his residence near Bachelor's Retreat, on last Saturday evening after a short illness. Dr. Miller was perhaps the oldest practicing physician in the county and had enjoyed an extensive and lucrative practice over thirty years. He was one of our best citizens and enjoyed the confidence and esteem of all who knew him. His loss as a physician will be greatly felt in his neighborhood and as a pure and upright citizen by the people of the County and State. He leaves a widow and several children who have our sympathy in their sad bereavement.

Thursday August 1, 1878:
Married - On the 7th of July, by the Rev. H. M. BARTON, at the residence

of the bride's father, UPSON MARTIN, JOHN LEE, JR., to Miss ELIZA MARTIN, all of Oconee.

Married - July 25th, 1878, by Rev. NIMROD SULLIVAN, Mr. BEATIE OAKLEY to M(rs.) NANCY OWENS, all of Oconee.

Married - On Sunday, the 28th day of July, at Mountain Rest, S. C., by W. A. KING, Esq., Mr. THOMAS BROWN, of Randolph County, Alabama, to Miss EMMA BOWER, of Oconee.

We regret to announce the death of Mr. JOHN HARDIN, one of our best citizens, on the 25th ult. Mr. Hardin was in his 66th year, and leaves many friends to mourn his death.

Thursday August 8, 1878:

State of South Carolina, Oconee County. - In the Court of Probate. Sale or Partition of the Real Estate of CLAYTON JENKINS, deceased, situated in the said county on Rockey Fork creek, waters of Chauga Creek, waters of Tugaloo River. GEORGE M. JENKINS, Plaintiff, vs. ELIZABETH JENKINS, MARY JANE CHAMBERS, JAMES G. JENKINS, ARY AMANDA RAGLAND, URIAH JENKINS, EPHRAIM COBB and BENSON TURNER, Defendants.

Oakway Locals - Mrs. N. J. PRICE, consort of Maj. N. PRICE, died very suddenly on Sunday evening of the 28th ultimo and was buried at South Union. On Tuesday after Rev. E. M. MERITT preached the funeral to a large number of weeping friends. Mrs. Price was an excellent, pious and intellectual lady, a kind and affectionate mother and neighbor. She leaves a weeping husband and seven or eight distressed children. She had been a constant member of the Methodist Episcopal Church South for several years.

JAMES O. SANDERS died this morning at 4 o'clock from an affection of the bladder, after a severe illness of two weeks. He was a quiet, industrious and good citizen, leaving a wife and children to mourn their loss.

Thursday August 15, 1878:

Married - August 5th, 1878, by the Rev. NIMROD SULLIVAN, Mr. JEREMIAH L. FRADY to Miss ELIZABETH OAKLEY, all of Oconee.

We are glad to see Prof. W. H. VERNER on a visit to his old home in Oconee. Prof. Verner is from Tuscaloosa, Alabama, the seat of the State University and five other colleges. He expects to remain some time in Oconee.

We have received intelligence of the death of Mr. ALEXANDER GLENN, an aged and highly esteemed citizen of our county, which occurred at his residence, near Fair Play, on last Sunday night. Mr. Glenn had been in a feeble health for a number of years and by reason of this and his advanced age was confined chiefly to his house for a considerable period before his death. He had long been a consistent member of the Presbyterian Church, and exemplified in life those Christian graces which are the fruits of a heart at peace with God and man.

State of South Carolina, Oconee County - Mortgagee's Sale. - By virtue of the power conferred upon me in the Mortgage given me by ELIZABETH KNIGHT, now ELIZABETH WILLIAMS, on the 16th of April 1877, of the tract of land etc,etc. H. S. VANDIVIERE Mortgagee

Died, in Anderson County, July 31, Rev. A. RICE, one of the oldest ministers of the Baptist denomination in South Carolina.

Died in Greenwood, S. C., July 28, Gen. JAMES GILLAM, age 87.

Thursday August 22, 1878:

We regret to announce the death of Mr. FRED TIEDEMAN, of Charleston, which took place at the residence of Mr. C. H. ROCHAU, of Walhalla, on the 20th instant. He was the victim of that insidious disease consumption. The funeral services will be held at the Lutheran Church on Friday, conducted in both English and German.

We learn that Dr. D. E. FOUTZ died at Horse Cove, N. C., on Tuesday, the 20th, of consumption. He was the proprietor of the celebrated horse powders, which have a world wide reputation. He was a native of Baltimore, Md., and had recently gone to Horse Cove for his health. His remains will no doubt be carried to Baltimore for interment.

JOSEPH THOMPSON REID, son of GEORGE T. and L. J. REID, of Abbeville County, died on the 19th instant, in Walhalla, at the residence of Col. W.C. KEITH, aged four years and fifteen days. Joseph was a promising child, winning the hearts of all about him by his affectionate disposition and remarkable intelligence. He was the joy and pride of his parents, who had centered the broken ties, severed in the death of his little brother a year ago, on this child. Death is at all times a sad thing, but how ainfully sad is the death of a child, in the full possession of consciousness and physical strength. During his illness he was patient, submitting to all painful efforts for his relief, but with an apparent look as if they were useless, and only delaying him on his way to God to meet his little brother. He had in health frequently spoken of his journey, and it ought to be solace to his parents to know that their earthly treasure has been transplanted to heaven, where he will be safely kept watching and waiting their coming. How many piteous lamentations for loved ones lost to earth would be turned to joy could we realize the true aim and purpose of life, and see with the eye of faith what Christ has made death to become. This, however, is above frail humanity, and death always brings its train of mourners.

Miss E. GRIMSHAW, of Whiteside Cove, North Carolina, died on Tuesday the 20th and her body was brought to Walhalla on Wednesday and deposited in the Presbyterian Church during the night, preparatory to shipment to Greenville for burial. We did not learn the cause of her death.

Thursday August 29, 1878:

Battle Creek Locals - Mrs. SALLIE PITTS, wife of H. M. PITTS, died on the 17th instant and was buried on the 18th, at Damascus Church.

ALECK DEWET, was hung at Darlington on the 9th inst., for the murder of WILLIAM WARREN in 1871. At the gallows he lost all self-control. and after baffling the executioner several times jumped off the drop and died of strangulation.

Mr. L. B. MASHBURN, of this county, died at his home at Oconee Station, on Thursday, the 22nd inst. Mr. M. was a native of Macon County, N. C. and was said to be a good citizen and a kind neighbor. He had reached the ripe age of sixty years. His disease was consumption.

Thursday September 26, 1878:

Married - At the residence of the bride's father, Mr. FRANK GRAHAM, on Thursday evening, 12th of September, 1878, by Rev. H. N. HAYS, Mr. JAMES MOORE and Miss MARGARET GRAHAM, both of Oconee county.

We learn from our exchanges the intelligence that Mrs.MC GOWAN, wife of Gen. S. MC GOWAN, died at her home in Abbeville last week. Mrs. McGowan was the daughter of Judge WARDLAW, one of the purest and ablest of our ante-war judiciary, and exemplified in life those virtues which adorn the character of a wife and mother.

ERNEST L. JONES, a native of Rockingham County, North Carolina, but for some time a resident of West Union, died at Phinney's Hotel on Wednesday evening the 18th inst., from the amputation of his leg and its diseased condition before the operation. The operation was performed on Tuesday before by Dr. MAHER, of Newberry, assisted by Dr. WILLIAMS of Walhalla, and the patient revived and seemed at first to be improving. The amputation was rendered necessary from an old wound received during the war at Winchester, Virginia, in 1864. It had once healed, but again broke out, growing worse every year, debilitating and poisoning the system. He

delayed the amputation too long. It was thought there would be a chance
for life under the operation, while without it no hopes of recovery were
entertained. The matter was fully understood by him and he desired to
take the risk under the operation. The amputation was skillfully performed, but his general debility and the poison in the system from a sore,
so bad and of such long standing, produced death. His body was buried by
the Masonic fraternity in the Baptist Churchyard at Walhalla on Thursday
evening with the peculiar ceremonies of that ancient order.

State of South Carolina, County of Oconee. - In the Court of Common Pleas
Summons of Relife - Complaint not served. - MALINDA MILLER, CAROLINE HO-
NEA, Plaintiffs, vs. SIDNEY DAVIS and others, Defendants. To SIDNEY DAV-
IS, EDWARD HONEA, JOHN F. MILLER, REBECCA DAVIS, ELIZA PICKENS, heirs-
at- law of JOHN E. DAVIS, deceased; heirs-at-law of A. P. DAVIS, deceased.
SUSAN ANDING, F. H. DAVIS, W. R. DAVIS, Defendants in this action. Parti-
tion of the real estate of JOHN E. DAVIS, deceased.

Thursday October 3, 1878:

Married - On the 12th of September, 1878, by Rev. FLETCHER SMITH, near
Westminster, Mr. WM. H. BALLINGER and Miss TALULAH F. JENKINS, all of
Oconee.

Married - On the 22d of September, 1878, at the residence of JOHN M. DOW-
IS, Esq., Habersham county, Ga., by Rev. Mr. CURTIS, Mr. WM. DOOLEY and
Miss DORCAS POTETT.

Obituary - Died, September 30th, 1878, ELEY WALKER, son of Mr. and Mrs.
J. L. SHANKLIN, aged one year and five months.

Death of Dr. J. W. KIBBEE - Highlands, N. C.   September 30.
Messers. Editors: This community has suffered an irreparable loss in the
death of Dr. J. W. KIBBEE. The Doctor had invented a fever cot with
which he had performed some remarkable cures. The ravages of the yellow
fever were such as to work on his sympathies in such a way that he finally decided to go to New Orleans and work in the cause of humanity. He
had unlimited confidence in his cot and treatment of yellow fever, as he
had reason to be, for four years ago at Memphis he was quite successful
in treating it. Some six weeks ago he went to New York to complete arrangements in the manufacture of his fever-cot, and while there worked
very hard in order to hurry to New Orleans. He finally reached that city
at night, and being anxious to get to work, he reported to the Board of
Health the next morning and immediately took charge of some cases. He
had the satisfaction of seeing a promising young man speedily recovering,
but alas! at the expense of his own life. His quick change of climate
and jaded and over worked system made him an easy victim of the pestilen-
tial miasma. He was taken down suddenly with the fever on the 19th of
September and died four days after. He had the tenderest of care and
after he died all possible honors were paid to his remains. Words are
inadequate to express the heroism of such a character and posterity will
hold him in honorable rememberance. He left a wife and three children
here and they are surrounded with many sympathizing and aching hearts.
The people here had become attached to him, for he was of a cheery nature
and had a pleasant word for everyone. He had become known and had gotten
quite a practice, extending into Jackson County and to South Carolina.
The loss is severe to Highlands, for he was an enthusiastic admirer of
the country and climate, and had he lived would have given valuable aid
in building up the country. But for God's ways are not our ways. Bx

Locals - We regret to learn that Mrs. BARBARA ALBERTSON, of Brasstown,
died of consumption on the 14th ultimo, in the 40th year of her age.

Mrs. MARY FEASTER died at Jacksonville, Fla., September 23, in her 78th
year. She formerly lived at Feasterville, in Fairfield county, S. C.
She has relatives living in this county to whom her death will be a sad
bereavement.

Thursday October 10, 1878:

Locals - C. BECHTLER died in Charlotte, N. C., on the 27th ultimo. He will be recollected by ante-war readers, as the man who made one dollar gold pieces before the war.

A. J. HINKLE, one of the "moonshine raiders" on the revenue officers in Pickens County, and who was convicted at the last term of the United States Court at Greenville, died in jail at that place last week.

ANDREW LONG lost his life in this county on Saturday last, in working a sorghum mill. His head was caught in the machinery and crushed to pieces. He died instantly.

Thursday October 17, 1878:

Married - By the Rev. A. COKE SMITH, at the residence of the bride's mother, in Pickens county, on Thursday afternoon, October 3, 1878, Mr. THOMAS C. ROBINSON, of Greenville and Miss ELLA, only daughter of Mrs. BAYLAS CLAYTON.

Thursday October 24, 1878:

Married - At Central, S. C., September 22, 1878, by Rev. Mr. DAWSON, of Pendleton, Mr. JOHN WRIGHT and Miss SUSAN SMITH.

Married - September 29, 1878, by the same, Mr. WALTER CASEY, of Central, and Miss ALICE JONES, of Anderson.

Married - On the 20th inst., at the bride's father, by Dr. J. P. SMELTZER, Mr. JOHN F. SULLIVAN to Miss ABBIE M. WIEBENS, both of Walhalla,S.C.

Thursday October 31, 1878:

Married - On Tuesday, October 22d, 1878, at the residence of Mrs. H. T. BROWN, Townville, S. C., by Rev. W. H. STRICKLAND, Mr. J. L. TRIBBLE and Miss EMMA E. FEASTER.

Thursday November 7, 1878:

State of South Carolina, Anderson County - In Probate Court. Petition for Partition. Mrs. MARY M. ISBELL, Plaintiff, vs. NANCY M. CLEVELAND, MARY E. GLENN and others. Sale at public auction of the real estate of Rev. SAMUEL ISBELL, dec'd., 160 acres more or less situated in Oconee county on the waters of Big Beaverdam Creek.

Thursday November 14, 1878:

Locals 0 Mrs. UBERNICKEL died in Walhalla last Monday and was buried in the Lutheran churchyard on Tuesday. She was thirty four years old, a worthy mother and wife, and leaves a husband and several children to mourn her untimely death.

Married - At the residence of the bride's father, Capt. ANDREW HUNTER, near Townville, on Thursday evening the 7th inst., by Rev. J. R. RILEY, Mr. JAMES L. FARMER and Miss AGNES LULA HUNTER.

Married - At the Baptist Church, Walhalla, on the evening of the 7th inst. by Rev. L. W. WINGO, Mr. J. W. SHELOR and Miss M. L. NEVILL, all of Walhalla.

Married - On the 7th inst., by Rev. FLETCHER SMITH, Mr. ANDERSON C. BROWNE and Miss ANNIE M. HUBBARD, all of Oconee.

Thursday November 21, 1878:

Maj. JOSEPH M. ADAMS, of Oconee County, died on last Friday morning, after a long and distressing illness. He was an excellant gentleman and an accomplished scholar. For some years previous to the war he was the principal of the flourishing male academy in Anderson, and was a thorough and successful instructor. After the war Major Adams was admitted to the bar and practiced law as a partner of Gen. S. McGOWAN at old Pickens Court House until he deceided to follow agricultural pursuits, and accor-

dingly removed to his plantation near Perryville, in Oconee county. For
the past two years he has been in declining health, so that his death
was not altogether unexpected. On Friday last his remains were interred
in the family burial ground at Deep Creek, in this county, after solemn
funeral services conducted by Rev. J. S. MURRAY. His family have the
sympathy of this community in their bereavement. "Anderson Intelligencer"

Married - On Tuesday the 12th inst., at the residence of the bride's
father, by the Rev. J. B. DAVIES, Mr. JOHN M. HENDRIX, of Walhalla, to
Miss EMMA E. COOK, of Mount Pleasant, Cabarrus County, N. C.

Married - At the residence of the bride's father, in Walhalla, on the
evening of the 19th inst., by Rev. J. G. BOEHM, Mr. JOHN ROSE to Miss
JULIANNA BAUMGARTEL.

Married - At the residence of the bride's father, Dr. THOS. L. LEWIS,
Walhalla, on the evening of the 19th inst., by Rev. J. J. NEVILLE, Mr.
O. L. HENRY, of Elbert County, Ga., and Miss JULIA LEWIS.

Locals- We regret to announce the death of Col. F. E. HARRISON, of Andersonville. He died on Monday last of disease of the throat. Col. Harrison was one of the best citizens of this section. (see below obit.)

Thursday November 28, 1878:

Married - On Wednesday evening, the 20th inst., near Westminster, at the
residence of the bride's father, W. F. PARKER, Esq., by Rev. S. L. MORRIS,
Mr. G. W, GREEN and Miss TECOA PARKER.

Death of Rev. W. W. SANDERS - The following sad information contained on
a postal card to Mr. J. W. STRIBLING, of our town, will be read with
feelings of surprise and sorrow. Mr. Sanders was well known to our people: Lynchburg, Va., November 25, 1878: Dear Brother: Yours of the 25th
found Bro. W. W. Sanders inour town where he had come to build up his
health. He had long been suffering from severe periodical attacks of
billious fever, and came to our "hill city" hoping that the mountain air
would restore him. But alas! alas! all was of no avail, and our dear
Sanders died to day about 1 o'clock. His remains will be sent to Tuscaloosa, Ala., tomorrow. How sad, how very, very sad! While the leaders
are falling the privates must close the ranks and press on. You knew
him and do not need that I speak of him. "He walked with God and God
took him." Yours truly, R. R. ACREE

Death of Col. F. E. HARRISON - This distinguished citizen of Anderson
county, died of laryngetis with typhoid fever, at his residence at Andersonville last Saturday night at twelve o'clock. Col. Harrison's military record for courage and efficiency was all that the most ambitious
could desire. He entered the Confederate Service as Captain of company
D., ORR's Regiment, at Sandy Springs, in July, 1861, and served as Captain and the immediate offices until he was promoted to the command of
his regiment. In command of one of the finest regiments in the service,
he took a high stand as a military officer, and much beloved and respected by his subordinates. At the battle of Gaines Mill, in 1862, near
Richmond, he was so seriously wounded that it was for several months before he could resume his position in the field, and finally, owing to
the effects of which, as well as his failing health, he was compelled to
resign his commission, and return to his family an invalid. ....a
member and Elder in Roberts' Presbyterian Church.....married three times;
first, to Miss ROSS, of Pendleton; second, to Miss PERRIN, of this
place, the daughter of Hon. T. C. PERRIN; third, in February last, to
Miss COTHRAN, of this town. The latter survives him and to whom the
sympathies of this community go out warmly in her great loss. ....as he
lived at his old family homestead of Andersonville, but after he married
in Abbeville, we had the pleasure of meeting him....a gentleman of the
old school...courteous, dignified and modest. ..(brief eulogy)..
                                        "Abbeville Press and Banner"

Locals - Mr. JORDAN BURNS, who resides near Townville, died recently in
his 67th year.

134

A little child of Mr. H. B. J. W. SCHRODER, living near our town, died on Tuesday of last week, of diphtheria.

Mr. WM. SUMMER, of Newberry, died on the 25th inst. Mr. Summer was well known and was a most useful citizen. He was editor of the "Southern Planter" before the war.

Mr. A. L. LAWTON, of Calhoun's mills, Abbeville, was instantly killed last Sunday evening by the kick of a mule. The man who puts his trust in a mule is not wise.

The wedding ceremonies, uniting Col. J. C. HEMPHILL, handsome and distinguished editor of the "Abbeville Medium", to Miss R. M. TRUE, of Flushing, New York, took place on the morning of November 19th, in the Methodist Episcopal Church - the rites being solomnized by the Rev. E. H. TRUE, assisted by Rev. Mr. PERRY.

A sad event has occurred in our town. Capt. F. WIEBENS, one of the oldest German citizens, died of lingering disease on Monday last. When the war broke out, although too old for active service, he volunteered "for the war", and remained in the army as long as his health would permit. The heart of Capt. Wiebens was large and in the right place. He suffered for months, but died calmly and peacefully. The funeral service and burial took place during the storm on Tuesday afternoon. The old soldier has fought his last battle. Peace to his soul!

Thursday December 5, 1878:

Married - At the residence of the bride's mother, Mrs. W. C. LEE, in Walhalla, on Sunday morning, December 1, 1878, by Rev. J. R. RILEY, Capt. J. H. SLIGH to Miss SALLIE R. LEE.

Married - By Rev. E. L. SISK, at the residence of the bride's mother, December 1, 1878, Mr. W. E. CLEVELAND to Miss SALLIE BRUCE, all of Oconee.

Married - By Rev. B. HOLDER, at the residence of the bride's father, on Thursday, November 7, 1878, Mr. WM. KING to Miss SUSAN MASON, all of this county.

Married - By the same, at the residence of the bride's father, on Thursday, November 21, 1878, Mr. GEORGE RANSOM, of Oconee county, to Miss AMANDA BROWN, of Anderson county.

Married - Sunday morning, December 1, 1878, at the residence of the bride's father, Mr. NOAH GRANT, by Rev. H. N. HAYS, Mr. JOHN MILLER to Miss SUSAN GRANT, both of Oconee county.

Locals - Mrs. JANE ANDERSON, an old citizen of this county, resident near Bachelor's Retreat, died at her home recently. She had a long time previous to her death been non compus mentus. In her younger days she was noted for her peculiar, eccentric and strange though good character.

Thursday December 12, 1878:

Married - At the residence of the bride's father, W. G. SMITH, Esq., at Sandy Springs, Anderson county, on Thursday evening, December 5th, 1878, by Rev. THOMAS DAWSON, of Pendleton, Mr. JAMES T. MC CORKLE of Central, and Miss AUGUSTIE M. SMITH.

Married - At the residence of the bride's mother, Mrs. ELVA SMITH, on Sunday evening, December 8th, 1878, by Rev. H. N. Hays, Mr. NOAH TOLLE-SON to Miss SALLIE SMITH, both of Oconee county.

Locals - Died, on the night of the 6th inst., near Pickens Court House, Mrs. H. J. ANTHONY.

Died, suddenly at Central, in Pickens county, on the night of the 2d instant, E. BLEVIN ALEXANDER.

Death is at all times sad. This feeling is intensified when the death
of one who was beloved by all passes away. We are thus impressed in an-
noucing the death of Mrs. JULIA MAXWELL, of this place, wife of Mr. SAM-
UEL MAXWELL. Her death was very sudden of disease of the heart. Mrs.Max-
well had passed the medium of life. During this period, by her gentle
manners and Christian graces, she had won the respect and affection of
all who knew her. Her remains were buried on Sunday, an inclement day,
in the Baptist Church graveyard, after the beautiful Episcopal buryal
services were read by Rev. Mr. LOGAN. The large attendance attested the
deep feeling of the community. Many of her old servants, who had been
brought with her in her youth from her home in the low country, followed
her sadly and in grief to the grave. Her bereaved family and friends
have the sympathy of the entire community.

Rev. TOLIVER ROBERTSON, of Laurens, died in Laurens, on the 3d inst., in
the 78th year of his age. He was a faithful and dearly beloved soldier
of the cross.

Thursday December 19, 1878:

Married - At NEVILL & HOLLEMAN's mill on the 7th inst., by W. J. NEVILL,
Esq., Mr. CHRISTIAN SHUNEMAN to Mrs. M. M. WHITE, all of Oconee county.

Married - On Tuesday evening, the 10th inst., at the residence of JACK-
SON DEATON, by Rev. BURREL WALL, Mr. JACKSON DEATON to Miss SUSAN HARBERT,
all of Oconee.

Also, at the same time and place, Mr. WELBURN CARVER to Miss ELIZABETH
HUTCHINS, all of Oconee.

Obituary - Died, suddenly, at her home in Walhalla, S. C., of heart
disease, December 6th, 1878, in the fifty-fourth year of her age, JULIA
SUSANNAH MAXWELL, the wife of SAMUEL E. MAXWELL. (Also see obit. above)
........lengthy eulogy follows, signed by "S".

Thursday December 26, 1878:

Married - At the residence of Col. W. C. KEITH, Walhalla, on Thursday
morning, December 19th, 1878, by Rev. J. R. RILEY, Mr. R. W. SHELOR and
Miss SALLIE R. REID, all of Oconee county.

Married - At the residence of the bride's father, Rev. D. H. KENNEMUR,
on Thursday evening, December 19th, 1878, by Rev. H. N. HAYS, Mr. HARRI-
SON MORGAN, of Oconee county, and Miss CYNTHIA A. KENNEMUR, of Pickens
county.

Locals - JOHN MILFORD, one of the oldest citizens of the county, died at
his residence, near Westminster, last Thursday night. We are informed
he was eighty-seven years old.

Thursday January 2, 1879:

Locals - An old and respected German fellow citizen, by the name of Mr.
JOHN REAULETTER, was accidentally burned to death one day last week.

An old widow lady, by the name of Mrs. _____ FREDERICKS, living in the
lower portion of the county, died at an advanced age last _____.

Married - At NEVILLE & HOLLEMAN's mills, by J. W. HOLLEMAN, Esq., on the
18th of December, 1878, Mr. RILEY SWAFFORD to Mrs. ARTA QUARLES, all of
Oconee.

Married - On the 24th of December, 1878, at the residence of the bride's
father, CALLAWAY STONE, Esq., by Rev. J. J. NEVILLE, Mr. JOHN MARTIN to
Miss MAGGIE STONE, both of Oconee county.

Married - December 26th, 1878, at the residence of Maj. N. PRICE, by Rev.
E. L. SISK, Mr. J. F. MC WHORTER, of Pickens, to Miss JANE BRUCE, of
Oconee.

Married - By Rev. J. O. LINDSAY, D. D., December 24th, 1878, at the residence of A. M. NORRIS, Mr. H. B. ZIMMERMAN, of Westminster, S. C., to
Miss LAURA E. MC LIN, of Anderson county, S. C.

Thursday January 9, 1879:

Married - On Sunday morning, January 5, 1879, by Rev. JUNIUS J. NEVILLE,
Mr. JOSEPH T. MARTIN to Miss MARTHA EMMA WYNN, both of Oconee county.

Married - On the 26th of December, 1878, by ISAAC WICKLIFFE, Esq., Mr.
ELLIOTT K. BREWER to Miss E. J. JONES, all of Oconee county.

Married - In Midway, Sunday evening, January 5, 1879, by Rev. J. R. RILEY,
Mr. H. HILLIAN to Miss MARY SNIPES.

Locals - Mr. THOMAS R. SHELOR died at his residence, in Georgia, on the
30th ultimo, after a lingering illness, at an advanced age. Mr. Shelor
was a native of Virginia. He removed to this State when a young man and
identified himself thoroughly with the people of his adopted state. By
industry and energy he accumulated a handsome property, and reared a most
interesting family. Some years ago, disgusted with the political condition of the State, Mr. Shelor removed to Georgia, where, notwithstanding
his advanced age, he commenced to rebuild the fortune which had been so
badly wrecked by the results of the war. Mr. Shelor was an honest man,
and leaves many friends here and in his new home to mourn his loss.

Thursday January 16, 1879:

Locals - Died, on Saturday evening, January 4th, 1879, Mrs. FRANCES DICK-
SON, wife of DAVID DICKSON, Esq., of our county. Mrs. Dickson had been
sick for a long time with dropsy, from which she died. She was buried
at New Chauga Baptist Church. Mrs. Dickson is said to have been a most
excellent woman, a good wife, a kind neighbor and an exemplary Christian.

Thursday January 23, 1879:

Married - On Wednesday, January 1st, 1879, at the residence of the brides
father, J. C. C. TURNER, Esq., by Rev. A. COKE SMITH, Mr. C. M. MC PHAIL,
of Anderson county, to Miss MARY E. TURNER, of the City of Greenville.

Married - At Biemann's Hotel, Walhalla, S. C., January 18, 1879, by H. A.
H. GIBSON, Esq., Mr. L. L. CLISBY, of Mulberry, Tennessee, to Miss EMMA
M. HARRELL, of Knoxville, Tennessee.

Married - On Thursday evening, January 16, 1879, at the residence of Mrs.
M. L. GAILLARD, by Rev. S. B. JONES, D. D., Hon. GEORGE R. CHERRY, of
Oconee county, to Miss SALLIE CRESWELL, of Anderson county, S. C.

Married - At Abbeville Court House, S. C., on Wednesday morning, January
15th, 1879, by Rev. JOHN KERSHAW, Mr. D. A. SMITH, of the "Keowee Courier", to Miss KATE SMALL, of Abbeville.

Thursday January 30, 1879:

Married - On Thursday evening, the 23rd inst., at the residence of the
bride's father, J. W. HOLLEMAN, Esq., by Rev. J. R. RILEY, Mr. JOHN C.C.
BOGGS, of Pickens county, to Miss JULIA D. HOLLEMAN, of Oconee county.

Thursday February 6, 1879:

Married - On the 24th of January, 1879, by the Rev. BURRELL WALL, at his
residence, Mr. ANDREW DAVIS to Miss ZILLAH LEATHERS, all of Oconee county.

Obituary - In Memory of Mrs. CATHERINE DODD - On last Sabbath night Mrs.
Catherine Dodd, wife of THOMAS DODD, an estimable woman and "Mother of
Israel", fell asleep in Jesus at the advanced age of seventy-five years.
She was a member of Fairview Methodist Church, having cast in her lot
with the people of God more than thirty-five years ago. About a year
ago she had a partial stroke of paralysis, from which she never entirely
recovered, being confined to her bed most of the time since. One week be-

fore her death she grew rapidly worse. Fearing her end was approaching her friends sent for a minister of the Gospel, who conversed with her freely about dying,.........lengthy eulogy follows, signed by S.L.M.

Thursday February 13, 1879:

Obituary - Departed this life on the 15th of January, 1879, ANNIE C., daughter of J. W. and M. J. SHELOR. Being an invalid all her life, she suffered most intense pain, from a complication of diseases, for several days before her death. S.

Thursday February 27, 1879:

Married - In Henderson County, on the 13th inst., W. A. MC COY, Esq., of Franklin, N. C., to Miss MARY GRAVES, of Henderson County, N. C.

Locals - We are pained to record the death of Mrs. LOUISE MC WHORTER, wife of Mr. W. A. MC WHORTER,...this sad event took place suddenly at her home in Georgia on Sunday night last. Mrs. McWhorter had many relatives and friends in this county who will be grieved to learn of her death. (More complete obituary follows)

Thursday March 6, 1879:

Married - On the 2d day of March, 1879, by the Rev. NIMROD SULLIVAN, Mr. JOHN S. KISER, of Oconee, to Miss MARTHA P. HANVEY, of Greenwood, Abbeville county.

Married - At the residence of the bride's father, Mr. THOMAS HARPER, on Thursday evening, February 27th, 1879, by Rev. H. N. Hays, Mr. J. N. HOPKINS and Miss IDA HARPER, both of Oconee county.

Married - On the 27th of February, 1879, at the residence of the bride, by Rev. WASHINGTON SMITH, Mr. ISAAC LEE to Miss JANE KOKER, both of Oconee county.

Obituary - LOUISA M. MC WHORTER, wife of W. A. MC WHORTER, was born in Pickens District, S. C., November 30, 1844, and died in Franklin county, Georgia, February 23, 1879, being in her thirty-fifth year. She leaves a husband and nine children to mourn their irreparable loss. ...in early life she united with the Presbyterina Church, of which she was a zealous member until after her marriage, when she joined the Methodist Episcopal denomination, this being the adopted church of her husband. Only a short time before her death the family had moved to a pleasant home in Georgia, where she, with her husband and children, had anticipated many years of happiness. ....(lengthy eulogy).....signed by F.B.D.

Obituary - Died, in this county, at 5 o'clock P.M., on the 4th day of January, 1879, at the age of 58 years, 2 months and 28 days, Mrs. FRANCIS DICKSON, daughter of E. H. and A. HUGHES, and consort of DAVID DICKSON, Esq. Mrs. Dickson was born in Spartanburg county, South Carolina, October 6th, 1820, and was baptized into the fellowship of the Holly Spring Baptist Church by Rev. BARACK CHAMBERS in 1845, and was married to David Dickson June 11th, 1848, to whom she was a faithful wife until death. ....(lengthy eulogy followed by poetry)....Mrs. Dickson left a husband bereft and lonely and brothers and sisters with many friends, who unite with them in their grief and extend them sympathy in their loss. E.L.S.

Locals - Died, in Walhalla, on Monday evening, from paralysis, Mr. ROBT. M. WRIGHT, son of Mrs. A. M. WRIGHT, of our town. His body was carried to Pendleton on Tuesday morning for interment.

Died, at the residence of JACOB BUSCH, on Tuesday evening, the 4th inst., Mr. FRITZ SCHRODER, formerly of Columbia, S. C. Cause of death, consumption.

Thursday March 13, 1879:

Death of THOMAS ADAIR - One by one the old land marks are passing away.

Died at his home in Walhalla, on Monday last, after a lingering illness
of several months, Mr. Thomas Adair, in the 56th year of his age. Mr.
Adair was an honest and upright citizen, respected and esteemed by all
who knew him for his many noble qualities of mind and heart. Being born
and reared in this county, he was known by most of our people, among whom
he had many and intimate friends. He was an inoffensive man and delighted, when in his power, to do acts of kindness to those who needed his
assistance, He was a good neighbor, kind, obliging and generous. For
twenty-five years he has been an active and working citizen of our town,
taking a lively interest in all matters pertaining to her welfare and
prosperity. For some months past his health began to fail him, and since
Christmas he has been unable to do any work. He however kept up and until
last Friday, when he went to bed to rise no more. He became, we are told,
unconscious soon after going to bed and gradually grew worse until death
came and relieved him of his sufferings. He died of the dropsy of the
heart......he leaves a wife and seven children to mourn their loss......
The remains of the deceased were buried with appropriate Masonic honors
in the Baptist church yard on Tuesday afternoon.

Death of Mrs. H. W. KUHTMANN - It is with sadness we have to chronicle
the sudden and unexpected death of Mrs. H. W. Kuhtmann, which took place
at her home, near Walhalla, on Monday last. She had been sick, as we are
informed, for two or three days, and died from congestion of the lungs.
She was an excellent lady, loved and respected by those whose pleasure
it was to know her. Her funeral took place at the Lutheran Church on
Wednesday morning, and her body was buried in the beautiful cemetery
back of the church. We leave for others, who knew her better than we do,
to write a more fitting and suitable tribute to her memory.

Thursday March 20, 1879:

Married - At Long Creek Church, February 17, 1879, by Rev. LEMUEL CHAM-
BERS, Mr. JAMES ADAMS to Miss SALLIE ROTHELL, all of Oconee county.

Married - February 23, 1879, at Tugaloo Valley, by T. J. RAMSEY, Esq.,
Mr. W. S. ROTHELL to Miss ARGINE BOATWRIGHT, all of Oconee county.

Married - March 2, 1879, by Rev. ROBERT COBB, Mr. OLIVER S. STANDRIDGE
to Miss L. C. ROTHELL, all of Brasstown Valley, Oconee county.

Married - At the residence of the bride's father, R. M. MORRIS, Esq., on
Wednesday, the 19th of February, 1879, by Rev. JOHN ATTAWAY, Mr. ELISHA
SUMMERELL, of Oconee county, to Miss EARNEST MORRIS, of Anderson county.

Thursday March 27, 1879:

Married - On the 6th inst., by Rev. FLETCHER SMITH, Mr. C. A. BRUCKE to
Miss MARY HUBBARD, all of Oconee.

Married - On the 16th inst., by Rev. DRURY KNOX, at the residence of W.
J. SUTTLES, Mr. J. W. VISSAGE to Mrs. _____SUTTLES, all of Oconee.

Locals - Died, on Saturday morning, at 1 o'clock, RUFUS, infant son of
J. N. RUTHERFORD, from inflammation of the bowels, aged five months and
eleven days. Funeral services by Rev. J. W. BROWN at 3 o'clock Sunday
evening. Burial at Bethel beside his little brother and sister, JOSEPH
W. and ESSIE L., who preceded him to the grave only eighteen months ago.

Thursday April 10, 1879:

Locals - Mrs. SUSAN M. LEWIS, relict of the late JESSE P. LEWIS, died of
paralysis, in this county on the 24th March, in the 84th year of her age.
Her remains were interred in the bury-ground at the Stone Church, Rev.
Dr. MARTIN, of Abbeville, conducting the funeral services. Mrs. Lewis
was a good woman, a devoted and consistent member of the Presbyterian
Church for many years and died lamented by all who knew her. To the family and relatives we extend our sympathies. (Note: Susan M. Lewis was
born 5 Feb. 1807 according to her tombstone in the Old Stone Church Cemetery...cme) (Jesse P. died 12 Oct. 1845; bur. O.S.C. cemetery)

<u>Thursday April 17, 1879</u>:

Obituary - Died, at Toccoa City, Ga., January 26th, 1879, in her seventy-second year, Mrs. SARAH ABBOTT. The deceased had suffered intensely at intervals for a long time with that fearful disease, rheumatism. At her death, her's was a life full of good works as well as years. In her the church has lost one of its oldest and brightest lights, having been for many years a consistent member of the Methodist Episcopal Church. The subject of this notice was widely known and loved for her kind heart and Christian piety.......(eulogy signed by "D")

Married - On the 10th day of April,1879, by the Rev. NIMROD SULLIVAN, Mr. JOSEPH E. REID to Miss MARY E. FITZJERALD, all of Oconee.

Locals - We regret to announce the death of Dr. W. TURNER HOLLAND, which occurred at his residence in Anderson County, on Monday morning from paralysis. Dr. Holland had long been an invalid, but his tall figure and genial countenance, as he appeared in health years ago, will be remembered by very many of our citizens. Dr. Holland lived many years in our county following his profession and had many admirers. His body was buried at Rock Springs Church on last Tuesday.

<u>Thursday April 24, 1879</u>:

State of South Carolina, Oconee County - In the Court of Common Pleas. Summons for Partition of Real Estate, Relief, etc. YOUNG DAVIS, Plaintiff, vs. WILLIAM B. DAVIS, C. D. DAVIS, ELIZABETH B. ELSTON, LETTY ANN FISHER, LAURA J. MASHBURN nee DAVIS, JOHN S. DAVIS, EFFIE LEE DAVIS, WALTER G. DAVIS, MARY D. DAVIS, HATTIE DAVIS, MATTIE DAVIS, WADE B. DAVIS, MARY L. HOLMES nee DAVIS, SALLIE B. DAVIS, NANNIE M. DAVIS, HARVEY A. DAVIS, BEATRICE E. DAVIS, Defendants. Absent defendants - WILLIAM B. DAVIS, C. D. DAVIS, JOHN S. DAVIS, ELIZABETH B. ELSTON. Partition of the real estate of HARVEY DAVIS, deceased.

State of South Carolina, Oconee County - In the Court of Common Pleas. Complaint for Partition, Relief, etc. AMANDA E. LILES, Plaintiff, against WM. HENRY LILES, FRANCES M. LILES, CHARLES L. LILES, WM. J. COWAN, WM. LATMER WHISENANT, MARY ANN WHISENANT, DAVID L. LILES, WM. J. LILES, CHARLES O. LILES, JOHN D. LILES, JESSE J. LILES, MARY JANE FRANCES LILES and CHARLES W. MASON, Defendants. Non-residents: CHARLES W. MASON, WM. J. COWAN, DAVID LEWIS LILES, WM. J.LILES, CHARLES O. LILES, JOHN D. LILES, JESSE J. LILES and MARY JANE FRANCES LILES.
State of South Carolina, Oconee County - Court Common Pleas. Summons. ELIZABETH COUNTS, Plaintiff, against JOHN HYDE, as executor of the last will of MARY A. SCOGGINS, deceased, SARAH A. HYDE, wife of JOHN HYDE and W. B. SCOGGINS, defendants.

In Memoriam - (4 lines poetry)...Fell asleep in Jesus on the 10th of March, 1879, Mrs. MARY A. KUHTMAN, wife of H. W. KUHTMAN and daughter of the late RICHARD S. SMITH, of Charleston, S. C. She, in memory of whom I write, was a native of Charleston, but many years since left the fair "Old City by the Sea", a spot she loved so well, for a home in the upper portion of our State. Who shall say how her heart bled on leaving those to whom she was attached by the ties of blood and affection?....(long eulogy with more poetry and signed by "A".)

<u>Thursday May 1, 1879</u>:

Locals - Gen. JAMES SIMONS, of Charleston, died in that city on the 26th inst. Gen. Simons occupied during his long life many high positions of honor and trust in the State.

Mrs. JANE RUSSELL, wife of Mr. W. W. RUSSELL, of Anderson, died on Monday last. Mrs. Russell was a daughter of JOHN B. SITTON, Esq., of Pendleton, and was a most estimable lady. She leaves a husband and six small children to mourn her loss.

<u>Thursday May 15, 1879</u>:
(see following page)

140

Married - On April 3d, by T. S. RAMSAY, Esq., on Tugaloo River, Mr.DAVID
N. PITTS to Miss SALINA LONG, all of Oconee.

Married - on the 3d day of May, by the same, Mr. WM. RAINS to Miss RINDA
LILES, all of Oconee.

Married - At Fair Play, S. C., on the evening of May 6th, Miss MARY A.,
daughter of Mr. J. B. HUDGENS, to Mr. W. C. MC CARLEY, of Townville, S.C.
by the Rev. J. R. RILEY.

Thursday May 22, 1879:

State of South Carolina, Oconee County - In the Court of Probate.
Petition and Complaint to prove Will in due form of Law.
LUCINDA A. MARTIN, as Executrix and CYNTHIA MARTIN, as Executrix, of the
Last will and testament of SHIELDS B. MARTIN, dec'd, Plaintiffs, against
FRANCIS M. MARTIN, DICKSON M. MARTIN, ROBERT A. MARTIN, ELIZABETH A. HAR-
VEY, EMILY HARRIS, LUCRETIA R. CAIN, ADALINE HARDIN, HARRIETT M. MARTIN,
MARY E. MARTIN, MARTHA L. LUMPKIN and the heirs-at-law of JOHN C. MARTIN,
dec'd, (names unknown), Defendants.

Locals - Mr. JACOB HOOD, a Presbyterian minister of Macon, N. C., is dead.

Thursday June 5, 1879:

Locals - Mr. LEMUEL PERRY, an old and esteemed citizen of Pickens county,
died on the 16th of May in the 65th year. He had been confined to bed
for fifteen months and died from paralysis. He has children and relatives
in this county who will regret to hear of his death.

The infant son of Mr. and Mrs. GEO. T. REID died at Hodges, in Abbeville
county, on the 28th ultimo, from dysentery, after an illness of one week.
This is the third little son they have buried, two of them within the
past twelve months. The family have our deepest sympathies in their sad
bereavement.

Thursday June 12, 1879:

Married - At the residence of the officiating officer, on Sunday, June 1,
1879, Mr. A. J. GREEN, of Anderson County, to Miss E. E. CARROLL, by J.
B. SANDERS, Esq., of Oconee County.

Thursday July 3, 1879:

Death of R. STYLES STRIBLING - We are called upon to lament the death of
Mr. R. Styles Stribling, a promising young man of our county, who breathed his last in this place Sunday afternoon, after an illness of several
weeks. Mr. Stribling was a student of Adger College. His body was interred on Monday in the cemetery at Richland Church. (A lengthy "In Memoriam" follows in the July 17th issue.)

Obituary - Near Walhalla, S. C., little JOHNNIE, son of Mr. J. W. and
Mrs. SALLIE S. HOLLEMAN, fell asleep in Jesus June 21st, 1879, aged nearly sixteen months....(poetry following)

Locals - Mrs. JAMES ADAMS, an estimable lady of our county, died on the
1st inst. and was buried at the Westminster graveyard.

Thursday July 17, 1879:

Death of Col. ELIJAH ALEXANDER - We are pained to announce the death of
Col. Elijah Alexander, at Pendleton, on the 12th inst. Col. Alexander
had resided at Pendleton for a number of years. His fine robust health
had been prostrated by disease, and for years he had been confined to
his room. However, he never lost his accustomed cheerfulness or desire
to see his many friends. He represented his district in the Legislature
for a number of years, to the great satisfaction of his many friends and
the common good of the country. He was sincere in his friendships,...
affectionate...leaves numerous family connections and friends to mourn
his loss.

Thursday July 31, 1879:

Locals - An infant child of Mr. GARNER, a citizen of our town, died last week.

We have information of the death of Miss LUCY HUTCHINS, residing near Walhalla, within the past few days. She had been sick several weeks with fever.

We are informed that Mr. LEWIS GAILLARD, an old citizen of our county, died at his residence a few miles from Walhalla on the 30th inst. from paralysis. He had been confined to his bed for a length of time.

We regret to state that Mrs. MARTHA COBB, wife of Mr. PINCKNEY COBB, died in our town last Sunday morning from the effects of child birth. The deceased was a daughter of Mr. RHODUM DOYLE, of our county, and had for years been a consistent member of the Methodist Church. The husband and relatives have our sympathy in their sad bereavement.

Thursday August 14, 1879:

Obituary - Died, at Walhalla, S. C., on Sunday morning, July 27th, 1879, in the 39th year of her age, Mrs. MARTHA COBB. She had been in feeble health for more than a year previous to her death, but her last illness was only for a few days, during which her sufferings were great, almost beyond description. ....dutiful daughter, loving sister, devoted wife, ...long eulogy signed by "L".

Locals - Mr. MOSES CANTRELL died suddenly one night last week. The cause of this death is unknown.

Thursday August 21, 1879:

Locals - We have been informed that a little boy, the son of Mrs. BRUCKE, died in Walhalla on Saturday night.

We regret to announce the death of Mrs. JAMES MC CAREY, which occurred at the residence of her husband on Thursday, the 14th inst., after a protracted illness. Mr. McCarey had been a resident of our town less than two years, when he was called on to mourn this great and irreparable loss. Who can estimate the loss of a father or mother? much less of a husband or wife? .... she leaves a husband and several children...... many friends......remains were carried to Charleston on Friday, the 15th inst., for burial in the soil of her early home.

DIEDRICH BIEMAN, JR., son of Mr. and Mrs. HENRY BIEMAN, died at the residence of his parents near Walhalla, on Sunday morning, the 17th inst., at 2 o'clock A.M. His remains were interred in the Lutheran Church yard on Sunday afternoon at 5 o'clock, after an impressive funeral sermon by Dr. SMELTZER.

Married - On Tuesday, August 12th, 1879, by the Rev. J. WALTER DICKSON, of the M. E. Church, South, Mr. WM. ALEXANDER DICKSON to Miss MARY ELIZABETH MC CARLEY, both of Townville, S. C.

Thursday August 28, 1879:

An article on the murder of ALEXANDER BRYCE, JR., by unknown persons. (Later issues names several persons arrested for the act.)

State of South Carolina, Oconee County - In the Court of Common Pleas. Summons in Partition - ANDREW C. BROWN, Plaintiff, against Mrs. JAMES TODD, widow, JOHN TODD, children of ELIZABETH STEELE, names unknown, JAMES TODD and THOMAS TODD, sons of WM. TODD, dec'd, SARAH E. ERSKINE, WM. J. ERSKINE, MARGARET E. MARKHAM nee ERSKINE, JOHN R. ERSKINE, MARTHA J. ERSKINE, JULIA E. ERSKINE and NEWTON E. ERSKINE, sons and daughters of JANE E. ERSKINE, dec'd., LELA TODD, daughter of CATER TODD, dec'd., NEWTON H. BROWN and JAMES L. BROWN, sons of Mrs. M. E. BROWN, dec'd.,Defendants. Absent defendants Mrs. JAMES TODD, JOHN TODD, JAMES TODD and THOMAS TODD, SARAH E. ERSKINE, MARGARET E. MARKHAM nee ERSKINE, WM. J.

ERSKINE, LELA TODD, NEWTON H. BROWN, and children of ELIZABETH STEELE, names unknown. Partition, relief of the real estate of JAMES TODD, dec'd.

Thursday September 4, 1879:

Locals - We regret to announce that Mr. PETER BROWN, of Fork township, died at his home on August 27 after only a few days severe illness from something like brain fever.

Thursday September 18, 1879:

Locals - We regret to learn that Mr. AUGUSTUS HOLWAYS died at the residence of his mother, near Walhalla, on Wednesday morning, the 17th inst., of consumption. This is the third and last son of Mrs. Holways, all of whom have died within the past few years, two having died this year. The remains of Mr. Holway(s) will be interred in the Luthern graveyard on Thursday evening, at 3 o'clock.

Thursday September 25, 1879:

Locals - Mr. WESTON HAYES died recently in Anderson, in the 60th year of his age. Mr. Hayes taught school for several years in Oconee and was well known to many of our readers as a writer for the press and teacher.

Thursday October 2, 1879:

Oakway Locals - S. M. HARBIN had a man by the name of JOHN DORR working in a well last Saturday, when the rope broke with a tub of mud and fell on Dorr in the well and bursted his skull, killing him at once.

Locals - Col. G. M. NETHERLAND, of Toccoa, Ga., died on the 22d ultimo. He leaves a wife and one child.

Mr. W. H. COLBURN, of Charleston, who came here for the benefit of his health, died at Mr. PITCHFORD's boarding house on Tuesday last, of Chronic diarrhoea. He was comparatively a young man and leaves a wife and one child. His body was carried to Charleston on Wednesday morning for interment.

Thursday October 9, 1879:

Married - September 15, 1879, by Rev. E. L. SISK, Mr. WILLIAM JOHNSTON to Miss JANE GOODWIN, all of Oconee county.

Married - At the residence of Hon. EDMUND HERNDON, September 16, 1879, by Rev. E. L. Sisk, Mr. SAMUEL HUBBARD, of Georgia, to Miss ISSAQUENA HERNDON, of Oconee county.

Locals - We regret to chronicle a sad event which occurred in our county a few miles Northeast of Walhalla, on the 5th inst. Mr. ADGER CRENSHAW, a young man of seventeen years of age, a son of Mr. SAMUEL CRENSHAW, Sr., while playing about an overshot water wheel at a mill near his home, fell between an arm of the wheel and the pillar and had his head crushed, causing almost instant death. He was buried at the Baptist Church yard in Walhalla on Tuesday afternoon at 2 o'clock.

Died - We regret to announce the death of Mr. D. G. HUMBERT, which sad event occurred at the residence of his father-in-law, Dr. GILLILAND, at Easley, on the evening of the 24th ult. Mr. Humbert was a native of Laurens County, but a few years since located at Easley, in this county, where he engaged in teaching school up to the time of his death. Last year he married the daughter of Dr. R. J. GILLILAND, and had just fairly entered upon the threshold of a happy and useful life. He was a young man of education, and had been blessed by his Creator with a bright in= tellect. His walk in life was upright and honorable. To his young wife and other relatives we tender our heartfelt sympathies. "Pickens Sentinel"

Thursday October 23, 1879:

(see following page)

Death of Mrs. JAS. T. MC CORKLE - Mrs. James T. McCorkle nee Miss MAMIE
AUGUSTA SMITH, eldest daughter of Mr. and Mrs. W. G. SMITH, of Sandy
Springs, Anderson county, S. C., entered into rest on October the 17th,
1879, at Central, in Pickens county, S. C............she had united her
destiny, a few months before, with an amiable companion.....member of
the Baptist church...........(lengthy eulogy)...........(poetry)..........
Mrs. McCorkle was a sister of our associate, Mr. D. A. SMITH, to whome
we extend our deepest sympathies in his sad bereavement.

Obituary - Died, on Thursday, October 2, 1879, at her residence in Greenville, S. C., Mrs. ELIZABETH HENRIETTA GRADY, wife of WM. S. GRADY, and
the eldest daughter of Dr. J. W. EARLE. To her family and friends, who
knew her well no comment on this sad event would be necessary. The memory of the loved and lost stirs emotions of sorrow in the hearts of the
surviving father and mother, brother and sisters, and bereaved and devoted husband, that no words can express. She has left four infant
children, the oldest too young to realize the greatness of his misfortune,
the youngest a babe only three months old. Relatives and numerous friends
.......The funeral of Mrs. Grady showed the respect of the community....
the Mayor of the city and other highly respected citizens acted as pall
bearers. At the Baptist Church, of which she was a member, Dr. JAS. C.
FURMAN spoke on the occarion to a numerous assembly of people. ....
Dr. Furman had visited with Mrs. Grady during her sickness.....she had
lingered for four weeks with typhoid fever.......lovely and beautiful in
person, mind and spirit; sensible, candid, loving, truthful, unaffected.
......Her remains rest beside the graves of her parental ancestry and
kindred in Springwood Cemetery.

Married - On the 14th inst., by ISAAC WICKLIFFE, Esq., Mr. JAMES R. MOR-
GAN, of Pickens, to Miss JOSEPHINE BARKER, of Oconee county.

Thursday November 13, 1879:

Death of SAMUEL LOVINGGOOD - The old heads are passing away and in the
death of Col. Samuel Lovinggood, which occurred on Tuesday morning, the
11th inst., another link which connects us with the past history of our
county has been broken. We can now almost count on our fingers the few
men of prominence who live to connect us with the old regime. We had
known Col. Lovinggood since our earliest recollection, remembering him
in our boyhood as a successful miner in Cheohee. He was born in Elbert
County, Georgia, and removed to South Carolina years ago and settled in
Cheohee, where he married the daughter of JAMES LAY, a leading citizen
of that section. He soon after lost his wife, leaving one daughter, on
whom he bestowed a liberal education, giving her every advantage money
coulf obtain. He was bold and fearless, advising the young, and speaking his mind freely but kindly. He started in life poor, but by a course
of strict honesty, economy and perseverance, he had, before the war, accumulated a large property, much of which his sound judgement enabled
him to carry through the war. For several years he has resided in Walhalla with his daughter and been engaged in the banking business, having
been the first and last President of the Walhalla Bank, and after its
dissolution continuing with W. C. ERVIN a private bank. Through a long
life of over seventy years success attended all his undertakings. After
the war he was generous in settling by compromising with his creditors,
taking fifty cents on the dollar of what was due him and giving his creditors time to make money and pay without sacrificing their property,
when he might have pressed their property to sale and bought it for a
trifle. Strictly sober and temperate in all things, he was highly respected in this community and will be greatly missed. Col. Lovinggood
represented old Pickens District in the Legislature one or two terms,but
he had no political aspirations and sought no preferment in that line.
His remains will be interred at Cheohee on Wednesday, where they will
rest by his wife until the last trump shall awake the dead to life.

Death of Miss LAURA NEVILL - We regret to chronicle the death, from consumption, of Miss Laura Nevill, on last Friday morning, the 7th inst.
Miss Nevill was the second daughter of our fellow citizen, WM. H. NEVILL
and was admired for her many excellant and ennobling qualities. She was
young, talented, lovely and amiable, the pride and joy of her fond parents. She has been called away.....services in the Baptist Church on

Saturday morning by the pastor of the church, the body of Miss Nevill was deposited in mother earth from which it came, to sleep until the resurrection morn.

Married - On Sunday, the 9th inst., by ISAAC WICKLIFFE, Esq., Mr. HILARY C. JONES to Miss LOUISA ELIZABETH BREWER, all of Oconee county.

Thursday November 20, 1879:

Married - At the residence of the bride's mother, Mrs. LAY, near Central, in Pickens county, on the evening of November 12th, by Rev. HUGH MC LEES, of Pickens county, Mr. JESSE C. DOBBINS, of Anderson county, and Miss CARRIE LAY, of Pickens county.

Married - By Rev. E. L. SISK, November 16th, 1879, at the residence of the bride's mother, Capt. J. C. SAGE, of Atlanta, Ga., to Miss SUE P. JONES, of Oconee.

Married - On Sunday the 16th of November, 1879, at New Hope Church, by Rev. H. N. HAYS, Mr. LAWRENCE CRANE and Miss MARTHA HUNNICUTT, both of Oconee.

Thursday November 27, 1879:

Married - On November 19th, 1879, by the Rev. FLETCHER SMITH, Mr. ROBERT FERGUSON to Miss MARY M. IVESTER, all of Oconee county.

Locals - We regret to state that Mr. N. G. BULWINKEL, a citizen of our town, died suddenly last Sunday evening from cramp colic. He was taken sick about noon on Saturday, while at work, and had to be hauled home, living only a little over twenty-four hours. Mr. Bulwinkel was a young man of industrious habits. His funeral services were conducted by Dr. J. P. SMELTZER at the Lutheran Church on Tuesday morning at 10 o'clock, after which his remains were buried in the Lutheran Cemetery.

Thursday December 4, 1879:

Married - At the residence of the bride's father, Mr. NOAH GRANT, on Sunday evening, November 30th, 1879, by Rev. H. N. HAYES, Mr. R. A. MOORE and EUGENIA GRANT, both of Oconee county.

Thursday December 11, 1879:

Married - At the residence of the bride's mother, Mrs. MARY ELROD, December 4th, 1879, by Rev. A. W. MC GUFFIN, Mr. A. B. MC GUFFIN to Miss ANNER ELROD, both of Oconee.

Married - On the 30th of November, 1879, by D. B. CARTER, Esq., Mr. DANIEL LEE to Miss MARY GRAHAM, both of Oconee.

Married - At the residence of the bride's mother, on Wednesday evening, 26th of November, by Rev. JUNIUS J. NEVILLE, Mr. JOHN MULCKE, of Pickens, to Miss KATIE EMMERSON, of Oconee.

Married - At Pendleton, S. C., on Wednesday evening, December 10th, 1879, by Rev. I. W. WINGO, Rev. G. T. GRESHAM, pastor of the Baptist Church, Walhalla, and Miss SEPTIMA SLOAN, of Pendleton, S. C.

Thursday December 18, 1879:

Married - On the 7th of December, 1879, by D. F. CARTER, Esq., Mr. JOHN S. HALL to Miss SARAH HOLMES, both of Oconee county.

Married - In the Presbyterian Church in Walhalla, on the evening of the 11th of December, 1879, by the Rev. S. L. MORRIS, Mr. DAVID DICKSON to Mrs. SARAH E. CRAIG, both of Oconee county.

Married - At the residence of the bride's father, Mr. JAMES FOWLER, on Sunday evening, the 14th December, 1879, by Rev. H. N. HAYS, Mr. MARION JONES to Miss MARY FOWLER, both of Anderson County.

Thursday December 25, 1879:

Married - On the 4th of September, 1879, by Rev. L. D. SEUELL, Mr. W. A.
MC WHORTER, formerly of Oconee County, S. C., to Miss LAURA J. NEAL, of
Franklin County, Ga.

Married - On the 18th inst., by Rev. FLETCHER SMITH, Mr. T. C. DODD to
Miss IDA COMPTON, all of Oconee county.

Married - On the 11th of December, 1879, at the bride's father, Rev. H.
N. HAYES, by Rev. B. HOLDER, Mr. THOMAS DODD, of Pickens county, to Miss
ROSELETTE HAYES, of Oconee.

Locals - Mrs. POLLY KIZER, of our town, who has been in feeble health
for several months past, died on last Friday morning. Her remains were
deposited in the Baptist graveyard on Saturday afternoon, Rev. Mr. GRES-
HAM conducting the services.

Thursday January 1, 1880:

Death of Mrs. Dendy - We are pained to announce the death of Mrs. ELIZA-
BETH DENDY, relict of the late JAMES H. DENDY, Esq. This sad event occurred at her home in this county on Thursday night, the 25th of December. Mrs. Dendy was a native of this county, and was in the seventy-six
year of her age at the time of her decease. She was widely known as a
useful member of society, and her death is a source of almost universal
sadness and grief. We are not sufficiently acquainted with the character and virtues of the decease to do justice to her memory. We leave
that sacred trust for the hand of friendship and affection.

Terrible Homicide Near Fair Play - We learn that TURNER OSBORNE, JR., and
DAVID BRADBERRY, in passing the residence of RICHARD COMPTON, on Friday
evening last, near Fair Play, in this county, had a difficulty with Compton in reference to his dog. Compton and his wife were in their home
when one of these persons fired a pistol at them. The ball struck Mrs.
Compton in the abdomen, producing death the next day. Osborne was arrested and made his escape on Saturday morning. Bradberry has been arrested
and is now in jail. We learn that Osborne fired the fatal shot. Efforts
are being made, we learn, to re-arrest Osborne. Trial Justice SEABORN,
acting Coroner, with a jury, held an inquest over the body of Mrs. Compton. The jury returned as their verdict that she came to her death by
a shot fired either by Osborne or Bradberry.

Married - On the evening of the 25th of December, 1879, by H. A. H. GIB-
SON, Esq., Mr. LEWIS WILSON to Miss AMELIA RICHIE, all of Oconee.

Thursday January 8, 1880:

Death of Mr. Thomas M. Stribling - We regret to state that THOMAS M.
STRIBLING, and old and esteemed citizen of our county, died at the residence of his son in this county on Wednesday, the 31st ultimo, in the
seventy-fourth year of his age. Mr. Stribling through a long life had
uniformly borne a character for industry and integrity and was counted
among our best citizens. No one could point to a single blemish in his
character, while at all times he was found among those who strove to promote the highest interests of his county and State. By his industry,
economy and integrity, he accumulated a fair property and brought up a
large family. Mr. Stribling had been on the decline for several years
and suffered much with patience and fortitude, though most of the time
he was able to visit with his children and friends. He was of a social
dispostion and was well posted in the past history of our county, so
that his company was pleasant and instructive. He had been a member of
the Baptist Church for several years and died in the bright hope of the
Christian. Hisremains were interred in the family burying ground on his
old homestead with appropriate funeral services.

Married - On the 5th of January, 1880, by H. A. H. GIBSON, Esq., Mr. E.
H. KIRBY and Miss ELIZABETH HILLIARD, all of Oconee.

Married - At the residence of the brides'father, Mr. THOMAS CAIN, December 15th, 1879, by J. W. HAULBROOK, Mr. JAMES BEARDEN to Miss EMMA CAIN, both of Oconee.

Married - December 23d, 1879, by J. B. SANDERS, Esq., at the residence of the bride's mother, Mrs. E. A. PRITCHARD, Mr. H. J. MYERS to Miss E. A. PRITCHARD, all of Oconee.

Married - At the Westminster Baptist Church, on Sunday evening, 4th inst., by Rev. E. L. SISK, Mr. A. P. FREEMAN and Miss CORDELIA SISK, daughter of the officiating minister.

Married - On January 4th, 1880, by Rev. HUTTO, at the residence of the bride's mother, Mr. C. L. G. ELROD to Miss A. J. PRITCHARD, all of Anderson county.

Married - By Rev. E. L. Sisk, December 31st, 1879, at the residence of Mr. PICKENS COLE, Mr. JOSEPH BATES to Miss LULU PRITCHARD, all of Oconee.

Locals - Mr. COLUMBUS SCRUGGS, formerly a resident of West Union, died at Seneca City on Wednesday, the 31st instant, of disease of the heart.

Columbia, S. C., December 27- An old gamecock raiser and fighter, named JIM CHAPPELL, was killed in a cockpit at Newberry, on Christmas night by a man named BILL HARP. A nephew of the murdered man, PRESS CHAPPELL, was also shot in the mouth by the same party and will probably die.

Thursday January 15, 1880:

Married - At the residence of the bride's father, Mr. DAVID ELROD, Tuesday 23d of December, 1879, by Rev. H. N. HAYES, Mr. WM. ELROD and Miss MARY ELROD, both of Anderson county.

Married - At the residence of the bride's father, Mr. EDWARD HONEA, Thursday evening, January 8, 1880, by Rev. H. N. Hayes, Mr. ROBERT HAYES and Miss FANNIE HONEA, both of Oconee county.

Thursday January 22, 1880:

Long article on the killing of JOHN BARNES, an old man, by MILTON W. W. NICHOLSON in White Water township.

Married - On the 11th of January, 1880, at the residence of the bride's mother, by the Rev. YORK GOODLETT, Miss LAURA NORTON to Mr. ANDERSON EVANS, colored.

Thursday January 29, 1880:

Locals - Article on the shooting and murder of JESSE HORN, laborer, by THOMAS O. PARKER, son of W. F. PARKER, and about 18 years of age.

Thursday February 5, 1880:

Married - On the evening of the 29th of January, 1880, by WM. J. STRIBLING, Esq., at the residence of the bride's father, Mr. ROLAND WATKINS to Miss MARY PUTMAN, both of Oconee.

Thursday February 12, 1880:

In Memoriam - Mrs. ELIZABETH KNOX DENDY, wife of JAMES H. DENDY, deceased, was born August 29th, 1804, and died December 25th, 1879, of pneumonia, at her residence, near Richland Church. She and her husband were among the original number who founded Richland Church nearly fifty years ago. She is, with one exception, the last one of that number that passed away and constituted the last link which bound the church of the present with the past. Even previous to the organization of the church she had consecrated herself to the service of her blessed Redeemer.....She was the mother of twelve children, of whom eight survive her, having reared her own children, her step children, her grandchildren and lived to see her great grandchildren. ....(lengthy eulogy).....For more than a year her failing health.......signed by "S.L.M."

Married - At the residence of the bride's mother, Mrs. JANE GARRISON, Sunday, February 8, 1880, by Rev. H. N. HAYES, Mr. JOHN SHEARLEY and Miss SUSAN GARRISON, both of Anderson county.

Married - At the residence of the bride's father, Elder HOLDER, February 15th, 1880, by Rev. J. F. STONE, Mr. DEMETRIUS H. DAVIS and Miss ADALINE HOLDER, both of Oconee county.

Married - At the residence of the bride's father, Mr. JOHN B. STEPHENS, Thursday evening, February 12th, 1880, by Rev. H. N. HAYES, Mr. JOHN A. GARRISON and Miss SALLY L. STEPHENS, both of Anderson county.

Married - At the residence of the bride's father, Mr. LEFELL JONES, on Wednesday February 11th, 1880, by Rev. B. HOLDER, Mr. EDWARD ELROD, of Central, Pickens county, to Miss EMMA JONES, of Oconee county.

Locals - A murder was committed in Laurens county on the 14th inst. by J. MARTIN stabbing and killing J. M. PARKER, who had previously shot Martin in the stomach. Martin is considered fatally injured. So the ball rolls.

Thursday February 26, 1880:

Death of Mrs. Nevill - We regret to state that Mrs. SARAH R. NEVILL, wife of WM. J. NEVILL, Esq., of our County, died last Friday morning, the 20th inst., after a lingering illness. Death is at all times sad, but when a wife and mother is cut off in the prime of life, it leaves an aching void which no time can supply. Mrs. Nevill was as remarkable for her Christian virtues as for those domestic qualities of head and heart which lend ornament and happiness to the family circle. Whenever and wherever known she was esteemed, and in her death her husband and family have the heartfelt sympathies of this community, where she had long been known and lived. Her remains, after appropriate funeral services, by Rev. I. W. WINGO, of Pendleton, were interred in the Walhalla Baptist Church graveyard, a large gathering of our citizens attesting their regard for the dead by their presence.

Married - On Thursday, the 19th day of February, 1880, at the residence of the bride's grandfather, at Pickens Court House, S. C., by Rev. ROBERT NALL, of Greenville, S. C., Miss BETTIE GRIFFIN, of Pickens, to Mr. JAMES FINDLAY, of Greenville.

Thursday March 4, 1880:

Married - On Wednesday evening, February 25, 1880, by Rev. H. M. BARTON, at the residence of the bride's aunt, Mrs. R. P. STRIBLING, Mr. THOMAS R. COLSTON, from Rome, Ga., to Miss SUE E. HARKEY, of Oconee county.

Locals - Mrs. EVE BURDETT, aged 84 years, died on the 26th of February, 1880, after a few days illness and was buried at South Union. She was a native of Abbeville County - a peaceable, quiet and kind lady. She leaves a large number of children to mourn her loss.

Died - THEODORE D. WAGNER, a prominent merchant of Charleston, and once a member of the firm of JOHN FRASER & Co., died in that city last week.

The Wedding Bells - Mr. WILLIAM CRAWFORD and Mrs. M. A. WYNN, both conscientious and long time officers of the State Lunatic Asylum, Mr. Crawford being the efficient supervisor and Mrs. Wynn has been creditably filling the responsible position of housekeeper at the institution, were last evening united in holy wedlock, at the Marion Street M. E. Church, by the pastor, Rev. J. L. STOKES. After the ceremony, a reception was tendered by the bride and groom to their many friends, at the residence of the Hon. JOHN A. ELKINS, which passed off very pleasantly. The happy pair were the recipients of pleasing tokens of remembrance and good will, in the form of presents of substantials as well as articles of ornament, and have the best wishes of a host of friends for their united happiness on their further journey through life. Mr. Crawford has been

connected with the institution in various capacities for about thirty
years. "Columbia Register"

Thursday March 11, 1880:

Anderson County Items - Capt. WILLIS ROBINSON died at his residence in
Pendleton on Thursday, the 26th of February last, after a short illness
from heart disease. Capt. Robinson was a native of Kentucky, but removed to this State in 1832, settling in old Pendleton District, and
soon became a popular, influential and prominent citizen, so that in
1838, he was elected a member of the South Carolina Legislature from
that District, of which the present County of Anderson formed a part.He
was at the time of his death seventy-eight years of age.

Locals - Mr. JAMES MALONE, an old and respectable citizen, living near
South Union in this county, died on the 3d inst., after a lingering illness of over twenty years duration.

Thursday March 18, 1880:

Death of H. (HOUCK) O. SLIGH - We are sorry to record the death of Mr.
H. O. Sligh, the second son of Capt. J. H. SLIGH, of our town. Mr.Sligh
though an invalid from his early boyhood up to manhood, was one of the
most enterprising and active young merchants. He had just passed his
twenty-second birthday and had already made for himself, by diligence
in business, a fine reputation among his business associates and custo-
mers. For the past few months he has been more or less confined to his
bed from severe attacks of rheumatism of the heart. On Tuesday morning
last the pains became more and more severe, and though the pains yielded
for a short time to the skill of the physician, they soon returned with
more severity and ended his young life about 5 o'clock P.M. After funeral services in Walhalla he is to be buried at the family burying ground
near Mr. S. Y. STRIBLING, on Thursday afternoon.

Married - On the 26th of February, 1880, at the bride's residence, by
the Rev. ANDREW W. MC GUFFIN, Mr. Q. M. FOSTER to Miss C. A. COLLINS,
all of Oconee.

Married - On Friday evening, the 5th of March, 1880, at the residence
of the bride, by the Rev. ELIAS JENKINS, Mr. MARK ADAMS to Mrs. CATHAR-
INE GOODE, both colored, of Oconee county.

Married - At the residence of the bride's father, Mr. JOHN GRISSOP, on
Thursday evening, March 11, 1880, by Rev. H. N. HAYES, Mr. KENNON B.
POORE and Miss ELIZABETH GRISSOP, both of Oconee county.

Thursday March 25, 1880:

State of South Carolina, County of Oconee - In the Court of Common Pleas.
Summons for Partition of Real Estate. JACOB ALEXANDER, Plaintiff, vs.
MARY ALEXANDER, widow of JAMES ALEXANDER, deceased, ELIAS F. ALEXANDER,
JORDAN ALEXANDER, DAVID ALEXANDER, brothers, and NANCY ANN MADDEN, sis-
ter of JAMES ALEXANDER, dec'd., MARTHA WATSON, MARY MC CALL, PENDLETON
ALEXANDER, REBECCA HUDSON, PICKENS ALEXANDER, VANCE ALEXANDER, TALLULAH
ALEXANDER and SIOTHA ALEXANDER, children, and JENNIE ALEXANDER, widow
of MICAJAH ALEXANDER, dec'd., DANIEL D. ALEXANDER, WILLIAM ALEXANDER,
SARAH FRAZIER, LUCINDA ALEXANDER, THOMAS ALEXANDER and JACOB ALEXANDER,
children, and CHARLOTTE ALEXANDER, widow of ISAAC ALEXANDER, dec'd.,and
DANIEL PERRITT, ELIZABETH ANN PERRITT and LERINA PERRITT, children of
MELISSA PERRITT, dec'd., DANIEL WATSON, JAMES WATSON and ELIZABETH WAT-
SON, children of ELIZABETH WATSON, dec'd., and THOMAS E. MADDEN, Defen-
dants. Partition of the real estate of JAMES ALEXANDER, dec'd.

Married - On Tuesday evening, 23d of March, 1880, at the residence of
the groom's father, by Rev. GEO. T. GRESHAM, Mr. H. O. CRENSHAW and Miss
J. E. SHANAHAN, all of Oconee county.

Locals - We understand that PICK TURNER, the witness who swore so might-
ily in the MOORE-BRYCE case, at our last court, died recently.

Thursday April, 1, 1880: (next page)

Married - At the residence of Mr. JOHN LIDDELL, on the 18th of March,
by Rev. T. E. DAVIS, Mr. WARREN R. DAVIS to Miss JULIA A. LIDDELL, all
of Oconee co.

Locals - We regret to announce the death of MAY OSTENDORFF, infant daughter of our townsman, J. HENRY OSTENDORFF, which occurred on Tuesday last
from pneumonia, after a brief illness. The deceased was nine years old
and had for a considerable time been a sufferer from an injury sustained several years ago. She bore her sufferings with the patience and
resignation worthy of a Christian of maturer years....................
her remains were interred in the Lutheran Churchyard on Wednesday at
3 o'clock P.M., with appropriate funeral services.

Death of Mrs. Pitchford - It is with feelings of much sadness we have
to chronicle the death of another one of our most esteemed and valuable
citizens, Mrs. MARGARET PITCHFORD, wife of WESLEY PITCHFORD, who died
on last Sunday morning the 28th of March, 1880, with typhoid pneumonia,
after a long and painful illness of about six weeks. ....
Mrs. Pitchford was well known to our people, having been born and
brought up in the county.............To the bereaved husband and motherless children we extend our deepest sympathies and trust that He, who
doeth all things well, will comfort and cheer their broken and mourning
hearts. Her funeral took place at the Baptist Church on Monday afternoon at 2 o'clock. At the tolling of the churchbell business in town
was appropriately suspended and our citizens repaired to the church,
where every available space was soon occupied. We noticed, too, in the
front of the church and standing in the doors a number of our colored
friends present who desired to pay their respects to the lamented dead.
The choir, led by Miss ADA CLABAUGH, sung a beautiful hymn as a volun-
tary, after which Rev. A. W. MOORE read the ....burial service of the
Methodist Church. .....Rev. HUGH STRONG offered up a comforting prayer
.........the body of Mrs. Pitchford was conveyed to the graveyard and
deposited.....with a prayer at the grave by Rev. GEO. T. GRESHAM.......

Thursday April 8, 1880:

Married - March 31, 1880, at the residence of the bride's father, JAMES
BEARD, Esq., by Rev. G. T. GRESHAM, Miss ANNA BEARD, of Oconee, and Mr.
THOMAS SCRUGGS, of Fairfield County, S. C.

Married - At the residence of Mr. LIPP, on the 1st of April, 1880, by
E. P. VERNER, Mr. JAMES PUTMAN to Miss JOSEPHINE LIPP, all of Oconee co.

Married - On the same evening, by the same, at the residence of Mr.
HAMBLETON PUTMAN, Mr. BRACK LIPP to Miss FLORENCE PUTMAN, all of Oconee
county.

Married - March 18th, 1880, at the residence of Squire RUSSELL, Tugaloo
Valley, by Rev. E. L. SISK, Mr. JOEL E. JONES, of Oconee, to Miss EUGEN-
IA POWELL, of Franklin county, Ga.

Thursday April 15, 1880:

Locals - Mr. THOMAS CAIN, of this county, died on the 9th inst., after
a protracted illness. His age is sixty-eight years. He was buried at
Center Church. Mr. Cain leaves a large train of relatives and connections to mourn their loss.

Capt. SAMUEL BUSCLARK died near Walhalla on Monday night last, in the
seventy ninth year of his age. He had lived at the same place for nearly fifty years and was well known to many.

Again we are called upon to chronicle another sad dispensation of Providence in the death of little WILLIE HODGES, of Greenwood, S. C. This
event occurred on Tuesday morning last at about 5 o'clock, at the residence of Mrs. DAVIES, of Walhalla. This interesting little girl was
the niece of our esteemed Professor, Mr. S. P. BOOZER. The little girl
had become so much attached to her uncle and aunt, Professor and Mrs.
Boozer, that she made her home with them and they loved, and cared for
her, as if she had been their only child. Willie was a bright, merry,

happy child and had every prospect of growing up into beautiful womanhood. But it was appointed otherwise. Fell disease laid hold upon her
and after some two weeks of intense suffering her gentle spirit entered
into rest. The body of little Willie Hodges was carried to Greenwood
of Wednesday morning, where it will be deposited in the family burying
ground at that place.

Death of Mrs. ANNIE SLOAN MAXWELL - (scripture and lengthy eulogy).....
she was the consort of Professor BENJ. SLOAN, which occurred suddenly
at Walhalla last Sunday, about 5 o'clock P.M. Mrs. Sloan was a kind
and gentle mother, an affectionate wife and had been a member of the
Baptist Church for many years. ....She was the daughter of Mr. JOHN
MAXWELL (note: the caption of the obituary evidently was misquoted..cme)
long and favorably known to our people for his sterling integrity throu'
a long and useful life. Maj. Sloan, her husband, was a graduate with
distinction of West Point, a Professor in Adger College and considered
one of the best scholars in our State, always genial and pleasant, but
kindly firm in the discharge of all his duties. They had one child, a
daughter, who mourns a dear mother,...................services were
conducted by Rev. G. T. GRESHAM at Pendleton last Tuesday and her remains were there deposited in the family burial ground, where they will
rest until the last trump shall summon the dead to life.

Thursday April 22, 1880:

Townville Items - BENJAMIN FRANKLIN, third son of Mr. and Mrs. JAMES A.
and JOHANNA GANTT, of this place, died on the 9th inst., after a very
short illness of diabetes, aged 16 years and 15 days. He was a kind
good boy, and had in him elements that would have made him a useful man.

Thursday April 29, 1880:

Married - At the residence of the bride's father, on Sunday the 24th,
by H. A. H. GIBSON, JR., Mr. JOHN T. CRAIN to Miss NANCY M. KELLEY, both
of Oconee.

Thursday May 6, 1880:

Locals - We regret to learn that Mr. GEORGE KILLIAN, one of our oldest
and most respectable citizens, died at his residence in Chatuga Township
on Saturday night last, in the 80th year of his age. Mr. Killian was a
native of North Carolina, but had been a resident of this section for
many years.

Thursday May 13, 1880:

MINNIE VAN DIVIERE, age 11, and daughter of H. S. and ROSE VAN DIVIERE,
was buried in the Baptist church yard at Walhalla on Thursday, 6th inst.

Thursday May 20, 1880:

Married - On the 2d of May, 1880, by D. F. CARTER, Esq., Mr. DAVID
HOLMES to Miss TERRISSA BOATWRIGHT, all of Oconee county.

Thursday May 27, 1880:

Seneca City Items - Mr. RUFUS CASEY, aged 81 years, 3 months and 12 days
died at the residence of his son on Saturday morning, the 23d. Mr. Casey was born in Spartanburg, but has been a resident of this and Anderson county for twenty years.

Married - At the residence of Mr. ELIJAH FOSTER, May 10th, 1880, by Rev.
W. A. HODGES, Mr. WILLIAM D. JAMES to Miss LILA B. JOHNS, only daughter
of the late Dr. JOHN JOHNS, both of Oconee county.

Locals - Mr. B. WILKIE BELL, father of Dr. B. W. BELL, died at Franklin,
N. C., in the 91st year of his age. Mr. Bell was highly respected and
loved by all who knew him.

Thursday June 10, 1880:

Seneca City Items - Mrs. SUSAN PATTERSON, wife of Mr. JOHN PATTERSON, died at her home, at Maxwell's Bridge, recently. She was buried at Shiloh.

Thursday June 24, 1880:

Married - By Rev. WASH. SMITH, Mr. JOHN POINTER and Miss S. J. COX, all of Oconee county. (day and date illegible)

Married - At the residence of Mrs. L. LAWRENCE, on Wednesday, 16th inst., by Rev. J. R. RILEY, Mr. WARREN GIGNILLIAT to Miss SUE LAWRENCE.

Married - At the residence of Mr. DAVID NORTON, the bride's father, in Hamburg, N. C., by Rev. C. B. FUGATE, SR., Mr. AMOS E. TAYLOR and Miss BELZONA NORTON, May 9th, 1880.

Seneca City Items - LUTHER C. HARBIN, only child and son of Mr. and Mrs. W. L. HARBIN, died on Saturday evening, June 13th.

Thursday July 8, 1880:

Married - At the residence of the bride, on Sunday morning, July 4th, 1880, by Rev. H. N. HAYES, Mr. JOHN B. HUBBARD, formerly of Columbia, S. C., and Miss ELIZA FREDERICKS, of Oconee county.

Locals - Mr. WM. FANT, of Central, Pickens county, died recently in the seventy-seventh year of his age.

Mr. ZEPHANIAH SMITH, of Pickens county, aged seventy years, died at his residence in that county on the 25th ultimo.

Thursday July 15, 1880:

Locals - We regret to learn that Mrs. J. J. HOOPER died at her residence in West Union on Tuesday night last of consumption. She leaves a devoted husband, a large circle of grief-stricken children, and many friends to mourn their loss. She was buried at the Baptist Church on Wednesday afternoon.

Thursday July 22, 1880:

Life of Rev. THOMAS DAWSON - Died, at Pendleton, S. C., on Tuesday, June 29th, 1880, at 9 o'clock A.M., Rev. Thomas Dawson, aged 90 years, 3 mo's and 25 days. Thomas Dawson, son of JOSEPH and ELIZA DAWSON, was born on the 4th day of March, A.D., 1790, at Lyme, Regis, Dorset County, England. At the age of eight years he was sent to school at Wellington, where he staid three years, and then to Mr. Paul in Castle Cary. After leaving this school, he was apprenticed to his grandfather and uncle, who were linen drapers in Maidstone, Kent. His grandfather and father were "Freedmen", a distinction in England entitling them to vote at elections; and his object in being apprenticed was to attain that privilege for himself; but his grandfather dying before the expiration of the apprenticeship, he did not acquire the right. He then, at the age of eighteen, went to London and served as a clerk in a large dry goods store for three years, then went into business on his own account as a dry goods merchant, but was unsuccessful. So, failing in this, he entered the British army, Fourth Regiment of Foot, and was a Lieutenant at the time of the battle of Waterloo, but was not engaged in that battle, having been detailed as a recruiting officer in England. After this battle the British army was reduced and Lt. Dawson was placed on the retired list at half pay, which pay he continued to receive for a considerable time after he came to America. On leaving the army he returned to London in order to learn the Lancasterian system of teaching, after acquiring which he went to Boston, England, and taught school. Whilst there he made application to William Lodge, A.F.M., to be made a Mason, but having decided to come to America, and the vessel on which he had engaged his passage being ready to sail, his application was never acted upon. He sailed from Liverpool early in the year of 1818 and arrived in New York, whence he went to Philadelphia and thence to Georgetown, District of Columbia, at which

place there was being held a tri-ennial convention of Baptists, and he
was, with the Rev. HUMPHREY POSEY, appointed by that convention to teach
the Indians in Western North Carolina, which appointment was with the
sanction of JAMES MONROE, then President of the United States. Mr. Dawson arrived on Hiwassee River in February, 1819, and was engaged in teaching the Cherokee and Creek Indians for three or four years. He was married to Miss MARY LEWIS, of New Jersey, who was also a teacher, and whom
he had previously met in Philadelphia. In 1823 he left Hiwassee, moved
to Pendleton District in South Carolina and settled on Fuller's Creek,
now in Oconee County, and near Perkins Creek Baptist Church. He was ordained a minister in 1824 and preached not only at Perkin's Creek Church
but all through the mountainous parts of Pendleton District. He afterwards bought a plantation on Martin's Creek, now known as Harper's tan-
yard place. Whilst residing here he attached himself to Shiloh Church
and then to the Pendleton Baptist Church, at which place his membership
remained to his death. From Martin's Creek, he removed to Barnwell District and preached most of the time as a missionary in Barnwell, Colleton,
Sumter and the upper portion of Charleston District. Whilst residing in
Barnwell he made application to Egeria Lodge, No. 71, A.F.M., at Ridge-
ville, and the degrees of sumbolic masonry were conferred on him by that
lodge. He was made a Royal Arch Mason by Union Chapter, No. 2, in Charleston, and had the Council degrees conferred on him by A. G. MACKEY in
Orangeburg. Mr. Dawson was subsequently employed by the Charleston As-
sociation to preach to the negroes on Edisto Island, where he remained
until the Confederate war broke out, when he was compelled to leave and
removed to George's Station on the South Carolina Railroad, where he remained one year and thence went to Orangeburg. At the close of the war,
he removed to Pendleton village and affiliated with Pendleton Lodge, No.
34, A.F.M., April 13th, 1867. His funeral services were conducted by the
Rev. Mr. HUTTO, of the M. E. Church, at the Pendleton Baptist Church, on
the 30th of June, 1880. After the services in the church he was buried
by Pendleton Lodge, No. 34, A.F.M., and assisting brethren, with the usual Masonic honors. W. H. D. GAILLARD

State of South Carolina, Oconee County - In the Court of Common Pleas.
Summons for Relief, etc. - JAMES H. RUTLEDGE, as administrator of the
Estate of L. B. RUTLEDGE, dec'd., Plaintiff, against PARTHENIA SNEAD,NAN-
CY SULLIVAN, EMILY CROMPTON, SARAH RUTLEDGE, HARRIET RUTLEDGE, the heirs-
at-law of JOSEPH RUTLEDGE, dec'd., number and names unknown, and JOHN S.
VERNER, as Receiver of the estate of JAMES LAY, dec'd., Defendants. Also
ELIZABETH HEADY, Sale of a tract of land, 150 acres, on Craven's Creek,
waters of Little River in Oconee County.

Thursday August 5, 1880:

Locals - Mrs. SARAH HALL, wife of WILLIAM HALL, died at her home, six
miles below Walhalla, on Tuesday, July 27th. Mrs. Hall was born in February 1809, and at her death was over 71 years of age. She had been declining for several years. At the age of twenty years she united with
the Presbyterina Church, of which she remained a consistent member until,
at a ripe old age, death claimed the body and the Saviour, in whom she
had so long trusted, the spirit. Her remains were buried, after appropriate services by Rev. J. J. NEVILLE, at the family burying grounds on
T. J. HALL's farm.

We are again called on to record the death of one of our oldest citizens,
Mr. ALEXANDER NEVILL, died at his residence, two miles above Walhalla,
on Sunday, the 1st inst., in the eighty-seventh year of his age. His
father was a soldier in the Revolutionary War, and afterwards resided for
a time in Abbeville County, where Alexander was born. When Alexander was
about one year old his father removed to this section of the State and
settled where the deceased lived to the time of his death. He had, there
fore, lived in the same house for about eighty-five years and was an eye
witness to the growth and development of this section from a wild waste
of forest, the home of wolves, bears and other wild beasts, to a prosperous and thrifty farming community, dotted with schools, colleges and
enterprising towns and intersected by railroads. Mr. Nevill was a quiet,
inoffensive, industrious citizen, and by his industry accumulated a fair
property for this section. During his long residence in the same neighborhood, we never heard of his having an enemy or anyone speaking harsh-

ly of him. He was, withal, truly patriotic and took great interest in the welfare of his State, turning our and polling his vote at all elections, not withstanding _____(blurred)----. He brought up a family of eight children, six of whom are still living, nearly all of them in this county, and doing well. His widow, who has trodden the pathway of a long life, with him, is still living at the old homestead. After appropriate funeral services by Rev. S. L. MORRIS, his remains were interred at the family burial ground near his home.

Thursday August 19, 1880:

Seneca City Items - Married , near the residence of the bride's father, on the evening of August 8th, by Rev. H. N. Hayes, Mr. C. T. HOPKINS to Miss M. T. PHILLIPS.

Thursday August 26, 1880:

Seneca City Items - The infant son of GEORGE R. CHERRY died recently.

Married - At the residence of the bride's father, by Rev. W. W. ABBOTT, on July 29, Mr. FRANK LUMPKINS and Miss SALLIE WADE, all of Oconee co.

Married - On August 12th, by Rev. W. W. Abbott, at the residence of the bride's father, Mr. JOHN SANDERS and Miss VINA SANDERS, all of Oconee co.

Married - August 15th, at the residence of the bride's father, by Rev. W. W. Abbott, Mr. D. A. GIBBS and Miss MARTHA COX, all of Oconee co.

Married - At the residence of the bride's father, by Rev. T. E. DAVIS, August 23d, Mr. JOHN MANOTTE, of New York, to Miss CAMPBELL, of Seneca City.

A Sad Death - Westminster, August 24th, 1880:
It is with sore regret that I have to announce the death of little HAMPTON, daughter of S. P. STRIBLING, which occurred at the residence of her father, on the 21st inst., after a short illness. She was not yet four years of age and was very bright and happy. Death is at all times sad, but most of all when one is lost who is just becoming interesting. In this instance we are doubly struck with the force of the following language: "Our days are as the grass,/Or like the morning flower,/If one sharp blast sweep o'er the field,/It withers in an hour." Her remains, after appropriate religious services, by Rev. WM. MC WHORTER, were deposited in the Richland cemetery. G.T.S.

Thursday September 2, 1880:

Locals - Married , on Sunday evening, August 29th, 1880, in the Walhalla Baptist Church, by Rev. J. P. SMELTZER, Mr. GEO. PINCKNEY COBB to Mrs. SALLIE JANE SLOAN, both of Oconee county.

THOMAS E. PATTERSON was arrested last week, near Westminster, under a warrant, for the murder of CHARLES W. KING, near Waterloo, in Laurens county, some twelve years ago, and is now in jail at Walhalla. He has confessed the killing, but claims that it was done in self defence. The prisoner will be transferred to Laurens for trial.

Thursday September 16, 1880:

Locals - We regret to learn that Mr. JAMES TURNBULL died at the residence of Capt. W. F. PARKER on Friday last. He was an old man about 70 years of age, well known to many of our readers. His funeral was preached by Rev. M. MORRIS last Sunday at Richland.

Thursday September 23, 1880:

Locals - Died, at Fort Madison, S. C., September 18, 1880, SAMUEL D., youngest son of JAMES A. DOYLE, Esq., aged 23 years, 3 months and 9 days.

Thursday October 14, 1880:

(see next page)

154

Obituary - NARCISSA ABBOTT, wife of SIMPSON ABBOTT, departed this life
October 3, 1880, after a long illness. She was 66 years old. She joined the Baptist Church October 2, 1841, and was a consistent member. She
was baptized by JOSEPH GRISHAM. She lived a Christian life and always
filled her seat in church. She leaves a husband, one son and grandchildren and many friends to mourn their loss; but their loss is her eternal
gain. ....Her funeral was preached by Rev. A. W. MC GUFFIN from 2d
Cor., 5th chapter, 1st verse.........She was interred at the old family
burying ground at Captain JOHN ABBOTT's old place. G.W.P.

Locals - Married, on the 22d of September, at the Lawn, Cobourg, the residence of the bride's father, by Rev. H. BRETTARGH, and afterwards at St.
Peters Church. by the Rev. J. D. CAYLEY, T. GRIMSHAWE, Esq., of Whiteside, North Carolina, to. ELIZABETH FRANCES, daughter of Colonel BOULTON,
of Toronto, Canada.

Maj. T. P. BENSON, formerly conductor on the Anderson branch of the
Greenville and Columbia Railroad, but for sometime proprietor of the Palmetto House, a popular hotel at Spartanburg, died suddenly on the 9th
·inst. between 4 and 6 o'clock. A dispatch to the "Greenville News", says
....."At 4 o'clock he was in his usual health, and retired to a chamber
on the third floor of the hotel for rest. When found at 6 o'clock life
was extinct."

Thursday October 21, 1880:

Married - on Wednesday, October 13, 1880, at the residence of the bride's
father, by Rev. Wm. MC WHORTER, Mr. W. C. HARKEY, to Miss MAGGIE DICKSON,
all of Oconee.

Mr. JOSEPH KAY, residing near Westminster, died recently of typhoid fever.
he was buried at Westminster. Mr. Kay was an excellant young man, respected and beloved by all who knew him.

Thursday November 4, 1880:

Married - On the 31st of October, 1880, by the Rev. NIMROD SULLIVAN, Mr.
J. LOUIS SPOONAGLE to Miss MARY FRICKS, all of Oconee county.

Married - On the 24th day of October, 1880, by the Rev. Nimrod Sullivan,
Mr. JOHN W. ABBOTT to Miss LULU WHITE, all of Oconee.

Married - At the residence of the bride's grandfather, A. TAYLOR, Esq.,
on Sunday afternoon, 31st of October, 1880, by Rev. G. H. CARTER, Mr.
GEORGE W. HAYES to Miss CANDACE DEHART, all of Walhalla.

Married - On Sunday morning, October 17th, 1880, at the residence of the
bride's father, by Rev. H. MILTON ALLEN, Mr. W. T. PATTERSON to Miss M.
M. CRAWFORD, daughter of Capt. S. M. CRAWFORD, all of Oconee county.

Locals - We regret to chronicle the death of Mrs. JULIA S. SCHRODER,
which occurred at the residence of her mother, Mrs. C. KNEE, of this
place, on Monday last. Mrs. Schroder had been an invalid for some time
from the effects of a stroke of paralysis, and which caused her death.
Her funeral services took place at the Lutheran Church on Wednesday afternoon.

Thursday November 11, 1880:

Married - On the 23d of October, 1880, by Rev. B. HOLDER, Mr. THOMAS PAT-
TERSON, of Oconee county, to Miss CAN, of Anderson county.

Married - By the same on October 27th, 1880, Mr. THOMAS NIMMONS to Miss
AMANDA SANDERS, all of Oconee county.

Thursday December 2, 1880:

Married - At the residence of the bride's mother, Mrs.M. D. GEORGE, on
Tuesday morning, November 30, 1880, by Rev. S. L. MORRIS, Mr. R. T. STEW-
ART, of Pickens co., to Miss NAMOI L. GEORGE, of Walhalla.

Married - By Rev. S, L. MORRIS, November 11th, 1880, at the residence of the bride's mother, Mr. H. L. COE, of Atlanta, Ga., to Miss SALLIE L. HUGHES, of Oconee.

Married - By D. H. CARTER, Esq., on the 7th of November 1880, Mr. JAMES C. ELLARD, of Oconee, to Miss POLLY HAYS, of Habersham county, Ga.

Married - November 25, 1880, at the house of GEORGE DODD, by Profs. RILEY and STRONG, Mr. MILES NORTON CANNON and Miss ELLA VASHTI NEAL.

Married - By the same clergymen, the same evening, at the home of the bride, Mr. JOHN T. WALT and Miss JEANNETT HAWKINS, all of Oconee County.

The infant son of Mrs. N. F. ARNOLD died at the residence of J. E. HENDRIX, in the town of Walhalla, on the night of the 29th ult. Its body was carried to Pickens County for interment.

State of South Carolina, Oconee County - In the Court of Common Pleas. Summons for Relief - LUCINDA CLINKSCALES, MIRIAM MILFORD, ANNA T. MCCLURE nee ADDIS and ELIZA ADDIS, Plaintiffs, against H. R. GASTON, as Executor of the last will of SAMUEL ADDIS, deceased, WM. J. ADDIS, HARRIET M. TANNERY nee BROWN, SUSAN MASON, child of SUSAN MASON, nee ADDIS, deceased, and HARRISON J. COLE, LUTHER COLE, ROXANNA COLE, MARTHA A.COLE, ELLIS COLE, ALLICE COLE, GARNETT COLE and LULA COLE, children of HESTER E. COLE, deceased, Defendants. Sale of the real estate of SAMUEL ADDIS, deceased.

(The next item should be included in the October news)
October 28, 1880 - Locals:
W. H. BURDETT, of Oakway, was in town on Monday last, paying his taxes and looking after other business. Mr. Burdett is now 105 years old, and voted his first Democratic ticket in Edgefield county over 80 years ago, and has voted the Democratic ticket ever since. He says that his experience with the Democracy, makes him love the name, and he that votes contrary is not a true patriot.

Thursday December 9, 1880:

Married - By Rev. JAMES L. MARTIN, at Seneca City, S. C., on the morning of Thursday, December 2d, 1880, at the residence of the bride's brother, (Hon. J. W. LIVINGSTON), Mr. W. JOEL SMITH and Miss SALLIE LIVINGSTON, all of Abbeville Court House, S. C.

Married - By the same, (assisted by Rev. J. W. HUMBERT) at Cokesbury, S. C., on the evening of Thursday, December 2, 1880, at the residence of the bride's father, Rev. A. E. NORRIS, of Johnston, Edgefield county, S. C., and Miss JULIA E., (daughter of Capt. CHARLES SMITH) of Cokesbury.

Married - November 24th, 1880, at the residence of Mr. HUGH BLAIR, by Rev. E. L. SISK, Mr. J. E. PHILLIPS, of Oconee, to Miss FANNIE BLAIR, Tuscaloosa, Ala.

Married - On the 17th of November, 1880, at the residence of the bride's father, Mr. S. H. OWENS, by Rev. WM. MC WHORTER, Mr. JOHN R. STEELE to Miss ANNA OWENS, all of Oconee.

Married - By the same on the 17th of November, 1880, at the residence of the bride's mother, Mrs. HARRIS, Mr. A. C. HUDGENS to Miss EUGENIA HARRIS, all of Oconee.

On Saturday, the 4th inst., a terrible affray occurred near Maybinton, in Newberry County, between the Messrs. THOMAS, (father and two sons) of Union County, and Mr. JOHN LYLES, of Newberry County, in which Mr. JAMES THOMAS, the father, was wounded fatally in the left side and has since died, and the sons received scalp wounds by pistol shots from the hands of Mr. Lyles, and Mr. Lyles was killed by a blow on the head with a cudgel in the hands of JAMES THOMAS, JR. Lyles is a son-in-law of JAMES THOMAS, SR., and the difficulty grew out of a family feud.

Locals - We regret to learn that EDGAR THOMPSON, son of A. W. THOMPSON,

died on Saturday, the 4th inst., at the residence of his father in Seneca City. He had barely entered on the threshold of life, being about
sixteen years of age, and was a youth, who by his good conduct merited
and won the respect of all his acquaintances. His remains were interred
at Seneca City on Sunday the 5th inst.

Hon. JAMES D. TRADEWELL, a prominent lawyer of Columbia, died on Wednesday, the 24th ult.

Thursday December 16, 1880:

Married - On the 5th of December, 1880, by Rev. Fletcher Smith, Mr. J. H.
HARBIN to Miss F. E. DAVIS, both of Oconee.

Married - On the 14th of December, 1880, by Rev. S. L. Morris, Mr. J. L.
FENNELL, JR. to Miss FANNIE L. DENDY, both of Oconee.

Married - At the residence of Mr. F. L. SITTON, on the evening of the
9th inst, December, 1880, Mr. OSCAR HARRIS to Miss SALLIE JONES, by Rev.
J. R. Riley, both of Oconee.

Locals - An interesting ceremony was performed at the residence of Senator BROWN, in Atlanta, on the first instant, ...Dr. SPALDING united in
the holy bonds of wedlock, Mr. WM. M. ADDINGTON, of Franklin, N. C., to
Mrs. LOU GRISHAM, formerly of Walhalla. This happy couple were in town
last week on their way to their home in Franklin.

Rev. T. P. BELL, pastor of the Baptist Church at Anderson, and Miss ADA
C. CLABAUGH, of Talladega, Alabama, were united in holy bonds of wedlock
on December 8, 1880,...Miss Ada was well known in Walhalla.

Thursday December 23, 1880:

Married - December 19th, 1880, at the residence of the bride's father, by
Rev. E. L. Sisk, Mr. J. B. BARTON, of Georgia, to Miss ELLA POOL, of
Oconee, S. C.

Married - On Sunday the 19th inst., by I. Wickliffe, Esq., Mr. JOSEPH
CRAIN to Miss FRANCES E. HAMMOND, all of Oconee.

Locals - Mr. STEPHEN D. KEITH, of Pickens, fell from his horse last week
and died from the effects of the injuries received. He was subject to
attacks of palpitation of the heart.

We regret to learn that Mr. H. D. ROCHESTER died suddenly recently at his
residence near Pendleton. Mr. Rochester was one of our best citizens and
leaves a family to mourn his loss.

Mr. SAMUEL A. ROWLAND, of Central, an employee of the Air Line Railroad,
was crushed to death between some cars at Charlotte, N. C., on Tuesday,
the 21st inst. He lived only a few minutes. Young Rowland was an active
and very promising young man and leaves many relatives and friends to
mourn his untimely death.

On last Friday the Trustees of Walhalla Lodge, Knights of Honor, No. 284,
paid to the wife of Mr. F. N. ARNOLD, deceased, $2,000, being the amount
for which his life was insured in this order. Mr. Arnold had been a member of the order about two years and had paid into the Widow and Orphan's
Benefit Fund $22. He died from consumption October 1st, 1880.

Article on the marriage of W. J. STRIBLING and Miss LIZZIE NORTON, daughter of Col. J. J. NORTON, on the 15th of December at Col. Norton's residence.

Death of JOHN N. GEORGE - It becomes our painful duty to announce the
death of Mr. John N. George, Auditor of this county, which occurred at
his residence near Walhalla, on Monday the 20th inst. Mr. George, in
point of age, was in the prime of life, but he had for many years been
of feeble constitution. In 1861 he joined company E, Orr's Regiment of
Rifles as a volunteer, and served with that regiment until the armies of

157

the Confederate States were disbanded, making an unexceptionally good soldier. Since the restoration of peace he has been engaged in farming and school teaching, until 1878, when by a highly flattering vote he was recommended for the office of Auditor of this county, which position he filled satisfactorily, to the time of his death, having been again recommended by a popular vote for reappointment for the next two years. Mr. George was a quiet and peaceable citizen, strictly honorable in his dealings and had won the esteem of all by his unassuming demeanor. He had been a consistent member of Bethel (Presbyterian) Church for a number of years, and exemplified in his walk and conduct the profession of his faith. He was confined to his bed only one week, his feeble frame yielding a ready harvest to that rapid and dread disease, pneumonia. He leaves a wife and five little children, a truly helpless family, to mourn his death. We are sure they have the warmest sympathy of this whole community in their sad affliction.

Thursday December 30, 1880:

State of South Carolina, Oconee County - In the Court of Common Pleas. Summons for Relief - ELIJAH SANDERS, SARAH WILSON, ELIZABETH ROCHESTER, ALEXANDER WILSON and L. A. PERRY, Plaintiffs, against F. L. MOODY, B. J. MOODY, ALICE WILSON, DANIEL VAN BUREN MOODY, A. V. MOODY, EMMA EATON, ALICE M. MOODY and JOHN R. MOODY, Defendants. Sale of the real estate of MARTIN MOODY, dec'd.

Thursday January 6, 1881:

Obituary - Died, in Walhalla, on the 29th of November, 1880, little JOSEPH NEWTON ARNOLD, the infant son of Mrs. L. E. ARNOLD, aged two years and nineteen days. (Poetry by Miss MAGGIE G. SIMMONS, age 12 follows)

Thursday January 13, 1881:

Married - At the residence of the bride's grandmother, Mrs. M. HIX, on January the 9th, 1881, by Elder J. H. STONE, Mr. J. A. MILLER, of Oconee to Miss ANNA E. LANE, of Georgia.

Married - On January 6th, 1881, by Rev. J. S. WEST, Mr. J. E. ORR to Miss S. E. GREEN, all of Oconee.

Married - On the 10th ult., by Rev. FLETCHER SMITH, Mr. MITCHELL SISKIE to Miss CATE LEAHEA, of Oconee.

Locals - We regret to announce the death of Mrs. J. N. ADAMS, which occurred in our town on Sunday night. She had been suffering from consumption a long time and her death was not unexpected. She had been connected with the Baptist Church at this place a number of years and her remains were interred in the churchyard on the 11th inst., after appropriate funeral services.

Thursday January 20, 1881:

Married - On the 30th of December, 1880, by Rev. FLETCHER SMITH, Mr. HENRY MC MAHAN to Miss LINA A. TAYLOR, both of Oconee.

Thursday January 27, 1881:

Locals - Mr. RHODUM DOYLE died suddenly at his residence in this county on the 24th inst., of disease of the heart.

We regret to learn that the little son of Mr. C. A. FISCHESSER, LUCIA, died yesterday of diptheria.

Thursday February 24, 1881:

Townville Items - Mr. SAMUEL M. HARBIN, an industrious and respected resident of Center Township, died December 23d, of paralysis, aged about 35 years.

Mr. NATHAN SHERIFF, until recently a citizen of Oconee, died suddenly at his son's residence near here on the 23rd ult., aged 76 years.

Locals - Mr. BUSCH, a young man living near Walhalla, died on last Monday, and was buried in the Lutheran Church cemetery on Tuesday afternoon.

Married - In Hood county, Texas, January 1881, Mr. GEORGE W. ABBOTT to Miss JANE HUMPHREYS, formerly of Oconee.

Thursday March 10, 1881:

Locals - Mrs. NANCY JAMES, a very aged lady, said to be one hundred and eleven years old, died at her home on Choestoe, in the Southern portion of this county, last week.

Mrs. MARY M. SLOAN, wife of Mr. S. G. SLOAN, died at the home of her husband in Cheohee on Wednesday, 2d of March. Mrs. Sloan leaves a little infant only a week old and six other small children to mourn her loss.

Mr. PAUL C. SMITH, of Virginia, was married last Thursday, the 3d inst., to Miss LIZZIE PITCHFORD, second daughter of Mr. WESLEY PITCHFORD, of Walhalla. The marriage ceremony was performed by Rev. C. D. MANN, pastor of the Methodist Church at this place. The wedding came off quietly at 7½ A.M., and our happy young friends left for Richmond, Va., by way of Columbia on the 9 o'clock train of the Blue Ridge Railroad.

Married - At the residence of the bride's mother, near Mt. Airy, Georgia, by Rev. C. W. IRWIN, on the 23d of February, 1881, Mr. G. E. PITTS, of Westminster, S. C., and Miss LULA BROWN, eldest daughter of Mrs. M. S. BROWN.

Thursday March 31, 1881:

Obituary - Mrs. SARAH CURTIS, consort of the late JOHN CURTIS, was a native of Pickens county, S. C., of that portion of the county now called Oconee. She was the daughter of Mr. NATHAN BOON. She was born November 18th, 1803, and died at the residence of her daughter in Seneca City, January 25th, 1881. Consequently her age was seventy-seven years, two months and seven days. ....a member of the Baptist Church.... (long eulogy and scripture, followed with 4 verses of poetry, signed by J.R.R.)

Married - At the residence of the bride's father on Sunday, the 27th instant, by ISAAC WICKLIFFE, Esq., Mr. JOHN M. CRAIN to Miss SARAH E. HAMMONDS, all of Oconee County.

Thursday April 7, 1881:

Mrs. BERTIE SIMS, wife of JOSEPH M. SIMS, of York county, committed suicide on the 28th ultimo by hanging herself with a cord. She was thirty years old, left one child and had been for sometime in a delicate state of health.

W. B. SANDERS, who was the second of Colonel CASH in the CASH SHANNON duel, died Tuesday morning at Sanders depot, in Sumter county.

Thursday April 14, 1881:

Long article on the death of Gen. M. W. GARY, of Edgefield.

Thursday April 28, 1881:

Married - On Thursday evening, April 21st, 1881, at the residence of the bride's parents, in Charleston, by Rev. L. MULLER, Mr. H. D. A. BIEMAN, of Walhalla, S. C., to Miss CATHERINE H. RIEPPE, of Charleston, S. C.

Married - In Greenville, S. C., on the 21st inst., by Rev. J. J. WOOLAHAN, Miss VIRGINIA EARLE, of that city, to Mr. CHARLEY MC ALISTER, of Charleston.

Married - On the 17th inst., by ISAAC WICKLIFFE, Esq., at the residence

of the bride's father, Mr. JAMES RAINS to Miss FLORENCE ELLA BROCK, all
of Oconee county.

Locals - Mr. JAMES ROACH, an old citizen of this county, who resided on
Chauga Creek, died on Sunday morning last, aged about seventy years.

Thursday May 5, 1881:

Married - April 28th, 1881, at the residence of WM. ROWLAND, the bride's
father, by Rev. T. E. DAVIS, Mr. JOHN DAVIS and Miss MARY F. ROWLAND,all
of Oconee county.

Locals - Gen. JOHN S. PRESTON, an old and highly esteemed citizen of Columbia, died at his residence on the evening of the 1st inst., in the
73d year of his age. He was a brother of the distinguished orator, WIL-
LIAM C. PRESTON, and was a native of Virginia, though he removed to this
State before his years of maturity. He represented Richland County in
the State Senate before the war, but sought no political position of late
years. At the time of his death he was President of the Central National
Bank and Chairman of the Board of Trustees of the South Carolina University.

The Rev. JOHN I. BONNER, D. D., the well known President of the Due West
Female College, and for many years the editor of the Associate Reformed
Presbyterian, died at his residence in Due West on Friday evening, the
29th ult., at the age of 59 years. He was a native of Alabama, but spent
the active portion of his life in South Carolina.

Thursday May 12, 1881:

Obituary O JESSE JENKINS, the subject of this notice, died at his residence in Oconee county on the 8th of April, 1881, of dropsy, aged seventy years. He leaves a widow and many friends to mourn his loss, but they
can draw consolation from the fact that from his past life they have as-
surances that their loss is his eternal gain. ......illness of several
months.....consistent member of the Baptist church...worthy father......
funeral services conducted by Revs. ROYSTER and KNOX....(long eulogy and
2 verses of poetry signed by "A Friend".)

Thursday May 26, 1881:

Married - On the 25th inst., in the city of Greenville, by Rev. J. R.
RILEY, Mr. JOHN D. SHELDON, of Oconee, to Miss LIZZIE DORROH, daughter of
Dr. JOHN F. DORROH.

Married - At the residence of T. L. REID, on the 17th of May, 1881, by
Rev. J. E. CARLISLE, Mr. JAMES N. PHINNEY, of Walhalla, and Miss CARRIE
F. DARBY, of Anderson county.

Killed by Lightning - Last Thursday, near Clayton, Mrs. ALEXANDER, from
Habersham county, while sitting in her room with her three children, was
struck by lightning and instantly killed. The children, it is thought,
were fatally injured.

Thursday June 2, 1881:

Locals - Died, near Walhalla, on the 30th ult., Mrs. MINA MYERS, in her
77th year. Her death caused from a fall sometime ago, by which her hip
was dislocated. She was buried on the 31st ult., in the Lutheran cemetery, after appropriate services in the church.

Nearly a year ago Mr. SIDNEY B. SMITH, of Boston, came to Walhalla in
the last stages of consumption. He was accompanied by his wife and children. Mr. Smith lingered until the 28th ult., when he died. His remains
were carried to Boston by his faithful wife and will be deposited in
their native soil.

Thursday June 9, 1881:

Married - In Marion Street Church, Columbia, S. C., June 1st, 1881, by

the Rev. J. L. STOKES, Mr. J. C. RUSSELL, of North Carolina, to Miss MAT-
TIE E. MESSER, of Oconee county, S. C.

Obituary - Died, on the 20th of December, 1880, Mrs. NANCY BLACKWELL,
aged 84 years. She had been unwell for several months and died of consumption. At the time of her death she was a member of the Holly Springs
Baptist Church and had been a consistent member of the church about 44
years. She was a native of Spartanburg county and had been living in O-
conee county about 30 years.

Thursday June 23, 1881:

Townville Items - Dr. DAVID A. SIMMONS, with his wife and two children,
who has been on a few weeks visit to relatives in this vicinity, returns
to his home this week near Sherman, Texas. In the spring of 1866 the
doctor emigrated from here to where he was born and reared, being a son
of the Rev. DAVID SIMMONS, now also living in Texas, to Iowa, where he
stayed three years, but owing to the rigorous climate he went South and
settled permanently in Grayson County, Texas. He has succeeded well in
his adopted country, having amassed a very considerable property and having withal an extensive practice. The doctor entered the Confederate
service as a member of the famous ORR's Regiment, with which he remained
until the battles of the Wilderness, where he was seriously wounded and
rendered unfit for further active service.   D.

Locals - Mrs. ESTHER ROBERTSON, relict of JAMES ROBERTSON, died at her
residence in Oconee county, near Fall Creek, on the 21st inst., in the
78th year of her age.

Mrs. ELIZABETH ELROD, died June 15th, at the residence of her son, D. A.
ELROD, in Anderson county. Mrs. Elrod was in the ninety-third year of
her age. She lived a consistent member of the Methodist Church for seventy-five years and died in peace. Her remains were placed in Sandy
Springs cemetery.

Thursday June 30, 1881:

Funeral Notice - Died, near Walhalla, S. C., June 28th, 1881, ANNA GER-
TRUDE, youngest daughter of JOHN J. and ELIZABETH M. SMITH, aged twenty
months. The funeral will take place this (Thursday) morning, June 30th,
at the family burying ground, near W. J. NEVILLS.

Locals - Mr. JAMES B. HAILEY, SR., living on the MAXWELL estate, near
Townville, in this county, died Sunday morning, the 26th inst., after a
lingering illness of several weeks. He leaves a wife and eight little
children.

Thursday July 7, 1881:

Locals - We are called upon to chronicle the sudden death of Mr. EDWARD
SCHRODER, who resided near this place. He had been ill only a few days
and died on Monday morning from typhoid pneumonia. He was a son of Mr.
JACOB SCHRODER and leaves a young and interesting family with many relatives to mourn his sudden death. Funeral services at the Lutheran church.

Thursday July 14, 1881:

Locals - On the 6th inst., Mr. GEORGE HENDRICKS, aged about 84 years, was
burned to death near his residence in Pickens county. It seems he was
clearing a place for a turnip patch when his clothes took fire and no aid
being near he was overcome and when found was dead.

We regret to state that Mrs. RIEKOFF, of Charleston, died last Friday at
the residence of her nephew, JOHN J. ANSEL, in Walhalla. She had lately
come from her home in Charleston in bad health, and with the view of re-
cuperating her strength. Her death at the time was unexpected. Her remains were removed on Saturday to her home in Charleston for interment.

The family of one of our neighbors has passed through severe affliction,

161

greater perhaps than any other in the county: HENRY HOLWAYS, the father, aged sixty years, was killed in the Confederate army at Savannah, November 12, 1864, by a cannon ball. All of his children, six in number, have also died. TEIDORA, a lovely infant daughter, eighteen months old, died in 1851. JOHN, a son, a few months old, died in 1866. WILLIAM, aged twenty years, died November 2, 1876. HENRY, aged twenty-seven years, died September 18, 1878. AUGUSTE, aged twenty-three years, died September 17, 1879. HANNAH, aged twenty-three years, died July 6, 1881. The four last named died of consumption. The only member of the family left is the mother, aged, feeble and alone, who stands on the brink of the grave. The hearts of all our citizens go out in sympathy and sorrow to the heart-broken mother.

Thursday July 28, 1881:

Married - July 24th, 1881, by the Rev. NIMROD SULLIVAN, Mr. WILLIAM ALEXANDER FRICKS to Miss PHEBE LOUISA HYDE, all of Oconee county.

Thursday August 11, 1881:

Locals - Mrs. ELIZABETH HAMILTON, aged lady of Pickens county, died near Walhalla on Sunday morning last.

We regret to learn that Mrs. MARTHA A. LAWRENCE, wife of Mr. WARREN D. LAWRENCE, of Mississippi, died at his residence in that State, June 8, 1881, in the 52nd year of her age.

Thursday August 18, 1881:

Locals - Rev. D. J. MILLAN, formerly of Walhalla, died August 7th.

Thursday September 1, 1881:

Locals - Died, August 16th, 1881, LOUIS DENDY, infant son of Mr. and Mrs. J. L. SHANKLIN, aged nine months and fifteen days.

We regret to state that the infant daughter of JOHN J. ANSEL, of our town, died last Sunday night after a protracted illness. She was about 18 months old.

Thursday September 22, 1881:

Locals - Married, on the 11th of September, 1881, at the residence of the bride's father, by Rev. Mr. CATRON, Mr. J. M. CARTER, of Walhalla, and Miss LILLIE SANDERSON, of Clay county, N. C.

SOLOMON RAMEY was shot and almost instantly killed on Whetstone, in this county, on the afternoon of Sunday last, by WM. HIGGINS. A previous difficulty had taken place between these persons a few days before the last, when Ramey and perhaps others had ill used Higgins. On Sunday afternoon, Ramey, in company with his two brothers, LOGAN and TIM, and DAVID WAULS, went to Higgins house and forced an entrance into it. Deceased and Higgins were both armed and fired at the same time. Ramey was shot in the forehead, the ball passing through his head and lodging behind the brain. Higgins was shot just above the hips, the ball lodging in him where it now is. Ramey is dead and Higgins is now in jail. Trial Justice SHELOR, in the absence of the Coroner, held an inquest over the body of Ramey. DAVID WAULS, LOGAN RAMSEY(sic) and TIM RAMSEY(sic) were held for trial on a charge of riot, etc.

Thursday September 29, 1881:

Locals - JAMES D. TURNER, was shot and instantly killed by JAMES F. WALSH in the Waverly House, Charleston, on the 26th inst. Pistols were used by both in the fatal fight. The cause of the difficulty is unknown.

Thursday October 20, 1881:

Married - By Rev. C. D. MANN, October 13th, 1881, at the bride's grandfathers, Mr. A. TAYLOR, Walhalla, Mr. WM. PELL and Miss MONDANE C. WALKER .

Married - By Dr. J. P. SMELTZER, October 18th, 1881, at the bride's father, Mr. JACOB SCHRODER, Dr. WM. E. LAKE, of Newberry, to Miss JULIA A.
SCHRODER, of Walhalla.

Townville Items - An infant daughter of Mr. and Mrs. J. A. MARTIN died on
the 13th inst. Mr. and Mrs. L. O. BRUCE also recently lost an infant
child by death.

Thursday October 27, 1881:

Locals - Married, on the 23d of October, 1881, by Rev. E. JENKINS, WM.
CLARK to FANNIE WILLIAMS, colored, of Walhalla.

Thursday November 3, 1881:

Death of Mr. C. Jones - The death of Mr. CHRISTOPHER JONES, which occurred at his residence at Tomassee, on the evening of November 1st, 1881,
from inflammation of the bowels, is a source of deep regret to his many
friends and acquaintances. He had been ill but a short time and his
death was unexpected. His loss is regarded as a public calamity at this
time, as he was one of those active, progressive public spirited men,
whose presence and influence were ever ready and ever felt in whatever
concerned or promoted the moral, educational and material progress of the
county. He possessed large means for this countty and his hand was ever
ready to devote a liberal portion to every public enterprise and his
voice and influence were freely given to the same end. Mr. Jones was an
energetic worker in raising means and stimulating our people to send a
full exhibit to the varied products and resources of our county to the
Atlanta Exposition, of which he was one of the Vice-Presidents from this
State, believing such a course would direct labor and capital to this
section. He kept up a constant correspondence with manufacturers in the
North and in England, and was looking to have a large delegation of cap-
italists visit our county during the exposition. Mr. Jones was quiet
and unobtrusive as a citizen, neither meddling with politics nor seeking
political preferment, but voting and quietly using his influence at all
times for the election of competent men to office and for an honest and
economical administration of the government. Few men can be found who
filled in a higher degree the true measure of a worthy citizen than Mr.
Jones. He has gone, but his example in public spirit and liberality in
all enterprises of a public character are well worthy of remembrance and
imitation. Mr. Jones was a native of Abbeville coun ty and a graduate
of the South Carolina College in the palmy days of that institution. After his graduation he went to Mexico, where he spent a number of years,
and by industry and business qualities amassed a large fortune. During
the war he returned to this country and purchased from Mr. ELAM SHARPE
the Tomassee plantation, then and now one of the largest, most fertile
and valuable plantations in the county. Soon after this he married a
daughter of Mr. A. B. GRANT, of Cheohee, and settled on his farm. He
has continued to reside there until his death, devoting himself to farming and public improvements. Mr. Jones was not only well educated, but
he had traveled extensively and had gathered from observation and experience valuable information on all subjects. He was between fifty and
sixty years of age and leaves a wife and several children to mourn his
loss.

Professor DAVID DUNCAN, A. M. - One of the most thorough and probably the
oldest, of South Carolina's scholars has passed away. Professor DAVID
DUNCAN,A.M., Emeritus Professor of Ancient Languages and Literature in
Wofford College, died at his home in Spartanburg on Sunday, October 30,
at the advanced age of 80 years. Professor Duncan was a native of Ireland and a graduate of Glasgow University, but had long claimed South
Carolina as his home and had claimed by her as an honored and trusted citizen. A ripe scholar and a Christian gentleman, Professor Duncan had
been connected with Wofford College ever since its foundation, more than
a quarter of a century ago, and had greatly contributed by his learning
and influence to the high moral and intellectual standard which is the
just boast of that institute. Prof. Duncan leaves worthy representatives
of his honored name in his two sons, the Hon. D. N. DUNCAN, Solicitor of
the Seventh Circuit, and Prof. W. W. DUNCAN, of Wofford College.

Townville Items - Married - at the residence of the bride's father, on
the 20th ult., Mr. B. FRANK MOORE and Miss WILLIE F., youngest daughter
of WM. HOLCOMBE, Esq., Rev. JOHN R. RILEY, officiating.

On the 3d inst., MOSES MC AULAY and CLARA MC GEE, both of African descent, were married.

Married - By Rev. Dr. J. P. SMELTZER, November 8, 1881, at the house of
the bride's parents, Mr. L. D. BRENNECKE to Miss FANNIE P. BRAZEALE,both
of Walhalla, S. C.

Married - October 27, 1881, at the residence of the bride's father, Mr.
JACOB BUSCH, near Walhalla, by Rev. WM. PILZ, Mr. HENRY D. RITTER to Miss
TENA M. BUSCH, all of Oconee county.

Long article on the particulars of the death of a young man named NELSON
HOOPER in an accident while working on the railroad. His body was sent
to his father's home in Walhalla and buried in the Baptist cemetery.

Locals - ELIJAH FOSTER, one of the oldest citizens of the county, died
on Sunday last. He had suffered greatly from rheumatism for several years
past. Mr. Foster was an honest hard working man and was much respected
by all who knew him.

We regret to chronicle the death from typhoid fever, on the 2d inst., of
W. A. ADDINGTON, which occurred at his home near Franklin, N. C. Mr.
Addington was formerly a citizen of our town and doing business here and
his many friends will regret to hear of his demise.

Mrs. A. ATKINSON, of Williamston, S. C., writes us that Mr. CHRISTOPHER
JONES, her brother, was a native of Columbia, instead of Abbeville, as
announced by us last week in noticing Mr. Jones' death, and that he was
66 years old.

Thursday December 22, 1881:

Married - On the 7th inst., by Rev. FLETCHER SMITH, Mr. FRANK J. TAYLOR
to Miss SALLIE MC MAHAN, of Oconee.

Married - On the 12th of December, 1881, by the Rev. NIMROD SULLIVAN, Mr.
WM. DORSEY to Miss CATHARINE KELLY, all of Oconee county.

Married - In Spartanburg, at the residence of Mrs. C. M. SLIGH, December
15th, 1881, by the Rev. H. J. MORGAN, Mr. JOHN L. HARLEY, of Orangeburg
to Miss MINNIE L., daughter of the late Rev. J. L. MC GREGOR, of the
South Carolina Conference.

Locals - We regret to chronicle this week the death of Mrs. ELIZABETH
ANN HARPER, wife of Mr. THOMAS HARPER, of Seneca City. She died on the
10th inst. Mrs. Harper was a worthy member of the Baptist Church for
many years.

Mrs. ANNA CLEVERS, an aged German lady, died at the residence of her son-
in-law, MARTIN WENDELKIN, on Monday evening at 6 o'clock. She was ninety years old and had been so afflicted for several years that her death
was not only expected, but must have been a relief to her. All must die
and when anyone reaches that extrordinary age they are far beyond the allotted period. She was the mother of the first wife of JACOB SCHRODER
and predeceased him only a few hours. She came to this country at the
age of 70 years. Her remains were interred in the yard of the Lutheran
Church, of which she had long been a member, on Wednesday, the 21st inst.

Mr. JACOB SCHRODER, one of our oldest and most prominent German citizens,
died at 3 o'clock on Tuesday evening, at his residence in West Union, in
the 75th year of his age. He had been suffering for several years from a
painful disease of the kidneys, which assumed some weeks ago a typhoid
form from which he died. His death was easy and peaceful and from his
exemplary life, his friends and family feel assured that his sufferings

are over and he is now enjoying a blessed immortality. Mr. Schroder left
the old country at the age of eighteen years and with less than twenty
five cents in his pocket came to Charleston, and after gathering a little
means went into the coal and family grocery business. His father was a
poor man and it is related of Jacob that when the officers of the law
were about to sell the bed from under his sick mother Jacob pledged himself, then a mere youth, to pay the debt off. As soon as he made the
means he returned to the old country, paid the debts of his father and
brought him a home. His long life illustrates the Christian promise....
.........He was one of the original members of the German Colonization
Society, which came here in 1850, bought large bodies of lands and plan-
ted a colony of Germans and built up Walhalla. Mr. S. was the last President of the Society and wound up its business with credit to himself and
to the satisfaction of all. When he came here he had large means, built
valuable mills and five or six houses in Walhalla, among them the large
American Hotel building. He done much for our county in this way and was
at all times public spirited. He lived beyong the allotted period of
time...all regret his death.....he had thirteen living childen born to
him, of whom he leaves nine surviving him. His remains will be interred
on Tuesday, the 22d inst., at 11 o'clock in the yard of the Lutheran
Church, of which he had been a consistent member.

Thursday January 5, 1882:

Married - By Rev. A. W. MC GUFFIN, December 21, 1881, Mr. JOHN BURDETTE
to Miss SUSAN O. ADAIR, all of Oconee.

Married - By Rev. McGuffin above, on December 22d, Mr. JAMES H. WILSON
to Miss ELIZABETH I. DRIVER, all of Oconee.

Married - By Rev. T. E. DAVIS, on December 18, Mr. D. A. CAMPBELL to Miss
MARTHA MOORE, all of Oconee.

Married - On the 18th December, 1881, by J. W. HOLBROOKS, Esq., W. A.Mc-
DONALD of Oconee and Miss LOU ROWLAND, of Hart county, Ga.

Maj. W. K. BRADLEY died at his residence in Abbeville county on the 30th
of December. He was a man of mark, having served two terms as a member
of the Legislature, and at the time of his death was President of the
Atlantic and French Broad Railroad Company.

Locals - Mr. J. S. WILSON, of Abbeville, has departed for parts unknown,
leaving a wife and one child.

Mr. JASPER WILLIAMS, an old and respected citizen of Anderson County,died
on Monday last. He was buried with Masonic honors at the New Lebanon
Baptist church on Tuesday.

We are pained to announce the death of Mrs. SUSANNA K. SLIGH, relict of
the late DAVID SLIGH. She was buried in Walhalla on Monday last. Mrs.
Sligh was a native of Newberry and had passed her three score and ten.

Mrs. ELIZABETH A. BURNS, wife of Mr. B. W. BURNS, died on the 21st of December last. She had been an invalid, confined to her bed, for a long
time.

Thursday January 12, 1882:

A Sad, Sad Scene - Mrs. L. LAWRENCE and Mrs. JULIA A. FOLGER, two sisters,
died at the residence of the latter at Pickens Court House on Wednesday,
the 4th inst., within less than two hours of each other. These ladies
were daughters of PLEASANT ALEXANDER, deceased, once the Sheriff of Pickens District, and were the companions of many ladies now living in Walhalla, who deeply regret their sad deaths. Mrs. Lawrence was the widow
od Dr. J. N. LAWRENCE, who died during the war, and who, by reason of the
emancipation of slaves, lost all of his property and left his widow with
three daughters with but scanty means of support. Mrs. Lawrence by industry and economy brought up her children, gave them a fair education
and gained and retained the esteem of all good citizens. Though such
women are to be found here and therein the South, who, brought up in lux-

ury, have met the reverses of fortune with a firm heart and a steady
trust in Providence, still they deserve a degree of credit few can truly
estimate. It is so natural in such cases to yield to repining that the
wonder is more to do not do so, but with Mrs. Lawrence there was no yielding, but a constant effort to give her children all the advantages with-
ing her reach. Prior to her death she had been living at Seneca City for
several years and was in the fifty second year of her age. She lived to
see all her daughters grown and two of them married and settled in life.
The death of Mrs. Folger, wife of JULIUS FOLGER, of Pickens, is rendered
peculiarly sad by reason of her leaving four children, the youngest but
a few weeks old, and also because she was in the prime of life, being
but thirty eight years old, with a promising future before her. While
all must die, yet when the mother looks upon her little children, like
olive plants about the fireside, how sad to leave them before their minds
are formed or their morals confirmed. There cannot be a mother whose
heart does not go out in sympathy toward the widowed husband and motherless children. This, we know, is the feeling of many in this community,
who have known Mrs. Folger since childhood, and have associated with her
in the school room and family. How sad indeed that two sisters, one on
a visit to the other, should die in the same house within so short a time
of each other. Truly in life we are in the midst of death. The remains
of Mrs. Lawrence were brought to Seneca City and after funeral services
by Rev. J. R. RILEY, were interred in the cemetery at that place. The
remains of Mrs. Folger, we understand, were buried at Pickens.

Locals - Miss HANNAH SEABORN, a daughter of the late Major GEORGE SEA-
BORN, and a most estimable lady and accomplished lady, died in Pendleton
on the morning of Monday, the 26th December, after a protracted illness
from consumption.

One of the most notable and pleasant incidents of the week in our town
was the marriage on Tuesday morning, January 10, 1882, at 8½ A.M., at the
residence of the bride's aunt, Mrs. R. A. HUNTER, by Rev. W. G. NEVILL,
assisted by Rev. S. L. MORRIS, Mr. R. P. WUARLES, of Ninety-Six, and Miss
LULA NEVILL, of Walhalla, sister of the officiating minister. The happy
couple left at once for Charleston on a short tour, after which they will
reside in Ninety-Six.

Thursday January 19, 1882:

Married - On the 12th inst., at the residence of the bride's father, A.
J. MARET, near Fair Play, by Rev. A. W. MC GUFFIN, Mr. WILBURN O. ALEX-
ANDER and Miss SALLIE M. MARET, all of Oconee.

Married - At the residence of the officiating clergyman, Rev. H. N. HAYS,
on Thursday eveing, January 12, 1882, Mr. WILLIAM T. ABBOTT and Miss MARY
MARGARET HAYS, both of Oconee.

Crimes and Casualties - W. H. LOCKE, a defaulting postmaster at Eugala,
Alabama, committed suicide on the 15th instant.

A passenger train on the Virginia Midland Road ran into a slide on the
15th inst., killing JOHN MINTON, of Alexnadria, wounding some of the em-
ployees and smashing the engine.

FRANK PIERCE, a seaman, of the schooner "Elizabeth", was run over and instantly killed by a lumber train at Port Royal on the 16th inst. His
body was mangled and the head torn from the trunk. He is supposed to
have been drunk and gone to sleep.

Mr. CHARLES P. LESESNE, a son of CHANCELLOR LESESNE, died suddenly of
apoplexy on the 15th inst. He had been exerting himself to get a wagon
unloaded and its contents moved to the top of the hill at which he had
stalled and on a sudden complained of fatigue and soon after fell down
and died.

An accident occurred at the South Carolina Railroad yard in Charleston
on the 16th inst., by which DENNIS R. BRENNAN, a worthy man, lost his
life. He was attempting to pass between two of the cars while in motion
by junping the bumper and after failing twice, fell on the third attempt

166

across the rails and the cars passed over his abdomen completely severing the body. Before the train could be stopped twenty four wheels had passed over his body.

Thursday January 26, 1882:

Married - January 19, 1882, at the residence of the bride's father, near Tallulah Falls, Ga., by Rev. S. L. MORRIS, Mr. GEORGE T. STRIBLING, of Westminster, S. C., and Miss HATTIE WEST, of Georgia.

Married - At the residence of the bride's father, Mr. NOAH GRANT, on Sunday, 22d January, 1882, by Rev. H. N. HAYS, Mr. CLAYTON GREAR and Miss SELAH S. GRANT, both of Oconee.

Locals - Col. JOHN T. SLOAN, of Columbia, formerly a resident of Pickens District, celebrated the 50th anniversary of his marriage on the 20th instant.

Thursday February 2, 1882:

Married - On Sunday, 29 January, 1882, by Rev. HUGH STRONG, Mr. A. J. WILSON to Miss E. J. WHITE, both of Oconee county.

Thursday February 9, 1882:

Married - On January 1, 1882, by Rev. WM. MC WHORTER, Mr. STEPHEN J. EDGAR and Miss LUTITIA CONLEY, all of Oconee county.

Married - On January 26, 1882, by the same, Mr. DAVID HALL and Miss DORA DAVIS, both of Oconee county.

Married - At the residence of the bride's father, Mr. PINCKNEY TANNERY, on Sunday, January 29, 1882, by Rev. H. N. HAYS, Mr. ROBERT A. HAYES and Miss ELIZA TANNERY, both of Oconee county.

Locals - JOHNATHAN CROW, of the Cheohee section of our county, died suddenly on the 2d inst., of heart disease.

Thursday February 16, 1882:

Married - January 19, 1882, at the residence of the bride's father, in Oconee county, by Rev. D. H. KENNEMUR, Mr. THOMAS POWERS, of Pickens county, to Miss SARAH BOGGS, of Oconee.

State of South Carolina, Oconee County - In Court of Common Pleas. Summons for Relief - SARAH E. JENKINS, Plaintiff, against JOHN B. SANDERS, as administrator of the estate of JESSE JENKINS, dec'd, WILLIAM F. JENKINS, ELIZA COLE, NANCY MC WHORTER, HARIET PERKINS, SALLIE SANDERS, H. D. A. BIEMAN and HENRY B. SCHRODER, Defendants. Settlement of the estate of JESSE JENKINS, dec'd.

Thursday March 9, 1882:

Married - February 28, 1882, by Rev. G. H. CARTER, Mr. MARSHAL L. ALEXANDER, of Oconee county, to Miss ROXANA NICHOLSON, of Rabun co., Ga.

Thursday March 16, 1882:

Death of Alexander Bryce, Sr.- Colonel ALEXANDER BRYCE (SR.), died at his residence near Rich Mountain, in this county, on Wednesday, the 8th inst. at the advanced age of about 80 years. He had for several years been in declining health and nothing but an iron constitution could have sustained him to his great age. In his early years he lived in the neighborhood of Muddy Springs, and though poor and uneducated, it was said no man ever exceeded, if equaled his popularity. During his long life he bore the reputation of an honest man. His great fault was aspiration to office and in not a few instances it was gratified by the votes of the people. In the militia he rose step by step by election from the office of Corporal to that of Colonel. In 1852 he was elected to the office of Sheriff of Pickens District, which he held four years. In 1868 he was e-

lected and became a member of the Republican Convention to frame a constitution and from that time affiliated with the Republican party of the
county. He was defeated both for the Senate and House after that, once
by a small majority. Both before and since reconstruction he filled the
office of Magistrate and Trial Justice, the latter under the Republican
Administration. Whatever faults he may have had were of the head and not
the heart, and all who knew him well will admit he lived and died an honest man, one true to his friends and kind to his enemies.

Locals - Died, of paralysis, at his son's residence in Newberry, on Monday last, Mr. S. K. KINARD.

Thursday March 23, 1882:

Married - Saturday evening, 11th inst., by Rev. H. N. HAYES, Mr. JOHN H.
BONDS and Miss AMANDA HAGOOD, both of Anderson county.

Married - At the residence of the bride's father, Mr. ROBERT HOWELL, Sunday morning, March 12, 1882, by Rev. H. N. Hays, Mr. JAMES BOLT and Miss
HANNAH HOWELL, both of Anderson county.

Married - At the residence of the bride's father, Mr. JOSEPH MOORE, Sunday evening, 19 March 1882, by Rev. Hays (above), Mr. JAMES T. BARNETT
and Miss JULIA MOORE, both of Anderson county.

Locals - BYRON G. JOHNSON, Esq., of Fort Worth, Texas and Miss JULIA M.
JOHNSON were married by Rev. WM. G. NEVILL at 2½ P.M. Tuesday, 21 March
1882, at the residence of the bride's father, Dr. L. B. JOHNSON, Walhalla,
S. C. They left on the morrow for their Texas home.

Thursday March 30, 1882:

Death of Wm. Bearden - WILLIAM BEARDEN, the old gunsmith, died suddenly
at his residence, near Oakway, in this county, on Monday, the 20th day
of March, 1882, of disease of the heart, aged nearly seventy-two years.
Mr. Bearden was a native of the county, having been born, lived and died
in the same neighborhood. Although Mr. Bearden had never held any public
position, he was well known to many of our citizens. He had been a member of the Baptist Church for more than forty-six years, his declining
years having been made happy by reason of his long converse and sojourn
with the church. Mr. B. reared a considerable family, his wife and sev-
en children having survived him. In his youth he learned the trade of
gunsmith and followed it more or less during his long life. There is a
lesson in the life of Mr. B. from which the youth of the country may profit: He commenced life in the section of country where he died, then
known as the least fertile, and by patient labor and economy he made a
good living and accumulated something to smooth the downward road of life.
Mr. B. had many friends, who, with his family and relatives, sadly mourn
his death.

Death of John Dowis - JOHN DOWIS, another one of our oldest citizens,died
on Tuesday on the Coffee Road, three miles above Walhalla. He was a little over eighty-two years of age and had been through life an honest, so=
ber and industrious citizen, accumulating by labor and economy a fair
living, besides bringing up eight children, most of whom he survived. Mr.
Dowis lived for a few years in Anderson county, and we believe resided in
Georgia a short time, but most of his long life was spent in old Pickens
District, where he had many friends and acquaintances. Up to within a
few years he was stout and healthy and was able to go about his farm and
to Walhalla, until some two months prior to his death, and even last week
he rallied sufficiently to come to town in his buggy. He could neither
read nor write, but was a man of sound judgement and a good friend and
neighbor to those about him. Such men, succeeding under his disadvantages
and there are but few who do, with a good education would have left a
mark behind them. He had been a member of the Baptist Church for many
yearsm and in May, 1877, connected himself with the Walhalla Baptist
Church by letter.

Locals - Mr. A. P. REEDER and Miss ANNIE BLACK were married in West Union
on the 19th inst., by Judge Wickliffe.

Thursday April 6, 1882:

Locals - Mrs. SALLIE L. HUTCHISON, wife of Dr. T. C. HUTCHISON, died suddenly in West Union on Sunday morning last. Mrs. Hutchison was about 37 years of age and a native of Fairfield County, in this State. Those who knew her intimately bear strong testimony as to her high Christian character and abiding faith in a crucified Redeemer. As a mother she was gentle, kind and loving, exercising her parental authority with judgment and wise forethought leaving an indelible impress for good on the minds and hearts of her children. She was a devoted and consistent member of the Baptist Church. She leaves a devoted husband and seven children to mourn their irreparable loss, to whom we extend our tenderest sympathies. She was buried on Monday afternoon in the Walhalla Baptist Church cemetery after solemn and impressive funeral ceremonies in the church by Rev. C. D. Mann.

Married - At the residence of Mr. JOHN S. GOODMAN, March 29th, 1882, by Rev. G. H. CARTER, Mr. ROLAND COBB and Miss IDA M. GOODMAN.

Married - At the residence of the bride's father, Mr. H. D. ROWLAND, at Central, Pickens county, March 22d, 1882, by Rev. H. M. ALLEN, Mr. A. D. BELOTTE and Miss KATE ROWLAND.

Thursday April 13, 1882:

Married - At the residence of the bride's father, Mr. JAMES LEE, on the 6th inst., by Rev. D. W. HEAD, Mr. FREDERICK WILLIAMS, of Anderson county, and Miss MARY LEE, of Oconee county.

Locals - We regret to learn of the death of Mrs. MARIA E. SMITH, wife of W. G. SMITH and mother of one of the proprietors of the "Courier", which occurred at her residence near Sandy Springs, in Anderson County, on Sunday morning, April 9th, 1882. Mrs. Smith was a daughter of JESSE LEWIS, one of the early settlers in the neighborhood of Sandy Springs, and at the time of her death was in the 68th year of her age. In early life she connected herself with the Baptist Church of Old Lebanon and continued a consistent member up to her death. She leaves a husband and three children, besides many friends, to mourn their loss. Her remains were interred in the family burying ground on Monday morning in the presence of the entire community, which turned out to testify their appreciation of her many virtues and elevated traits of character.

Thursday April 20, 1882:

Married - April 16, 1882, by the Rev. NIMROD SULLIVAN, Mr. DAVID KING to Miss MARTHA REID, all of Oconee.

Mrs. LOU SHELOR, wife of JOSEPH W. SHELOR, Esq., died in Walhalla, at the residence of her brother-in-law, JESSE W. STRIBLING, on Saturday the 15th inst. at 10 o'clock P.M. Mrs. Shelor was a daughter of W. J. NEVILLE, and was only twenty-three years old at the time of her death. She had been married a few years and leaves a husband and little daughter two years old, as also a large number of relatives and friends to mourn her loss. Mrs. Shelor had been in declining health for over a year, and was confined to the house and bed several months prior to her death. She had been a consistent member of the Walhalla Baptist church from early youth, and illustrated in her life and conduct, as well as in the fortitude with which she endured her sufferings, those christian graces, which mark the true disciple. Death is at all times sad, but doubly so in the case of the young just entering on the threshold of life and bound to the earth by strong social and family ties. It is an event, however, which must befall every living soul, and being so it is a great consolation to her friends to know and feel that by her example as well as by her profession, her death was but an entrance into life eternal. Her remains were buried in the Baptist Churchyard on Monday at 11 o'clock A.M. after appropriate funeral services by Rev. Mr. CARTER, pastor of the church. A large concourse of friends and acquaintances were present to pay the last tribute to her christian character and social worth.

Thursday April 27, 1882: (next page)

Married - On the 16th inst., by D. F. CARTER, Esq., Mr. JOHN S. PHILLIPS
and Miss ADA A. CARVER, both of Oconee.

Locals - Capt. JOHN A. SMALL, a brother-in-law of D. A. SMITH, of the
Courier, died at Sardis, Mississippi, on the 9th of last January. Capt.
Small was a native of Abbeville county and served during the late war as
Quartermaster of Col. BLACK's Regiment of Cavalry. After the close of
the war he removed and settled in Mississippi, where he died. It seems
that three or more letters were written to the relatives of the deceased,
both at Abbeville and Walhalla, no one of which was received, and only
last Tuesday did they first hear the sad intelligence. Capt. Small leaves
a wife and several children.

Thursday May 4, 1882:

Married - By Rev. FLETCHER SMITH, on the 27th of April, Mr. JOHN T. ROPER
to Miss DISA JOHNSON, both of Oconee.

Married - On 27th ult., by Rev. JOHN OWEN, Mr. D. C. ALEXANDER to Miss
JANE HOLDEN, all of Oconee.

Locals - Miss MARY SMITH, daughter of JOHN J. SMITH, our County Auditor,
died of consumption at the residence of her father, near Walhalla, on Wednesday evening, the 26th ult., in the 24th year of her age. Miss Smith
had been a member of the Methodist Church for several years. She was a
young lady of many excellant and noble traits of character and during
the sickness of her sister, who preceded her to the grave only a few
months ago, she was her constant companion night and day, and showed a
self-sacrificing spirit to duty which is scarcely if ever found in this
day and time. Miss Smith has many friends and admirers. Her remains
were interred at the Baptist Church graveyard on Thursday afternoon, the
27th ult., after appropriate funeral services by Rev. C. D. MANN, assisted by Rev. G. H. CARTER. A large assemblage of the citizens of Walhalla and neighborhood were present to pay a last sad tribute to her memory.

Thursday May 11, 1882:

Locals - Mrs. MARY SANDERS, wife of J. B. SANDERS, Esq., departed this
life at Oakway, in this county, on May 6th, 1882. She had just finished
her 57th year, being a corpse on her birthday. She was buried at Center
Church on Monday, where she had been a member of the M. E. Church, South,
since 1846. She was an affectionate wife and mother and all who knew
her loved her. May the Lord comfort the bereaved husband and motherless
children.

Thursday May 18, 1882:

Married - May 15, 1882, by the Rev. NIMROD SULLIVAN, Mr. WILLIAM BROOM
to Miss ANNA WHITMAN, all of Oconee county.

Married - On the 4th inst., by Rev. H. N. HAYS, Mr. THOS. DALTON to Miss
JULIA HAMILTON, both of Oconee county.

Thursday May 25, 1882:

Locals - Mr. JAMES PARKER, formerly of West Union, died recently at Piedmont, Greenville county, of pneumonia. Mr. Parker was well known to our
people and respected by them as a good citizen.

Thursday June 1, 1882:

Locals - Miss SOPHIA PARKER, a young lady well known in our community,
died last week at the Piedmont Factory of typhoid fever. She was the
daughter of Mr. JAMES PARKER, whose death we announce last week.

Messrs. JOSEPH and WM. REID, the former of Chickasaw County, Mississippi,
and the latter of the Argentine Republic of South America, have been on
a visit to their relatives and friends in this section. They left this
country in 1824. They were impressed with the rapid growth and improvement of this section. Mr. Wm. Reid has been a resident of South America

for more than twenty-five years.

Mr. CHRISTIAN MICHALUS, an old German citizen of our town, met with a fatal accident on last Thursday afternoon, as he was going down the steps of his daughter's house. It seems that there was a small round stick of wood on the steps and as Mr. Michalus started down his foot struck the stick of wood, which began to roll, causing him to fall with great force to the ground. The fall, it is thought, caused the rupture of some blood vessel near the heart, and death ensued in six or seven hours after the accident. Mr. M. was 79 years old and came from Germany and settled at Walhalla about 27 years ago. He leaves a wife and several children.

Thursday June 29, 1882:

Locals - Mrs. EUGENIA NORRIS, a most estimable and Christian woman, died on Sunday morning last. Mrs. Norris was the wife of Mr. R. E. NORRIS, who lives near Westminster in this county. She leaves a family of seven children and many friends to mourn their loss. She was buried on Monday at Westminster cemetery after funeral services by Rev. C. D. MANN.

Thursday July 6, 1882:

Locals - Miss SUE BALLENGER, niece of Capt. A. J. BALLENGER, living near Westminster, died on Sunday morning last from consumption and was buried on Monday morning at Westminster cemetery.

Thursday July 13, 1882:

Married - On the 9th inst., by Rev. H. N. HAYES, Mr. CHARLES WHITE to Miss ANNIE BUSBY, all of Anderson.

Mr. LAWRENCE LENHARDT, one of the oldest and wealthiest citizens of Greenville county, died suddenly one day last week on the road to his mill, some five miles from the city. He was 90 years old and the verdict of the jury was death by the visitation of God.

Thursday August 3, 1882:

Locals - Mr. HORATIO FIELDS, a citizen of Oconee and a soldier of the war of 1812, died on the 26th of July. He was one of the oldest citizens of the county.

We regret to announce the death of Dr. J. W. SPEARMAN, of Seneca, which sad event took place in that town on the 29th of July. Dr. Spearman was a native of Newberry, but for many years had made his home in Oconee. He had been in bad health for years and finally died of consumption.

Thursday August 17, 1882:

Locals - Miss OVALINE C. SHARP, a daughter of JOHN SHARP, Esq., died at his residence on Sunday morning last, and on the same day ROBERT KELLY, a grandson of Mr. Sharp and raised by him, died at the same place. Miss Sharp was the only child that this aged couple had still single and therefore her death makes the loss more heavy for them, as they are quite feeble. The deceased were buried at Bethel Presbyterian Church graveyard and funeral services were conducted by Rev. HUGH STRONG.

Thursday August 24, 1882:

Locals - Mr. STEPHEN BALDWIN, one of our oldest and most respectable citizens, died at his residence in this county on the 20th inst. He was over 80 years of age.

Thursday August 31, 1882:

State of South Carolina, County of Oconee - In the Court of Common Please. Summons for Relief (Complaint not served) - S. P. DENDY, as Administrator, Plaintiff, against MILLEY GRANT, widow, ELIZABETH WELDON, MARTHA BROWN, MARY A. PALMER, PATTEN F. GUESS and JOSEPH GUESS, heirs-at-law, and R. L.

B. CONNELLY, Grantee of GEORGE GRANT, deceased, Defendants. Foreclosure of a mortgage on the real estate of GEORGE GRANT, dec'd.

State of South Carolina, County of Oconee - In the Court of Common Please. Summons for Relief -LEMUEL V. PITTS, as administrator of the personal estate of WILLIAM PITTS, deceased, and heir-at-law of said dec'd, DAVID PITTS, DANIEL PITTS, REUBEN PITTS, HARIETT PITTS, SARAH HERRING nee PITTS, AMANDA PITTS, IDELLA PITTS and MELINDA PITTS, Plaintiffs, against EMILY PITTS, HARIETT PITTS, MATILDA CHRISTIAN nee PITTS, NANY LILES nee PITTS, KEITH PRICE, GARVIN S. PRICE, TURNER CRENSHAW, FANNIE GERMAN nee CRENSHAW, ALICE HARRINGTON nee CRENSHAW, RINLEY nee DAVIS, ELLEN SAWYER nee DAVIS, ALICE CAIN nee DAVIS, WARREN R. DAVIS, CHARLES J. DAVIS, IDA DAVIS and H. D. A. BIEMAN, Defendants. Sale of the real estate of WILLIAM PITTS, dec'd.

Locals - Married , on the 27th inst., by Rev. B. HOLDER, Miss KATIE ALEX-ANDER to Mr. THOS. HARPER, all of Oconee.

Thursday September 7, 1882:

Locals - WILLIAM COOK, one of our oldest citizens, died recently at his residence near Tunnel Hill.

Thursday September 14, 1882:

Locals - Married, on the 31st ult., by Rev. J. R. EARLE, Mr. SAMUEL L. CLEVELAND, of Oconee, to Miss HATTIE SUTTLES, of Anderson.

Thursday September 21, 1882:

Mr. JESSE MULKEY, an old and respected citizen of our county, died recently of dropsy of the chest. He was 76 years old.

Mr. NATHAN HUNTER, living above Walhalla four or five miles, departed this life on Friday night last, the 15th inst. Mr. Hunter was a good citizen, a native of Newberry county and was eighty-two years old.

Married - On the 13th September 1882, by J. W. HAULBROOK, Esq., JOSEPH T. MARTIN and Miss SARAH M. EMERY, both of Oconee county.

Thursday September 28, 1882:

Married - In Townville Presbyterian church September 24, 1882, by Rev. H. STRONG, Mr. W. A. BOWEN and Miss ANNA PITTS, both of Oconee county.

Married - On 21 September 1882, at the residence of Mr. Z. GIBSON, by A. B. GRANT, Esq., Mr. J. N. GROGAN and Miss TALLULAH V. GIBSON, both of Oconee county.

Thursday October 5, 1882:

Married - At the residence of the bride's mother, September 28, 1882, by Rev. C. D. MANN, J. B. SANDERS, Esq., to Miss BETSEY HERBERT, both of Oconee.

We regret to learn that Mr. BRY FRETWELL, an old and highly esteemed citizen of our county, died at his residence near Whetstone on the 29th ult. He was ill only a few days from some affection of the kidneys and died in otherwise good health. He removed from Anderson to this county years before the war and has always been an upright, quiet, unobtrusive citizen. He engaged in farming and stock raising and had accumulated by industry a fair property.

Thursday October 19, 1882:

Married - On Tuesday, October 3, 1882, at the residence of Mr. E. CLEVE-LAND, by W. K. SHARP, Esq., Mr. F. ALONZO DANIELS, of Anderson county, to Miss SALLIE CLEVELAND, of Oconee.

Mr. JOHN ANSEL, one of the earliest settlers of Walhalla, died at his

residence on Saturday evening at 6 o'clock of something like rheumatism
of the heart. His death was sudden and painless, being ill but a few
minutes, though he had been complaining for some time. To him, it seems,
death was not unexpected, as he told some friends last weel he would not
live but a few days and had picked out his coffin and given instructions
about its trimming. Mr. Ansel was born in Wurtenburg, Germany, December
18, 18815, and came to the United States about 1838. He resided in Charleston several years and removed to this county under the auspices of the
German Colonization Society and continued to live here until his death.
Mr. A. was a cabinet maker and was remarkably skillful in his calling,
having followed it in several Northern cities, in Charleston and in Walhalla. His work was polished and faithfully executed. He is said to have
made the first raised top coffin in the United States and understood all
kinds of fine work. He is said to have been the oldest German Mason in
the State, having been a member of the Order since 1847. He also belonged
to the Order of Odd Fellows. Mr. Ansel was an industrious, upright citizen, a kind father, a reliable friend, kind hearted and liberal in all
things in proportion to his means. He leaves two sons and several daughters, as also many friends to mourn his loss. His funeral services were
conducted by Dr. J. P. SMELTZER in the Lutheran Church on Monday at 11
o'clock A.M., at the close of which the Masonic fraternity took charge
of his remains and interred them in the adjoining yard with their usual
impressive ceremonies.

Thursday October 26, 1882:

Mr. TILMAN C. MAGEE died at this residence, near Fair Play, in this county, on the 19th inst., in the 82d year of his age. Mr. Magee had lived
at his present home near forty-eight years. He had been married twice and
leaves a considerable family and many friends to mourn their loss. He had
been for years a member of the Baptist Church and was a faithful member
to the end.

A Happy Social Event ("Hartwell, Ga. Sun") - On the evening of the 18th
inst., were united in marriage at the residence of Mrs. M. STEELE, Oconee
county, S. C., J. R. RILEY, D. D., officiating, Mrs. S. J. DENDY and Dr.
CHARLES A. WEBB, of Hartwell, Ga. (Further details follow)

Thursday November 2, 1882:

Long article on the death of GEORGE R. CHERRY, at his residence on Seneca
River.

A very pleasant little celebration of the marriage of JOHN D. CAPPLEMAN,
formerly of this place, but now of Charleston, to Miss JULIA A. PIEPER,
took place at the residence of the bride's father, our fellow townsman,
Mr. H. W. PIEPER, on last Thursday afternoon, October 26, 1882, at 2
o'clock.

Thursday November 23, 1882:

We are pained to chronicle the death of Miss AMANDA JONES, which occurred at her home in Fort Madison, Tuesday morning, 21st inst., at half
past 1 o'clock. While on a visit to relatives in Mississippi last summer she contracted malaria, which terminated in congestive fever, of
which she died.

Thursday November 30, 1882:

Married - At the residence of the bride's father, Mr. JAMES B. MYERS,
November 26th, 1882, by F. A. DANIELS, Notary Public, Mr. F. M. BRUCE
and Miss SARAH MYERS, all of Oconee county, S. C.

Thursday December 7, 1882:

Long article on the murder and robbery of WILLIAM JOHN HUNNICUTT.

Married - On Tuesday evening, 28th ult., by Rev. J. P. SMELTZER, Mr. C.
R. D. BURNS and Miss BERTHA H. SCHRODER, both of Oconee.

Thursday December 14, 1882:

Married - On Sunday, the 10th inst., by F. A. DANIELS, Notary Public, Mr. J. Y. BURNS and Miss CORNELIA THRASHER.

Married - On Sunday, the 10th inst., by the same, Mr. WM. THRASHER to Miss MARY BURNS.

Married - On Tuesday, December 8, 1882, by Rev. JOHN ATTAWAY, Rev. LANDY WOOD, of the South Carolina Conference, and Miss CARRIE McC., daughter of Mr. MILTON REESE, of Anderson county.

Thursday December 21, 1882:

Married - On Tuesday, December 19, 1882, by Rev. C. D. MANN, Mr. G. B. STEWART to Miss ALICE MC LANE. Both persons were from Georgia.

Married - On the 3d inst., by JAMES T. REID, Notary Public, Mr. W. H. DUNSON, from Knoxville, Tennessee, to Miss ANNA STONE, of Oconee.

Thursday December 28, 1882:

Married - On the 16th inst., by Rev. D. H. KENNEMUR, Mr. ELIJAH GOLDEN to Miss NARCISSA MORGAN, both of Oconee.

Married - On the 21st inst., by the same, Mr. J. N. MULKEY, of Oconee, to Miss ETTA BREWER, of Pickens.

Thursday January 4, 1883:

Married - On the 31st December 1882, at the residence of W. F. DODD, by ISAAC WICKLIFFE, Esq., Mr. JOHN F. TAYLOR to Miss AGNES HAWKINS, both of Oconee.

Married - In Atlanta, Ga., on the evening of December 19th, 1882, at the residence of Mrs. SARAH TOMPKINS, by _____, Mr. CHARLES REYNOLDS, of Jamestown, New York, and Miss BETTIE SHACKELFORD, formerly of Oconee co.

Thursday January 11, 1883:

Married - On the 7th inst., at Holly Springs Church, by Rev. ROWLAND COBB, Mr. BAYLUS E. CHAMBERS to Miss MARY BLACKWELL, all of Oconee.

Married - Near Monticello, Fairfield county, S. C., December 14, 1882, by Rev. J. L. HIDE, Mr. JOHN M. HALL, of Oconee county, to Miss A. M. BELL, of Fairfield county.

Married - At the residence of Rev. J. C. NEESE, the bride's father, Bowersville, by Rev. J. H. GROGAN, on the 6th of December, Mr. F. B. DOYLE and Miss LULA NEESE. Doyle, like a sensible man, built a house and furnished it ready to cage his bird. A more handsome couple were never united in Hart. "Hartwell Sun"

Thursday January 18, 1883:

Married - At Shiloh Church Sunday evening, January 14, 1883, by Rev. H. N. HAYS, Mr. THOMAS GRISSOP and Miss LENA WELCH, both of Seneca City, S. C.

Married - In West Union, at the residence of the bride, January 10, 1883, by Rev. J. P. SMELTZER, Mr. JAMES W. SADLER and Miss MAGGIE E. SCHRODER.

Married - On Thursday evening, 11th inst., at the residence of the bride's father, J. B. SANDERS, Esq., Oakway, S. C., by Rev. C. D. MANN, Mr. HANDY MARET to Miss LENA SANDERS.

Married - On the 9th inst., by JAMES T. REID, Notary Public, Mr. J. G. MAULDIN, of Pickens, to Miss C. M. WOODEN, of Oconee.

Married - November 21st, 1882, near Carnesville, Ga., by Rev. J. F. Goode,

Mr. J. J. HALEY, of Townville, S. C., to Miss R. L. ALLGOOD, of Carnesville, Ga.

Mrs. BARBARA MC JUNKIN, wife of C. M. MC JUNKIN, Editor of the "Palmetto Yeoman", died on the 13th of January, of cancer.

Thursday January 25, 1883:

Married - On January 7th, by Rev. S. A. GARY, at his residence, Mr. G. B. STEVENS, of Oconee county, to Miss SALLEY D. FERGUSON, of Pickens.

Col. WARREN D. WILKES, a well known, and, at one time, prominent citizen of this county, died at his residence in the Eastern part of the county on last Friday, the 12th inst., after a severe illness of several months from nervous prostration. Col. Wilkes was a man of fine mind, and a most eloquent orator in years gone by. His life was an evenful one, beginning with a trip to Kansas and residence there during the agitation and election preceding the admission of that Territory as a State. He returned here afterwards and practiced law until the war, when he went out with the Palmetto Sharpshooters and served to the close of the war. After the war he returned to Belton to practice law. He was elected in 1872 to the Legislature, and after the expiration of his term served as Trial Justice for several years. During latter years his health has been quite poor, and for months before his death was an invalid. His funeral services were performed by Rev. MIKE MC GEE at Shady Grove Church, and his remains placed to rest in the churchyard there on last Sunday. "Anderson Intelligencer"

The eldest daughter of Judge COTHRAN died at Abbeville Monday night, 8th inst. She was the wife of Mr. J. ALLEN SMITH.

Thursday February 1, 1883:

State of South Carolina, County of Oconee - In the Court of Common Pleas. Summons for Relief - J. BAYLIS PALMER, Plaintiff, against ELIZA ANN H. WILLIAMS, JESSE PALMER, J. PRESTON PALMER, MARTHA SMITH, LUCINDA SLEDGER, W. H. BUTLER and JAMES and JOHN PALMER, sons of W. PALMER, dec'd, Defendants. Partition of a lot or parcel of land in Oconee county on the Walhalla and Bachelor's Retreat road, 16 acres more or less, among the heirs-at-law of AMANDA SLAUGHTER PALMER, dec'd. Absent defendants: J. PRESTON PALMER, MARTHA SMITH, LUCINDA SLEDGER, JOHN and JAMES PALMER.

Married - On the 21st of January, 1883, by D. F. CARTER, Esq., Mr. JAMES L. BRIGHT to Miss ISABELLA STANDREDGE, both of Oconee county.

Married - On Thursday evening, January 25th, 1883, by Rev. WM. MC WHORTER, at the residence of the bride's mother, Mr. C. E. O. MITCHELL and Miss MARY E. HOLCOMBE, youngest daughter of Mrs. ELIZABETH HOLCOMBE, all of Oconee.

Mrs. AMANDA KILBURN, wife of Mr. WALLACE KILBURN, died at her residence near Westminster, on last Friday night, the 26th inst. Mrs. Kilburn had been in declining health for several months, a victim of consumption. She leaves one child. Her remains were buried on Sunday in the Baptist graveyard at Westminster.

DAVID DUNLAP, one of our oldest and most respectable citizens, died on the 24th inst.

Mrs. FERRABY MC FETRIDGE died at the residence of JOHN CLAUS, near Fairview on the 26th inst. Mrs. McFetridge was one hundred and five years old.

Thursday February 8, 1883:

We regret to announce the sudden death of Rev. NIMROD SULLIVAN on Tuesday evening at 8 o'clock in the 85th year of his age.

Thursday February 15, 1883:

Married - At the residence of the bride, by Rev. J. V. EVANS, Mr. HENRY

M. SKINNER, of Highlands, N. C., to Miss MATTIE O. NICHOLSON, of Chattooga Valley, Ga.

Married - On the 11th inst., by Rev. MILTON SANDERS, Mr. C. B. MORTON to Miss ALLICE CHASTAIN, both of Oconee county.

Thursday February 22, 1883:

We regret to learn that Mr. ANDREW HOLMES, a well known and highly respected citizen of our county, died at his residence, on Long Creek, on last Wednesday, the 14th inst, of pneumonia.

Thursday March 1, 1883:

Married - At Acworth, Ga., on the 21st of February, 1883, by Rev. A. G. THOMAS, Mr. E. D. REYNOLDS, of Atlanta, to Miss NELLIE GROGAN, of Acworth.

Married - At the residence of the bride's mother, in Anderson county, S. C., January 15th, 1883, by Rev. J. R. RILEY, Mr. JOHN S. PATTERSON, of Oconee county, to Miss MARY ANN MC CRARY.

Married - At the residence of the bride's father, Mr. W. J. HIX, February 27th, 1883, by Rev. G. H. CARTER, Mr. JOE W. SHELOR, of Walhalla, and Miss LIZZIE HIX, of Fair Play.

We regret to learn that Mr. JOHN C. CHERRY, of Pendleton, died near that place on Thursday night last. We have not been able to hear what disease caused his death. Mr. Cherry was well advanced in years and had never married.

ALFRED G. INMAN, the Emanuel co., Ga. man who murdered and robbed his wife, was lynched after attending her funeral.

Thursday March 8, 1883:

Married - On the 1st inst., at the residence of the bride's father, by Rev. J. M. SANDERS, Mr. JOHN W. MILLER to Miss NARCISSA E. ABBOT, both of Oconee.

We regret to announce the death of Miss SALLIE GAILLARD, daughter of Capt. A. D. GAILLARD, on Saturday, the 3d inst., of consumption. The deceased was buried at Bethel Church on Sunday afternoon.

Mr. LAWRENCE C. BEST, of Allendale, was killed on the 24th ult., by Mr. DUPREIS, the town marshal, while the latter was defending himself from an attack with a knife.

DUDLEY M. DU BOSE, ex-member of Congress from Georgia, died from paralysis at Washington, Ga., Friday. General DuBose married the only daughter of ROBERT TOOMBS, but she died several years ago. He leaves four grown children- two sons and two daughters.

Thursday March 15, 1883:

An Inquiry - A Postal was recently addressed to our Clerk of Court, asking about the descendants of one AARON CLEVELAND. As we have several families in our county by the name of Cleveland, we have concluded to publish the contents of the letter, as it may result in great benefit to some of the family if we have such in our county. The postal is as follows: 74 Hamilton Street, Cleveland, Ohio. February 27, 1883. Dear Sir: I wish to find a trace of the descendants of Aaron Cleveland, born 10th of November, 1766, in Norwich, Connecticut, who went to South Carolina and died there leaving children. If there are any persons by the name of Cleveland known to you, please send me their address by return postal, and greatly oblige, H. G. CLEVELAND.

Married - At the residence of BALUS HIX, in Fair Play, by JAMES SEABORN, T. J., Mr. P. N. LINDSEY to Miss CARRIE RAMAGE, both of Oconee.

Married - On the 8th inst., at the residence of the bride's father, by

ISAAC WICKLIFFE, Esq., Mr. ANDREW D. LESLEY, of Pickens county, to Miss ELIZABETH REBECCA FRASIER, of Oconee county.

A little son of Mr. CHARLES H. NIEBUHS, of our town, died last week, it is said, of something like meningitis. This is the first case we have heard of in our county.

Died, at her residence at Oakway, S. C., Mrs. MARY CAIN, aged about 80 years, after severe illness of long standing. Mrs. Cain lived a life of industry and quietness among her acquaintances. She leaves 14 grandchildren and about 20 great grandchildren to mourn for her. She died on Friday, the 9th inst. and was interred at New Bethel Church, after a funeral discourse by Rev. A. W. MC GUFFIN.

LAMAR STARKE, a well known citizen of Columbia, died in that city on Saturday.

Thursday March 22, 1883:

The friends and relatives of Miss JULIA CAPPELMANN will be grieved to learn that she died at the residence of her father, in Walhalla, on Tuesday night, after a short illness. Her remains will be buried at the Lutheran Church on this (Thursday) afternoon, at 3 o'clock.

Thursday March 29, 1883:

As we go to press we learn of the death of Mr. BALUS HIX, of Fair Play, in this county, after a severe illness of several days. He was one of the pillars of Beaverdam Baptist Church.

Thursday, April 5, 1883:

We record the following deaths from pneumonia which occurred last week: HARRISON LEATHERS, a young man, a son of ASA LEATHERS, after a short illness. BENJAMIN KNOX, a young man, a son of ROBERT KNOX, buried at New Hope Church last week. JACKSON DEATON, about sixty years old.

Thursday April 12, 1883:

Married - At the residence of T. D. ALEXANDER, on Sunday, April 8, 1883, by Rev. A. W. MC GUFFIN, Mr. WILLIAM ADAMS to Miss DORA DICKSON.

Married - On the 10th inst., at the residence of Mr. JOSEPH JENKINS, brother of the bride, in Newberry county, by Rev. R. N. WELLS, Col. JOHN L. BLACK, late of Fairfield, to Miss E. T. JENKINS.

A statement is made that DAVID A. KEASLER, of Pendleton, was thrown from his buggy, near Central, last week, and killed. Now it is stated that he was murdered and robbed, and that his murderer, a negro, has been arrested and committed to jail at Anderson.

Thursday April 19, 1883:

State of South Carolina, Oconee County - In the Probate Court. Settlement of the estate of ELIZABETH MARTIN, deceased. G. W. BURNS, Administrator, Plaintiff - vs. YANCY WHITE, JANE HAYES, THOMAS CLEVELAND, MARY RICE, JANE CLEVELAND, SARAH DANIELS and E. CLEVELAND, Defendants.

The Death of Mr. Howe - Columbia, April 15 - The Rev. GEORGE HOWE, D. D., L.L.D., died at his residence in this city, at half-past 5 o'clock this afternoon. Two weeks ago today Dr. Howe was thrown from his carriage and his leg broken. He was doing well, and his recovery hoped for until yesterday, when he had two nervous chills and thenceforth sank rapidly. His relapse was so sudden that absent members of his family could not be summoned in time to reach here before his death.

Miss LUCY P. PHILLIPS, sister of JOHN S. VERNER, was married by the Rev. CHARLES PHILLIPS at Chapel Hill, N. C., on the 9th inst., to Mr. M. H. RUSSELL, of Rockingham, N. C.

177

Thursday April 26, 1883:

Death of Mrs. Sarah M. Bomar - Mrs. SARAH M. BOMAR, of Spartanburg, Died at the residence of her granddaughter, Mrs. GEORGE and WILLIAM BOMAR, on Augusta street, Greenville, Saturday morning, aged 75 years. The deceased lady was twice married, her first being JOHN BLASSINGAME and her second also, deceased, being JOHN BOMAR. She has been living for some time with her son, JOHN BLASSINGAME, Sheriff of Spartanburg, and came here to visit about two weeks ago. She was a native of Pendleton and a sister of JOHN T. SLOAN, Clerk of the House of Representatives of South Carolina. She was a member of the Baptist Church of Spartanburg and a faithful and con- scientious Christian. During her long life she invariably retained the esteem and respect of many warm friends and her decease will be deeply deplored. The remains will be taken to Spartanburg tonight. "Greenville News", April 15.

Married - On the 5th inst., in Cohaba Valley, Ala., by Rev. Mr. LAMBERT, Mr. LOUIS T. STALNAKER, of Virginia, to Miss FANNIE K. JAMES, of South Carolina, second daughter of Dr. B. S. and Mrs. LAVINIA JAMES.

Married - On Sunday evening, April 1, 1883, at the residence of the brides father, B. F. ROBERTSON, by Rev. C. D. MANN, Mr. THOMAS A. GRANT, to Miss ELLA ROBERTSON.

Married - In Charleston, S. C., on the 19th of April, 1883, by Rev. LU- THER PROBST, at the residence of the bride's father, Mr. J. GEORGE GUTE- KUNST to Miss HARRIET CAROLINE SONNTAG.

State of South Carolina, County of Oconee - In the Court of Common Pleas. Summons for Relief - JOHN M. DOWIS, as executor of the last will and tes- tament of JOHN DOWIS, dec'd, Plaintiff, against FRANCES M. DOWIS, MARY ELIZABETH RAMPEY, MARTHA J. BRADY, JOHN WELBORNE GRAY, MARTHA ADALINE DAVIS, MANNING GRAY, BERRY HINTON, and MARY J. SCOTT, Defendants. Absent defendants: MARTHA J. BRADY, JOHN WELBORNE GRAY, MARTHA ADALINE DAVIS, MANNING GRAY and MARY J. SCOTT. For construction of the last will and testament of JOHN DOWIS, dec'd, as to the rights of the widow, FRANCES M. DOWIS, under the will.

We met this morning our old friend, Mr. D. P. ROBINS, who reached Walhal- la Monday night from Helena, Montana Territory. He is on a visit to his father, Capt. ABLE ROBINS, and his other relatives.

Thursday May 10, 1883:

Married - On the 29th ult., by Rev. FLETCHER SMITH, Mr. JOHN M. DRYMAN, of Macon, N. C., to Miss JULIA A. KILLIAN, of Oconee, S. C.

Married - At the residence of the bride's father, Mr. J. E. HENDRIX, Wal- halla, S. C., on Tuesday evening, May 8th, 1883, by Rev. J. P. SMELTZER, Mr. ALEXANDER L. ROBERTS, of Charleston, to Mrs. LEWELLYN E. ARNOLD.

Thursday May 17, 1883:

Married - At the residence of the bride's father, on the 15th inst., by the Rev. H. STRONG, Dr. J. H. MILLER, of Cross Hill, S. C., to Miss LEELA E. S. BLACK, second daughter of Col. JOHN S. BLACK.

A six year old daughter of HARRISON WOOD, of Union, was burned to death by lighting a fire with kerosene last week.

Thursday May 24, 1883:

BENNETT MOODY, one of the best citizens of this county, died of paralysis at his residence in Cheohee on the 14th May, 1883, aged 75 years, 11 mos. and 18 days. He was faithful and punctual in the discharge of all the du- ties of life, as husband, father, Christian, neighbor and citizen. He had been for over forty years a consistent member of the Baptist Church and most of the time a deacon. His descendants revere his spotless char- acter and emulate his good works. They are comforted at his loss by the full assurance that he has gone...to eternal bliss.

Thursday June 14, 1883:

Mountain Rest Locals - I am sorry to state the death of Miss MATTIE HUN-
TER, who has been sick for the last three months. She bore her sickness
with great patience. She leaves a loving father and mother, six brothers
and two loving sisters and many friends to mourn her loss. Her last words
were, "Lord have mercy on us."

Thursday June 21, 1883:

Townville Items - Mrs. MOLLIE BOLEMAN, wife of G. N. C. BOLEMAN, died at
her home in Townville Thursday, the 7th inst., and was buried in the
graveyard of the Baptist Church.

Locals - Married, on Wednesday, June 13, 1883, by Rev. G. H. CARTER, Mr.
WM. J. NEVILL to Mrs. L. W. STRIBLING.

Thursday June 28, 1883:

Locals - Mrs. HODGE, an old lady of our town, died on last Sunday and
was buried in the Lutheran graveyard on Monday afternoon. She had been
sick quite a long time.

Thursday July 5, 1883:

Locals - Married = in Grace Church, Charleston, June 28, 1883, by Rev.
C. C. PINCKNEY, Mr. G. W. PRATT, of Walhalla, to Miss MAMIE DAWSON, of
Charleston.

Thursday July 12, 1883:

Locals - We learn that Mrs. SARAH C. LIDDELL, relict of the late GEORGE
W. LIDDELL, deceased, died recently at her home on Keowee River.

Thursday July 19, 1883:

The Anderson papers announce the death of Mrs. FANNIE CARPENTER, of consumption, on Tuesday, of last week, in the 35th year of her age. She was
the daughter of Rev. T. B. MAULDEN, deceased, of Oconee. She leaves four
little boys, her husband and many relatives and friends to mourn their
loss.

Thursday July 26, 1883:

A Son's Tribute - My mother, Mrs. MARIA E. BALLENGER, wife of Capt. J. A.
BALLENGER, was born and reared in Henderson County, North Carolina, and
to South Carolina in 1846, where she lived until her sudden death on the
13th of June, 1883, in her seventieth year. She was a pure and mature
Christian. ....her last letter to the writer gave evidence she
was ready to die...only a few days later the sad words were telegraphed.
....."Your mother is dead"......fatigued with execises she had taken that
warm June morning, she lay down to rest and woke up amid the songs of the
redeemed........eulogy signed by E.W.B.

Thursday August 2, 1883:

Married - In West Union, on Tuesday evening, July 31, 1883, by Rev. F. M.
MORGAN, Mr. WM. B. HUTCHINSON to Miss NORA MC CRACKIN, all of Oconee.

Mr. WILLIAM HALL died at his residence, in this county, on Friday night
last, of apoplexy, in the 70th year of his age. Mr. Hall was a native of
the county and one of our best citizens.

We regret that we are called upon to announce the death of MARION R.
MOORE, a son of Mr. JOHN B, MOORE, of this county, which occurred in Atlanta, Ga., on the 14th of July from typhoid fever. Mr. Moore was twenty three years old at the time of his decease, and had been in Atlanta
since the fall of 1881, first as agent for the Singer Sewing Machine Co.
and afterwards as agent of the WHEELER & WILSON Co., but at the time of
his death he was connected with the railroad business.

Thursday August 9, 1883:

Married - On Sunday, July 29, 1883, by Rev. W. C. SEABORN, at the bride's father, Mr. WM. C. SLUTER to Miss MARY J. HAYNES, both of Oconee.

Westminster Correspondence - Many people of our county will regret to hear that Mr. ALLEN TERRELL has sold his fine farm on Tugaloo River to Mr. A. ZIMMERMAN, and that he will move with his family at an early day to Texas.

We are sorry to record the death of Mrs. MARSHAL B. DENDY, which occurred on last Saturday, 4th inst. She leaves a large family to mourn her loss. She was buried at Richland Church on Sunday, Dr. Smeltzer conducting the service.

Thursday August 23, 1883:

Mrs. ELIZABETH LYLES, a lunatic, was sent to the State Asylum on the 21st inst.

"The Abbeville Press and Banner" announces that Mr. J. P. PHILLIPS, of Ninety Six, was presented by his wife on the 12th inst. with two sons and a daughter, weighing four, five and six pounds respectively. The little fellows are all stout, healthy and kicking. They are named PETER BERRY, WILLIE LAWTON and ANNA BOLIN. Mr. Phillips is a son of Mr. BERRY PHILLIPS of this county.

ANNIE MAY, infant daughter of Mrs. JULIA JOHNSON, died on Saturday morning last, aged about six months. Its remains were buried in the Lutheran cemetery on Sunday morning. (Followed by 3 verses poetry and 13 verses of poetry on August 30.)

Thursday August 30, 1883:

Married - On the 22d August, 1883, by Rev. JAMES MAULDIN, Mr. JORDAN MOORE to Miss DORA DURHAM, all of Oconee.

FENTON H. HALL, a native of Anderson, died at his home, Battle Creek, in this county, on the 12th day of August, in the eighty-third year of his life. He leaves a large number of relatives and many friends to mourn his loss.

Thursday September 6, 1883:

Death of Richard P. Quarles - RICHARD P. QUARLES was born Sept. 22, 1850 near Liberty Hill, Edgefield county, and died of typhoid fever at Ninety-Six, August 24, 1883, after an illness of about four weeks. The funeral was preached by the Rev. H. C. SMART .....his body laid to rest in the cemetery at that place. ...when quite a youth, he came to Abbeville as salesman to the store of J. W. TOWBRIDGE & Co., and some twelve or fourteen years ago he moved to Ninety-Six where he formed a co-partnership in the mercantile business with Mr. JOHN A. MOORE...continued several years....firm of Quarles, Moore & Co. was dissolved last fall...Mr.Quarles continued the business on his own account. ...also a member of the firm of Quarles & Co., at Abbeville. Assets of his estate, one half of which is in real estate, are estimated at about $40,000 with liabilities at about $15,000. He leaves no will. Messrs. H. P. GALPHIN and T. O. TURNER will be in charge of the store until an administrator can be appointed. Mr. Quarles married Miss LULA NEVILLE at Walhalla, in January 1881. He had built a handsome dwelling in Ninety-Six and was in the midst of his most prosperous carrer and the enjoyment of the affection of a noble young wife. ....''Abbeville Press and Banner''

Obituary - Beloved child ...the spirit of little SEP. SLOAN passed away in Seneca on the 1st day of September, 1883. She was born December 17th, 1871, eleven brief years ago, ...long eulogy followed by poetry.L.M. C.

Seneca City Correspondence - Solemn death has visited our place and taken from our midst Miss SEPTIMA A. SLOAN, eldest daughter of Dr. JAMES M.

SLOAN, aged 11 years, 8 mo's and 27 days. Little "Sep" breathed her last at 2 o'clock on Saturday morning, September 1st. Her remains were interred on Sunday at Pendleton beside her father. Services conducted by Rev. Mr. ERVIN. On Sunday morning every omnibus hack and buggy was pressed into use to convey her friends, schoolmates and playmates to her funeral. Yet many failed to get conveyance. Never has the writer witnessed such a flocking of little girls to pay the last tribute of their respect to their beloved one as was witnessed Sunday morning when little "Sep's" remains were started to their final resting place. M. (1 verse poetry)

Five verses poetry by Mrs. A. S. GOODMAN in memory of Mrs. LOUISA DENDY. (Her death recorded on August 9, 1883 - Mrs. MARSHAL B. DENDY.

Married - On the 30th of August, 1883, by Rev. WM. MC WHORTER, at the residence of Mr. JULIUS RAMSEY, Mr. H. DAVIS, of Georgia, to Miss A. HOPKINS of Oconee.

The heirs of ELIZABETH and MARGARET THOMPSON, deceased, who are said to have been connected with the "Scruggs" family of Virginia, but who lived in Pendleton district, South Carolina, prior to 1856, can hear something to their advantage by writing to Messrs. Christian & Christian, Richmond, Va.

State of South Carolina, Oconee County - In the Court of Common Pleas. Summons for Relief - FRANKLIN L. MOODY, plaintiff, against MARY A. MOODY, MARY M. NICHOLSON, A. JOSEPHINE KING, W. M. CANTRELL, MARY CANTRELL, JEREMIAH CANTRELL,Capt. C. CANTRELL, MARTHA L. ALEXANDER, JOHN M. MOODY and SARAH E. LAY, Defendants. Sale and partition of the real estate of BENNETT MOODY, dec'd.

Thursday September 13, 1883:

Married - August 30th, 1883, by Rev. J. A. SLIGH, Rev. W. W. DANIEL, of Seneca City, to Miss A. ROWENA AULL, daughter of Mr. JACOB L. AULL, of Edgefield county.

Mr. W. H. EATON, aged 32 years, died on Saturday morning last, 8th inst., and was buried on Sunday afternoon in the family burying ground after appropriate funeral services, conducted by Rev. J. S. WEST. Mr. Eaton leaves a wife and five children.

Mr. JESSE M. LEE, well known and formerly a resident of Walhalla, is engaged in the hotel business at Madison, Wisconsin, this summer. His house is on Lake Tonywatha, and his establishment the occasion of one of the biggest serenades by steamer of the season. Mr. Lee also runs one of the best hotels at Jacksonville, Fla., in the winter season, where he will be glad to see his friends.

State of South Carolina, County of Oconee - In the Court of Probate. Summons for Relief - MOSES CAIN as executor of the last will of WILLIAM CAIN, dec'd, plaintiff, against RICHARD CAIN, ROBERT CAIN, HANNAH BROWN, WM. CAIN, JR., MIRIAM CAIN, WM. HANDY CAIN, JANE HONEA, ANNA TERRIL,CHARLOTTE MARTIN, LUCRETIA CAIN, JO BERRY SANDERS as administrator of the personal estate of LEWIS CAIN, SR., dec'd, for partition among heirs of WM. CAIN, SR., dec'd.

Thursday September 20, 1883:

Mrs. KITTY JAYNES died at her home near Westminster this week at an advanced age.

FRITZ BRUCKE died on the night of the 17th inst., after a protracted illness. His remains were interred at Fairview Church on the 19th inst.

We regret to state that from a postal from Dr. J. H. DOYLE, of Granbury, Texas, information has been received of the death on the 13th of September, 1883, of Mr. DAVID S. STRIBLING, of fever. Mr. Stribling was a native of this county and lived for many years in the Fair Play neighborhood, exhibiting in his life and conduct those high and honorable traits of character, both in private life and as a citizen, which won the esteem

of all his neighbors. In 1866 he removed with his family to Texas where
he has since lived. Mr. S. was seventy years old at his death and had
been for many years a consistent member of the Baptist Church. He was the
father of our efficient Clerk of the Court and of W. J. STRIBLING, attor-
ney at law, at this place. All the rest of his children we believe, are
in Texas. Few men live to a greater age and fewer still have lived a more
exemplary life, as a husband, a father, a citizen and a Christian. He has
in this county two living brothers, M. S. STRIBLING and W. H. STRIBLING,
with a long line of relations of a remote degree. As there was regret
when he removed from this county at the loss of so pure and worthy a citizen, so now there will be general regret at the announcement of his
death in his distant and adopted State.

Married - At the residence of the bride's father, Mr. W. A. MILES, Walhalla, S. C., by Rev. G. H. CARTER, on Sunday, September 16th, 1883, at
3 o'clock P.M., Mr. W. H. ADAMS to Miss BETTIE MILES.

FARISH C. FURMAN, the celebrated farmer of Georgia, died at his residence
near Milledgeville on the 14th inst. after an illness of three weeks. He
was a native of Sumter county in this State and was thirty seven years
old. He married the daughter of Prof. JOSEPH LE CONTE, the distinguished geologist, whose writings are text books in many schools and colleges.
The experiements of Mr. Furman in cotton culture have been published extensively throughout the United States and show what can be accomplished
by thorough culture and fertilization. The death of such a man is a public calamity.

Thursday September 27, 1883:

Married - On Sunday, September 16, 1883, at the residence of Mrs. LODEN,
by G. V. HUNTER, Esq., Mr. KEELS COBB to Miss Q. VICTORIA LODEN, all of
Oconee.

Thursday October 11, 1883:

Married - At the residence of the bride's father, on Wednesday morning,
the 10th inst., by Rev. Dr. J. P. SMELTZER, Mr. J. CRAWFORD KEYS, of
Charleston, to Miss LIZZIE R., eldest daughter of Col. ROBERT A. THOMP-
SON, of Oconee.

Thursday October 18, 1883:

Married - On the 16th inst., at the residence of the bride's father, Mr.
W. A. BARRON, near Seneca, by Rev. H. STRONG, Mr. W. L. MC MAHAN and Miss
IDA BARRON, all of Oconee.

Thursday October 25, 1883:

Married - On Sunday, the 21st inst., at the residence of the bride's father, by ISAAC WICKLIFFE, Esq., Mr. WILLIAM PIERCE and Miss EMMA WILSON,
all of Oconee.

We are informed that THOMAS HUNTER, a son of SAMUEL HUNTER, of Bachelors
Retreat neighborhood, fell into a well about forty feet deep last Thursday, killing him instantly. His neck was broken. Mr. Hunter was a youth
about 17 or 18 years old and was an exemplary young man and Christian.
He was, at the time, engaged in fixing a wall around the well on which
to place the box and floor. (see more in below article...cme)

Thursday November 1, 1883:

THOMAS A. HUNTER, third son of Mrs. SAMUEL HUNTER,......born in Abbeville
county June 3, 1866, died in Oconee county October 18, 1883...made public
profession in Christ in his 14th year, uniting with the Presbyterian
Church. (long eulogy signed by "S")

Married - At the residence of the bride's parents, Walhalla, S. C., October 25, 1883, by Rev. J. F. PROBST, Mr. JOHN JOOST, of Jacksonville,Fla.,
to Miss MARY M. SEEBA.

Married - At the residence of the bride's mother, Walhalla, S. C., October 23, 1883, by Rev. C. D. MANN, J. HENRY PITCHFORD, Esq., to Miss LOLA C. BAUKNIGHT.

Married - On Thursday, the 25th October, at the residence of the bride's father, by Rev. W. C. SEABORN, Mr. JAMES T. ROWLAND to Miss MARY M. WEST, all of Oconee.

Married - On Sunday, October 28, at the residence of Mr. JOSEPH MULKEY, by the Rev. W. C. SEABORN, Mr. JAMES W. PERRY to Miss MARGARET M. GOULDEN, all of Oconee.

Mr. J. L. WARD, a young man living near Westminster, in this county, died on last Monday morning after a lingering illness of several months, of consumption. Mr. Ward was in the prime of life and it is to be regretted that one so young should thus be cut off so early. He was buried at the Westminster cemetery on Tuesday.

Mr. WESLEY COMPTON, who lives near Fair Play in this county, committed suicide on the 20th of October. S. H. JOHNS, the Coroner, held an inquest the next day over his body, and the verdict of the jury was that the deceased came to his death by an over dose of laudanum. Mr. Compton had been threatening, it is said, to take his own life for some time past.

An aged couple married at Toronto, Canada, on Thursday, GEORGE MC LAUGH-LIN, the groom, being 88 and his bride, 90 years of age.

Thursday November 15, 1883:

Married - Sunday evening, November 11, 1883, in Walhalla, S. C., by Rev. G. H. CARTER, Mr. JOHN J. THODE to Miss MATTIE SMITH.

Married - November 1, 1883, at the residence of the bride's father, Mr. JOSEPH BEARDEN, by Rev. J. H. STONE, Mr. J. L. MILLER to Miss L. J. BEARDEN, all of Oconee.

Married - In the Presbyterian Church at Cokesbury, Abbeville county, S.C. November 7, 1883, by Rev. R. D. SMART, of the S.C. Conference, Rev. WM. G. NEVILLE, of Ninty-Six, a native of Oconee County, to Miss VIRGINIA AIKEN, daughter of Hon. D. WYATT AIKEN.

Mr. JOHN RITCHIE, formerly of our town, but now living near Pendleton, Anderson county, lost a fourteen year old son last week from fever. He was buried at Sandy Springs burying ground on Saturday, 10th inst., Rev. Mr. HENCKEL officiating.

ROBERT M. STEELE, formerly of this county, died on the 16th of October of mountain fever and erysipelas at Fort McLeod, Northwest Territory of British America. He was a son of Capt. WILLIAM STEELE, of this county, and has a number of relations here. He left here in 1859 in company with several brothers for Montana, and has since that time made the Northwest his home. At the time of his death he was forty-three years old and was engaged in merchandizing.

TRIVIA

It seems that the publisher of the "Keowee Courier" was having a problem getting subscribers to pay and for others to purchase his paper. He chided them by inserting some humorous items in the columns. You don't see this these days.

"TO BORROW YOUR NEIGHBOR'S NEWSPAPER IS CHEATING THE PRINTER OUT OF HIS DUES. SUBSCRIBE FOR THE KEOWEE COURIER AND QUIT BORROWING."

"THE MAN WHO BORROWS A NEWSPAPER BELONGS TO A VERY ECONOMICAL FAMILY; HE IS A BROTHER OF THE FELLOW WHO TRIED TO COOK HIS DINNER BY USING THE SMOKE FROM HIS NEIGHBOR'S CHIMNEY."

"A MAN WHO WILL READ A NEWSPAPER THREE OR FOUR YEARS WITHOUT PAYING FOR IT, WILL PASTURE A GOAT ON THE GRAVE OF HIS GRANDFATHER."

"SOME PEOPLE HAVE ALTOGETHER AN ERRONEOUS IDEA OF WHAT IS MEANT BY A FREE PRESS. IT DOESN'T MEAN THAT YOU ARE TO TAKE A NEWSPAPER AND NOT PAY FOR IT."

Of no genealogical value, but a glimpse into the pranks played in the year 1878:

MIXED BABIES

Some time ago there was a dancing party given in a certain neighborhood in Texas, and most of the ladies present had little babies, whose noisy perversity required too much attention to permit the mothers to enjoy the dance. A number of gallant young men volunteered to mind the young ones while the parents indulged in an old Virginia breakdown. No sooner had the women left the babies in charge of the mischievous devils than they stripped the babies, changed their clothes, giving the apparel of one to another. The dance over, it was time to go home, and the mothers hurriedly took each a baby in the dress of her own and started, some to their homes, ten or fifteen miles off, and were far on their way before daylight. But the day following there was a tremendous row in the settlement. Mothers discovered that a single night had changed the sex of their babies, observation discovered physical phenomena, and then commenced the tallest female pedestrianism. Living miles apart it took two or three days to unmix the babies and as many months to restore the mothers to their natural sweet dispositions. To this day it is unsafe for any of the baby mixers to venture in the neighborhood.

"Keowee Courier"

Issue of October 31, 1878:

BILL LONGLEY, of Texas: The telegraph has already announced the execution at Giddings, Texas, on Friday last, of the notorious WILLIAM LONGLEY, for the murder of WILLIAM ANDERSON, a field hand, in March 1875. Upon reaching the gallows, and after the completion of all the preliminary arrangements, during which Longley surveyed the scaffold and gave directions how to tie the rope, a hatchet was asked for. Longley wanted to know if they were going to cut his head off. He walked up the stairs with a light, mimic military step a smile upon his face and a lighted cigar in his mouth. Fearing the steps might give way, when about half way up, he stopped and laughingly said he didn't want to "be crippled". After the sheriff read his death warrant, Longley took his cigar from his mouth and addressed the crowd saying: "Well, I haven't got much to say. I see a good many enemies around me, and mighty few friends. Hope to God you will forgive me. I will you. I hate to die, of course; any man hates to die. But I have earned this by taking lives of men who loved life as well as I do. If I have any friends here I hope they will do nothing to avenge my death and if they want to help me let them pray for me. I hear my brother is in the crowd. I hope he ain't, but if he is I hope he will not take anybodys life to avenge mine. I have done enough of that. I deserve this fate. It is a debt I owe for my wild, reckless life. When it is paid it will be all over with. I hope you will all forgive me. I will forgive you whether

you do so or not. May God forgive me." His arms and limbs were then pin-
ioned. He kissed the priests, shook hands with the officers and said,
"Good bye everybody". The black cap was then put on and the drop fell.
The body hung for eleven minutes, when the doctor declared life extinct,
and it was cut down and given to friends for interment.

Issue of December 7, 1882:

Locals - Mr. WILLIAM BURDITT, living thirteen miles below Walhalla, is
the oldest man in the county, if not in the State. He is now 105 years
old, as we are told. A few years ago, when over 100 years old, he would
ride horseback ten or twelve miles. He was then spry and jolly, enjoying
a horsewap as much as a youth would. He is a small man, of low statue,
and weighing less than 125 pounds.

Issue of September 20, 1883:

Locals - Mr. J. H. ELLIOTT informs us that a large hawk, measuring some
four feet tip to tip of wing, lit in his yard some time ago and got into
a fight with an old hen, when Mr. JAMES ROWLAND went out and caught the
hawk, who was so busy fighting as not to notice him. The hawk stuck his
spurs so deep into Mr. Rowland's hand that Mr. Elliott had to pull them
out. The bird was killed.

Issue of August 19, 1880:

Townville Correspondence - FRANK HOLLINGSWORTH has a very fine crop of
watermelons. A fair specimen measured 32 inches in length and 28 inches
in circumference.

"KEOWEE COURIER:
INDEX

Prepared by
Colleen Morse Elliott
Fort Worth, Texas

Abbot, Narcissa E. 176
Abbott, George W. 159
  James M. 43
  Jane 159
  John 44,155
  John W. 155
  Lulu 155
  Mary Margaret 166
  Narcissa 155
  Noah 43
  Sarah 140
  Simpson 155
  Solomon 28
  Temperance 13
  William 39,43
  William T. 166
  Willis W. 101,106
  W. W. 154
  Avarilla 85
Abercrombie, Clarinda 80
  Haynes 80
Ables, Mary 21
  Priestly 21
Acree, R. R. 134
Adair, Eliza 3
  Grafton 3
  Jno. 68
  John 3,7,10,28,87
  Martha Jane 87
  Rebecca 87
  Susan O. 165
  Thomas 138,139
Adams, Catharine 149
  C. C. 87
  Dora 177
  Eugene 62
  James 139
  Mrs. James 141
  Jasper 68
  Jesse 7
  J. M. 101
  Mrs. J. N. 158
  Joseph M. 133
  Lizzie P. 68
  Mark 149
  Mary 37
  Polly 7
  R. L. 37
  Sallie 139
  W. H. 182
  William 177
Addington, Lou 157
  W. A. 164
  Wm. M. 157
Addis, Anna T. 156
  Miss C. 54
  Eliza 156
  Esther 32
  Euinice 54
  Jas. E. 111
  Mary N. E. 88
  Samuel 54,81,156
  Sarah 101
  Susan 156
  William 101
  William M. 88
  Wm. J. 156
Agnew, M. Eliza 90
  S. W. 90
Ahrens, Johannes 58
Aiken, Daniel 128
  D. Wyatt 183
  Virginia 183
  Mary 65
Alberson, Nancy A. 45

Albertson, Barbara 132
Alexander, A. 1
  Amanda 101
  Angalina 22
  Ansalem 5
  Canba 105
  Caroline 111
  Celia A. 110
  Charlotte 149
  Cora Tulula 117
  Daniel 45,149
  Daniel M. 12
  David 117,149
  D. C. 170
  E. 10,47.51.52,54,55,78
  E. A. 67
  E. B. 47
  Mrs. E. B. 117
  E. Blevin 135
  Elias F. 72,149
  Ekijah 141
  Elijah E. 99
  Elijah Sr. 120
  Elisha 90
  Elizabeth 90,110
  E. m. 105,114
  Emalissa 113
  Miss E. S. 55
  Fountain 117
  Frank P. 129
  Georgia A. 129
  Hannah A. 12
  Hiram 110
  Isaac 149
  Jacob 149
  James 45,149
  Jane 170
  Jefferson 54
  Jennie 149
  J. M. 84
  Jordan 149
  Julia A. 165
  Katie 172
  L. 165
  Mrs. L. 112
  Laura 114
  Laura A. 79
  Lucinda 149
  Macajah 117
  Malinda 54
  Margaret Vinetta 129
  Marshal L. 167
  Martha 75,84
  Martha L. 181
  Mary 72,82,121,149
  M. C. 117
  Miss. M. E. 113
  Micahah 149
  Micajah, Jr. 117
  Mrs. - 160
  Miss. N. A. 111
  Nancy 104
  Nancy A. 70
  Nancy Ann 149
  Nettie 112
  Mrs. N. M. 67
  P. 1
  Patsy 74
  Pendleton 149
  Pickens 149
  Pleasant 165
  P. McD. 121
  Prier 101
  Prier, Jr. 40
  Prier, Sr. 75

Alexander, Roxana 167
  Rutha 47
  Sallie M. 166
  Sarah E. 55
  Siotha 149
  S. Mattie 125
  Susan 117
  Tallulah 149
  T. D. 177
  Thomas 45,149
  T. M. 22,117
  T. W. 113
  Vance 149
  Victoria 40
  W. E. 111
  Wilburn O. 166
  William 149
Alford, Joshua 51
Allen, Amanda J. 26
  Arabella C. 105
  Charles 1
  Elizabeth 8
  Hannah Elizabeth 71
  H. M. 169
  H. Milton 155
  James C. 91
  L. W. 8,26
  Sarah A. 1
  T. C. 71
  Thomas L. 105
  W. M. 71
Allgood, Alexander 116
  Alvin 116
  Banister 116
  Barnett H. 116
  Rebecca 111
  Miss R. L. 175
  Zilpha 90
Allison, A. D. B. 80
Ambler, Angus Marcellus 44
  Carlos Thaddeus 81
  James, Sr. 2
  J. H. 44,81
  Z. A. 44
Amick, Elizabeth 44
Anderson, A. J. 31
  Carrie H. 121
  Edmund 12
  Isaac 106,107
  Jane 135
  Mary P. 19
  Nancy R. 13
  Robert 19
  Wm. H. 12,13,121
Ansel, John J. 161,162,172
Anthony, H. J. 55,76,80,86,
  89,93
  Mrs. H. J. 135
  Margaret 70
Archer, A. H. 38
  Andrew H. 38,93,104
  Eugenia 93
  Hugh 34
  John E. 104
  John P. 2
  Malinda 104
  M. Ann 78
  Oliatta 93
  Parmelia T. 39
  Van 104
Ariail, Ira Onslow 24
  John 74,89,110,118
  Luke J. 24
  Nancy 24
Arnold, F. N. 157

Arnold, H. T. 32
  J. N. 78,79,86,89,92,99,
  103
  Joseph Newton 158
  Mrs. L. E. 158
  Mrs. Lewellyn E. 178
  Louisa M. 19
  Marcus M. 19
  Mrs. N. F. 156
  Ophelia A. 53
Arthur, T. S. 12
Asley, Jas. 67
Atkinson, Mrs. A. 164
Attaway, John 139,174
Auld, J. Freeman 29
Auld, Rachel 29
Aull, A. Rowena 181
  Jacob L. 181
Autrey, John 37

Babb, Clarinda 80
Bacon, John E. 73
  Rebecca 73
Bagby, Thomas, Jr. 50
Bailey, Allen 73
  R. T. 42
Baker, Adaline 93
  Adolpheus 34
  Crawford 18
  Daniel 30
  Ellender 188
  Harriet 81
  James 75
  John 18
  Lewellen 18
  Lucinda 18
  Richard 18
  Robert 18
  Sarah 93
  Sarah Ann 75
  William 18,93
Baldwin, Evaline 124
  Peggy 101
  Stephen 171
Balldon, Mary 13
Ballenger, Maria E. 179
Ballew, Celia R. 124
  David L. 124
Ballinger, Martha M. 45
  Sarah Ann 65
  Talulah F. 132
  Miss T. P. 53
  Wm. D. 45,65
  Wm. H. 132
Baltrell, Thomas 52
Bandy, Bryant 26
  Phoebe 26
Banks, Elmina 86
Bansemer, C. F. 26,28,37,
  58,66
Barker, Josephine 144
Barksdale, Eliza 77
  George 77
  Mary 77
Barnes, George 114
  John 147
  Lorenzo 114
  Martha 114
  Mary 4
  William 4
Barnett, Elizabeth 76
  James T. 168
  Julia 168
  M. C. 41
Barret, Arthur 9
  Mary 9
Barrett, Athalenda 113
  Benjamin 112
  David 112
  Jas. 113
  J. P. 71
  Milton 112

Barrett, William 112
Barron, Henry 102
  Ida 182
  I. T. 102
  John 102
  Josephine L. 98
  Mary 102
  Mary Eliza 89
  Thomas 102
  Samuel 102
  Stephen P. 98
  W. A. 182
  Wm. A. 89
Barth...20
Barton, Angalina 22
  Baily A. 8
  Benjamin 1,6,14
  Carolina 8
  Miss. C. D. 87
  Dorcas 6
  Eliza A. 51
  Ella 157
  H. M. 28,33,86,96,129,
  148
  James 126
  Jane 1
  J. B. 157
  J. M. 55
  Martha 126
  O. E. 6,12
  Parmelia T. 39
  Seth 12
  Wm. B. 14
Bates, Fleming 97
  Mary E. 33
  Polly 97
  Shelby 79
  Tabitha 79
Bauknight, Lola C. 183
Baumgartel, Julianna 134
Beacham, Eugenie A. 69
  James D. 69
Beard, Anna 150
  Carrie L. 121
  James 150
  Jas. M. 121
  Mary 31
Bearden, Emma 147
  James 147
  Joseph 183
  Levina 12
  Miss L. J. 183
  William 168
  John 51
  Matilda 51
Beasley, Wm. 53
Beatty, Susan 108
  Anna 126
Bechtler, C. 132
Beck, Carolina 13
  Marion J. 13
Bedford, J. M. 38
Been, Anderson 9
  Martha A. 9
Belcher...65
Bell...120
  Ada C. 157
  Miss A. M. 174
  B. W. 151
  B. Wilkie 151
  Catharine 13
  James A. 109
  Mattie 109
  Mondane C. 162
  T. P. 157
  Wm. 162
Bellotte, J. E. 111
  A. D. 169
  F. A. 28
  J. E. 43,44,66,74
  Kate 169
  Thos. D. 28

Belser, James E. 55
  W. M. 58
Benjamin, James 79
Benson, E. B. 79
  Elizabeth 43
  Thornton 43
  T. P. 155
Berrien, J. W. M. 65
Best, Lawrence C. 176
Bieman...37
  Catherine H. 159
  Diedrich, Jr. 142
  H. D. A. 159,167,172
  Henry 142
  Catherine 83
  Henry 83
Billingsley, H. A. 46
  Minerva 46
  Amanda 101
  Andrew J. M. 102
  Susan M. 102
  William 101
Bird, Arabella 28
Black, Annie 168
  Elizabeth 37,60
  Emerson 37
  Henry W. 127
  James J. 60
  Jane 37
  Jesse R. 101
  J. M. 32,60
  John 32
  John L. 177
  John R. 101
  John S. 178
  Leela E. S. 178
  Margaret M. 55
  Mary J. 101
  Nanthany 70
  W. D. 70
Blackburn, John 88
Blackston, Elizabeth J. 63
Blackstone, Elizabeth M. 63
  John H. 63
Blackwell, Mary 174
  Nancy 161
  Rhoda Ann 54
  Robert 54
Blair, Fannie 156
  Hugh 156
Blakely, Susan 86
Blalock, Mrs. R. 4
Bland...129
Blassingame, E. Jennie 72
  John 100,178
  John F. 97
  Lena E. 97
  Lucy E. 100
  Margaret 70
  W. G. 70
Bleckley, James 122
Blevin, Elizabeth 44
Bloodworth, Nancy 86
Boatmer, Sally 45
Boatwright, Argine 139
  Chesly 23
  Jas. 18
  Terrissa 151
Boehm, J. G. 134
Boggs, Aaron 104
  Andrew 104
  B. F. 79
  D. C. 65,69,76,78,89
  D. Chalmers 32
  Etta 104
  Henrietta R. 32
  H. W. M. 22
  James L. 104
  John C. C. 137
  Joseph G. 104
  Josiah 104
  Julia D. 137

Boggs, Mary C. 22
  Rosalie H. 79
  Sarah 104,167
  Thos. H. 25,46,51,75,76,
    79,89
Boleman, G. N. C. 179
  Mollie 179
Bolles, Elizabeth 1
  William 1
Bolt, Hannah 168
  James 168
Bomar, George 178
  Sarah M. 178
  William 178
Bonds, Amanda 168
  John H. 168
Bonham, James 41
  M. L. 41
  Sophia 41
Bonner, John I. 160
Boon, Nathan 159
  Sarah 159
Boone, Mary J. 12
Boozer, J. I. 49
  S. P. 150
Boroughs, J. H. 78
Bottoms, Elias 58
Botts, John M. 1
Boulton, Elizabeth Frances
  155
Bourn, C. J. 69
Bowden, A. B. 18,31,32,39,
  41,54,58
Bowen, Anna 172
  Miss D. J. 32
  John 43,126
  John H. 89
  M. A. A. 25
  Martha A. 90
  Mary E. 89
  Nancy 43
  Rebecca 111
  Robert E. 25
  T. H. 43
  W. A. 172
  William 43
  William Sr. 27
  W. R. 43
  W. T. 111
Bower, Emma 130
Bowlegs, Billy 62
Bowman, Elizabeth 52
  John G. 80
  John M. 52,64
Boyd, D. B. 19
  J. B. 106
  J. L. 51,127
  Lucy 106
  Margaret C. 127
  Mary 110
  Mary P. 19
  Wm. E. 110
Braday, Mrs. Sillar 11
Bradberry, David 146
Bradham, Daniel 59
  Stephen P. 58
Bradley, A. J. 64
  Ellen 63
  Emma 64
  Joel 63
  Sarah E. 41
  Thomas 41
  W. K. 165
Brady, Martha J. 178
Brandt, Louis H. 98
  Mattie C. 98
Brannon, James 22
  Jas. W. 100
  Nancy E. 100
Bray, M. C. 125
Brazeale, E. A. 125
  Eliza 28
  Elizabeth M. 63

Brazeale, Fannie B. 164
  Griffin 61
  Kenon 33
  L. Camilla 99
  Lucy J. 61
  Margaret A. 98
Brennan, Dennis R. 166
Brennecke, A. 37
  Fannie B. 164
  L. D. 164
Brettargh, H. 155
Brewer, D. S. 9
  E. J. 137
  Elizabeth 10
  Elliott K. 137
  Etta 174
  John 6,82
  Jas. 55
  Levi 6
  Louisa Elizabeth 145
  Mary 3
  Mary S. 104
  Nymay 6
  Rebecca 58
  Sarah 6
  Sarah Susannah 9
Brewster, Paul 67
  P. H. 43,67
  Susan M. 43,67
  William Fort 43
Brewton, Miss E. E. 41
Brice, C. S. 54
  Fannie 54
Bright, Isabella 175
  James L. 175
Brinkley...74
Brock, Amanda 99
  Eliza J. 105
  Florence Ella 160
  Mary M. 98
  Silas H. 105
  William 98
Brockman, Thomas P. 69
Brooks, Frances C. 111
  J. L. 49
  Martha A. 105
  Mary E. 78
Broom, Anna 170
  Arminda 4
  Daniel 4
  Elizabeth 7
  Emily 7
  M. 7
  Mary 37
  Nancy S. 108
  Thomas 129
  William 7,170
Brown...157
  A. E. 97
  Amanda 56,135
  Andrew C. 142
  Benjamin 93
  Daniel B. 13
  Deborah 34
  Elizabeth 64
  Emma 130
  E. T. 26
  F. C. 121
  Harriet M. 156
  Henry 76
  Miss. H. T. 133
  James L. 142
  John 56
  John L. 66
  John Peter 78
  Joseph N. 99
  Julia M. 97
  Julia S. 78
  J. W. 139
  Lizzie L. 99
  Louisa 101
  Lula 159
  Margaret E. 28

Brown, Martha 13,16,171
  Martha E. 26
  Mary G. 28
  Matilda 90
  Mrs. M. E. 142
  Melissa 11
  Mildred 120
  "Milly" (Cooper) 120
  Mrs. M. S. 159
  Nancy A. 9
  Nancy G. 66
  Newton H. 142,143
  Peter 143
  Robert C. 120
  T. 33
  Thomas 130
  W. H. 28
Browne, Anderson C. 133
  Annie M. 133
  J. M. 126
  Mary F. 126
Brownlee, E. 73
Bruce, Alice A. 70
  F. M. 173
  Jane 136
  Lizzie L. 99
  L. O. 163
  Sallie 135
  Sarah 173
  Thomas 99
Brucke...142
  C. A. 139
  Fritz 181
  Mary 139
Bryan, Wm. E. 128
Bryce...149
  Alexander, Jr. 142
  Alexander, Sr. 167
  M. A. 98
  Morgan H. 98
  Sarah 90
Bryson, C. P. 106
  Elvira S. 106
Buckester, Joel R. B. 45
  Nancy A. 45
Buist, E. T. 33
Bullwinkle, Mrs. C. D. 27
  Menke 27
  N. G. 145
  C. 16
Bunch, Andrew 121
Bunyard, Martha E. 105
  Wm. 105
Burdett, Eve 148
  W. H. 156
  John 165
  Susan O. 165
Burdine, Hamilton 4
  John 92
  John W. 32
  Jos. 92
  Louisa 4
  Lucinda 32
  Mason 12
  Patsy 92
  Richard 88
  Samuel 92
Burdit, Delilah 64
  Henry 64
Burditt, Susan C. 109
  W. H. 109
Burgess...94
  Nancy E. 76
Burket, E. H. 88
  Mary J. 56
  Rachel 88
Burkett, Cornelia C. 47
  M. E. 47
  W. 47
Burleson, E. 14
Burns, Bertha H. 173
  B. W. 165
  Cornelia 174

Burns, C. R. D. 173
  Elizabeth A. 165
  G. W. 177
  James 58
  Jordan 134
  Joseph 10
  J. Y. 174
  Mary 174
  Sarah 10
  Miss S. C. 104
Burrel, Bright 9
  Nancy A. 9
Burris, Milford 75
  Vashti 75
Burrows...75
Burton, Cecelia C. 115
  J. F. 115
Busby, Annie 171
Busch...159
  Jacob 138,164
  Tena M. 164
Busclark, Samuel 150
Bush, D. 124
  Ida E. 124
Buslark, Samuel 10
  Sarah Ann 10
Butler...77
  A. P. 19
  Emily 7
  Elizabeth 7
  James 41
  Sarah 41
  Sarah Jane 74
  W. H. 175
  Wm. Henry 74
Byars, D. D. 97,125
Byrem, Elisha 101
Byron, Sarah 68
  Wm. 68
Byrum, Elisha 99

Cain, Alice 172
  Emma 147
  J. M. 88
  Lewis, Sr. 181
  Lucretia 181
  Cucretia R. 141
  Mary 177
  Miriam 181
  Moses 181
  Richard 181
  Robert 181
  Robert M. 112
  Sarah L. 112
  Thomas 146,150
  William 181
  Wm. Jr. 181
  Wm. Sr. 181
  Wm. Handy 181
Calder, William 87
  Jennie 73
Calhoun, Florida 18
  John 114
  John, Jr. 91
  John C. 8,18,41,48
  Martha Cornelia 18
  Nancy 114
  Patrick 40,41
  Sarah 108
  Sarah C. 90
  Thomas P. 60
  Warren 108
  William L. 18,48
  W. R. D. 90
Callahan, J. W. 34
  Martha 34
Camanade, Susan 43
Cameron, Mary E. 115
  Robert 115
Campbell...154
  A. C. 68
  Archibald C. 82
  Caroline Matilda 12

Campbell, Collin 82
  D. A. 165
  H. E. 47,73
  Jincey E. 47
  John F. 41
  Lizzie P. 68
  Martha 165
  Mary 102
  Mary Ann 124
  Mary C. 67
  Nancy G. 66
  William 124
  Wm. H. 12
Can, Miss - 155
Cane, Francis 128
Cannon, Benjamin 16
  Carter 16
  Elijah 16
  Ella Vashti 156
  Harriet 53
  James 16,27
  James M. 106
  J. W. 90
  Mary 27
  Mary M. 98
  Miles Norton 156
  Sarah 90
  Silas K. 98
  Warren R. 53
  Washington 16
  Wm. R. 39
Cantrell, D. W. 98
  Jeremiah 181
  Mary 181
  Mary S. 98
  Moses 142
  Tabitha Ann 99
  William 99
  W. M. 181
Cape, Elizabeth 33
Capehart, Francis 114
  John 113
  Leonard 94
  Margaret 90
  Margaret Eliza 114
Cappleman, John D. 173
  Julia 177
  Julia A. 173
Cappock, E. S. 56
Capps, Andrew J. 39
  Nancy Ann 39
Caradine, Andrew 9
  Bird 9
  Hiram P. 9
  J. B. 111
  Jos. B. 111
  Susan 111
  Thomas 9
  Thos. C. 9
  Wm. G. 9
Carey, John W. L. 100
Carlisle, Arabella 28
  J. E. 160
  John M. 121
  Wm. 11
  Wm. B. 28
Carmack, J. N. 67
Carothers, J. N. 9
  W. W. 17
Carpenter, Alfred M. 93
  A. Monroe 80
  Elizabeth J. 80
  Fannie 179
  Fannie E. 112
  Jas. B. 112
  Nancy Ann 126
Carroll, Miss E. E. 141
  James 79
  Susan 79
Carter, D. B. 145
  D. F. 151,170,175
  G. H. 155,167,169,176,

Carter, G. H. 182,183
  Jm. M. 162
  Josiah 40,72
  J. W. 105
  Lillie 162
  Nannie L. 72
  N. H. 128
  Sallie R. 40
  Woody T. 28
Carver, Ada A. 170
  Elizabeth 136
  Hannah R. 43
  Hannah R. 43
  Henry 34
  Jabel 8
  John 43
  Kemly 8
  Welburn 136
Casey, Alice 133
  Rufus 151
  Sarah Ann 31
  Walter 133
Cash...159
Cater, Artemissa A. 26
Cato - (a freedman) 102
Catron...162
Cayley, J. D. 155
Chambers, Barack 138
  Baylus E. 174
  James H. 68
  Lemuel 139
  Mary 174
  Mary Jane 130
  Philip 8
Chaney, James S. 25
Chapman...71
  Benjamin P. 97
  Darcus Ann 98
  Dilley 21
  Eliza 103
  Elizabeth 43
  Enoch 72
  George I. 97
  George L. 70,71
  Israel 40,118
  Jacob 118
  James 55
  Joel 40,118
  Joseph 98
  Joshua 40
  Mary A. A. 66
  Nancy 72,86
  Nancy Ann 94
  Rebecca 100
  Samuel 118
  Sarah 97
  Wm. 86
Chappell, Jim 147
  Press 147
Charles, John 68
Chastain, A. 87
  Allice 176
  A. M. Cleveland 125
  Caroline 102
  Elizabeth 36
  George W. 75
  H. A. 111
  Hannah 36
  James 36
  John A. 125
  Lucinda 125
  M. 22,28,56,89
  Margarett 8
  Matilda 111
  Nancy Evaline 125
  Nancy R. L. P. 125
  Rachel L. 125
  Sarah 75
  Mrs. Thomas 129
  T. J. 36
Cherry, George R. 137,154,
  173

Cherry, John C. 176
    Lortie M. 102
    Sallie 137
Cheves, Langdon 20
Child, Sallie R. 58
Childers, Anne 36
    H. C. 74
    Licena 89
    Marshall 36
Chiles, James M. 58
Choice, Jefferson 83
Christian...181
    Matilda 172
Clabaugh, Ada C. 157
Clampet, Martha E. 26
Clark, E. 53
    Elizabeth 21
    Fannie 163
    James 63,83
Clary, Lewis 32
Clark, Thomas E. 21
    Wm. 163
Claus, John 175
Clayton, A. T. 36
    Mrs. Baylas 133
    Elizabeth L. 6
    Ella 133
    Hannah 1
    Jesse M. 1,90
    Joel H. 85
    John 1
    John J. 112
    John Thomas 1
    Margaret 1
    Martha A. 90
    Mary 66
    Melissa 6
    M. Elizabeth 56
    Philip 17
    R. C. 56
    Robert C. 1
    Stephen G. 1
    Miss. T. C. 36
Cleaveland, Elizabeth 25
    Mrs. M. E. 121
    W. T. 121,122
    Cleland, Sarah A. 34
Cleveland, Aaron 176
    Benj. 43
    Benjamin 77
    E. 172,177
    E. H. 109
    Elizabeth 41,48
    Fannie E. 94
    Francis H. 98
    Hattie 172
    H. G. 176
    Jane 177
    Jeremiah 77
    Jonathan R. 41,112
    J. R. 48
    Milla M. 109
    Nancy M. 133
    S. 94
    Sallie 135,172
    Samuel L. 172
    Sarah E. 112
    Susan F. 98
    Thomas 77,177
    W. E. 135
Clevers, Anna 164
Clinkscales, Lucinda 156
Clisby, Emma M. 137
    L. L. 137
Clyde, W. A. 99
Coachman, Cyrus 128
Coat...73
Coats, Henry 33
Cobb...39
    Ceclia C. 115
    Edmund 72
    Ephraim 130
    George Pinckney 154

Cobb, Ida M. 169
    John 69
    J. W. 115
    Kate 69
    Keels 182
    Louisa 66
    Martha 142
    Martha E. 26
    Pinckney 142
    Robert 139
    Roland 169
    Rowland 174
    Sallie Jane 154
    Vilanty 17
    Warren 66
    William 30
Cochran, Thomas R. 47
Cockrel, Alexander 40
Coe, H. L. 156
    Sallie L. 156
Coffee, Edward 43
    Jno. 68
Cogburn, Hyram 78
Coil, John 49
Colburn, W. H. 143
Cole, Allice 156
    A. S. 32
    Charlotte 128
    Eliza 167
    Ellis 156
    Esther 32
    Garnett 156
    Harrison J. 156
    Hester E. 156
    Lula 156
    Luther 156
    Martha A. 156
    Pickens 147
    Roxanna 156
Colelough, John A. 5
Colhoun, Nancy Isabella 1
Collett, Sarah J. 110
    Jane 99
Collings, Elijah 99
Collins, Miss C. A. 149
    E. 12,51
    James 29
    Sarah 43
Colly, Elizabeth 104
    J. B. 104
Colpetzer...41
Colston, Sue E. 148
    Thomas 148
Compton, Ida 146
    James E. 58
    Mary 3, 51
    Rebecca 58
    Richard 146
    Sarah 6
    Wesley 183
    Wm. B. 3
Cone, F. H. 65
Conley, Lutitia 167
Connell, Annie 43
    James 43
Connelly, R. L. B. 172
Conner...66
Cook, Anderson Barton 87
    Emma E. 134
    John C. 87
    Justina A. 87
    J. W. 75
    William 172
Cooper, Licena 89
    Mildred 120
    R. A. 89
Copeland, Arminda 3
    Lemuel J. 3
Corbin, Belona 127
    Francis Malone 127
    Lemuel T. 127
    Miss. R. E. 51
    Sarah Jane 127

Corbin, W. F. 127
    Wm. 127
    Wm. B. F.
Corn, John 40,72
Cornish, A. H. 34,69,78,
    113,116
Cory, Thos. Monroe 85
Cosgrove, Chas. 58
Cothran...134,175
    Jane 110
    Rebecca 111
Cottingham, Tristame 65
Cottrell, Victoria 40
Couch, Armanda Caroline 70
    Cynthia 53
    Jno. Q. A. 70
    Mary Ann 18
    Mary Jane 70
    Robert 18
    Sarah A. 70
Counts, Elizabeth 140
Cowan, James E. 8
    Lucinda E. 8
    Wm. J. 140
Cox, A. P. 86
    Miss. C. A. 88
    Caroline 86
    Edward 45
    E. H. 31,48,88,90
    F. A. 78
    Gabriel 45
    G. F. 45
    John 45
    Joshua 45
    Lewis 114
    Lizzie 53,75
    Malinda 15
    Marinda 45
    Martha 118,154
    Mary Ann 124
    Mary E. 78
    Mary Josephine 86
    Mordecai 15
    Robert 45
    Miss. S. J. 152
    Sophronia 52
    Wm. 75
    Wm. A. 62
Craig, Arthur 3
    Catherine 71
    John 71
    Laura F. 113
    Mary Melinda 3
    Robert T. 113
    Sarah E. 145
Crain, Frances E. 157
    John M. 159
    John T. 151
    Joseph 157
    Nancy M. 151
    Sarah E. 159
Crane, Amanda 74,114
    Ansel 91
    A. P. 60
    Davis 60
    Elizabeth 17,60
    Georgiana Amanda
    Melvina 5
    Harper 60
    Isaac 114
    Jasper 34
    Keziah 34
    Lawrence 145
    Margaret 60
    Martha 145
    Philoman 114
    Philemon Ansel 5
    Viney 114
    Wm. J. 17
Crawford, Belle 119
    James 119
    Jimmie 119
    Miss M. M. 155

Crawford, S. M. 155
  Susan 119
  Tom 73
  William 148
Crayton, Hattie N. 23
  Thomas S. 23
Crenshaw, Adger 143
  Alice 172
  Celia 102
  Celia A. 110
  Elizabeth 110
  Fannie 172
  Henry 99
  H. O. 149
  James A. 110
  Lucinda 30
  Mary J. 106
  Samuel, Sr. 143
  Sarah 99
  Tabitha 79
  Turner 172
  William 102
Cresap...67
Creswell, Sallie 137
Crews, Celia R. 124
  Thomas B. 124
Crockett...39
Croly, John 30
Crompton, Emily 153
Cross, J. M. 67
Crow, Johnathan 167
  Mary 4
Crumpton, Elizabeth 116
  N. A. 92
  Richard 116
  W. W. 92
Crutchfield...71
Cummings, A. W. 25
Cunningham, Robert 120
  Visa 120
Cureton, Jane C. 72
  P. D. 72
Curtis...132
  John 159
  Mary 4
  Namaan 108
  Sarah 159
  Thomas 56
  William 108

Dalton, Julia 170
  Thos. 170
Daner...47
Daniel, Mary E. 22
  Sumpter 89
  William S. 82,83
  W. W. 181
Daniels, F. A. 173,174
  F. Alonzo 172
  Sallie 172
  Sarah 177
Darby, Carrie F. 160
  Emaline 54
  Joseph 124
  Susan 124
Darnold, James A. 53
  L. J. 53
Darden, Miles 20
David, Jeff (Colored) 128
Davidson, John 3
  Permelia 3
Davies, J. B. 134
Davis...150
  Adaline 148
  Alice 172
  Andrew 137
  Anna 106
  A. P. 132
  Beatrice E. 140
  Catharine M. 124
  Charles J. 172
  D. A. 95

Davis, Daniel 51
  Demetrius H. 148
  Dora 167
  Effie Lee 140
  Elizabeth 25
  Ellen 172
  Emily M. 91
  Miss. F. E. 157
  F. H. 132
  Francis L. 39
  H. 181
  Harvey 122,140
  Harvey A. 140
  Hattie 140
  Ida 172
  James G. 62
  Jefferson 90
  John 160
  John E. 132
  John S. 140
  Julia A. 150
  Laura J. 140
  Lawrence O. 124
  Lettyann 66
  Maranda Jane 124
  Maria C. 80
  Martha 95
  Martha Adaline 178
  Mary 66,76,95
  Mary D. 140
  Mary L. 140
  Mattie 140
  Nancy 39
  Nannie M. 140
  Miss. N. T. 22
  Rebecca 132
  Safonsba 90
  Sallie 122
  Sallie B. 140
  Sidney 132
  Susan Amanda 62
  Susan F. 98
  T. E. 150,154,160,165
  T. F. 66,76
  Thomas 95
  Thomas R. 91
  Wade B. 140
  Walter G. 140
  Warren R. 122,150,172
  William 106
  William B. 140
  Willie Thompson 66
  William 124
  W. R. 24,132
  Young 39,140
  Zillah 137
Dawson...133
  Eliza 152
  Elizabeth 87
  Joseph 152
  Mammie 179
  Mary 153
  Thomas 135,152,153
Day, Addie 89
  Mary N. E. 88
Deal, Sarah L. 39
Deale, Ann 21
Dean, Anna 117
  Jesse 23
  Jesse L. 117
  Mary Melinda 3
  Russel 3
Deaton, Emily 48
  Jackson 136,177
  Susan 136
Ke Burgheim, Phillips
  Fahnenberg 55
Dedinger, Michael 62
De Graffenreid, T. H. 17
Dehart, Candace 155
Delany, Alfred 41
  P. H. 64

Dendy, Elizabeth 146
  Elizabeth F. 1
  Elizabeth Knox 147
  Fannie L. 157
  James H. 1,146,147
  Jennie 123
  Louisa 181
  Lou W. 91
  Lucy A. 104
  Marshal B. 180
  Mrs. Marshal B. 181
  M. B. 25
  M. L. 25
  S. Jennie 83
  Mrs. S. J. 173
  S. P. 171
  Susan 15
  Thos. H. 104
  W. H. 83
Dennenberge, Henry 97
Deveneau, Caroline M. 14
  Joseph M. 14
Dewet, Aleck 131
Dibble, F. I. 114
Dickey, Sarah 97
Dickinson, Anna 115
  Caroline C. 72
  Jeremiah 72
Dickson, Bratton M. 44
  David 137,138,145
  Dora 177
  Mrs. E. M. 116
  Frances 137
  Francis 138
  J. Walter 142
  Louisa P. 62
  Maggie 155
  Mary 26
  Mary Elizabeth 142
  Mary G. 28
  Matthew 44
  Michael 45
  Sarah Antoinette 35
  Sarah E. 145
  T. 35
  W. B. 28,44
  William 26,62,116,123
  Wm. Alexander 142
Dillard, Harrison 35
  James 38
  Margaret 35,42
Dobbin, J. C. 22
  Carrie 145
  Jesse C. 145
Docery, William 20
Doss, Caroline 40
  Catherine 137
  George 156
  G. W. 4
  Henry 123
  Ida 146
  Lizzie 53
  Margaret 123
  Martha E. 108
  Roselette 146
  Sarah I. 76
  T. C. 146
  Thomas 137,146
  Thomas, Jr. 53
  Thomas, Sr. 123
  W. F. 76,174
Dodge...118
Dodgen, John 4
  Mary 4
Dodson, Artemissa 87
Dolleson, Joseph 16
  Melinda 16
Donaldson, John 108
  Jospeh 21,108
  Sue 75
  T. O. 75
Donhoe, Cornelius 69

Dooley, Dorcas 132
  William 132
Dorr, John 143
Dorrah, John F. 160
  Lizzie 160
Dorsey, Anderson 35
  Andrew J. 1
  Catharine 164
  Elizabeth Jane 35
  Nancy Isabella 1
  William 164
Douglas...57
  Jonathan B. 19
Douglass...29
Douthit, Eugenie A. 69
Dow, Jesse E. 11
Dowis, Frances M. 178
  Jno. 43
  John 168,178
  John M. 132,178
  Sarah 43
Doyle, E. E. 113
  Eli R. 54
  E. R. 15
  F. B. 174
  James A. 55,154
  James H. 96
  Jas. A. 125
  J. H. 181
  John N. 96
  Julia F. 113
  Lizzie Jane 55
  Lou W. 96
  Lula 174
  Martha 55,96,142
  Mary 65
  M. S. 54
  O. M. 65
  Rhodum 142,158
  Samuel D. 154
  Susan 15
  Susan Reese 54
Dozier...24
Drane...12
Drennan, Mrs. M. D. 48
  Prudence 37
  R. Henry 48
  Wilson 37
  William L. 48
Driver, Elizabeth I. 165
Dryman, John M. 178
Du Bose, Dudley M. 176
  J. E. 90
Duke, Abraham 16
  Harriet 16
  Ransom 16
Dunbar, David 65
Duncan, B. N. J. 78
  Cynthia M. 108
  David 163
  D. N. 163
  Frnaklin 108
  Jane 76
  Margaret 78
  Mason 25
  Nancy Ann 25,39
  Robert 62
  W. W. 163
Dunlap, Celia 102
  David 175
  Delilah C. 54
Dunn, Elizabeth 27
  Sarah Ann 65
  William 27
Dunson, Anna 174
  W. H. 174
Dupreis...176
Durham, A. H. 93
  Andrew B. 46
  Artamissa 94
  Artamissa Narcissa 118
  Charles 97,120
  Dora 180

Durham, Francis Elizabeth
  118
  Jane 110
  J. C. 83
  John 110
  Joseph 63
  L. R. 105
  Malinda 83
  Martha J. 46
  Mary Ann 97
  Mary J. 93
  Melinda 45
  Nancy Jane 118
  Rebecca 120
  Sallie A. 105
  William 45
  W. O. 94
Duval, Francis 22
  John 71
  N. T. 22
Dyar, Sarah 116

Earle, Eliza Ann 1
  Elizabeth Henrietta 144
  J. R. 172
  J. W. 1,144
  M. B. 108
  Virginia 159
Easley, John A. Jr. 34
Eaton, Elizabeth Ann 33
  Emma 158
  G. W. 97
  Surry 108
  W. H. 181
Edens, Alexander 7
  John M. C. 124
  Samuel 7
  William 7
  W. D. 124
  William Jackson 124
Eddins, Martha 57 ·
  William 57
Edgar, Lutitia 167
  Stephen J. 167
Edge, Littleton 45
  Minerva 45
Edgeworth, Maria 2
Edings, Ephraim 121
Edwards, John 18
Elberson, D. 34
  John 34
Elenberg, Solomon 58
Elford, Charles J. 109
Elkins, John A. 148
Ellard, James C. 156
  Polly 156
Ellenburg, Susan 51
  Thos. J. 51
Ellinburgh, Susannah 86
Elliott, Allen R. 123
  David R. 123
  Elizabeth Ann 76
  Frances Caroline 72
  George W. 114
  Martha A. 72
  Mary E. 114
  Nancy 123
  Nathan W. 72
Ellis, Constantia C. 38
  Gideon 4, 40,61,69,75
  Jeremiah 116
  Patsy 116
Ellison, A. H. 118
  H. E. 86
  Lucretia 86
  M. Agnes 118
  Mary Jane 70
  William 70
Elmore, Franklin H. 8
Elrod, Anner 145
  C. L. G. 147
  D. A. 161

Elrod, David 122,147
  Edward 148
  Eleanor C. 70
  Elizabeth 161
  Emma 148
  George G. 70
  Lucinda 122
  Maranda Jane 124
  Mary 145,147
  William 147
Elston, Elizabeth B. 140
  John C. 109
  Sabina 109
Emery, Sarah M. 172
Emmerson, Katie 145
Engel, Mrs. Fred 76
Entriken, Lucretia 78
  T. D. 78
Ernest, Betsy 92
  Jacob 92
  May 51
Erskine, Jane E. 142
  John 22
  John R. 142
  Julia E. 142
  Margaret E. 142
  Martha J. 142
  Newton E. 142
  Sarah E. 142
  William J. 142,143
Ervin, George 114
  Isaac 114
  Nancy 114
  Thomas 114
  W. C. 144
  William 114
  Thomas 52
Evans, Anderson 147
  James 95
  J. V. 175
  Laura 147
  L. D. 95
  Sanford 78
Evatt, Adam 26
  Artemissa A. 26
Evins, Eliza E. 102
  Thomas A. 102

Fairchild, William L. 68
Fajen, Mrs. Augustus 97
Fant, Elizabeth 43
  Martha B. 89
  William 152
  William B. 43
Farmer, Agnes Lula 133
  James L. 133
Farrow, W. W. 128
Feaster, Emma E. 133
  Jacob 66
  Mary 132
  Miss. S. C. 66
Featherston, J. C. C. 89
Felton, Eliza 87
Fendley, Carrie 98
  Elvira 95
  J. W. 78
  Lewis 96
  Laura 114
  W. A. 114
Fennel, Miss. N. E. 52
  W. J. 97
  Fannie L. 157
  J. L. Jr. 157
  Mary A. A. 66
  William M. 65
Ferguson, Elisha A. 74
  Eliza 3
  James 3
  James, Sr. 60
  John 79
  M. Adaline 79
  Martha 51

Ferguson, Mary 74
  Mary M. 145
  Robert 145
  Salley D. 175
  William 17
Field, B. W. 21
  E. 21
  E. Jennie 72
  E. M. 21
  J. D. 21
  James M. 21
  Jeremiah 21
  John D. 21
  Martha J. 98
  W. G. 98
  William T. 72
Fields, Cornelia M. 1
  E. M. 1
  Horation 171
  J. H. 42
Fincher, Laura F. 113
Findlay, Bettie 148
  James 148
  Lewis 13
  Lucinda 18
  Mary Ann 13
  Thos. W. 18
  Charley 117
  Jos. 6
  Sarah Caroline 6
  Mary M. 92
  Susan 40
  W. T. 92
Finney...62
Fischesser, A. 94
  C. A. 158
  Lucia 158
  Mena 94
Fisher, John 68
  Letty Ann 140
  Patrick 73
  Wesley 44
Fitzgerald, Eli 91
  Margaret 91
  Mary E. 140
Fitzpatrick, Bird 69
  Michael 95
Fletcher, William 25
Flournoy, Thos. 56
Folger, Alonzo M. 90
  Julia A. 165,166
  Julius 166
  L. Camilla 99
  M. Eliza 90
  O. Cyrus 99
Folkes, James A. 61
Forbes, Adolphus 15
  Eliza 15
  Elmina 15
  George 15
  Jeptha 15
  Martha 15
  Nelson 15
  Ziporah 15
Ford, G. 59
  John T. 73
Forrester, Berry 61
  Elizabeth 18
  Harriet 52
  Lelitia L. 61
Forster, John 75
Fort, Tomlinson 65
Fortner, Ivy 22
Fortune, Caroline 53
  G. N. 94
Foster, Abial 113
  Edmund D. 104
  Elijah 151,164
  Mary S. 104
  Q. M. 149
  R. W. 70
  Sallie E. 106
  Susan 40

Fowler, Eddy Malinda 127
  G. 7
  James 145
  John 48
  Mary 145
  Nancy E. 32
Foxworth, J. 79
Fracheur, Lucinda 108
Fracheur, T. Dickens 108
Frady, Elizabeth 130
  Jeremiah L. 130
Francis, Sallie A. 98
Franklin, Drucilla 128
  George 128
Franks, Nehemiah 69
  R. P. 26,92
Fraser, John 148
Frasier, Elizabeth Rebecca
  177
  Sue E. 124
  William S. 124
Frazier, Sarah 149
Frederick, Sarah Ann 31
  Thomas M. 31
Fredericks...136
  Balus 106
  Cornelia 56
  Eliza 152
  George W. 111
  G. W. 111
  Harriet 106
Freeman, A. P. 147
  Cordelia 147
  David 95
  Drury 76
  Elvira 95
  Frances 36
  Malinda B. 33
  Nancy E. 76
Fretwell, Bry 172
  Josephene 103
Fricks, Frances 12
  Mary 155
  Mary Ann 9
  Matthias 9
  Phebe Louisa 162
  Rany 8
  Wm. Alexander 162
Frost, Anna 97
Fugate, C. B. Sr. 152
Fulks, Miss E. J. 123
Fullenwider, Henry W. 96
Fuller, Allen 74
  Eliza 74
  William 70
Fullerton, Louisa P. 62
Furguson, Delilah 109
Furman, Farish C. 182
  Richard 40

G_____Sallie 64
G_____T. R. 64
Gadd, Nancy Ann 126
  Robert 126
Gaillard, A. D. 176
  Lewis 142
  Mary E. 100
  Mrs. M. L. 137
  Sallie 176
  S. S. 102
  W. H. D. 153
Gaine, James A. 70
Gaines, Anna 102
  B. S. 100,102,105,109
  D. O. 33
  Edmund Pendleton 2
  Elisha 78
  Ella 121
  Frances 54
  Miss G. A. 53
  Hugh Oscar 78
  Lewis B. 33

Gaines, Lucy A. M. 36
  Maria 63
  Mary 15
  Mary A. 70
  Mary P. 14
  Reuben 53
  Robert 54
  Susanna 78
  Vashti 75
  W. B. 36
Gallaway, Evaline B. 124
Galphin, H. P. 180
Gantt...41
  Benjamin Franklin 151
  Highland Mary 124
  James A. 151
  Johanna 151
  Martin 68
  Richard 11
Gardner, Wm. 16
Garner...142
Garret, Elizabeth 88
  T. P. 88
Garrett, Angelina 72
  George Washington 72
  Jesse 39
  John 72
  Martha 106
  Mary 39
  Milton 106
  Stephen 106
Garrison, Delia Ann 42
  Elizabeth 27
  Jane 148
  John A. 148
  Sally L. 148
  Susan 148
Garvin, Azina M. 50
  David 61
  Etta 104
  F. L. 104
  Jane E. 78
  Martha F. A. 92
  Martha M. 78
  Nancy 61
  Thomas 73
  William T. 78
Gary, Eugenia A. 125
  M. W. 159
  S. A. 175
  Samuel A. 104
Gasaway, Elizabeth 1
  Henry 26
  James 26
  Matilda A. 19
  Rachel 26
  Wesley 26
  William 26
  W. W. 1
Gassaway, Anna 102
  James D. 63
  Jane 1
  Maria 63
  Wm. D. 102
  Wm. W. 1
Gaston, H. R. 156
  John 24
Gayle, John 68
George, John N. 106,157,
  158
  Mrs. M. D. 155
  Namsi L. 155
  Sarah 106
Gerard, Mary 31
  Thos. 31
Geurin, John 27
  Margaret 89
  Margaret E. H. 89
  Mary C. 27,74
  Nathaniel 89
Gibbs, D. A. 154
  Martha 154

Gibson, A. 90
  Augustus Napoleon 46
  Catherine 46
  H. A. 137
  H. A. H. 46,146
  H. A. H. Hr. 151
  James 28
  Keziah 34
  Margaret 90
  Sarah J. 69
  Tallulah V. 172
  Z. 172
Giddings, Wm. 18
Gignilliat, Sue 152
  Warren 152
Gilbert, Lettie Ann 17
  Lucretita 39
  Squire A. 39
Gillam, James 130
Gillespie, Elizabeth 93
  Jason 93
  Matthew 89
  Rachael 89
Gilliland, James 39
  J. Anna 48
  R. J. 48,143
Gilmer, Amanda F. 28
  R. A. 90
  Robt. A. 27
Gilstrap, Abraham 90
  Judith 76
  Louisa 90
  William 16,113
Giradeau, J. L. 72
Gissel, Hanche 32
  Josephine E. 32
  Lucy Amelia 32
Givens, Avarilla 80
  Harrison J. 80
Glazener, J. Riley 112
Gleason, J. H. 52
  Ophelia L. 52
Glenn, Alexander 130
  Mary E. 133
Glover, E. Toccoa 76
  Thomas J. 76
Glow, George 45
  Rhoda 45
Godfrey, Ansel 31
Goings, James 60
Golden, Elujah 174
  John 70
  Narcissa 174
  Thos. 35
Goode, Catharine 149
  J. F. 174
Gooden, Permelia 3
Goodlett, Mary 77
  S. D. 77
  York 147
Goodman, Mrs. A. S. 181
  Ida M. 169
  John S. 169
Goodwin, Jane 143
  Lidie A. 123
  Wm. D. 123
Goore, Mary H. 18
Gorden, Andrew 1
  Elizabeth 1
Gordon, Nancy 14
Gossett, John R. 95
Gotz, Mena 94
Goulden, Harriet 127
  Margaret M. 183
Graday...98
  Elizabeth Henrietta 144
  Wm. S. 144
  Wm. T. 58
  W. P. 109
Graham, Alexander 13
  Ananias 82
  Betsy 127
  Frank 131

Graham, Margaret 131
  Mary 145
  Temperance 13
Grant, A. B. 163,172
  Catharine M. 124
  Donald 84
  Elizabeth 21,34
  Eugenia 145
  George 34,172
  James B. 100
  John N. 127
  Leethe 127
  Martha 52
  Mary 100
  Milley 171
  Nancy 127
  Noah 135,145,167
  Selah S. 167
  Susan 135
  Thomas A. 178
  Thomas J. 20
  Zilpha 20
Graves...23
  Mary 138
  J. S. 57
Gray, Andrew 86
  Elizabeth 128
  John Welborne 178
  Manning 178
  Reubin 53
  Susannah 86
Gready, W. P. 104
Grear, Clayton 167
  Selah S. 167
Green...4
  A. J. 141
  G. W. 134
  James 47
  Mary 72
  Miss S. E. 158
  Tecoa 134
Gregory, John W. 19
  Willis T. 19
Gresham, Geo. T. 149,150
  G. T. 145,150,151
  Septima 145
Grey, Adaline 22
Grice, D. 106
Griffin, Alethea Ann 11
  Avarilla 46
  Avarilla A. 46
  Bailey 46
  Bailey B. 46
  Barton 46,117
  Benjamin 46
  Bettie 148
  E. H. 125
  Elihu H. 46
  G. B. 46
  James A. 90
  Jane B. 117
  Jane M. S. 46
  J. L. 79
  John 11
  Joseph 46
  Lucy J. 61
  Margaret T. 46
  Mantha F. D. 46
  Mary L. M. 46
  Nancy V. 46
  R. H. 46,61
  Rosannah M. 46
  Sargent 41,46
  Sargent J. 46
  Thomas V. 46
  Thos. 46
  William 46
  Zilpha 90
Griffith, Wm. 75
Grimes, S. D. 20
Grimshaw, Miss. E. 131
Grimshawe, Elizabeth F.
  155

Grimshawe, T. 155
Grisham, Joseph 16,82,155
  Mrs. L. M. 82
  Lou 157
  Martha Josephine 15
  William S. 15
  Wm. S. 9.12,17,19,25,
    33,35,43
  W. S. 1,2,6,56
Grishop, Sarah 62
Grissop, Elizabeth 149
  John 149
  Lena 174
  Thomas 174
Grogan, Henry 52
  J. H. 174
  J. N. 172
  Kate 117
  Nellie 176
  Sarah 52
  Tallulah V. 172
Grubbs, Miss. D. O. 33
  Nancy E. 33
Guerin, Abby 66
Guess, Joseph 171
  Patten F. 171
Guillemard, Arnold 40
Gunn, Annie 43
  David 24
Gurley, J. A. 80
  Joseph A. 9
  Minnie Florence 80
  S. M. 9,80
Gutekunst, J. George 178

Hailey, James B. Sr. 161
Hagood, Amanda 168
  Benjamin 32
  E. 42
  Eliza 32
  James E. 34,40,45,53,
    76,86,90,93
  J. E. 7,42,102,121,123
  Lelah C. 42
  Lidie A. 123
  Lydia 93
  Mary 121
Hal_, Belinda F. 90
Haley, J. J. 175
Hall, Caroline 8
  David 167
  Dora 167
  Elizabeth J. 58
  Fenton H. 180
  H. M. 8
  John M. 174
  John S. 145
  J. T. 37
  Martha J. 37
  Mary 86
  Sarah 145,153
  T. J. 153
  William 153,179
  Zachariah, Sr. 116
Hallum, Catherine 61
  Celestia B. 61
  Fair K. 61
  Margaret 9
  Thomas J. 61
  Thos. 9
  Thos. J. 40
  William 61
Hallums, Martha 34
Haltree, W. C. 86
Hamby, Mary 51
  Wm. J. 51
Hamilton, Amanda Caroline
  70
  Carrie 120
  D. K. 74
  Elizabeth 162
  Griffin 112
  Harrison 112

Hamilton, James A. 75
  Jane 84
  Jane C. 72
  Julia 179
  Lemuel 72
  Lou M. 120
  Malinda 112
  Malinda A. 75
  Miss M. A. M. 6
  Margaret 35
  McDuffie 70
  Rebecca J. 52
  Sarah J. 110
  Terrell 112
  Warren 112,120
  W. K. 6
  Wm. 110,112
Hamlin, J. R. 98,99,103,104,
  111,114,118
Hammett, Archelaus 88
Hammond...46
  E. 82
  Frances E. 157
  H. 36,82
  Herbert 100
  Ira 30
  Joshua 4
  Lucy A. M. 36
  Mary E. 82
Hammonds, Sarah E. 159
Hampton, Mary S. 33
  Wade, Jr. 33
Hancock, David 27
  Elizabeth 26
Hanks, J. A. R. 123
Harvey, Martha P. 138
  Harbert, Susan 136
Harbin, J. H. 157
  Luther C. 152
  Mary E. 106
  Samuel M. 158
  S. M. 143
  W. L. 152
Harden, Mary 64
Hardin, Adaline 141
  Eliza 123
  John 130
  Joseph 123
Hargroves, S. Jane 128
Harkey, Maggie 155
  W. C. 155
Harkin, Sue E. 148
Harley, John L. 164
  Minnie L. 164
Harp, Bill 147
Harper, Elizabeth Ann 164
  Henry 36
  Henry T. 73
  Ida 138
  Katie 172
  Lucinda 36,72
  Sarah J. 72
  Thomas 138,164
  Thos. 172
Harvey, Bartley 66
  Elizabeth A. 141
  Mary 66
Harrel, W. E. 40
  Emma M. 137
Harrington, Alice 172
  Y. J. 11
Harris, Charlotte 58
  Eleanor C. 70
  Emily 141
  Eugenia 156
  John 58
  J. P. 53
  Martha 53
  Nancy 76
  Oscar 157
  Richard 76
  Sallie 157

Harris, Sarah 76
Harrison, Andrew 34
  Anna E. 25
  Cornelia M. 1
  F. E. 94,134
  Francis 25
  James M. 77
  Mary 94
  Matilda 45
  Nancy E. 77
Hase, Malica 23
Haulbrook, J. W. 147,172
Hauskamp, Catherine 33
Hawkins, Agnes 174
  Caroline 40
  Jeannett 156
  John 40
  Newton S. 41
Hawthorne, Anna 105
  Miss. E. E. 105
  J. G. 40
  J. N. 105
  Sallie A. 105
  Susan 40
Hayes, Candace 155
  Eliza 167
  Fannie 147
  George W. 155
  H. N. 122,146,152,154,
  168
  Jane 177
  Robert 147
  Robert A. 167
  Roselette 146
  Weston 143
Haynes, Andrew 76
  Jesse 65
  Judith 76
  Mary J. 180
Hays, Anderson B. 76
  Elizabeth Ann 76
  H. H. 124
  H. N. 108,135,136,145,
  166
  Jack 2
  James 6
  James L. 108
  Mary Margaret 166
  Melissa 6
  Polly 156
Head, D. W. 169
  George 10
  James 26
  Jeptha 13
  Martha 84
  Minerva 10
  Sarah 13
Heady, Elizabeth 153
Hearon, Henry D. 72
Hembree, Alfred 12
  Elam 106
  Elijah 13
  James A. 88
  Lucy J. 12
  Martha J. 106
  Mary 13
Hemphill, J. C. 135
Henderson, Francis 116
  James W. A. 72
  William 116
Hendricks, Cynthia 53
  George 161
  John 53
Hendrix, Emma E. 134
  J. E. 156,178
  John M. 134
  Rachael 89
Henry, B. A. 59
  Beverly Allen 59
  Julia 134
  Mary A. 59
  O. L. 134

Henry, Samuel 127
Henton, John T. 52
Herbert, Betsey 172
Herd, Phoebe 44
Hernandez, Joseph M. 21
Herndon, Edmund 95,123,143
  Issaquena 143
  L. Susie 123
  Narcissa P. 95
Hester, Alfred 50
  Elizabeth 100
  Henry 6
  James B. 71
  Laura A. 100
  Lucettie 71
  Malinda 100
  Mary E. 100
  Melissa 6
  Stephen C. 100
  Thomas 3
Hide, J. L. 174
Higgins, Margaret 23
  W. A. 42
  Wilson 23
  Wm. 162
Hiles, Jacob 7
Hill, Charles D. 106
  D. A. 80
  Mary J. 106
  T. W. 80
Hiller, Blanche 112
Hillhouse, Esther L. 6
  J. B. 1,3,89,108
  Joseph B. 6
Hillian, H. 137
  Mary 137
Hilliard, Elizabeth 146
Hinkle, A. J. 133
  Alsey A. 90
  Elias 90
Hinton, Berry 178
  Fannie 54
  L. C. 54
  N. E. 52
Hireat, Emile 60
Hitt, Martha 93
  Thomas 93
Hix, Balus 176,177
  Gibson 77
  John 103
  Lizzie 176
  Mrs. M. 158
  Nancy 77
  Robert 40
  Sarah 40
  W. J. 176
  Wm. J. 121
Hobbs, Catharine 66
Hodge...179
Hodges, W. A. 151
  Willie 150,151
  Wm. 53
Hodgings, Elizabeth 76
Hoffman, Julius 18
  Tabitha 18
Hogan, John 67
Hoke, John E. 26
  Lillie 113
  Martha E. 26
  Robert F. 113
Holcombe, Arminda 117
  Charles 117
  E. C. 50
  Miss E. C. E. 98
  Elias 94
  Eliza 89
  Elizabeth 175
  Eliza E. 102
  Ella Jane 50
  Fannie E. 94
  Jonathan S. 91
  Mary E. 89,175

Holcombe, R. E. 89
  W. E. 50,102
  Willie F. 164
  Wm. 164
Holdbrooks, J. W. 165
  Mary Ann 122
Holden, B. F. 24
  Isaac 15
  Jane 15,170
  Jemima 24
  John 111
  Martha 15
  Mary Emmaline 111
  Mary M. 92
  William 15
Holder, Adaline 148
  B. 126,128,135,146,155,
  172
  Benj. 90
Holland, B. F. 61
  David T. 18
  Henry D. 8
  James Harrison 8
  John 53
  Martha 53
  Penelope 61
  W. Turner 140
Hollbrook, Caroline 21
  Wm. 21
Holleman...120,136
  Emma E. 88
  Jas. W. 88
  Johnnie 141
  Julia D. 137
  J. W. 136,137,141
  Sallie S. 141
Holley, James 105
  Martha A. 105
  Martha S. 76
  Mollie 105
Hollingshed...120
Hollingsworth, Deborah R.
  76
  Frances 36
  I. J. 76
  James I. 73
  John 36
  Lucinda 36
  Rebecca 115
Hollis, Edwin 30
Holly, Sarah Ann 65
Holmes, Andrew 176
  Caroline 21
  David 151
  Elizabeth 33
  Marshfield 33
  Mary L. 140
  Sarah 145
  Terrissa 151
Holsey, Hopkins "Tagalo"
  61
Holt, Anna 50
Holtzclaw, Rany 8
  William 8
Holways, Auguste 162
  Augustus 143
  Hannah 162
  Henry 162
  John 162
  Teidora 162
  William 162
Honea, Benson 76
  Caroline 132
  Edward 132, 147
  Fannie 147
  Jane 181
  Mary 64
  Sarah Ann Frances 64
  Viney E. 76
Honnea, Robert 14
Honnicutt, William John
  173

Hood, Jacob 141
Hooper, Cynthia 108
  Mrs. J. J. 152
  Nelson 164
Hopkins, Miss A. 181
  C. T. 154
  Miss D. A. 62
  Edward 100
  Ida 138
  James P. 103
  J. N. 138
  John S. 108
  Martha 103
  Martha E. 108
  Mary S. 100
Horn, Jesse 147
Horshaw, Louisa M. 44
Horton, Wm. 58
Houghton...113
Hounschild, Wm. 51
Howard, Abner 70
  Ann 79
  Caroline M. 14
  Henry 31
  Mary A. 105
  Nancy 70
  Tilman 79
Howell, Hannah 168
  Robert 168
Howerton, Joseph 53
Hubbard...120
  Annie M. 133
  Elzia 152
  Issaquena 143
  John B. 152
  Mary 139
  Robert H. 112
  Samuel 143
  Wm. 33
Hubburt, Philip 11
Huber, Jas. A. 28
Huckabee, G. W. 85
Hudgens, A. C. 156
  Ella 121
  Eugenia 156
  J. B. 141
  Mary A. 141
  T. A. 121
Hudson, Elizabeth 47
  John 95
  Margaret M. 55
  Rebecca 149
  Wyatt 55
Huff, Thos. 30
Hughes, A. 138
  A. C. 80
  A. H. 90
  Aserett 46
  E. 22,33,66,27
  Edward 46
  E. H. 138
  Elizabeth 9
  Elizabeth F. 1
  Elizabeth J. 80
  Francis 138
  George B. 13
  Hannah R. 43
  Harvey 9
  Henry R. 1
  Hester Ann 35
  John 61
  Joseph Sr. 20
  Louisa 4
  Louisa M. 44
  Lucinda 35,80
  Nancy J. 110
  Sallie L. 156
  Sarah 104
  Sarah A. 46
  Thomas B. 13
  Thomas J. 44
  T. J. 35

Hughes, W. J. 110
  Elizabeth J. 58
  T. J. 58
Hull, Carolina 10
  Caroline 32
  Catherine 9
  Daniel 9
  Daniel S. 32,116
  James 68
  John 10
  Miss L. J. 76
  Sarah 68
  Sarah E. 68
Humbert, D. G. 143
  J. W. 156
Humphreys, D. 116
  David 7,10,15
  Jane 159
  Wm. 73
Hunnicutt, Agnes 53
  Miss A. M. 4
  Elmina 74
  Ester 127
  Joberry 33
  J. R. 6,10,11,12,13,21,
  25,26,28,33,37,48,54,
  58,68,69,70,76,82
  Kate 126
  Martha 145
  Mary 33
  M. R. 126
  William 53
  Wm. J. 74
Hunt, Charles 79
  E. A. 31
  H. D. 31
  Henson 12
  James W. 12
  J. J. 93
  Lucinda 93
  Milla M. 109
  Nancy 93
  Ransom 109
  William 92
  Wm. 56,62,64,78
  W. R. 28
Hunter, A. 63,93
  Aeneas 97
  Agnes Lula 133
  Andrew 133
  G. V. 182
  Mattie 179
  Nathan 172
  Mrs. R. A. 166
  Samuel 182
  Thomas 182
  Virginia E. 109
  Wm. 93,105
Hutchins, Abner 37
  Constantia C. 38
  Elizabeth 136
  Lucy 142
  Nancy 37
  Robt. M. 32
  Sarah A. 32,127
  Wm. B. 38
Hutchinson, Wm. B. 179
  Sallie L. 169
  T. C. 169
Hutto...147,153
Hurt, Avarilla 80
  Miss D. A. 80
  Daniel 80
Hyde, Arminda 62
  Jacob 62
  John 140
  Phebe Louisa 162
  Sarah A. 140

Ingram, Seth 19
Inman, Alfred G. 176
Irwin, C. W. 159

Isbell, Julia 79
  Mary M. 133
  Robert 79
  S. 79
  Samuel 133
Isham, John 20
Isom, Spencer 51
Ivester, Anderson 85
  Arzela 85
  Charles Anderson 85
  Mary M. 145
Ivey, George 46

Jackson...104,105
  Zilpha 20
James...49
  Artamissa 94
  B. S. 178
  Fannie K. 178
  Jane E. 78
  John T. 78
  Lavinia 178
  Lila B. 151
  Martha M. 78
  Nancy 159
  Thos. A. Y. 120
  William 151
Jameson, J. 86
  Joshua 39,60
  Louisa 89
  Wilkinson 38
Janes, Celia 64
  D. S. 84
  Miss F. E. 41
  W. T. 84
Jarrat, Thomas B. 47
  Elizabeth 123
  Ida E. 124
  Patton 124
  Robert 123
  Sallie P. 123
Jaynes, Kitty 181
Jeanes, Mary S. 126
  W. F. 126
Jeans, Charlie B. 51
  Charlotte 58
  Eliza A. 51
  Sarah 10
Jenkins, Abner 77
  Anderson 77
  Arminda A. 34
  Caroline 32
  Clayton 130
  E. 163
  Miss E. E. 76
  Elias 149
  Elizabeth 130
  Miss E. T. 177
  Francis 77
  George M. 130
  Grafton 34
  James 77
  James G. 130
  Jesse 77,109,160,167
  John 77
  Joseph 177
  Martha J. 37
  Mary E. 98
  Nancy E. 77
  Rebecca 34
  Sarah E. 167
  Talulah F. 132
  Thomas 77
  Uriah 130
  William F. 167
  Williamson 77
Jennings, Julia 32
  L. R. L. 14
  Sallie E. 14
Johns, Jeremiah 97
  John 151
  Lila B. 151
  Nicey 32

Johns, Rebecca 97
  S. H. 64,183
  Z. 32
Johnson...120
  Annie May 180
  Bill 16
  Braxton R. 88
  Byron G. 168
  Caroline 102
  C. N. 17
  Disa 170
  Elizabeth 38,69
  Elvira S. 106
  James 30,102
  James H. 56
  John 20
  Julia 180
  Julia M. 168
  L. B. 113,168
  Leonora 67
  Mary 114
  Melvira J. 88
  Nancy 37
  Wm. 114
Johnston, Benj. J. 123
  B. 26
  Edward F. 98
  Eliza J. 105
  Jane 143
  L. Susie 123
  Mary E. 98
  William 143
Jones...39
  Alice 133
  Amanda 173
  Andrew 128
  Christopher 163,164
  Cornelia 12
  David 11
  Miss E. J. 137
  Emma 148
  Ernest L. 131
  Eugenia 150
  Francis 128
  Hartwell 11
  Hilary C. 145
  Jabez 72
  James B. 109
  James C. 73
  J. E. 109
  Joel E. 150
  John 102
  John D. 12
  John H. 59
  J. V. 109
  Leander 89
  Lefell 148
  Louis 50
  Louisa 89
  Louisa Elizabeth 145
  Lucinda J. 11
  Marion 145
  Martha M. 11
  Mary 11,145
  Mat. 50
  Matilda C. 11
  Nancy 11,102
  Rebecca C. 11
  Sallie 157
  S. B. 137
  Stephen A. 109
  Sue P. 145
  Susan C. 11
  Thomas H. 11
Joost, John 182
Jordan, Nicholas 35

Kannady, Martha 13
Kay, Joseph 155
  Miss M. J. 120
Keasler, David A. 177
  Henry 111

Keasler, Miss M. A. 111
  Narcissa 124
Keaton, Jane 90
  John 90
Keese, E. 124
  Sallie J. 124
Keith...121
  Broadwell W. 99,100
  B. W. 100
  Drucila 99,100
  E. L. 76
  Eliza Ann 1
  Elizabeth 8
  Elizabeth B. 61
  Elliott M. 61
  Marville L. 99,100
  Mary 99,100
  Mary R. 99
  Stephen D. 157
  Susannah 99,100
  Thomas J. 75
  W. C. 136
  W. L. 1,8
  Wm. L. 9,11
  Wm. C. 99
Keitt, L. M. 65
  Sue 65
Kelley, Ann 25
  Charles W. 87
  Ezekiel 108
  James T. 25
  Martha Jane 87
  Mattie A. 54
  Nancy M. 151
  Thomas 54
Kelly, Andrew 43
  Artamissa Narcissa 118
  Catherine 164
  Francis Elizabeth 118
  Henry 29
  James J. 43
  J. W. 43
  Nancy A. 62
  Nancy Jane 118
  Ransom 62
  Robert 171
  Simon 53
  Surry 108
  Susan Amanda 62
  Tarlton 108
  Wm. 118
Kendrick, Judith "Judy" 16
Kennedy, Callie P. 69
  Daniel J. 17
  Elizabeth 68
  Henrietta R. 32
  Jane H. 45
  J. L. 1,6,8,25,32,34,
    45,48,49,66,68,69,72,
    103,112,121
  Lettie Ann 17
  Mary M. 29
  Michael 29
Kennemore, Francis 116
Kennemuir, D. H. 12
Kennemur, Cynthia A. 136
  D. H. 43,53,57,70,72,
    75,136,174
Kershaw, John 137
Ketchum, R. C. 51
Key, Thos. G. 18
Keyes, James C. 101
  Robert 101
Keys, James Crawford 99
  J. Crawford 182
Kibbee, J. W. 132
Kilburn, Amanda 175
  Mis L. J. 53
  Wallace 175
Killian, George 151
  Julia A. 178
Kilpatrick, Benjamin F. 11

Kilpatrick, Clara 39
Kimbrell, Sarah E. 41
Kinard, S. K. 168
Kinkade, Geo. 105
King, A. Josephine 181
  Catherine 54
  Charles W. 154
  David 169
  E. E. 41
  Elizabeth Jane 35
  George L. 23
  G. H. 41
  G. W. 67
  Helena 23
  Henry 46
  Jas. Preston 67
  Jno. B. 120
  J. W. 103
  Lizzie Ann 103
  Louisa 88
  Lou M. 120
  Malinda 112
  Martha 169
  Mary 21
  Mary A. 111
  Melvira J. 88
  Peter 24
  Robert W. 88
  Robert 23
  Susan 135
  W. A. 130
  Wm. 35,135
  Wm. J. 112
Kirby, E. H. 146
  Elizabeth 146
Kirkoff, Frances 100
  John H. 100
Kirksey, Alethea Ann 11
  C. 11
  Christopher 61
  Isaiah M. 61
  Jared 61
  Jared E. F. 61
  Mary L. M. P. 61
  M. Elizabeth 56
  Robert 127
Kiser, John S. 138
  Martha P. 138
Kistler, P. F. 124
Kizer, Polly 146
Klenibeck, John H. 26
  Sophia 26
Knauff, W. J. 29
Knee, Mrs. C. 155
  Herman Heinrich 113
  Julia S. 155
  Mattie C. 98
Knice, Hermann C. 118
Knight, Elizabeth 130
  James 33
Knox...160
  Amanda 32
  Arthur R. 105
  Benjamin 177
  Drury 11,76,139
  Mrs. E. 117
  Elizabeth 90
  Frances J. 76
  Gerogiana Amamda Melvina 5
  John 4,5,7,8,9,13,17,18, 23
  John C. 90
  Margaret C. 127
  Mary C. 22
  Mathew 76
  Robert 127,177
  Sallie L. 105
  William 76
Koker, Jane 138
Koonce, Sarah F. 44
Kruse, J. G. C. 22
Kuhtman, H. W. 140

Kuhtman, Mrs. H. W. 139
  Mary A. 140
Kuhtmann, Anna W. 116
  H. W. 116
Kyle, Cahterine 10
  Henry 10
  Hunter 10
  James/Jas. 10
  John Laughlin 10
  Mathew 10
  Robert 10
  Wm. 10

Ladd, John 1
Laidy, Frances 100
Lake, Julia A. 163
  Wm. E. 163
Lambert...178
  John 52
Lancaster, Columbus 64
  Sarah 20
Land, Martha L. 68
  Melissa 32
  Wm. H. 68
Landers, Caroline M. 42
  R. P. 42
Dandrum, A. 62
  B. F. 124
  Rebecca 124
  Sallie J. 124
  Samuel 39
Lane, Anna E. 158
Langston, Betsey 108
  D. A. 62
  F. M. 62
  Lucy J. 11
  Martha E. 52
  S. H. 11
Lanier, Allen 127
  Bartley 127
  Bird 127
  Polly 127
  Pressley 127
  William 127
Lapoint, John 20
Latham, John L. 117
  Sarah 117
  Andrew P. 92
  Anthony G. 92
  E. A. 84
Lathem, Eliza A. 84
  Geo. 92
  John C. 84
  J. W. 92
  Polly 92
  Richard M. 92
  Robert Anderson 83
  Sam W. 92
  W. W. 84
Latner, Jno. Thomas 25
  Joseph T. 25
  Julia A. 25
Laurence, Elizabeth L. 6
  John M. 5
  Esther C. 6
Lawrence, James 122
  J. N. 165
  Mrs. L. 114,152,165
  Martha A. 9,162
  M. Rose 66
  Olivia Kate 114
  Sue 152
  Warren 128
  Warren D. 162
  W. D. 9
Lawton, A. L. 135
Lay, Carrie 145
  James 7,144,153
  Jane E. 111
  John 66
  Mary 7
  Sarah E. 181
  W. A. 111

Leahea, Cate 158
Leathers, Asa 177
  Harrison 177
  Susan C. 109
  Wm. G. 109
  Zillah 137
Le Conte, Joseph 182
Lee, Daniel 145
  Elisha 1
  Eliza 130
  Elizabeth J. 38
  Isaac 138
  James 169
  Jane 138
  Jas. F. 75
  Jesse M. 181
  John, Jr. 130
  L. B. 129
  Martha 9
  Mary 145,169
  Sallie R. 135
  W. C. 1,3,10,13,38
  Mrs. W. C. 135
Lendeman, Amanda C. 115
  Francis M. 115
Lenhardt, Lawrence 171
Lenox, W. J. 50
Le Roy, Elizabeth 48
  J. H. 28
  Susan 124
Lesesne, Chancellor 166
  Charles P. 166
Lesley, Andrew D. 177
  David 10
  Elizabeth Rebecca 177
  J. W. 97
  Lou J. 97
  Sarah Margaret 90
  Wm. A. 90
Lester...58
Lewis, Alsey A. 90
  Anthony B. 113
  Caroline C. 72
  Caroline Matilda 12
  Eliza E. 28
  Emalissa 113
  Henry 111
  Jacob 79
  James 90
  Jesse 169
  Jesse P. 139
  J. J. 72
  Joab 1,17
  John 93
  John T. 28
  John W. 1
  Josephine 111
  Julia 134
  Maria E. 169
  Mary 93,153
  Olivia Kate 114
  Phalba 111
  Phalby 1
  Richard 114,123
  Samuel W. 26
  Susan M. 139
  Thos. L. 134
  Vilanty 117
Liddell, George W. 179
  G. W. 95
  John 150
  Julia A. 150
  Mary E. 60
  Sarah C. 179
Liles, Amanda E. 140
  Charles L. 140
  Charles O. 140
  D. A. 37
  David Lewes 140
  Deborah 34
  Frances M. 140
  Jane 37
  Jesse J. 140

Liles, Jesse J. 140
  John D. 140
  Louisa 101
  Mary Jane Frances 140
  Nany 172
  Rinda 141
  Salina 97
  Samuel 101
  Wm. Henry 140
Lindsay, J. O. 137
Lindsey, Carrie 176
  P. N. 176
Lingo, A. J. 62
Lipp, Brack 150
  Florence 150
  Josephine 150
Littleton, Elizabeth W. 95
  John L. 95
Lively, Eliza 46
  Mark 46
Livingston, Clara 39
  J. W. 39,156
  Sallie 156
Lacke, W. H. 166
Loden, Q. Victoria 182
Logan...136
Lonas, John L. 25
  Maria L. 25
Long, Andrew 133
  Callie P. 69
  Elizabeth 48
  I. J. 69
  Jemima 68
  John 22
  Salina 141
  Susan 40
  Thomas D. 40
  Wm. Boyd 68
Looney, Martin 77
  Miriam 77
Looper, Anderson 125
  Daniel 117
  Jeremiah 93
  Jeremiah, Sr. 81,93
  Joseph 117
  Mary 81
  Polly 117
  Samuel 90
  Thomas 31,71,85
Loquet, C. 60
Lorton, John S. 39
Love, Ann 50
  John B. 25
  Maria L. 25
Loveless, James 15
  Sarah 15
Lovinggood, Samuel 144
Lovingood, Mary 7
  Samuel 7,23
Lowery, Arminda 62
  B. C. 126
  Kate 126
  Mary E. 106
  Mattie C. 86
  R. Y. H. 86
  William 106
Lowndes, Anna 97
  W. Pinckney 97
Lowry, Frances 48
Lumpkin, Martha L. 141
  Miss N. K. 13
Lumpkins, Frank 154
  Sallie 154
Lusk, E. C. 55
  E. S. 55
  N. B. 51
  R. E. 51
  Rebecca 127
Lyles, Elizabeth 180
  John 156
  John M. 55
  Mary 77

Lyles, Mary E. 55
  Matilda 90
  William 90
Lynch, Calvin 93
  C. F. 93
  D. 18
  G. M. 93
  Nathaniel, Sr. 91
  Sallie J. 109
  William J. 93
Lytle, Aleck 77

Mayberry, James 71
  W. 71
Mackey, A. G. 153
Magee, Maret 93
  N. A. 93
  Tilman C. 93,173
Magill, Daniel 67
  Mary C. 67
Madden, E. M. 53
  Louisa M. 19
  Nancy A. 70
  Nancy Ann 149
  Ophelia A. 53
  Thomas E. 149
  Thos. E. 70
Mahathey, Leatha F. 31
  Martin 31
Maher...131
Mahew, Chas. 41
  Mary A. 41
Major, Casander 116
Malone, James 149
Mann, C. D. 159,162,170,
  172,174, 178,183
Manotte, John 154
Mansell, Mary 104
  Matthew 104
Marchbanks, Margaret 16
Marcy, W. L. 20
Maret, A. J. 166
  Benjamin W. 100
  Elias J. 100
  Frederick S. 100
  Handy 174
  Joanna C. 100
  John W. 100
  Lena 174
  Lena E. 97
  Lucinda W. 100
  Sallie M. 166
Marett, Julia 79
  Wm. G. 79
Markey, Thos. 50
Markham, Margaret E. 142
Marshal, J. B. 46
  Vashti 46
Marshall, Richard 5
  Melissa 6
Martin...139
  Alfred 111
  Amanda J. 26
  A. R. 106
  Bird 117
  Caroline 117
  Charlotte 181
  Cynthia 141
  Dickson M. 141
  Edmund 17
  Eliza 130
  Elizabeth 177
  Francis 86
  Francis M. 141
  Harriett M. 141
  J. 148
  J. A. 163
  James L. 156
  James W. 96
  John 67,86,136
  John C. 141

Martin, Joseph T. 137,172
  Lucinda A. 141
  Maggie 136
  Martha 70
  Martha Emma 137
  Mary E. 141
  Robert A. 141
  Sallie E. 106
  Sarah Ann Frances 64
  Sarah M. 172
  Sheilds B. 141
  Thomas C. 70
  Upson 130
  Wm. 64
  W. P. 59
Mashburn, Laura J. 140
  L. B. 131
Mason, Annie 125
  Benjamin 93
  Burnetta 27
  Charles W. 140
  Elias 93
  Ezekiel 93
  Fanny 93
  Susan 79,135,156
Massey, D. M. H. 93
  Enoch 15
  James 31
  Lucinda 93
Masters, Elizabeth 54
  J. D. 90
  Sarah Margaret 90
Matheson, Betsy 127
  Robert 127
Mattison, Miss F. A. 29
Mattock, B. S. 58
Maulden, Narcissa 124
  R. N. 99
  Scarber 124
  T. B. 179
Mauldin, B. F. 61,78
  Miss C. A. 79
  Deborah R. 76
  Elizabeth 12
  Fannie E. 112
  Godfrey 104
  James 104,180
  J. G. 174
  Joab 76,104
  John G. 1
  Joseph Henry 12
  Lucettie 71
  Lucinda E. 8
  Mabry 117
  Martha Jane 1
  Milton 85
  Nancy 106
  Samuel 93
  T. B. 11,12,73,84,90,
  102,112
  Vardry 117
Maw, Malinda B. 33
  Robert E. 33
Maxwell...161
  Annie Sloan 151
  Baylis James 23
  Elizabeth 23
  G. Keels 99
  Mrs. G. L. 121
  J. H. 82
  John 23,122,123,151
  Julia 136
  Julia Susannah 136
  Mary 82
  Mary F. 99
  Samuel 136
  Samuel E. 136
  S. E. 70
  Miss S. M. 121
  Susan J. 70
May, Anthony 128

Maybin, Wm. 38
Mayfeild, Jane 120
  Pierson 120
Mays, Geo. W. 83
  Kate E. 29
  Lucinda 122
  Samuel E. 29
McAdams, James 78
  Nancy 78
McAllister, Arminda 10
  Arminda A. 34
  Charley 159
  David 34
  Elizabeth 17
  Francis 86
  Virginia 159
  William 10
McAulay, Clara 164
  Moses 164
McBryde, T. L. 32,53,79,82
McCall, Mary 149
  Samuel 97
McCallis, Mena 97
McCarey, Mrs. James 142
McCarley, Mary A. 141
  Mary Elizabeth 142
  T. A. 127
  W. C. 141
McCarroll, Miss E. A. 31
McCarty, Frasier 106
McCay, Jerusha A. 11
  Mary 95
  R. Catherine 13
  Wm. B. 13
McClanahan, B. Franklin 120
  Elizabeth 104
  George W. 120
McClellan, Henry 124
  Mary 124
McClendall, Britton 11
McClure, Anna T. 156
  Belle 106
McCorkle, Augustie M. 135
  James T. 135,144
  Mamie Augusta 144
McCoy, Mary 138
  Sarah 60
  W. A. 138
McCrackin, Arthur 48
  Frances 48
  Nora 179
  Sarah 101
  William 101,102
McCrary, Alfred 6
  Mary Ann 176
  Rebecca 6
McCulley, Amanda J. 26
  Mrs. E. 26
  S. 26
McDaniel, Calvin 94
  J. C. 42
  Levi H. 59
  Susan D. 42
McDavid, Allen 87
  Annie 87
McDearman, James 41
McDonald, Lou 165
  Lucy 106
  W. A. 165
McDow, Amanda 99
  John 99
  Mary 100
  Sidney 70
McDuffie, George 33
  Mary S. 33
McDunnie, Rachel 12
  Wm. 12
McEachern, Mary 58
McElroy, Eliza J. 33,103
  J. M. 103
McFall, Andrew N. 83
  Anna 47

McFall, John 15
  Julia E. 47
  Mattie C. 113
  Narcissa C. 15
  Rachel 29
  S. R. 29,47
McFetridge, Ferraby 175
McGanghey...104,105
McGee, Clara 164
  Mike 175
McGilvary, A. B. 56
  A. F. 87
McGowan...49
McGowan, S. 131,133
McGrady, John 60
McGraw, John 32
McGregor, Mrs. E. J. 125
  J. L. 164
  Minnie L. 165
McGuffin, A. B. 145
  Andrew 114
  Adrew W. 3,4,13,27,51,
  53,54,62,76,104,145,
  149,155,165,166,177
  Anner 145
  Burnetta 27
  Carolina 10
  E. E. 76
  James 27
  John H. 76
  L. J. 76
  Mrs. L. J. 97
  Martha 27
  Sallie 114
  Wm. S. 76
McIver, Alexander M. 9
McJunkin, Barbara 175
  Joseph A. 36
  C. M. 175
  W. T. 21
McKay, Harriet 106
McKee, Emily E. 58
  James A. 58
McKieman, Francis 73
McKinlay, Samuel Peter 95
McKinney, Amanda E. 89
  David 37
  D. M. 111
  Francis 51
  George W. 51
  James 28,51
  James D. 51
  J. H. 97
  J. H. C. 98,101
  John 51
  Josephine L. 98
  Mary 28,40,118
  Mary F. 37
  Mary Margaret 26
  Nancy 51
  Nancy Jr. 51
  Miss N. C. K. 113
  Preston 51
  Preston, Jr. 51
  Rebecca 111
  Sarah 51
  Thomas 40
  T. N. 113
  William 51
  Wilson 20
McLand Alice 174
McLaughlin, George 183
McLees, Hugh 145
McLin, Laura E. 137
McMahan, Caroline 112
  Henry 158
  Jesse 112
  Lina A. 158
  Sallie 164
  W. L. 182
McMasters, Ophelia L. 52
McMillan...67

McNeville, James 42
  Margaret 42
McPhail, C. M. 137
  Mary E. 137
McSwain, W. A. 82
McWhorter, David 126
  Miss E. A. 92
  Isaac 126
  James M. 92
  Jane 1,136
  J. F. 136
  John 27,37,126
  Laura J. 146
  Louisa M. 138
  Louise 138
  Lou J. 97
  Lucinda 32
  Mary 126
  Mary A. 87
  Matilda N. 71
  Moses 126
  Nancy 167
  Rachel W. 2
  Samuel 56
  Sam'l Y. 2
  Sarah 37
  Sarah A. 32
  Sarah L. 126
  Temperance 37
  W. A. 138,146
  William 113
  Wm. W. 10,14,15,25,29,
  32,33,37,55,58,68,83,
  91,97,118,124,126,154,
  156,167,175
McWilliams, Archibald 58
Meek, A. B. 97
Megee, Benjamin 87
Melton, Daniel 73
  Mary H. 18
  Samuel 82
  Samuel W. 17
Merck, Jas. 40
Meredith, Mary 66
Meritt, E. M. 130
Messer, Mattie E. 161
Meyer, Miss E. D. 118
Michalus, Christian 171
Mickler, Hassie M. 127
  J. P. 127
Midyett, B. S. 21
Miles, Bettie 182
  Eliza 32
  F. A. 32
  W. A. 182
Milford, John 136
  Miriam 156
Millan, D. J. 162
Miller, Anna E. 158
  Belinda F. 90
  C. W. 62
  Delilah C. 54
  Elihu F. 90
  Elizabeth Ann 33
  Florence 44
  George 67
  Georgie Ann 115
  H. 44
  Hugh 71
  J. A. 158
  James 54
  James R. 33
  Jane 9
  J. C. P. J. 98
  J. H. 178
  J. L. 183
  John 135
  John F. 132
  John W. 176
  Julia M. 97
  Malinda 132
  Mary 95

Miller, Morris 115
  Narcissa E. 176
  Sallie C. 78
  Sarah 62
  Sarah C. 95
  Susan 135
  Thos. 99
  Tilman 95
  T. S. 44,129
  William Y. 78
Millford, Anna M. 108
  W. J. 108
Milwee, Martha J. 46
Mimmis, J. R. 67
Minnegrode...105
Mingers, John 120
  Milly Ann 120
Minton, John 166
  Malica 23
  T. A. 101
  Z. 23
Mitchell...63
  C. E. O. 175
  John 71
  Martha 106
  Mary E. 175
  M. F. 105
  Newton 106
Mitchum, Jessie 127
Monroe, James 153
Monteeth, Galloway 36
Montgomery, Alexander 57
  Bob 88
  Mary Ann 94
  Thomas 63
Mood...84
Moods, F. A. 75
Moody, Alcie M. 158
  Amanda 23
  A. V. 158
  Bennett 23,84,178,181
  B. J. 158
  Daniel Van Buren 158
  Elizabeth H. 95
  Emily 99
  F. L. 158
  Franklin L. 181
  James 76
  Joel 35
  John M. 103,181
  John R. 158
  Joseph 55
  Martha 23
  Martha Jane 127
  Martha Louisa 35
  Martin 158
  Mary A. 181
  Rachel 35
  Rhoda 76
  Sarah 84,106
  Sarah Harriet 35
  W. F. 99
  Wm. 55
Moor, J. 13
  N. K. 13
Moore...23,65,73,149
  A. B. 20
  B. Frank 164
  Dora 180
  Eli, Jr. 54
  Emily 54
  Eugenia 145
  Evaline 124
  James 64,131
  James A. 69
  Jane 118
  John A. 180
  John B. 179
  Jordan 180
  Joseph 52,168
  Julia 168
  Malinda A. 75
  Margaret 131

Moore, Marion R. 179
  Martha 165
  Mary 64
  Nymay 6
  P. 66
  R. A. 145
  Rachel 88
  Rebecca J. 52
  Sarah 37
  Sarah J. 69
  Warren D. 124
  Willie F. 164
Moorehead, Alex. 43
  Henry 1
  Ira 120
  Susan 120
Morgan, Cynthia A. 136
  F. M. 179
  Harrison 136
  H. J. 164
  James A. 114
  James R. 144
  Josephine 144
  Miss M. A. 98
  Malissa 86
  Mary A. 41
  Mary Emmaline 111
  Nancy A. 114
  Narcissa 174
  R. F. 111
  Robert F. 86
  Sarah 75,79
  Stephen Clayton 86
  Susan 2
  Thomas D. 27
  William 79
Morris, Miss Earnest 139
  M. 154
  R. M. 139
  S. L. 128,134,145,154,
    155,157,166
Morrison, Robt. 53
Morse, Albert A. 45,76
  Ophelia 69
Morton, Allice 176
  C. B. 176
  Wm. M. 5,76
Moseley, Sam'l 12
Mosely, B. B. 35
  Kate E. 29
  Lucy 35
  Martha 11
  Sarah A. 35
Moss, Sarah Caroline 6
  Alexander H. 59
  Arretha S. 97
  Carrie 98
  Eddie 76
  Eliza 92
  J. Bayliss 6
  Jennie 73
  Margaret 11
  Martin 11,98
  Miss M. E. 76
  Wm. Warren 97
  Wilson 73
Mulcke, John 145
  Katie 145
Mulkey, Etta 110,174
  Jesse 172
  J. N. 174
  John H. 100
  Joseph 183
  Mary 110
  Sarah F. 100
Mull, Thomas 28
Mulleken, Jas. 15
  Malinda 15
Muller, L. 159
  Louisa 66
Mulligan, Mary 66
  Monroe 66
Mullinix, Elizabeth A. 36

Mullinix, John G. 36
  W. G. 92
  E. G. 53,62
  Elias 68
  Jackson 98
  J. H. 80
  Martha J. 98
  Mary S. 100
  Maveann C. 80
  Rachael 80
  W. 53
  W. G. 5,8,19,22,28,30,
    32,33,35,36,38,40,54,
    63,65,67,70
Murphee, Ann 25
Murphree, Elizabeth 78
  J. M. 37
  John 78
  Mary F. 37
  Susan 51
Murphy, Elizabeth 38
  Ellis 116
  Jane 116
  John E. 87
  Mary 51
  Sarah E. 55
  William 55
  W. J. 38
Murray, J. S. 134
Murry, J. Scott 6,7,8,19,
  23,70,78,121
  Lucy J. 12
Myer, Henry 9
  Mary Ann 9
Myers, Henry 12,14,126
  H. J. 147
  James B. 173
  Jno. 14
  Matilda 12,126
  Mina 160
  Nancy J. 110
  Sarah 173
  Sarah E. 112

Nall, Robert 148
Nally, Catherine 85
  L. F. 85
Nance, F. W. R. 121
Naves, George 45
  Jane 45
Neal, Ella Vashti 156
  Laura J. 146
  Margaret 123
  Mary 110
Neese, J. C. 174
  Lula 174
Netherland, G. M. 143
Netting, James 54
  Catherine 54
Nevilee, J. J. 127
Nevill, Laura 144,145
  Alexander 153,154
  Lula 166
  Miss M. L. 133
  Sarah R. 148
  W. G. 166
  W. J. 136,161
  Wm. G. 168
  Wm. H. 144
  Wm. J. 148,179
Neville, J. J. 128,134,136,
  153
  John C. 47
  Joseph G. 72
  Julia E. 46,47
  Junius J. 137.145
  Lou 169
  Lula 180
  Nannie L. 72
  Sallie R. 40
  Virginia 183
  W. J. 169
  Wm. G. 183

Neville, Wm. J. 40
Newell, J. A. 114
  Sallie 114
Newton, George M. 54
  Jerusha A. 11
  Nathan 11
Nichols, Charity 27
  John 27
Nicholson, Baylis 63
  Elizabeth 63
  Evan 15,24
  Evan J. 95
  Jane 15
  Jemima 24
  J. W. 111
  Mary M. 181
  Mattie O. 176
  Milton W. W. 147
  Roxana 167
  Susan 95
  William 15
Niebuhs, Charles H. 177
Nimmons, Amanda 155
  Jane E. 111
  Jas. E. H. 111
  Phalba 111
  Safonsba 90
  Thomas 155
Nix, E. J. 52
  Elizabeth 1
  Harriet 52
  Thomas 1
Nixon, Elizabeth 76
  Letitia L. 61
  Wm. H. 76
Norman, Harriet 123
  Henry 123
  Joshua 46
  Nancy 70
Norris, A. 124
  A. E. 156
  A. M. 137
  A. O. 11
  Miss D. 34
  Edward 95
  Eugenia 171
  John James 3
  Julia E. 156
  Lucy J. 11
  Mary 86
  R. E. 171
  William 86
North, Mrs. John L. 48
Norton, Belzona 152
  B. P. 29
  David 152
  J. J. 157
  Laura 147
  Lizzie 157
  Martha 15
  Miles M. 13
Nuckolls, David 69

Oakley, Beatie 130
  Elizabeth 130
  Nancy 130
O'Briant, Hannah A. 12
  James C. 12
  Sarah I. 6
O'Brien...8
O'Connell, J. J. 43
Odell, Abner 98,106
  Arta Omega 106,107
  Mary S. 106
Odom, Zion 51
O'Donnell, Bartley 73
Oliver, Miss M. A. A. 25
Oneal, Elizabeth 10
O'Neal, Agnes 53
  Elizabeth 9,50
  Ransom 50
  Ransom A. 10
  Sarah Susannah 9

O;Neal, Wm. Franklin 50
O'Neall, Joel T. 87
  Mary A. 87
  Mary Ann 13
  William Ross 13
Orr...134
  Alexander 52
  Cornelia 32
  Eliza Foster 13
  J. A. 32
  James L. 13
  J. E. 158
  Mary J. 13
  Saphronia 52
Osborne, L. A. 105
  Turner, Jr. 146
Ostendorff, J. Henry 150
  May 150
Overby, B. H. 75
Owen, John 170
  Martha 70
Owens, Anna 156
  Elijah 30
  Elizabeth 78
  Jane 26
  John 80
  J. M. 93
  Lucinda 30
  Nancy 130
  Parmelia A. 93
  Samuel H. 26
  S. H. 156
  Thomas 66
  William 66

Pace, Burrell 123
  Hannah 123
Palmer...8
  Amanda Slaughter 175
  Cornelius 62
  Helena 23
  James 175
  J. Baylis 175
  Jesse 175
  John 175
  J. Preston 175
  Mary A. 171
  Mary S. 126
  N. H. 44
  Rhoda 62
  W. 175
Parker...121
  James 170
  J. M. 148
  Sophia 170
  Tecoa 134
  Thomas O. 147
  W. F. 147,154
  W. P. 134
Parrott, J. C. 98
  Licena E. 98
Parsons, Azina M. 50
  C. C. 111
  F. V. G. 44
  J. C. C. 103
  Mollie E. 111
  Phoebe 44
  Sam'l A. A. 50
  W. J. 17,26,43,44,50,
    61,68
  Wm. J. 61
Passmore, Dinah 83
  Jane 83
  William 83
Patterson, Anna 106
  Miss C. C. 125
  John 152
  John S. 43,176
  Mary Ann 176
  Susan 43,152
  Thomas 155
  Thomas E. 154
  W. T. 155

Payne, Hester Ann 35
  John B. 35
  Lucretia 39
Pearce, Jefferson 9
  Sarah 39
Pearson, Arminda 90
  Wm. F. 109
Pegg, Eliza 28
  James H. 28
  Mary A. 70
Pelfree, Joseph 33
  Martha A. 33
Peltier, William 30
Pendleton, M. C. 77
Pendley, Andrew J. 89
  Lucinda M. C. 89
  Rosanna Abi 89
Penny, Henry H. 98
  H. H. 113
  Miss M. L. 25
Perkins, Amanda 32
  Hariet 167
  Wm. 32
Perrin...49
  Mary 94
  T. C. 134
Perritt, Burnell 37
  Daniel 149
  Eleanor 37
  Elizabeth Ann 149
  Lerina 149
  Melissa 149
  William T. 37
Perry...115,135
  B. F. 55
  C. C. 97
  Clark D. 109
  Elizabeth 121
  Elmina 74
  Emily E. 58
  Ephraim 51
  James W. 183
  L. A. 158
  Lemuel 141
  Margaret M. 183
  Martha 51
  Mena 97
  N. J. F. 39,121
  Samuel 51
  Susan 40
Peterson, J. F. 32
Petit, Jane E. 92
  Jas. E. 92
Petrie, John A. 71
Petty, Stephen 65
Phillips, Ada A. 170
  Anna Bolin 180
  Berry 180
  Caroline 117
  Charles 177
  Elisha 5
  Fannie 156
  George 33
  J. E. 156
  John S. 170
  Jonas, Jr. 26
  J. P. 180
  Levi 97
  Lizzie 75
  Lucy P. 177
  Mahala 26
  Mattie C. 86
  Miss M. T. 154
  Nathan 26
  Peter Berry 180
  Sophia 33
  Willie Lawton 180
Philpot, I. H. 125
Phinney, Carrie F. 160
  James N. 160
Pickens, A. C. 12
  Andrew 77
  Eliza 132

Pickens, Ezekiel 77
  F. W. 73
  Mary J. 12
  Rebecca 73
  Susan J. 70
  T. J. 70
Pickett, John B. 113
  Mattie C. 113
Pieper, F. W. 124
  H. W. 173
  Johannes 58
  Julia A. 173
  Maggie 124
  Wm. Henry 58
Pierce, Frank 166
  G. A. 78
  Mary 110
  S. B. 40
  William 182
  Wm. 28
Pike, Albert 53
Pilgrim, Amanda E. 89
  Eliza 46
  Wm. H. 89
Pilz, Wm. 164
Pinckney, C. C. 179
Pitchford...143
  J. Henry 183
  Lizzie 159
  Lola C. 183
  Margaret 150
  W. 74,75
  Wesley 150,159
Pitts, Anna 172
  Daniel 172
  David 172
  David N. 141
  Emily 172
  G. E. 159
  Harriett 172
  H. M. 131
  Lemuel K. 108
  Lemuel V. 172
  Lula 159
  Matilda 111,172
  Nancy 172
  Nancy S. 108
  Reuben 172
  Salina 141
  Sallie 131
  Sarah Ann 98
  William 125,172
Place, Charles W. 61
Poe, Mellie 74
Pointer, John 152
Polk, James K. 2
Pollard, T. P. 53
  W. W. 53
Pool, Ella 157
  Temperance 73
Poore, Elizabeth 149
  Kennon B. 149
Porter...20
  Basil S. 6
  C. C. 44
  James 63,98
  J. S. 88
  Porter, Malinda 44
  Mary S. 98
  Sarah I. 6
  Wm. 94
Posey, Humphrey 153
Potett, Dorcas 132
Potter, Mrs_ 62
Powell...58
  Alman 27
  Ashley 92
  Decatur 52
  Eugenia 150
  Martha E. 52
  Robt. 32
  Stephen 9

Power, Harriet 53
  James W. 89
  Martha B. 89
Powers, Sarah 167
  Thomas 167
Prather, J. W. 48
  J. Y. 48
  Mary Estelle 48
  P. H. 48
Pratt, G. W. 179
Pressly, E. E. 75
  John S. 87
Preston, John S. 160
  William C. 160
Price, Delia Ann 42
  Delelah 64
  Fannie 81
  Fielding 42
  Garvin S. 172
  James A. 20
  Jeremiah 9
  Keith 172
  Lucretia 78
  Martha 9
  Martha E. 105
  N. 130,136
  Mrs. N. J. 130
Prichet, John 117
  Rachel 117
Prince, James F. C. 92
  Martha F. A. 92
Pringle, J. Maxwell 68
Pritchard, Mrs. E. A. 147
  Lulu 147
Probst, J. F. 182
  Luther 178
Proyor, Samuel 109
  Sarah Ann 109
Puckett, John B. 126
  Mary F. 126
Pullen, Mary 33
Putman, Florence 150
  Hambleton 150
  James 150
  Josephine150
  Mary 147

Quarles, Arta 136
  David 63
  Jackson 65
  Margaret 63
  Richard P. 180
  Sarah Ann 65
Quarterman, J. M. 19
Quillian, J. M. 54
Quitman...53

Rackley, John L. 121
  Melissa 121
  Reddin 121
  Warren 121
  W. Benson 121
Ragland, Amy Amanda 130
Rains, Florence Ella 160
  James 160
  Rinda 141
  Wm. 141
Ramage, Carrie 176
Ramey, Logan 162
  Solomon 162
  Tim 162
Rampey...115
  Elizabeth 178
Ramsay, T. S. 141
Ramsey, Alexander, Sr. 125
  Juluis 181
  Logan 162
  Mary 65
  R. J. 139
  Tim 162
Randolph...120
  C. 74

Raney, Hugh 61
Rankin, Eddie 76
  Edward, 13,114
  Eliza 108
  John 7
  John M. 76
  Mary 114
  Mary M. 29
  Minerva 10
Nathaniel 7
  Sarah 13
  William 10
Ransom, Amanda 135
  George 135
Raredon, Carolina 8
Ray, Ann 21
  F. E. 41
  John T. 41
  W. D. 78
  Wm. 21
Reams, Martha 103
Reauletter, John 136
Reaves, Rebecca 6
  Wiley 1
Redman, Melinda 120
  Richard 120
Reed, C. 41
  J. P. 78
  Julia S. 78
  Thomas 39
Reeder, Annie 168
  A. P. 168
  James H. 106
  Samuel C. 110
Reese, Carrie McC. 174
  Elizabeth 93
  Jeptha 36
  Lewis 120
  Milton 174
Reeves, Malinda 54
Reid, Alfred M. 117
  Carrie 98
  Clayton N. 117
  F. M. 4
  George M. 42
  George T. 131
  Geo. T. 141
  Hugh 9
  Isabella 16
  James T. 98,174
  John H. 2
  Joseph 16,170
  Joseph E. 140
  Joseph Thompson 131
  Lawrence O. 117
  L. J. 131
  Martha 169
  Mary E. 55,140
  Nancy 9
  Oliver C. 117
  Sallie R. 136
  Samuel 121
  Samuel C. 42
  Sarah E. 68
  Susan 2
  Thomas B. 43
  T. L. 160
  Warren 17
  Willie 121
  Wm. 68,170
  Wm. W. 4,85,86
Reynolds, Bettie 174
  Charles 174
  E. C. 176
  Nellie 176
  W. C. 94
Rhodes, Wm. 53
Rice, A. 8,28,54,126,130
  Caroline 8
  Ibzan J. 25
  Isaac 60,111
  Mary 177

Rice, Nannie I. 111
Richards, Eliza 121
  R. T. 121
Richardson, Mary 74
  Mary R. 29
  Matthias B. 118
  Matti J. 118
Richey, D. D. 54
  Emaline 54
  Margaret 63
Richie, Amelia 146
Rickman, Jesse 105
  Jesse 105
  Sarah 105
Rider, Caroline 13
  Nathaniel 70
  Nathany 70
  Roland 98
  Sarah Ann 98
Ridgeway, James A. 64
Ridgley, Thomas H. 91
Ridley, Elizabeth 36
Ried, Caroline D. 87
  James T. 87
  Samuel 87
Rickoff, Mrs. - 161
Rieppe, Catherine H. 159
Rigdon, Sarah 68
Riggins, Andrew R. 85
  Gizzeal 85
Riley...156
  Daniel 25
  John R. 164
  J. R. 133,135,136,137,
  141,152,157,160,166,
  173,176
  Margaret 78
  Nancy Ann 25
Rinley...172
Riordan, Patrick 72
Ripley, Mrs. V. A. 75
Ritchie, John 183
Ritter, Henry D. 164
  Tena M. 164
Rivers, Frank 88
  John 22
Roach, Catharine 66
Roach, Henry 39
  James 160
  Jennie 78
  Sarah 39
  W. M. 66
Roberts...79
  Alexander L. 178
  Gus 72
  Jack 72
  Melvina 117
Robertson, Arretha S. 97
  B. F. 32,178
  D. J. 32
  Eliza E. 28
  Ella 178
  Esther 161
  James 28,161
  Malinda 44
  Toliaer 136
Robins, Abel 61,87
  Able 178
  Arminda 3
  D. P. 39,40,51,52,54,
  62,63,65,68,102,113,123,
  124,178
  Eliza 87
  Levi N. 2,10,13,18,24,
  31,63,78,81,87,88,97,
  98,105,114,117
  Susannah 3
Robinson, Ames 37
  Mrs. E. E. 128
  Elijah 92
  Eliza 93
  Ella 133

Robinson, George E. 58
  George, Jr. 93
  Hardy 93
  Henrietta 92
  James 51,93
  Jane 26
  John 93
  John A. 93
  John W. 42
  Joseph 93
  Nancy 93,116
  Nelly 37
  Michel 41
  Randall 93
  Rebecca 42
  Richard 93
  Sallie R. 58
  Thomas C. 133
  Warren D. 61
  William 53,93
  Willis 149
  W. J. 116
Rochau, C. H. 130
Rochester, Arminda 90
  Cornelia 56
  Elizabeth 108,158
  H. D. 157
  Jas. 90
  Sarah F. 100
  Wm. D. 56
  Wm. T. 108
Rogers, David 37
  Edward 37
  Felix 48
  Frances E. 18
  Hugh 37
  James 37
  John 37
  Leonard 36,47,51,90,92,
  98
  Leonard 84
  Mary 124
  Miss N. A. 92
  Permelia G. 125
  R. 59
  Sarah C. 90
  William 37
  Zachariah 37
Roland, Sue E. 124
Roper, Anerson 86,89
  Anna 85
  Arminda 85
  Charles 61
  Chas. 85
  Disa 179
  Elijah 85
  John T. 170
  Lucinda 61
  Margaret L. 85
  Melinda 7
  Sarah 86,89
  Tyre L. 7
Rose, John 134
  Julianna 134
Ros...134
  A. W. 39,74,78
  George F. 98
  Jesse R. 98
  John 98,129
  Lunsford 98
  Moses 77
  Patrick 41
  Sallie C. 78
Rothell, Argine 139
  Miss. L. C. 139
  Rhoda Ann 54
  Sallie 139
  W. S. 139
Rowland...17
  H. D. 169
  James 3
  James T. 183

Rowland, Kate 169
  Lou 165
  Mary F. 160
  Mary M. 183
  Samuel A. 157
  Wm. 160
Rowlinstone, Ophelia 69
  Peleg 69
Royster...160
Rudler, John 36
Runion, J. M. 32
Runnels, H. G. 30
Rushing, M. R. 67
Rusk, Mary 82
  Rachel W. 2
  Thomas J. 2
  Thomas. J. 21,22
Russell, Jane 140
  J. C. 161
  Malinda 127
  Mattie E. 161
  M. H. 177
  Squire 150
  William S. 4
  W. W. 140
  Miss D. S. 84
Ruston, Jesse L. 18
Rutherford, Essie L. 139
  J. N. 139
  Joseph W. 139
  Rufus 139
Rutledge, Harriet 153
  James H. 153
  Joseph 153
  L. B. 153
  Sarah 153

Sackett...65
Sadler, I. N. 51
  James W. 174
  Maggie E. 174
Sage, J. C. 145
  Sue P. 145
Salmon, H. M. 93
  Ward 93
Samples, John 114
  Judith 114
Sanders, Amanda 155
  Arabella C. 105
  Betsey 172
  Elijah 158
  Elizabeth 10,38,100,
  118
  Francis C. 118
  Hannah 106
  James 118
  James O. 130
  Jane 90
  J. B. 20,66,73,85,87,
  102,112,122,128,141,
  147,170,172,174
  J. M. 176
  Jo Berry 181
  John 154
  John B. 167
  John W. 118
  Joseph Orr 118
  K. R. 109
  Lena 174
  Marcus 105
  Margaret 118
  Martha 106
  Martha J. 106
  Martha Jane 118
  Mary 170
  Milton 176
  Rachel 12
  Sallie 167
  Sarah 101
  Sarah L. 112
  Squire 10
  Vina 154

Sanders, W. B. 159
    Wm. Sr. 38
    William 118
    W. W. 134
Sanderson, Lillie 162
Sandford, Rhoda 62
Sargent, A. B. 52
    Elizabeth 104
    Sarah 52
Satterfield, A. B. 85
    Anna 85
    Anne 36
    Arminda 85
    Sarah 68
Sawyer, Ellen 172
Schroder, Bertha H. 173
    Edward 161
    Fritz 138
    J. B. J. W. 135
    Henry B. 167
    Jacob 161,163,164,165
    Julia A. 163
    Julia S. 155
    Maggie E. 174
Schumann, John 121
Schumpert, Mrs. R. N. 56
Sciley, Thomas 51
Scleton, Bailus 86
    Sarah 86
Scoggins, Mary A. 140
    W. B. 140
Scott, Christopher 7
    Mary J. 178
    Sue 49
Scruggs...181
    Anna 150
    Columbus 147
    Thomas 150
Seaborn...146
    Annie 125
    George 166
    Hannah 166
    James 125,176
    Mollie 34
    W. C. 180,183
Seawright, Robert 112
Seeba, Mary M. 182
Senn, James 93
Sevell, L. D. 146
Shackelford, Bettie 174
Shanklin, Ann E. 66
    Eley Walker 132
    J. A. 66
    J. L. 113,122,132,162
    Joseph Doyle 122
    Julia D. 122
    Julia F. 113
    J. V. 66
    Louis Denby 162
Shanahon, Miss J. E. 149
Shannon...159
Sharp, Annie 87
    Francis F. 25
    J. J. 76
    John 8,29,41,76,100,171
    Matilda C. 25
    M. E. 76
    Ovaline C. 171
    Van Buren A. 87
    William De Witt 25
    W. K. 172
Sharpe, Elam 163
    Geor. W. 20
    Peter 75
    V. A. 80,87,90,92
Shaw, James 70
    J. W. 45
Shealer, Joseph R. 10
    Rebecca 10
Shearley, John 148
    Susan 148
Shearman, A. F. 60
    Mary E. 60

Shed, Miss C. 92
    Emily 54
    Joel 12
    Rebecca 12
    Rhoda 76
Shehane, C. F. R. 19
Sheldon, Amanda 99
    John D. 160
    Lizzie 160
    Mary F. 99
Shelor, Alex. 49
    Annie C. 138
    Joe W. 176
    Joseph W. 169
    J. W. 133,138
    Lizzie 176
    Lou 169
    M. J. 138
    Miss N. R. 108
    R. W. 136
    Sallie R. 136
    Sue 49
    Thomas R. 137
    W. R. 116
Sheriff, Nathan 158,159
Sherman, Mary 39
Shields, J. A. 19
Shippard...78
Shoultz, Israel 20
Shrum, Elvira G. 75
Shrum, Jacob 75
Shuneman, Christian 136
Sibley, Amory 2
Sickles...101
Siebern, Frances 12
    Henning 12
Simkins, J. Eldred 31
Simmons, David 161
    David A. 161
    Elizabeth 34
    Isham 39
    Jordan 52
    Maggie G. 158
    Martha 52,126
    Nathan 64
    Samuel 64
    James 140
Simpson, Elizabeth 68
    Frances C. 111
    Francis M. 111
Sims, Andrew C. 57
    Bertie 159
    Elizabeth S. 57
    Joseph M. 159
Singleton, John W. 85
    Mary Joannah 85
    Nancy 76
    S. A. 85
    W. B. 36,70,72,89,90,
    105,111
Sisk...136
    Cordelia 147
    E. L. 135,143,145,147,
    150,156
    S. 37
Siskie, Cate 158
    Mitchell 158
Sitton, C. J. 80
Edward 80
    F. L. 157
    J. B. 80
    John B. 140
Skates, Matthew 103
Skinner, Henry M. 175,176
    Mattie O. 176
Sledger, Lucinda 175
Sligh, Mrs. C. M. 164
    David 165
    H. (Houck) O. 149
    J. A. 181
    J. H. 135,149
    Sallie R. 135

Sligh, Susanna K. 165
Sloan, A. J. 19
    Amanda 98
    Amanda C. 125,126
    Annie 151
    Benj. 151
    B. F. Sr. 105
    David U. 32
    Eliza 92
    Emily 19
    Essie M. 45,65
    James 118
    James M. 180,181
    Jas. M. 109
    J. B. E. 34
    Jimmie 118,119
    John N. 109
    John S. 98
    John T. 45,167,178
    J. T. 65
    Julia 32
    Mary M. 159
    Mollie 34
    R. E. 121
    Sallie 118
    Sallie J. 109
    Sallie Jane 154
    Sep 180
    Septima 145
    Septima A. 180,181
    S. G. 159
    Theodore B. 109
    Thomas M. 4
    Thos J. 57
    T. J. 92
    William D. 106
    Wm. D. 108,109
Sluter, Wm. C. 180
Small, D. A. 170
    John A. 170
    Kate 137
    Matilda 51
Smart, J. C. 180
    R. D. 183
Smeltzer...142
    J. P. 133,134,154,163,
    164,173,174,178,182
Smith, A. Coke 133,137
    Adaline 117
    Alvin 9
    Armelia 74
    Anna Gertrude 161
    Arminda 4
    Artemissa 87
    Augustie M. 135
    Barnet 108
    Calvin 9
    Charles 156
    Celia 64
    C. McKendree 94
    D. A. 137,144
    Daniel S. 116
    Eliza 103
    Elizabeth 10,48,61
    Elizabeth M. 161
    Elizabeth S. 57
    Elva 135
    Fletcher 26,88,97,98,
    104,105,112,123,125,
    132,133,139,145,146,
    157,164,170,178
    G. W. A. 1
    Harvey 117
    Henry 4
    Jacob 41
    J. Allen 175
    James 13
    James D. 33
    Jas. 48
    Jemima 68
    Jerry 64
    J. M. 70

Smith, Joanna 12
  Job. F. 79
  John 12,13,46,103
  John C. 116
  John J. 161,170
  John M. 87
  John R. 86
  Julia E. 156
  Kate 137
  Lizzie 159
  Lizzie Ann 103
  M. Adaline 79
  Mamie Augusta 144
  Maria E. 169
  Martha 175
  Martha A. 54
  Martha Jane 1
  Mary 170
  Mary A. 140
  Mary D. 58
  Mary E. 33
  Mattie 183
  M. T. 103
  Nathan 77
  Oayk C. 159
  Persifer F. 40
  Rebecca 12
  Richard S. 140
  Sallie 135,156
  Sarah 40,41,52,86
  Sarah I. 76
  Sidney B. 160
  Smallwood 41
  Sophia 41
  Susan 86,133
  Thos. 58
  Valentina 13
  Vilenda 120
  Wash. 152
  Washington 138
  W. G. 135,144,169
  W. Joel 156
  Wm. Taylor 33
  Zephaniah 152
Smithson, D. E. 52
Smyer, Jacob 36
Snead, Amanda 98
  Archie L. 125,126
  Benjamin H. 125,126
  Martha B. 125
  Parthenia 153
  Phillip 126
  Samuel 126
  Wm. 126
  Wm. B. 125,126
Snipes, Mary 137
  Robt. M. 120
Snow, Fountain 22
Snyder, John Ludwig 81
Somervile, Elizabeth
  Fitzgerald 50
  M. C. 50
  Wm. G. 50
Sondley, Richard 33
Sonntag, Harriet Caroline
  178
Sosebee, Jane 55
  John 30
Southerland, Amos L. 21
  Esther 7
  Pascal 7
  William 56
Southwick, Patsy 92
  T. H. 92
Spalding...157
Spann, H. R. 40
Sparks, Sue 65
Spearman, J. W. 171
Spears...99
  C. H. 90,100
Spencer, Amanda 56
  Emily 48

Spencer, James M. 56
  Robert 48
Spoonogle, J. Louis 155
  Mary 155
Stadtler, Malinda Carver
  63
  Martin 63
Stalnaker, Louis T. 178
Stancil, Calvin H. 94
  Nancy Ann 94
Standredge, Isabella 175
Standridge, Oliver S. 139
Stanley, Jennie 78
  W. B. 78
Stansell, E. G. Jr. 86
  Elmina 86
Starke...67
  Lamar 177
Starritt, V. Rose 51
Steele, Anna 156
  liza J. 33,103
  Elizabeth 142,143
  Esther 6,12
  James 6
  John R. 156
  Joseph G. 125
  J. Thomas 79
  Laura A. 79
  Mrs. M. 173
  M. Agnes 118
  Margaret 42,123
  R. E. 114
  Robert A. 42
  Robert E. 103
  Robert M. 183
  Robt. Jr. 33
  Sarah Antoinette 35
  S. Jennie 83
  S. Mattie 125
  Thomas J. 35
  W. D. 4,6,11,12,13
  William 106,126,183
  Wm. D. 42
Stegall, Mary Ann 94
  William 94
Stewart...126
  Adaline 93
  Alice 174
  Canba 105
  David A. 128
  E. C. 103
  Eliza 77
  Fannie 81
  G. B. 174
  George W. 93
  Gizzeal 85
  Isaac 81
  John 94
  Licena E. 98
  Margaret L. 85
  Mollie E. 111
  Namoi L. 155
  R. A. 111
  Robert 105
  Robt. Jr. 25
  R. T. 155
  Samuel D. 103
  S. Jane 128
  Susan 94
  Watson 98
Stephens, A. B. 120
  J. B. 60
  John B. 148
  Sarah 60
  Sally L. 148
Stevens, G. B. 175
  Joanna 12
  Salley D. 175
  Samuel 12
Steward, Josephine 111
Stillman...32
Stillwell, Wm. 41

Stilwell, Tabitha 18
Stoddard, Wm. 80
Stokes...115
  J. L. 148,161
Stone, Anna 174
  Athalenda 113
  Callaway 136
  Elizabeth 87
  Isaac 87
  J. H. 158,183
  Maggie 136
  Susan 94,95
Stovall...87
Stow, Sallie E. 14
Stowers, F. G. 99
  Francis Gaines 101
Stratton, W. H. 114
Stribling, Anna 128
  Carrie 98
  David S. 101,181
  George T. 167
  Hanpton 154
  Hattie 167
  J. C. 109
  Jesse 11
  Jesse W. 169
  J. W. 134
  Lizzie 158
  Lou, W. 91,96
  Mrs. L. W. 179
  Mary 11
  Mary Eliza 89
  Mary D. 110
  M. S. 116,128,182
  Miss R. E. 116
  Robert 117
  Mrs. R. P. 148
  R. R. 91
  R. Styles 141
  S. P. 154
  S. Y. 149
  Thomas M. 146
  Thos. M. 110
  Virginia E. 109
  W. H. 182
  W. J. 157,182
  Wm. H. 89,98
  Wm. J. 147
Strickland, Abraham 60,67
  James 60
  W. H. 133
  Strong...156
  A. B. 172
  H. 178,182
  Hugh 150,167,171
Strother...55
  Hassie M. 127
  William H. 127
Stuart, Elizabeth 88
Stubblefield, Milton 40
Stuber, Madison 82
Stuckey, D. Ladson 72
Suggs, Jess 7
  Lotty 7
  Robert 128
Sullivan...115
  Abbie M. 133
  A. P. 76
  D. B. 69
  Miss E. A. 89
  Elizabeth 69
  James 99
  James H. 120
  J. F. 128
  J. H. 97,105,112
  John F. 133
  Mary 99
  Minrod 169
  N. 98
  Nancy 153
  Mimrod 6,7,33,130,138,
  140,155,162,164,175

Summer, Wm. 135
Summerell, Earnest 139
  Elisha 139
Suttles, Hattie 172
  John 129
  Mattie A. 54
  W. J. 54,139
Sutton, Jeremiah 26
  Sarah 26
Swafford, Arta 136
  Riley 136
Swift, Amanda F. 28
Swiney, John 43
  Sarah 43
Swords, Amelia 74
  C. A. 74
  John S. 29
  Rebecca 97
Symmes, Nettie 112
  Whitner 112

Tabor, Narcissa P. 95
  W. M. V. A. 95
Taliaferro, Caroline 53
  Charles P. 53
Tannery, Eliza 167
  Harris M. 156
  Melissa 32
  Pinckney 167
  W. K. 32
Tarrar, Mrs. A. 4
Tate, John 120
  Vilenda 120
Tatham, J. F. 98
  Margaret A. 98
  Sallie A. 98
  W. C. 98
Taylor, A. 155,162
  Abner C. 44
  Abraham 102
  Agnes 174
  Amos E. 152
  Belzona 152
  David S. 197
  Frank J. 164
  Isham W. 15
  John F. 174
  Josephine 103
  Lina A. 158
  Madison 103
  Narcissa C. 15
  Sallie 164
  Sarah 52
  Susan M. 102
  Wm. 44
Teague, John 73
  Miss M. E. 97
  Temperance 73
Telford, Elizabeth 52
Templeton, Addie 89
  D. C. 89
  Miss E. C. 103
  M. A. M. 6
  W. A. 6
Terrel, John C. 82
Terrell, Aaron 84
  Allen 180
  J. Clark 11
  Lucy A. 104
  M. Allen 104
  Melissa 11
Teril, Anna 181
Terry, Carrie E. 26
  John McDowell 26
  J. Wesley 26
  Reuben L. 29
Thackston, John S. 95
  Mary 95
Thode, John J. 183
  Mattie 183
Thomas, A. G. 176
  Anna 126
  James 156

Thomas, James, Jr. 156
  J. B. 36
Thomason, Bartlett 92
  Alice A. 70
  A. W. 124,156
  Cornelia 12
  Dennis 44
  Edgar 156,157
  Elizabeth 9,181
  Elizabeth J. 38
  Fleming 9
  G. McD. 109
  Henry G. 109
  John W. F. 70
  J. W. F. 38
  Lilly 124
  Lizzie R. 182
  Margaret 181
  Robert A. 51,182
  Rob't. A. 100
  Sarah 22
  Sarah F. 44
  V. Rose 51
  Waddy 12
  H. H. 34
  M. 7
  Mary L. 7
Thrasher, Cornelia 174
  Mary 174
  Wm. 174
Thrift, J. W. 105
  Sarah 105
Thruber, F. H. 19
  Matilda A. 19
Thurston, Mrs. Edward 48
  James M. 80
  Maria C. 80
Thwing, Edward F. 83
Tiedeman, Fred 130
Tiel, J. 69
Tillinghast, R. L. 36
Tillman, John 83
Tisher, Chesley A. 66
  Lettyann 66
Todd, Amanda 57
  Blanche 112
  Carlile 76
  Cater 142
  George 57
  H. Cater 112
  James 142,143
  Mrs. James 142
  James Buchanon 57
  Jane 76
  John 142
  Lela 142,143
  Mattie 109
  Thomas 142
  Wm. 142
Togno, Joseph 56
Tolbert, William K. 120
Tolleson, Noah 135
  Sallie 135
Tompkins, Sarah 174
Toney, Wm. 28
Toombs, Robert 176
Torre, A. Della 45
Towbridge, J. W. 180
Towers, Leonard 95
Townsend, E. D. 101
Tradewell, James D. 157
Tranum, George 95
Trapp, John 22
Traynum, John P. 54
  Martha A. 54
Tribble, Emma E. 133
  J. L. 133
Trimmier, Mary L. 7
  T. G. 7
Trinchard, John B. 52
Tripp, Piety 120
  Richard H. 120
Trotter, Henry 39

Trowell, John H. 61
True, E. H. 135
  Miss R. M. 135
Tuck-A-Lixtah (Indian) 37
Tucker, Robert 86
  Tilghman 63
Turnbull, James 154
  J. Anna 48
Turner...17,128
  Benson 130
  D. McNeil 94,121
  D. McNeil, Jr. 129
  James D. 162
  J. C. C. 137
  Mary E. 137
  Mary J. 93
  Pick 149
  Richard 108
  Sally 108
  T. O. 180

Ubernickel...133
Uedard...74

Van de Graeff, Cormelia 32
  W. J. 32
Vandiver, Belle 30
Vandivier, H. S. 66
  M. Rose 66
Vandiviere, J. S. 130,151
  Minnie 151
  Rose 151
Van Rensalaer, Maria 72
Van Wyck, Augustus 105
  Leila G. 105
  Lillie 113
Vanzant, Amanda Jane 6
  Geo. Thomas 6
  George W. 66
  G. W. 66
  Harriet 6
  Jeptha 6
  Lavina Elizabeth 6
  Mary C. 66
  Robert William 6
  William 6
Vaughn, Joel 34
  Sarah A. 34
  William 24
Verner, E. P. 32,64,65,77,
  79,105,150
  John 2
  John S. 153,177
  Rebecca 2,10
  W. H. 130
Vick, Davidson 73
Vincen, David 8
  Margarett 8
Vinson, Viney E. 76
Visage, Elizabeth 108
Vissage, J. W. 139
Van Eitzen, D. 11
  Margaret 11

Wade...19
  Hampton 123
  Nancy 25
  Sallie 154
  Samuel 123
Wagner, Sarah Ella 78
  Theodore D. 148
  Theodore Dehon 78
Wakefield, Celestina 54
Walden, Lucinda 108
Wales, S. A. 50
Waldrupe, James 102
  Mary 102
Walker...14,37
  James 74
  Jane 74
  Jas. 74
  Jno. 68
  John 74

Walker, John W. 115
  Mary J. 115
  Mondane C. 162
Wall...14
  Burrel/Burrell, 48,52,
    54,75,90,92,136,137
  James 11
  Martha 11
  Martha L. 68
Wallace, Daniel 65
  Wilson 4
Walsh, James F. 162
  Wm. 125
Walsingham, John G. 52
Walt, Jeannett 156
  John T. 156
Walters, Anna M. 108
  W. E. 42,99,106
  Wm. 53
  Wm. E. 108
Ward, Amanda 74
  Daniel A. 76
  Harriet Mahala 104
  James 74
  J. L. 183
  Martha S. 76
Wardlow...131
Warley, Jacob 78
  Sophia 69
  Sarah Ella 78
Warren, William 131
Watkins, Jane 83
  Jesse 88
  John 88
  Joseph 83
  Martha A. 33
  Mary 147
  Roland 147
Watson, A. P. 70
  Daniel 149
  Elizabeth 149
  James 149
  John Overton 56
  Lucinda 61
  Martha 149
  Richard 56
  Sarah 86,89
Watt, Rebecca 42
Wauls, David 162
Weatherford, Jesse 4
Weatherly, T. C. 129
Webb, Charles A. 173
  E. F. 19
  Esther C. 6
  Kate 69
  T. J. 19
  Wm. E. 6
Webster, Daniel 34
  John 9
  Margaret 9
Welborn, Francis,(Miss) 59
  H. 59
  W. E. 59
  Wilkes 35
Welch, Lena 174
Weldon, Elizabeth 171
Wellborn, Joel 43
  Martha 43
Wells, R. N. 177
Wendelkin, Maggie 124
  Martin 164
  M. C. 124
Werner, Jas. J. 100
  Mary 100
West, Archibald 114
  Catherine 114
  Cynthia 114
  Hannah 36
  Hattie 167
  James Rogers 114
  Jasper 114
  John 103,114

West, J. S. 158,181
  Martin 114
  Mary M. 183
  Minerva 114
  Sarah Ann 75
  Stephen 114
  Susan Catherine 114
Weston, W. W. 71
Wheaton, Robert 20
Wheeler...179
  E. B. 71
Whisenant, Christopher 97
  George 97
  Jane 97
  Mary Ann 140
  Nicholas 97
  Robert 97
  Wm. Latner 140
Whistenant, Calloway 8
  Kemly 8
White, Annie 171
  A. P. 18
  Beaufort R. 100
  Belle 106
  Charles 171
  Miss E. J. 167
  Emma E. 88
  Frances E. 18
  J. B. 88
  John Blake 69
  Joseph 18
  Lulu 155
  Mary E. 100
  Mrs. M. M. 136
  Sarah 99
  Sarah Ann 10
  Sarah Jane 74
  Miss S. M. 9
  W. B. 99,108
  Wm. 10
  Wm. A. Jr. 92
  Wm. H. 74,80
  William N. 106,127
  Yancy 177
Whitefield, J. C. 37
  Sillar 11
  William 11
Whitfield, John C. 40
  J. T. 17
  Susan 40
Whiting, James H. 32
  Nancy E. 32
Whitley, Sarah L. 39
  Terry 39
Whitlock, Hattie N. 23
Whitman, Anna 170
Whitmire, Anna 93
  Daniel 63
  Elizabeth 63
  Jeremiah 93
  J. M. 31
  John 105,118
  Kate 117
  Leatha F. 31
  Mrs. L. F. 112
  Lucinda 18
  Mary 100
  Sallie L. 105
  Sarah 84
  Susan E. 118
  T. 117
  Wm. 18
  Wm. H. 84
Whitner, Elias E. 90
  Emma A. 90
  Essie M. 45,65
  E. Toccoa 76
  W. H. 45,65
Whitten, E. V. 62
  Malachia 56
  Mary J. 56
Whitworth, Nancy E. 33

Whitworth, Wm. H. 33
Wickliffe, Celestina 54
  Isaac 54,137,144,145,
    159,174,177,182
Wiebens, Abbie M. 133
  F. 135
Wiggenton, O. J. 40
  Ruth 40
Wigington, Ruth 118
Wiley...73
  Mollie 105
  Thos. 105
Wilkes, Mrs...66
  T. M. 14
  Warren D. 175
Wilkins, Leila G. 105
  Wm. W. 105
Williman, A. 124
  Highland Mary 124
Willard...115
  Rosalie H. 79
Willbanks, Henry D. 12
  Levina 12
Williams...131
  Andrew B. 118
  Charles 86
  Edward 26
  Eliza Ann H. 175
  Elizabeth 130
  Elvira G. 75
  Emma A. 90
  Fannie 163
  Frederick 169
  Jasper 165
  J. C. 90
  Jeremiah 75
  Jas. 102
  M. Ann 78
  Margaret 23
  Mary 26,169
  Mary Alice 127
  Mary Ann 18,122
  Sarah 76
  S. C. 66
  S. N. 104
  S. Newton 78
  Susan E. 118
  V. B. 76
  Wm. C. 122
  Wm. S. 66
Williamson, Charles 4
  Miss E. F. 19
Wilson...179
  A. J. 167
  Alexander 158
  Alice 158
  Amelia 146
  Arminda 10
  Charity 27
  Elizabeth 47,54,76
  Elizabeth I. 165
  Emma 182
  James H. 165
  J. M. 47
  J. S. 165
  W. J. 39
  Lewis 146
  Martha Malinda 127
  P. V. 76
  Robert 15
  Sarah 15,158
  Miss V. 36
  Wm. 54
Winchester, David 99
  J. M. 105
  Mary A. 105
  M. C. 111
  Nannie I. 111
  Tabitha Ann 99
Winfield, Jno. 23
Wingo, I. W. 145,148
  L. W. 133

Witherspoon, I. D. 44
Woeslin, Jacob 20
Wood, Alex. 79
    Carrie McC. 174
    Charles 79
    Harrison 178
    James 84,106
    John 79
    Joseph 79
    Landy 174
    Martha 84
    Nancy 106
    Robt. 79
Wooden, Miss C. M. 174
Woodin, Mary 99
Woodruff, G. W. 25
    Nancy 25
Woodward, Edward 62
Woody, J. K. 20
Woolahan, J. J. 159
Woolbright, J. P. 18
    Margaret E. 28
    W. S. 21,23,34,52,69,76
Worley, Walter 80
Wright, Mrs. A. M. 138
    J. H. 52
    John 133
    Robt. M. 138
    Susan 133
    Thomas J. 5
Wuarles, Lula 166
    R. P. 166
Wyly, Anna 128
    T. B. 128
Wynn, Mrs. M. A. 148
    Martha Emma 137

Yancey, John 69
    Thomas 69
Yarborough, Edward 46
Yearwood...62
York, Jerry 108
    Peggy 108
Young, Anna W. 116
    Caro 67
    Cyrus, Jr. 7
    Darcus Ann 98
    Elizabeth J. 63
    G. W. 27
    James 1,9
    Lotty 7
    Lucretia 86
    Mary Elizabeth 1
    Matti J. 118
    Robert Aiken 79
    Thos. L. 34
    Wm. J. 63
    Zachariah 125
Youngblood, G. A. 94
    Joseph 94
    Robert 116
    Samuel 94
    Sarah Ann 109

Zelle, Sophia 26
Zimmerman, A. 180
    H. B. 137
    J. H. 25,52,70,82
    Laura E. 137
    Mary E. 82

www.ingramcontent.com/pod-product-compliance
Lightning Source LLC
Chambersburg PA
CBHW021903020426
42334CB00013B/463